# Personality and Interpersonal Communication

Sage's *Series in Interpersonal Communication* is designed to capture the breadth and depth of knowledge emanating from scientific examinations of face-to-face interaction. As such, the volumes in this series address the cognitive and overt behavior manifested by communicators as they pursue various conversational outcomes. The application of research findings to specific types of interpersonal relationships (e.g., marital, managerial) is also an important dimension of this series.

# SAGE SERIES IN
# INTERPERSONAL COMMUNICATION
**Mark L. Knapp**, Series Editor

# Personality and Interpersonal Communication

Edited by James C. McCroskey
and John A. Daly

Sage Series in Interpersonal Communication

**Volume 6**

**SAGE** PUBLICATIONS
The Publishers of Professional Social Science
Newbury Park   Beverly Hills   London   New Delhi

*For information address:*

SAGE Publications, Inc.
2111 West Hillcrest Drive
Newbury Park, California 91320

SAGE Publications Inc.    SAGE Publications Ltd.
275 South Beverly Drive       28 Banner Street
Beverly Hills       London EC1Y 8QE
California 90212       England

SAGE PUBLICATIONS India Pvt. Ltd.
M-32 Market
Greater Kailash I
New Delhi 110 048 India

Printed in the United States of America

Library of Congress Cataloging-in-Publication Data


Personality and interpersonal communication.

   (Sage series in interpersonal communication ; v. 6)
     1. Interpersonal communication.   2. Interpersonal
relations.   3. Social interaction.   I. McCroskey,
James C.   II. Daly, John A. (John Augustine),
1952-     .   III. Series.
HM132.P428   1986       302.3'4       86-6651
ISBN 0-8039-2645-6
ISBN 0-8039-2646-4 (pbk.)

# CONTENTS

# SERIES EDITOR'S INTRODUCTION

The publication of this book represents a milestone. Although much of the empirical research in communication studies during the last 30 years has been infused with probes into personality, this book is the first to acknowledge this fact openly, to synthesize the work that has been done, and to point the way for future personality study in the communication discipline. It has not always been fashionable to admit the role of personality research in communication studies because the term itself is so closely identified with psychology and the study of the individual. Nevertheless, the use of tests to measure dogmatism, Machiavellianism, intolerance for ambiguity, need for approval, among many others, are frequently used in efforts to identify individual differences in communication research. Furthermore, several research programs developed by communication scholars have important implications for understanding the role of personality in interpersonal communication—for example, rhetorical sensitivity, interaction involvement, communication apprehension, communicator style, argumentativeness, and constructivism.

Clearly the persons who make interaction, the communicators, are basic units in the communication process—along with the messages, channels and situation. Thus if this book focused exclusively on the communicator per se, it would provide a much-needed perspective. But it does more than examine the person. Throughout the book, the authors acknowledge and grapple with Lewin's observation that interaction is a function of the person and the environment. This book, then, deals not only with communicator traits and communicator behavior but with the interaction of these with communication situations. The following are only a few of the difficult but fundamental issues addressed in this book.

- What kind of communication behavior is exhibited by people with various personality profiles?
- When we observe people communicating in a certain way, what personality attributions do we make?
- Is the elementary decision to talk or not to talk reflective of a personality trait?
- How does our self-concept affect our information-seeking behavior?
- Do people with different personalities process information differently?

- How can we distinguish between enduring personality traits and situationally based behavior?

*Personality and Interpersonal Communication* has several distinguishing features that should make it an important reference work for anyone in the social sciences interested in the study of interpersonal communication. It provides a historical perspective on the study of personality in communication research; it maintains a focus on communication behavior throughout that provides the reader with a clear understanding of the central issues; and it gives concise summaries and critiques of an extensive body of theory and research.

The publication of this book is timely. It reminds all of us who may overestimate the influence of the situation that the person is a critical part of the communication equation. The book does not ask the reader to choose between personality explanations and situational explanations— only to recognize that characteristics of the person may provide useful bases for interpreting outcomes. In this sense the book makes an important contribution to our understanding of the total communication event as well as to the specific study of individual differences. Daly says in Chapter 1 that "communication research emphasizing personality has had no obvious structure or 'master plan' associated with it." This book itself changes that assessment. It clarifies the structure of our past efforts and lays the foundation for planning the future.

Mark L. Knapp

# PREFACE

Since the beginnings of empirical research related to communication over a half-century ago, one of the central concerns of communication researchers has been the personality of communicators. In the beginning, most of this work was based on personality constructs drawn from the fields of psychology and sociology. While such borrowing continues into the present, in recent years communication scholars have increasingly devoted attention to personality constructs which have been generated within the field itself.

The present volume is an attempt to summarize much of the literature which has accumulated from these two approaches. The book is an outgrowth of the Symposium on Personality and Interpersonal Communication sponsored by the Department of Speech Communication at West Virginia University in March 1985. At that symposium the authors summarized initial drafts of the present chapters and received comments and criticisms from the other authors as well as audience members attending the meetings.

During recent years considerable controversy has emerged concerning the usefulness of the individual differences approach to the study of interpersonal communication. Situational research approaches have been suggested as a more appropriate alternative. The editors of this book (and, we believe, most of the authors as well) do not feel that this controversy has served the field of communication well. Interpersonal communication behavior is a function of both individual differences and situational factors as well as their interaction. Without negating the value of situational research, we believe that a reading of the chapters in this book will convince the astute reader of the value of communication research which focuses on individual differences, particularly personality-type differences. If this proves to be so, the book will be of significant service to the field of communication.

The book is divided into four parts: perspectives, communication orientations, social orientations, and information-processing orientations. In the first section Daly focuses on major models of personality structure and perceptual approaches to traits, the relationship between traits and behavior, and some of the methodological options relating to research on personality and interpersonal communication. Steinfatt provides an extensive analysis of research relating to personality variables originating outside the field of communication which have received much attention from communication scholars.

The second section is devoted to two sets of personality constructs which have originated within the communication discipline but have conceptual kin outside the discipline as well. McCroskey and Richmond direct attention to the construct of willingness to communicate and related constructs such as communication apprehension and shyness. Infante centers his attention on the constructs of argumentativeness, assertiveness, and verbal aggressiveness.

In the third section attention is directed toward social orientation. This approach involves a blend of constructs which have emerged from a variety of disciplinary backgrounds. Bell discusses such constructs as interaction involvement, empathic responding, self-monitoring, and rhetorical sensitivity, while Wheeless and Lashbrook center their discussion on the constructs of communicator style, androgyny, and social style.

The final section of the book recognizes the importance of individual differences in information processing in interpersonal communication. Berger centers his discussion on self-conception, while Burleson focuses on cognitive complexity.

As editors we are deeply indebted to a number of people without whose efforts this book would not have been possible. We are particularly grateful to the individuals who contributed the chapters which appear on the following pages.

We decided to do an edited book rather than attempt to complete this enormous task alone. Once that was decided, we drew up a list of the people we thought would be able to write the best chapters. The authors who provided the chapters of this book were our first choice in every case. We also wish to acknowledge the critical contribution of Dean Thomas J. Knight of the West Virginia University College of Arts and Sciences in approving the funding of the original symposium. The interaction among authors which this provided made all of our work better.

James C. McCroskey
John A. Daly

# Part I
# PERSPECTIVES

# 1

# Personality and
# Interpersonal Communication
## Issues and Directions

### JOHN A. DALY

The purpose of this book is to summarize research and theory on personality and communication. The chapters that follow deal with specific dispositions and their import for communication. This chapter attempts to frame much of the research that is summarized in later chapters by introducing a few important conceptual issues in the field of personality as they relate to communication scholars.

This chapter focuses on a limited number of topics. Many of the issues found in typical personality texts (e.g., psychodynamic theories, clinical assessment and modification of traits, phenomenological approaches to personality, and personality as cause or effect of behavior) are not examined for reasons of brevity as well as relevance. The topics that are examined are those which probably have the greatest importance to communication scholars. They include a brief review of the major models of personality structure and perceptual approaches to traits, a survey of theory and research on the relationships among traits and behavior, a brief introduction to some of the methodological options in personality research as they arise in typical communication projects, and a short discussion of the various roles that personality plays in communication.

## THE TRAIT CONCEPT

The concept of a disposition entails an enduring tendency to behave, think, or feel in a certain way. A trait is, in Guilford's (1959) words, "any distinguishable, relatively enduring way in which one individual differs from others" (p. 6). Traits differ in a number of ways. Some are broad, some narrow in their focus. Some emphasize social characteristics, others highlight more cognitively oriented variables. Some are defined primarily by people's responses to questionnaires, others are more often recognized by their behavioral manifestations. Some are conceptualized as part of a larger scheme, while others stand alone. But whatever the differences, the underlying assumption is similar: People differ in systematic ways from one another. Traits attempt to define the meaningful ways in which people differ.

Some researchers have attempted to distinguish between traits, as enduring dispositions, and states, as situationally specific responses. For instance, Zuckerman (1983) suggests that states and traits can be distinguished on four grounds: (1) traits have high retest reliabilities while states do not; (2) a state should have a moderate correlation with its related trait, that is, a sampling of states over time should yield a summed score highly correlated with the related trait; (3) a trait should correlate more highly with other similar traits than with its related state, and the state response should correlate more highly with similar state responses than with the trait associated with it; and (4) traits should not be affected by transient changes, whereas states may be so affected. The differences between trait and state are, in actuality, primarily differences of emphasis. Personality scholars tend to emphasize the trait over the state. In recent years, however, the distinction has become increasingly blurred. Many approaches to personality today, for instance, are emphasizing the aggregation of state responses as indicators of traits (e.g., Buss & Craik, 1984).

One of the knottiest problems is defining a personality variable. Personality constructs seem to proliferate at an incredible rate. One can hardly avoid finding some aspiring new construct described in some journal each month. For the most part, these new constructs are unrelated to one another, created either because of some specific need of an investigator (e.g., a measure is created to serve as a covariate in an experiment) or because the researcher saw an unassessed individual difference in people and opted to create a construct and measure.

While most of the traits found in typical studies of social behavior are conceptually independent, there have been some attempts to systematically categorize and determine central constructs. For instance, Cattell (1965) proposes 16 basic traits, while Murray (1938) offered 20. Norman (1963), on the basis of factor analysis, arrived at five, and Eysenck (1967) suggests three. Peabody (1984) has devised five groups of traits under the labels of achievement, affiliation, adjustment, assertiveness, and impulsiveness (controlled versus expressive). In an integration of interpersonal traits—the ways in which individuals differ from one another "in terms of what they do to each other" (p. 396)—

Wiggins (1979) proposes a circumplex model composed of 16 trait clusters that combine into eight major groups. The clusters are: ambitious, dominant, arrogant, calculating, cold, quarrelsome, aloof, introverted, lazy, submissive, unassuming, ingenuous, warm, agreeable, gregarious, and extroverted. In a series of studies, Wiggins (1979) found impressive evidence supportive of a circumplex model for these traits.

## MEASURING TRAITS

While there are a variety of techniques available to the communication scholar for assessing personality characteristics, the predominant approach is the self-report. Respondents complete a questionnaire composed of items conceptually and empirically related to the characteristic in question. Clearly, there are limitations to this technique. For instance, respondents may not answer accurately or truthfully, and in the case of most self-report tests used in communication research, there is no foolproof method for detecting such biased responses. People will often provide responses that place them in a favorable light (Daly & Street, 1980).

Some self-reports are transparent in revealing what they measure. For example, measures of self-esteem that include items like "I like myself," or questionnaires on shyness that include items like "I am shy," conspicuously display the construct they are tapping. Other self-report techniques are less transparent. For instance, communication researchers interested in cognitive complexity often have subjects describe a person or event. The number of different constructs a subject comes up with is a measure of his or her complexity. This sort of assessment has less bias associated with it, at least in terms of the obviousness of what is being assessed. Daly, Bell, Glenn, and Lawrence (1985) offer another self-report technique for assessing individual differences in the way people represent conversations. They had subjects sort through a number of short conversational excerpts and judge them on the perceived similarity. The similarity judgments were then used in a multidimensional scaling that yielded two underlying dimensions: one that emphasized the surface features of the episodes, and the other emphasizing the underlying communication event that occurred in the episodes (e.g., politeness or disagreement). Subjects received scores on both dimensions. This indirect method for assessing a personality dimension avoided many of the potential biases common in self-reports. There are other techniques available (e.g., forced-choiced measures and "bogus-pipeline") that, although they are seldom used in communication studies, nevertheless offer ways for assessing personality dimensions while avoiding many of the problems often associated with self-reports.

An alternative to self-reports is observer ratings. In some investigations, people familiar with a person judge that person on some disposition. This technique also has limitations. Observers, for example, may be biased, may not observe certain acts (particularly private ones), or may have different perceptual definitions of dispositional characteristics than the observed individual. In spite of these problems, there is evidence that observer ratings and self-reports of some behaviors are positively related (Buss & Plomin, 1984), although observers generally report lower frequencies than those offered by self-reports.

Reliability is established by assessing internal consistency and consistency over time. Validity is typically established in three ways: first, by correlating the trait with other traits based on the expectation that similar traits ought to correlate highly and that dissimilar traits should have a more limited association (Campbell & Fiske, 1959); second, by comparing self-reports on the trait with observers' reports of the individuals' standing on the continuum represented by the trait; and third, by predicting and then observing behavioral correlates of the trait.

One limitation of most scaling techniques for personality variables is that scores are based on sample characteristics. The critical issue is the relative standing of individuals, and this emphasis does not permit judgments about a specific person. While a person's absolute manifestation of a disposition may be constant, his or her relative standing can change due to changes in other members of the sample. Or the person's absolute manifestation of a disposition might change while his or her relative standing remains constant if all other members in the group change. This problem has led Buss and Craik (1984), among others, to suggest alternatives to traditional scales. They propose an index of behavioral frequencies for a disposition.

Trait measures also reflect underlying assumptions about the units of personality. The vast majority of traits are dimensional variables thought to be possessed, to some degree, by all individuals. Thus continuous distribution is assumed. Alternatively, some personality variables may better be viewed as class variables, where differences are distributed into discrete classes (e.g., there are two classes of people) and a continuous distribution is not assumed (Gangestad & Snyder, 1985).

## PERCEIVING PERSONALITY

While much of personality theory and research focuses on traits that distinguish people from one another, one area emphasizes instead the conceptions people hold about the personalities of others. Regardless of whether people actually have traitlike dispositions, people seem to believe that they do. Two major topics fit within this area: implicit personality theory and trait attributions.

### Implicit Personality Theory

Our language is filled with terms that are essentially descriptive of traits. Allport and Odbert (1936) found almost 18,000 trait words in English. Traits are part of the way people construe their social world. In the mid-1950s a major concern was how people form impressions of others. Following Ash's (1946) investigation, scholars attempted to determine the relationships that people perceive among trait terms. Under the rubric of *implicit personality theory* (Bruner & Tagiuri, 1954), a number of investigations were conducted to determine the underlying structure of people's beliefs about personality (e.g., Rosenberg & Sedlak, 1972; Wishner, 1960). Debates ensued about a variety of issues, including whether the structures people had for traits represented idealized versions of how people are or if they actually reflected the interrelationships of people's dispositions (Schneider, Hastorf, & Ellsworth, 1979). More recently, debates have emphasized the potential dialectic approach that most people have to making personality impressions (e.g., Lamiell, Foss, Trierweiler, & Leffel, 1983). A second issue was whether the interrelationships observed reflected mostly the semantic relations among behavior categories rather than the actual co-occurrence of behavioral traits (e.g., Shweder & D'Andrade, 1980; see also Romer & Revelle, 1985). In communication research, Norton (1980) and Sypher (1980) have debated this issue. Neither concern has yet been resolved to the satisfaction of most.

A variant of implicit personality theory has been introduced by Cantor and Mischel (1979). They suggest that people may organize their trait perceptions into categories, labeled *prototypes*, that allow them to parsimoniously organize their impressions of others (Pryor, Kott, & Bovee, 1984). These categories are hierarchically organized. For example, within the prototype of extroversion may lie other traits (e.g., outgoing, talkative), as well as behavioral representations of the traits. The memorability of traits and behaviors closely related to a particular prototype is generally greater than that of traits and behaviors that are incompatible with the prototype (Cantor & Mischel, 1977; see also Hastie & Kumar, 1979). Prototypes serve as guides for organizing knowledge about others. In judging others, people tend to rely on central or prototypical features (Mischel & Peake, 1982).

## Trait Attribution

People often attempt to explain why individuals behave as they do when trying to determine "who they are." These attributions can be organized in a number of ways. A particularly important way of arranging attributions about others' behavior is by whether the observed behavior was due primarily to situation or to disposition. In many cases, people overemphasize the importance of dispositions and underemphasize the role of situational considerations in judging others' behavior. On the other hand, when judging their own behavior, they often tend to highlight situational aspects and deemphasize dispositional causes (Jones, 1979; Jones & Nisbett, 1971): "I do what I do because of the situation; you do what you do because that is the way you are." Storms (1973) demonstrated this effect. Two people interacted while two others observed the conversation. The actual interactants made relatively more attributions to the situation than did the observers. The primary explanation for this pattern is familiarity: The person is more familiar with the self (and with the self in the particular setting) than the observers and thus makes more attributions to the situation and fewer attributions to the self. When people are unfamiliar with a subject, they usually rely on traits (Jones & Nisbett, 1971). More recent research has challenged this notion (e.g., Monson & Snyder, 1977; Monson, Tanke, & Lund, 1980), suggesting that greater familiarity should lead to stronger trait attributions. Kerber and Singleton (1984) have attempted to resolve the conflict. They have demonstrated that while there is a tendency for actors to make more situational attributions for their behavior than observers, there is no difference in the amount of trait attributions made by actors or observers.

The tendency for observers to overemphasize trait explanations has often been used by critics of personality research. They suggest that personality scholars may themselves suffer from this tendency (labeled the "fundamental attribution error") when they see personality as a meaningful way of understanding people.

## PERSONALITY AND BEHAVIOR

Probably the most consistently debated concern in the conceptual literature on personality in recent years is the relationship between disposition and behavior. This concern, always present in the literature, was well enunciated in Mischel's (1968) text. In his review of personality and behavior, Mischel argues that the evidence for a link between dispositional tendencies and behavior is relatively weak. In the first place, people are not *consistent* across situations. One would anticipate that if there were true personality variables, they ought to be evidenced in a variety of situations. If a person were shy, one would expect to see shy behavior in a number of situations. Some communication scholars have also taken this position. Hewes and Haight (1979) sought to demonstrate that predispositions to verbal behavior (a personality dimension tapping people's tendencies to enjoy and engage in verbal activity) are not consistently reflected in a group of behaviors that should be evidence of that trait if cross-situational consistency is assumed. In later work, Mischel (Mischel & Peake, 1982; Peake & Mischel, 1984) drew a distinction between *temporal stability* (consistency over time) and *cross-situational consistency*, arguing that while temporal stability may be achieved, cross-situational consistency is generally weak (see also Conley, 1984a). Second, Mischel has observed that traits have poor *predictability*. He notes that the typical correlation between a personality variable and the individual behaviors purportedly related to that variable is weak, averaging around .30. The magnitude of this correlation is not impressive, accounting for less than 10% of the variance in prediction.

A bevy of responses followed and continue to this day. One was to suggest that Mischel's critique was too all-encompassing. First, such criticisms are best restricted to social-behavioral variables, since cognitive abilities and styles generally show cross-situational consistency. Second, there is good evidence for the long-term stability of many traits. Conley (1984a, 1985) has demonstrated high levels of stability across a number of traits for periods of up to 40 years. The most consistent were traits associated with intelligence. Personality traits had moderate consistency. Only self-opinion (e.g., morale) had low levels of consistency over long time periods. Moss and Susman (1980) have demonstrated similar levels of consistency for traits, as has Block (1977). In his own defense, Mischel (1977) argues that most cases of consistency occur with judgmental or self-perception data, not with actual behavior.

Other responses to Mischel emphasized that low correlations were present only in undifferentiated cases. When characteristics of situations and people are considered together, correlations increase. A final reply focused on the nature of the behavioral criteria. Here, instead of emphasizing single behaviors in specific settings, a pattern of behavior across situations usually correlates well with dispositions and reveals good cross-situational consistency. The issues of situation, person, and behavior spawned by the Mischel critique are important, and each is reviewed briefly.

## Situation

One of the primary issues in personality research which was highlighted by Mischel's critique concerns the role of situation in personality studies. The major issue—whether it is the situation or the person that best explains behavior—is one that dots the history of personality work (Snyder & Ickes, 1985). Some scholars have suggested that situations account for the vast majority of variability in behavioral prediction and that traits are relatively unimportant. They assume that behavioral differences are a function of the immediate environment rather than traitlike structures. Some proponents of this position argue that traits are really nonexistent in people; rather, they are part of the implicit belief systems of perceivers. Others suggest that situations are preeminent in behavior prediction; thus, while dispositions may exist, they are essentially irrelevant to behavior.

While situations clearly play a major role in affecting behavior, a situationalist perspective has not received either strong empirical or conceptual support. First, systematic conceptualizations of situations are not well developed. Indeed, there are a virtually unlimited number of situational characteristics that could, directly or indirectly, affect behavior. While some scholars have started to identify some of the major components of situations (e.g., Forgas, 1979, 1981, 1983; Fredricksen, 1972; Magnusson, 1982), much remains to be accomplished. Until that search is refined, little functional knowledge of the systematic impact of situations can be parsimoniously obtained. Second, when the role of situational variables is examined by itself, research suggests that these account for little more of the variation in behavior than traits. Funder and Ozer (1983) raise this concern. Taking a series of classic studies often used to demonstrate the importance of situational characteristics for behavioral prediction, they computed the magnitude of effect due to situation and found it to be only slightly larger than that associated with traits. The point of Funder and Ozer's (1983) study and others like it (e.g., Bowers, 1973; Golding, 1975; Sarason, Smith, & Diener, 1975) is that situational characteristics alone are not much better at predicting outcomes than are traits. Further, situational characteristics and dispositions often make independent contributions to behavior prediction. The fact is that dispositions do account for some variation in behavior over and above situations, and to dismiss them is to reduce, unnecessarily, behavioral predictability.

Few scholars today argue that situation alone, in every setting, can account for the entire behavioral pattern of an individual. On the other hand, many scholars suggest that optimal predictability for behavior comes from focusing on the complex interrelationships among traits and situations. This can be demonstrated by comparing situations where personality traits are highly correlated with behavior and those where they are not. For instance, when people are placed in settings where they are highly self-focused, the correlation between disposition and behavior is much higher than when they are in settings where self-focusing is low. Pryor, Gibbons, Wicklund, Fazio, and Hood (1977) have demonstrated this using sociability as the personality trait.

A second situational characteristic affecting the relationship between traits and behavior may be the degree to which a situation constrains behavior (Snyder & Ickes, 1985). Some situations are highly constraining and thus require certain behaviors regardless of what an individual would prefer to do. Other settings are more open to people freely selecting their behavior. Behavior in a highly constrained setting is likely to be mostly a function of the setting's requirements. Thus the correlation between disposition and behavior should be low. Alternatively, in less constrained settings the correlation should be more substantial. Various studies have supported this expectation (Mischel, 1977; Monson, Hesley, & Chernick, 1982). Another characteristic may be the competency demands of the situation. Mischel (1984, 1985) describes research with children suggesting that greater behavioral consistency occurs when the situational requirements exceed children's competencies. In communication research, one relevant characteristic may be the degree of acquaintanceship among interactants. Parks (1980) found that communication apprehension was associated with anxiety in settings where subjects were unacquainted with other interactants but was unrelated to anxiety when others were well known to the subjects.

A related and more conceptually based approach which emphasizes the role of situations falls under the rubric of *interactionism* (Magnusson & Endler, 1977). The basic tenet of interactionism is that traits, by themselves, offer little predictability about behavior. When combined with situations, however, the interaction between a trait and situation can account for a sizable chunk of the behavioral variation. Interactionism is not a new idea (Endler, 1984). It reflects Lewin's (1936) brief formula

B = f(P,E) which translates to: Behavior is a function of person and environment. Empirical evidence for the importance of an interactionist approach has been offered by Bowers (1973). He surveyed a group of studies that provided estimates of the relative contributions of situation, disposition, and their interaction on behavior and found that traits and situations each accounted for approximately 10% of the variation in prediction. The interaction of situation and disposition also accounted for an additional 20% of the behavioral variance. Other studies (e.g., Argyle, Furnham, & Graham, 1981; Magnusson & Endler, 1977) offer further evidence supporting the substantial contribution made by disposition and situation together. Contradictory results have been reported by Sarason, Smith and Diener (1975) in an extensive survey of personality studies and by Gifford (1981) in a study of sociability.

Scholars interested in the relationship between situation and disposition have also examined what may be labeled the *selection* bias. People often select situations that match or emphasize their traits (Snyder & Ickes, 1985). For instance, extroverted individuals might place themselves in settings where extroversion is encouraged, while their introverted counterparts might choose situations requiring less social interaction (Diener, Larsen, & Emmons, 1984; Emmons, Diener, & Larson, 1985; Furnham, 1981). Daly and McCroskey (1975) found that high communication apprehensives anticipated selecting occupations having low communication requirements when contrasted with the occupations preferred by low apprehensives. Daly and Shamo (1978) demonstrated that same pattern for choices of academic majors based upon writing apprehension. Snyder and Gangestad (1982) showed that high self-monitors preferred a group discussion setting that offered clearly defined normative expectations—a setting where they could easily adapt to the requirements of the situation. Alternatively, low self-monitors, who conceptually are less responsive to situations and guided more by their dispositional tendencies, preferred settings that permitted them to display their trait tendencies. These findings led to the conclusion that "individuals systematically choose to enter and to spend time in those social situations and interpersonal settings that are particularly conducive to enactment of their characteristic behavioral orientations" (Snyder & Gangestad, 1982, pp. 133-134). Kahle (1980) has demonstrated a similar selection bias for locus of control, as has Zuckerman (1974) for sensation-seeing and Diener et al. (1984) for the need for order. Moreover, in some settings people may try to modify the situation so that it more closely matches what they would prefer in terms of their disposition. Thus, the extrovert, upon entering a quiet party, may become particularly boisterous, trying to change the social gathering's tenor into one with more social interaction—what he or she would prefer.

A final conceptual model emphasizing situations is the *template-matching* approach, proposed by Bem and Funder (1978) as a means for testing hypotheses about how individuals behave in specific situations. Perhaps the easiest, if not the best, way of explaining this approach is by describing the methodology. The first step is to devise *templates*—personality descriptions of the ideal (hypothetical) person who should behave in some distinctive way in a particular situation. Second, one obtains self-descriptions of personality from a sample of individuals (these descriptions could also be ratings from people who know the individuals). Third, one matches the self-descriptions obtained in the second step with the templates created in the first. People should display the behaviors associated with the templates they most closely match. This procedure has been used successfully in a number of studies (e.g., Bem, 1983a; Funder, 1982) but has also received some criticism (Mischel & Peake, 1982, 1983).

### Person

One distinction that dots personality theory is that between idiographic and nomothetic approaches to the study of dispositions. A nomothetic approach seeks general laws of personality having wide applicability, while an idiographic approach emphasizes that people are different and that personality is organized in different ways for different individuals (e.g., Rushton, Jackson, & Paunonen, 1981). Each person may show a stable pattern of behavior across situations, but it is impossible to compare people because behavioral patterns may be unique to the individual. While idiographic models are conceptually reasonable, they undermine attempts at generality. To say that everyone is different undercuts the basis of personality, which, by definition, seeks consistencies among people. A halfway point between the idiographic and nomothetic approaches is one that emphasizes that people differ in the degree to which they are consistent in their behavioral tendencies.

People differ in the degree to which they behave in accordance with their dispositions. Some people's behavior is highly consistent with their traits; others are far less consistent. For instance, the behavior of people who are high self-monitors should conceptually be less in accord with their traits than should the behavior of low self-monitors (Snyder, 1974). Snyder (1983) summarizes research supporting this prediction. At the same time, Cheek (1982) has demonstrated that the acting component of the self-monitoring scale is the primary contributor to greater consistency among low self-monitors in comparing peer reports and self-reports of traits. Another personality variable that may affect the relationship between traits and behavior is private self-consciousness (Fenigstein, Scheier, & Buss, 1975). A number of studies have found that highly private self-conscious individuals demonstrate far greater consistency between trait and behavior than less private self-conscious individuals (e.g., Scheier, Buss, & Buss, 1978; Underwood & Moore, 1981; see also Wymer & Penner, 1985).

Bem and Allen (1974) have argued that people vary in their degree of behavior-trait consistency. For any personality trait, some people will be cross-situationally consistent, while others won't be. In one study they asked students how cross-situationally consistent they were on two traits (friendliness and conscientiousness). Using a variety of behavioral indices in various situations, Bem and Allen (1974) found that students who described themselves as cross-situationally consistent on a trait did indeed have more consistency in their behavior across situations (especially in friendliness) than students who said they were inconsistent. Mischel and Peake (1982) found that individuals classified as consistent on the basis of their own reports demonstrated more temporal stability in rated behaviors (but not actual behaviors) associated with conscientiousness than people who said they were not consistent. Kenrick and Springfield (1980) have demonstrated a similar role for consistency (see also Rushton et al., 1981). Some recent evidence has cast doubt on Bem and Allen's findings on mathematical grounds (Tellegen, Kamp, & Watson, 1982) and empirical grounds (Chaplin & Goldberg, 1985; Paunonen & Jackson, 1985) even as other researchers (e.g., Diener & Larsen, 1984) have found that some individuals are generally more consistent across situations than others.

Another way of emphasizing the role of the person in traits is to highlight the importance of what have been labeled ''self-schemata'' (Markus, 1977). People who are involved in some dimension of personality (i.e., who feel the dimension important and/or hold extreme positions on the dimension) tend to have well-developed and highly organized schemata for that dimension. Having a strong schema for a disposition increases the likelihood that the disposition will be reflected in perceptions, memory, inferences, and behavior (Fiske & Taylor, 1984). While potentially quite useful in understanding personality, there are conceptual and methodological problems unresolved at this time (Burke, Kraut, & Dworkin, 1984).

## Behavior

One important trend in recent research and theory on personality has been a reconsideration of the nature of the behavioral indicants of personality. There have been two major strands of research in this area: multiple act criteria/aggregation and act frequency. Each emphasizes that single behaviors are not good representations of a disposition. Single behaviors in a single setting are too likely to be affected by the many situational factors present. Instead, a pattern of behavior across time, observers, and settings better represents a dispositional tendency. Proponents of these approaches suggest that the proper concern of scholars interested in personality is the general tendencies of individuals and not their specific behavior in specific situations.

## Multiple Act Criteria/Aggregation

Research on the relationship between attitude and behavior suggests that the two must be matched in their levels of generality if substantial correlations are to be obtained. Strong associations are observed between general attitudes and general behavioral patterns as well as between highly specific attitudes and behaviors. When the generality of behavior and attitude are not congruent, however, correlations are modest at best. The same pattern of matching should be true of personality traits and their behavioral indicants. A disposition is a *general* tendency to behave in some fashion and consequently should be predictive not of a single behavior but of a general pattern of behavior across various settings. Jaccard (1974) introduced the idea to personality, and Daly (1978) applied it to communication work. Consider Figure 1.1 as a model of the multiple act criteria.

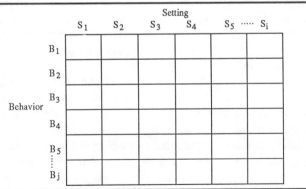

**Figure 1.1 Multiple Act Criteria**

Suppose we wanted to correlate shyness, as a disposition, with behavioral indicants of shyness. One dimension is composed of the different behaviors that might represent shyness (e.g., reduced talkativeness, fewer intimate disclosures, less argumentativeness); the other dimension is made up of the observation periods or settings (e.g. a classroom, a social conversation, or a job interview). The two dimensions, taken together, offer four different behavioral indices. The first (a single cell) is a single act in a single observational period (e.g., did the shy person demonstrate less talkativeness in a specific classroom setting on Monday, December 12th? The second (summing down a column) is a collection of different behaviors, all representative of the disposition in question, observed at one time (e.g., on Monday, December 12th, in the classroom, did the shy person generally demonstrate less talkativeness, less argumentativeness, fewer intimate disclosures, and so on?). The third index sums across observation times for a single behavior (e.g., in classrooms, interviews, and social interactions, does the shy person demonstrate less talkativeness?). The fourth index incorporates different behaviors during different observation periods (in classrooms, interviews, social interactions, is the shy person less talkative, argumentative, and disclosive?).

With the latter three criteria, summing does not imply that the person must demonstrate every behavior (or in every observation period even display a behavior). Rather, the issue is one of preponderance: Shy people should show more of the behaviors more of the time than nonshy individuals. The multiple act criteria approach proposes that a general disposition will have its strongest correlation with multiple acts observed across a number of observational periods (the fourth indicant). The weakest correlation should be between the general disposition and a single behavior assessed during one observational period. The point here is that personality variables represent general tendencies; the behavioral criteria should be as general as the disposition. When a very general disposition is correlated with a very specific indicant, one would expect a weak relationship.

Closely tied to the multiple act model is one emphasizing aggregation. This approach draws directly from test theory for its impetus. Test theory posits that the best indicator of an individual's performance is a highly reliable measure that has temporal stability. Epstein (1979, 1980, 1983), as well as others, argues that one would obtain larger reliabilities (that is, greater consistency) for dispositions if the behavioral criterion was an aggregation of behaviors across time and setting. Just as one typically averages across subjects in an experiment for purposes of obtaining reliable estimates, so too by taking sample of behaviors across time and setting one can obtain a more reliable index of behavioral tendencies. Error of measurement is reduced and small inconsistencies tied to idiosyncratic aspects of the different situations are controlled through averaging. A number of scholars have demonstrated that when personality traits are correlated with an aggregated behavioral index, the correlation among the two is substantial (e.g., Woodruff, 1984). They have also demonstrated that the aggregation of data across time results in much greater stability and consistency than the use of unaggregated data (Diener & Larsen, 1984; Small, Zeldin, & Savin-Williams, 1983). Cheek (1982) has demonstrated that aggregation over raters and items yields stronger correlations between self-ratings and peer ratings. Aries, Gold, and Weigel (1983) found that dispositional dominance was strongly correlated with a collection of behaviors displayed during small group interactions. Individual behaviors had much weaker correlations with disposition. Moskowitz (1982) found temporal stability for dominance behaviors in children over an eight-week period. However, methodological issues have been raised about this approach (Day, Marshall, Hamilton, & Christy, 1983; Paunonen, 1984).

While there is good supportive evidence for the multiple act/aggregation approaches, there are also certain problems that need to be addressed. For instance, in the typical study, behaviors are simply summed within and across observation periods. Treating each behavior as equal may be a questionable procedure. Moreover, the selection of behaviors and the choice of observation periods and settings have not receive sufficient attention. As a result, we may lose sight of the importance of understanding and predicting single behaviors in particular situations. The best measure that aggregation or multiple acts can provide is an average behavioral tendency, and while that may suffice in many cases, there are times when specific response predictions are needed. When summing across various characteristics of situations, one can forget that situations still play an important role in behavioral prediction.

## Act Frequency Approach

In the act frequency approach (Buss & Craik, 1983, 1984), a disposition is represented by the frequency with which an individual engages, over time, in behaviors representative of that disposition. Acts can take a number of forms (e.g., physical actions, intentions, and stylistic tendencies), occur within differing contexts, and vary in the degree to which they represent the construct. In Buss and Craik's approach, representative acts for a disposition are obtained in a multistep sequence where various acts are nominated as indicators of a disposition, then rated for prototypicality, and sorted to assess the degree to which they represent more than one disposition. After obtaining a collection of acts, frequency estimations are obtained. A number of procedures are available, including self-reports, observer ratings, and mechanical recordings. By emphasizing absolute frequencies and eschewing additional scaling methods, the act frequency approach permits comparisons that are not typically found in personality work. With most techniques, the only permissible comparisons are relative ones; people are compared vis-à-vis other people (Lamiell, 1981). In the act frequency approach, no reference to a group is necessary. Conceptually, there is a true zero point in the act frequency approach.

Frequency data allow the investigator to derive a number of different indicants. One might, for instance, collect frequency data on an individual for some disposition from two equal time periods. As the ratio of the two frequencies approaches unity, support emerges for an enduring tendency on the part of the subject. Computing a mean ratio across a group of people yields a *modal human tendency* with respect to the disposition. Frequency information allows comparisons among groups (e.g., cultures, age groups, generations, or societal categories) to examine whether there are group differences in the rate with which a given disposition appears. Children, for example, may have a larger rate of quarrelsome acts than adults. Moreover, different personality dimensions can be compared. Thus one might discover that the rate of sociable acts is four times greater than the rate of aggressive acts in some population. Finally, the impact of different situational characteristics can be assessed (e.g., in public settings the rate of submissive behaviors is less than it is in private settings).

There are a number of similarities among the behavioral approaches. For instance, the act frequency approach emphasizes multiple act criteria insofar as a variety of behavioral indicants over time are tabulated to form a composite frequency estimate. As is the case with the multiple act approach, specific behavior predictions are not made; instead, predictions are made of general tendencies as evidenced by frequencies of a collection of acts representing the disposition. In addition, in many construals of personality an assumption is made that a trait is best represented by a group of highly correlated behaviors. Neither the multiple act approach nor the act frequency approach makes this assumption, since it is conceivable that two people might engage in totally different behaviors, both of which are highly representative of the trait in question.

## COMMUNICATION AND PERSONALITY

So far in this essay, attention has been directed to certain major conceptual themes in personality. In this section, the different roles that personality plays in communication are described. Underlying this exposition is the basic question of why communication scholars ought to be interested in personality in the first place. What does personality research have to contribute to our understanding of communication? And, just as important, although less often considered, what does communication scholarship have to offer personality research and theory? Personality per se is the domain of psychologists. It should be the focus of communication scholars only insofar as it affects, or is affected by, communication.

The research summarized in the chapters that follow clearly indicates that personality and communication are inherently intertwined. Traits are correlated with communication-related variables in meaningful ways. They account for significant variation in communication behavior as well as communication-based perceptions. At the same time, communication plays an important role in the development and maintenance of dispositional tendencies. Psychological and sociological explanations of the etiology of many personality variables emphasize the critical role of communication. Self-concept theories inevitably posit the interactive nature of social interaction and the formation of self-valuing. Developmental models of shyness, assertiveness, sex-role beliefs, altruism, locus of control, loneliness, and many other dispositions almost always incorporate aspects of social interaction in some form (e.g., reinforcement via communication, development of communication skills, or communication of norms) as a major contributory correlate.

In communication scholarship, personality variables play a number of roles. First, they serve as useful covariates in some investigations. By statistically covarying certain dispositions, better evidence of the role of situational characteristics or experimental manipulations can be demonstrated. A communication scholar might, for instance, be interested in the degree to which certain situational characteristics affect talkativeness. Since communication apprehension (or some variant; see Daly & McCroskey, 1984) affects talkativeness (Daly & Stafford, 1984), the scholar may decide to assess participants' apprehension as part of data collection in studies where talk is considered, and then covary out the effect of apprehension. Statistically, covariance controls the effect of the personality variable. Any effects that remain after the disposition has been partialed out can reasonably be attributed to variables other than dispositional apprehension (although one needs to be cautious due to potential interactive effects of some trait and some situational or experimental manipulation).

A second, and related, role that personality variables play in communication research is as predetermined factors in communication studies. To continue with the hypothetical study of talkativeness, apprehension could be built into the study as a component of the investigation. Subjects could be classified as high or low in communication apprehension, and the independent effect of apprehension—as well as the joint effect of apprehension and situation or experimental manipulation—could be probed. In contrast with covariance analysis, designing the study to incorporate a personality variable allows the investigator to examine the independent impact of that trait on talkativeness, as well as the interactive effects of apprehension and situation on talkativeness. One might find that under certain circumstances, apprehension is correlated with talkativeness, while in other settings there is no relationship (an interactionist position).

Communication researchers also develop and validate traits that have direct relevance to communication. These communication-oriented traits focus on dispositional tendencies to do (or not do) something related to communication. Thus scholars in communication devise operationalizations of such things as communication apprehension and its many variants (Daly & McCroskey, 1984), communicator style (Norton, 1983), and argumentativeness (Infante, Chapter 4, this volume). These scholars face all of the issues addressed so far in this chapter. One common step in projects focusing on the validation of a construct is correlating a particular disposition with others presumed to be relevant to the trait. Thus we see studies where communication-oriented personality constructs such as communication apprehension (e.g., McCroskey, Daly, Richmond, & Falcione, 1977; McCroskey, Daly, & Sorensen, 1976) or loneliness (Bell & Daly, 1985) are correlated with other personality variables. Another variant of communication scholarship is the application of traits, devised both in other disciplines and communication, to communication-related concerns. This is probably the most common way in which communication scholars involve themselves in personality work. In some cases, investigators correlate a personality dimension (e.g., Machiavellianism, self-esteem, loneliness, assertiveness, sex-role, or cognitive complexity) with some communication outcome (e.g., compliance-gaining strategies, affinity seeking, or persuasiveness). The focus is on the individual and the choices made as a function of disposition.

An alternative approach is to focus on the relationships among interactants as a function of their traits. Issues such as the complementarity

of traits among interactants become highly relevant (e.g., the consequences of a highly cognitively complex individual interacting with
either another highly complex person or a less complex one). One can
argue with justification that this interactive approach is the proper
domain for communication scholars interested in personality, since the
interaction among people is the central focus of this sort of work. How
do two people, similar or different on some dimension of personality,
mesh in a conversation? Does complementarity in personality dispositions enhance communication outcomes? Research of this type is only
beginning to appear in the journals, but it certainly represents a fruitful
direction for communication scholars. It is truly focused on communication.

## DIRECTIONS FOR PERSONALITY
## IN COMMUNICATION SCHOLARSHIP

Communication research emphasizing personality has had no obvious
structure or "master plan" associated with it. Each individual investigator selects his or her favorite trait and proceeds to explore the
measurement, manifestations, or consequences of the disposition without
much regard for how it fits within some larger domain of communication-related traits. Very simply, integrative models of communication-
oriented traits have not been devised. Even though hints of such models
exist in both communication (Bochner, Kaminski, & Fitzpatrick, 1977)
and psychology (e.g., Wiggins, 1979), it is easy to apply Wiggins's
(1980) commentary to communication research:

> The last 25 years of personality study may be characterized as a period of
> construct elaboration in which a variety of single dimensions of
> personality (e.g., authoritarianism, achievement, aggression) have been
> studied in depth. . . . Despite the considerable advances that have been
> made in understanding specific dimensions of personality, there has been
> a notable absence of a generally accepted theoretical framework.
> (pp. 285-286)

While there are some notable exceptions to this lack of integration
(e.g., Norton, 1983), for the most part there is a narrow focus to
scholarship on personality in communication. A telling case of this lack
of conceptual structure came about when the present book was in its
organizational stages. There was no conceptual frame within which the
different variables could be organized. Instead, the different dispositions
were simply grouped on the basis of gross similarity. At some point, an

integrative model will be necessary, one that effectively summarizes past and present research, structures variables of common interest to communication scholars, and highlights unexamined, but critical, areas of concern. While there is nothing wrong with focusing on single variables, it would be an important step forward for communications scholars to develop a typological framework for future work.

Even more important than a conceptual model for the structure of communication-related personality variables are well-developed theoretical formulations for the place of personality in communication research. How, when, and why do dispositions affect the ways in which people communicate? It is not sufficient simply to suggest that shy people talk less because they are shy, or to argue that lonely people are less happy because they have less than the desired number of interactions. In each case, the reason for the effect is identical to the definition of the trait. A better explanatory model needs to be posited, one that describes conceptually the manner in which communication and personality are related. More broadly, it is important to identify the places and situations in which personality plays a vital role in communication. Why do dispositions appear important in some settings and unimportant in others? In short, what are the conceptual boundaries for personality scholarship in communication?

One trend in contemporary personality scholarship is the identification of specific behavioral indicants of different dispositions. In the various behavior approaches to personality reviewed earlier (e.g., multiple act, aggregation, and act frequency), it is critical that the investigator identify a group of behaviors that have some relevance to a trait. Communication scholars need to consider which communication behaviors are most representative of the traits they wish to explore. However, the field of communication has spent an inordinate amount of time devising trait measures and far too little time conceptually and empirically developing behavioral indicants of those traits. This is especially problematic because generally when trait measures fail to correlate adequately with behaviors, investigators rush to indict the trait, forgetting that many times the trait has significantly stronger conceptual and empirical bases than the behaviors involved in the study.

Behavioral indicants can vary in their level of specificity, ranging from broad communication characteristics (e.g., shy people show less involvement) to highly specific behaviors (e.g., shy people engage in fewer head nods while listening). In recent years, one tendency in communication research has been to focus more on the actual behaviors exhibited when people communicate. Under a variety of labels (e.g., conversational analysis, dominance, and compliance-gaining), research has begun to identify behavioral measures for dispositional tendencies related to dominance and influence, affinity, and social integration, among others. Not only is it important to discover reliable and valid behaviors as correlates for trait measures, but newer conceptualizations of traits, such as act frequency, demand added emphasis on the specification of behaviors related to traits. It may be that by focusing more on the behavioral displays of traits, many of the concerns associated with self-report measures will be of less critical importance.

An alternative trend, but just as important, is the increasing concern by communication scholars regarding the cognitive aspects of communication and personality. Very little has been accomplished in this area, but it represents a critical new direction. It may be that people have communication-related cognitive dispositions. The search for ways of measuring these dispositions and of identifying their correlates has only recently begun. One approach has been to examine individual differences in the ways people organize information about conversations. Daly et al. (1985) have devised two measures to assess what they term conversational complexity. In one procedure, subjects completed a sorting task that produced measures of the degree to which they construed underlying structural aspects of conversation, as well as the extent to which they focused on surface features of conversations. Not surprisingly, people who represented conversations in deeper ways (focusing on underlying features) demonstrated a high degree of involvement in and enjoyment for social interaction. A second procedure, mimicking research on cognitive complexity, assessed the differentiation that subjects had for the concept of conversation. Those with greater differentiation were more conversationally involved and less apprehensive.

McCroskey and Richmond (Chapter 3, this volume) have begun to emphasize a stronger cognitive orientation to their research on communication apprehension. Berger (Chapter 7) and Burleson (Chapter 8) have also comprehensively related a number of different cognitive personality differences to communication. More broadly, communication scholars can examine the prototypes that individuals have for communication and their implicit theories of communication.

Future scholarship also needs to focus more on the links between communication and the development and maintenance of dispositions. Even though there is evidence for strong hereditary bases for basic temperaments (Buss & Plomin, 1984), communication in the child's social environment is likely to have substantial and long-lasting effects on disposition. Very little work within the communication discipline has emphasized the ways in which communication-related traits develop. It is a fertile area for future pursuits.

## REFERENCES

Allport, G. W., & Odbert, H. W. (1936). Trait names, a psychological study. *Psychological Monographs, 47*(1).

Argyle, M., Furnham, A., & Graham, J. A. (1981). *Social situations.* Cambridge: Cambridge University Press.

Aries, E., Gold, C., & Weigel, R. (1983). Dispositional and situational influences on dominance behavior in small groups. *Journal of Personality and Social Psychology, 44*, 779-786.

Asch, S. E. (1946). Forming impressions of personality. *Journal of Abnormal and Social Psychology, 41*, 258-290.

Bell, R., & Daly, J. A. (1985). Some communicator correlates of loneliness. *Southern Speech Communication Journal, 50*, 121-142.

Bem, D. J. (1983a). Constructing a theory of the triple typology: Some (second) thoughts on nomothetic and idiographic approaches to personality. *Journal of Personality, 51*, 566-577.

Bem, D. J. (1983b). Further déjà vu in search for cross-situational consistency: A response to Mischel and Peake. *Psychological Review, 90*, 390-393.

Bem, D. J., & Allen, A. (1974). On predicting some of the people some of the time: The search for cross-situational consistencies in behavior. *Psychological Review, 81*, 506-520.

Bem, D. J., & Funder, D. C. (1978). Predicting more of the people more of the time: Assessing the personality of situations. *Psychological Review, 85*, 485-501.

Block, J. (1977). Advancing the psychology of personality: Paradigmatic shift or improving the quality of research? In D. Magnusson & N. S. Endler (Eds.), *Personality at the crossroads* (pp. 37-63). Hillsdale, NJ: Erlbaum.

Bochner, A., Kaminski, E., & Fitzpatrick, M. (1977). The conceptual domain of interpersonal communication behavior: A factor analytic study. *Human Communication Research, 3*, 291-302.

Bowers, K. S. (1973). Situationism in psychology: An analysis and critique. *Psychological Review, 80*, 307-336.

Bruner, J. S., & Tagiuri, R. (1954). Person perception. In G. Lindzey (Ed.), *Handbook of social psychology* (Vol. 2). Reading, MA: Addison-Wesley.

Burke, P. A., Kraut, R. E., & Dworkin, R. H. (1984). Traits, consistency, and self-schemata: What do our methods measure? *Journal of Personality and Social Psychology, 47*, 568-579.

Buss, A., & Plomin, R. (1984). *Temperament: Early developing personality traits.* Hillsdale, NJ: Erlbaum.

Buss, D. M., & Craik, K. H. (1983). The dispositional analysis of everyday conduct. *Journal of Personality, 51*, 393-412.

Buss, D. M., & Craik, K. H. (1984). Acts, dispositions, and personality. In B. Maher & W. Maher (Eds.), *Progress in experimental personality research* (Vol. 13, pp. 242-301). New York: Academic Press.

Campbell, D., & Fiske, D. (1959). Convergent and discriminant validation by the multitrait-multimethod matrix. *Psychological Bulletin, 56*, 81-105.

Cantor, N., & Mischel, W. (1977). Traits as prototypes: Effects on recognition memory. *Journal of Personality and Social Psychology, 35*, 38-48.

Cantor, N., & Mischel, W. (1979). Prototypes in person perception. In L. Berkowitz (Ed.), *Advances in experimental social psychology* (Vol. 12). New York: Academic Press.

Cattell, R. B. (1965). *The scientific analysis of personality*. Chicago: Aldine.

Chaplin, W. F., & Goldberg, L. R. (1985). A failure to replicate the Bem and Allen study of individual differences in cross-situational consistency. *Journal of Personality and Social Psychology, 47*, 1074-1090.

Cheek, J. M. (1982). Aggregation, moderator variables, and the validity of personality tests: A peer-rating study. *Journal of Personality and Social Psychology, 43*, 1254-1269.

Conley, J. J. (1984a). The hierarchy of consistency: A review and model of longitudinal findings on adult individual differences in intelligence, personality, and self-opinion. *Personality and Individual Differences, 5*, 11-25.

Conley, J. J. (1984b). Relation of temporal stability and cross-situational consistency in personality: Comments on the Mischel-Epstein debate. *Psychological Review, 91*, 491-496.

Conley, J. J. (1985). Longitudinal stability of personality traits: A multitrait-multimethod-multioccasion analysis. *Journal of Personality and Social Psychology, 49*, 1266-1282.

Daly, J. A. (1978). Communication apprehension and behavior: Applying multiple act criteria. *Human Communication Research, 4*, 208-216.

Daly, J. A., Bell, R., Glenn, P., & Lawrence, S. (1985). Conceptualizing conversational complexity. *Human Communication Research, 12*, 30-53.

Daly, J. A., & McCroskey, J. C. (1975). Occupational desirability and choice as a function of communication apprehension. *Journal of Counseling Psychology, 22*, 309-313.

Daly, J. A., & McCroskey, J. C. (1984). *Avoiding communication: Shyness, reticence, and communication apprehension*. Beverly Hills, CA: Sage.

Daly, J. A., & Shamo, W. (1978). Academic decisions as a function of writing apprehension. *Research in the Teaching of English, 12*, 119-126.

Daly, J. A., & Stafford, L. (1984). Correlates and consequences of social-communicative anxiety. In J. Daly & J. McCroskey (Eds.), *Avoiding communication: Shyness, reticence, and communication apprehension* (pp. 125-144). Beverly Hills, CA: Sage.

Daly, J. A., & Street, R. (1980). Measuring social-communicative anxiety: Social desirability and the fakability of scale responses. *Human Communication Research, 6*, 185-189.

Day, H. D., Marshall, D., Hamilton, B., & Christy, J. (1983). Some cautionary notes regarding the use of aggregated scores as a measure of behavioral stability. *Journal of Research in Personality, 17*, 97-109.

Diener, E., & Larsen, R. J. (1984). Temporal stability and cross-situational consistency of affective, behavioral, and cognitive responses. *Journal of Personality and Social Psychology, 47*, 871-883.

Diener, E., Larsen, R., & Emmons, R. (1984). Person × situation interactions: Choice of situations and congruence response models. *Journal of Personality and Social Psychology, 47*, 580-592.

Emmons, R. A., Diener, E., & Larsen, R. (1985). Choice of situations and congruence models of interactionism. *Personality and Individual Differences, 6*, 693-702.

Endler, N. S. (1984). Interactionism. In N. S. Endler & J. M. Hunt (Eds.), *Personality and the behavioral disorders* (Vol. 1, pp. 183-219). New York: John Wiley.

Epstein, S. (1979). The stability of behavior: I. On predicting most of the people much of the time. *Journal of Personality and Social Psychology, 37*, 1097-1126.

Epstein, S. (1980). The stability of behavior: II. Implications for psychological research. *American Psychologist, 35*, 790-806.

Epstein, S. (1983). Aggregation and beyond: Some basic issues in the prediction of behavior. *Journal of Personality, 51*, 360-392.

Epstein, S. (1984). A procedural note on the measurement of broad dispositions. *Journal of Personality, 52*, 318-325.

Epstein, S., & O'Brien, E. J. (1985). The person-situation debate in historical and current perspective. *Psychological Bulletin, 98*, 513-537.

Eysenck, H. J. (1967). *The biological basis of personality*. Springfield, IL: Charles Thomas.

Fenigstein, A., Scheier, M. F., & Buss, A. A. (1975). Public and private self-consciousness: Assessment and theory. *Journal of Consulting and Clinical Psychology, 43*, 522-527.

Fiske, S. T., & Taylor, S. E. (1984). *Social cognition*. Reading, MA: Addison-Wesley.

Forgas, J. P. (1979). *Social episodes: The study of interaction routines*. London: Academic Press.

Forgas, J. P. (1981). Affective and emotional influences on episode representations. In J. P. Forgas (Ed.), *Social cognition: Perspectives on everyday understanding*. London: Academic Press.

Forgas, J. P. (1983). Episode cognition and personality: A multidimensional analysis. *Journal of Personality, 51*, 34-48.

Fredricksen, N. (1972). Toward a taxonomy of situations. *American Psychologist, 27*, 114-123.

Funder, D. C. (1982). On assessing social psychological theories through the study of individual differences: Template matching and forced compliance. *Journal of Personality and Social Psychology, 43*, 100-110.

Funder, D. C. (1983). The "consistency" controversy and the accuracy of personality judgements. *Journal of Personality, 51*, 346-359.

Funder, D. C., & Ozer, D. J. (1983). Behavior as a function of the situation. *Journal of Personality and Social Psychology, 44*, 107-112.

Furnham, A. (1981). Personality and activity preference. *British Journal of Social and Clinical Psychology, 20*, 57-68.

Gangestad, S., & Snyder, M. (1985). "To carve nature at its joints": On the existence of discrete classes in personality. *Psychological Review, 92*, 317-349.

Gifford, R. (1981). Sociability: Traits, settings, and interactions. *Journal of Personality and Social Psychology, 41*, 340-347.

Golding, S. L. (1975). Flies in the ointment: Methodological problems in the analysis of percentage of variance due to person and situations. *Psychological Bulletin, 82*, 278-288.

Guilford, J. P. (1959). *Personality.* New York: McGraw-Hill.

Hastie, R., & Kumar, P. A. (1979). Person memory: Personality traits as organizing principles in memory for behavior. *Journal of Personality and Social Psychology, 37*, 25-38.

Hewes, D. E., & Haight, L. (1979). The cross-situational consistency of communicative behaviors. *Communication Research, 6*, 243-270.

Jaccard, J. J. (1974). Predicting social behavior from personality tests. *Journal of Research in Personality, 7*, 358-367.

Jaccard, J. J., & Daly, J. A. (1980). Personality traits and multiple act criteria. *Human Communication Research, 6*, 367-377.

Jackson, D. N., & Paunonen, S. V. (1985). Construct validity and the predictability of behavior. *Journal of Personality and Social Psychology, 49*, 554-570.

Jones, E. E. (1979). The rocky road from acts to dispositions. *American Psychologist, 34*, 107-117.

Jones, E. E., & Nisbett, R. E. (1971). The actor and the observer: Divergent perceptions of the causes of behavior. In E. E. Jones, D. E. Kanouse, H. H. Kelley, R. E. Nisbett, S. Valins, & B. Weiner (Eds.), *Attribution: Perceiving the causes of behavior.* Morristown, NJ: General Learning Press.

Kahle, L. R. (1980). Stimulus condition self-selection by males in the interaction of locus of control and skill-chance situations. *Journal of Personality and Social Psychology, 38*, 50-56.

Kenrick, D. T., & Dantchik, A. (1983). Interactionism, idiographics, and the social psychological invasion of personality. *Journal of Personality, 51*, 286-307.

Kenrick, D. T., & Springfield, D. O. (1980). Personality traits and the eye of the beholder: Crossing some traditional philosophical boundaries in the search for consistency in all of the people. *Psychological Review, 87*, 88-104.

Kerber, K. W., & Singleton, R. (1984). Trait and situational attributions in a naturalistic setting: Familiarity, liking, and attribution validity. *Journal of Personality, 52*, 205-219.

Lamiell, J. T. (1981). Toward an idiothetic psychology of personality. *American Psychologist, 36*, 276-289.

Lamiell, J. T. (1982). The case for an idiothetic psychology of personality: A conceptual and empirical foundation. In B. Maher & W. Maher (Eds.), *Progress in experimental personality research* (Vol. 11, pp. 1-64). New York: Academic Press.

Lamiell, J. T., Foss, M. A., Larsen, R. J., & Hempel, A. M. (1983). Studies in intuitive personology from an idiothetic point of view: Implications for personality theory. *Journal of Personality, 51*, 438-467.

Lamiell, J. T., Foss, M. A., Trierweiler, S. J., & Leffel, G. M. (1983). Toward a further understanding of the intuitive personologist: Some preliminary evidence for the dialectical quality of subjective personality impressions. *Journal of Personality, 51*, 213-235.

Lewin, K. (1936). *Principles of typological psychology*. New York: McGraw-Hill.

Magnusson, D. (1982). Situational effects in empirical personality research. In A. Kossakowski & K. Obuchowski (Eds.), *Progress in psychology of personality*. Amsterdam: North-Holland.

Magnusson, D., & Endler, N. S. (Eds.). (1977). *Personality at the crossroads: Current issues in interactional psychology*. Hillsdale, NJ: Erlbaum.

Markus, H. (1977). Self-schemata and processing information about self. *Journal of Personality and Social Psychology, 35*, 63-78.

Markus, H. (1983). Self knowledge: An expanded view. *Journal of Personality, 51*, 543-565.

McCroskey, J. C., Daly, J. A., Richmond, V. P., & Falcione, R. (1977). Studies of the relationship between communication apprehension and self-esteem. *Human Communication Research, 3*, 269-277.

McCroskey, J. C., Daly, J. A., & Sorensen, G. (1976). Personality correlates of communication apprehension: A research note. *Human Communication Research, 2*, 376-380.

Mischel, W. (1968). *Personality and assessment*. New York: John Wiley.

Mischel, W. (1977). The interaction of person and situation. In D. Magnusson & N. S. Endler (Eds.), *Personality at the crossroads: Current issues in interactional psychology*. Hillsdale, NJ: Erlbaum.

Mischel, W. (1983). Alternatives in pursuit of the predictability and consistency of persons: Stable data that yield unstable interpretations. *Journal of Personality, 51*, 578-604.

Mischel, W. (1984). Convergences and challenges in the search for consistency. *American Psychologist, 39*, 351-364.

Mischel, W. (1985, August). *Personality: Lost or found? Identifying when individual differences make a difference*. Paper presented at the meeting of the American Psychological Association, Los Angeles.

Mischel, W., & Peake, P. K. (1982). Beyond déjà vu in the search for cross-situational consistency. *Psychological Review, 89*, 730-755.

Mischel, W. & Peake, P. K. (1983). Some facets of consistency: Replies to Epstein, Funder, and Bem. *Psychological Review, 90*, 394-402.

Monson, T. C., Hesley, J. W., & Chernick, L. (1982). Specifying when personality traits can and cannot predict: An alternative to abandoning the attempt to predict single-act criteria. *Journal of Personality and Social Psychology, 43*, 385-399.

Monson, T. C., & Snyder, M. (1977). Actors, observers, and the attribution process: Towards a reconceptualization. *Journal of Experimental Social Psychology, 13*, 89-111.

Monson, T. C., Tanke, E. D., & Lund, J. (1980). Determinants of social perceptions in a naturalistic setting. *Journal of Research in Personality, 14*, 104-120.

Moskowitz, D. S. (1982). Coherence and cross-situational generality in personality: A new analysis of old problems. *Journal of Personality and Social Pyschology, 43*, 754-768.

Moss, H. A., & Susman, E. J. (1980). Longitudinal study of personality development. In O. G. Brim & J. Kagan (Eds.), *Constancy and change in human development.* Cambridge, MA: Harvard University Press.

Murray, H. A. (1938). *Explorations in personality.* New York: Oxford University Press.

Norman, W. T. (1963). Toward an adequate taxonomy of personality attributes: Replicated factor structure in peer nomination personality ratings. *Journal of Abnormal and Social Psychology, 66*, 574-583.

Norton, R. (1980). The illusion of systematic distortion. *Human Communication Research, 7*, 88-96.

Norton, R. (1983). *Communicator style.* Beverly Hills, CA: Sage.

Parks, M. (1980). A test of the cross-situational consistency of communication apprehension. *Communication Monographs, 47*, 220-232.

Paunonen, S. V. (1984). The reliability of aggregated measurement: Lessons to be learned from psychometric theory. *Journal of Research in Personality, 18*, 383-394.

Paunonen, S.V., & Jackson, D. N. (1985). Idiographic measurement strategies for personality and prediction: Some unredeemed promissory notes. *Psychological Review, 92*, 486-511.

Peabody, D. (1984). Personality dimensions through trait inferences. *Journal of Personality and Social Psychology, 46*, 384-403.

Peake, P. K., & Mischel, W. (1984). Getting lost in the search for large coefficients: Reply to Conley. *Psychological Review, 91*, 497-501.

Pennebaker, J. W., & Epstein, D. (1983). Implicit psychophysiology: Effects of common beliefs and idiosyncratic physiological responses on symptom reporting. *Journal of Personality, 51*, 468-496.

Pryor, J. B., Gibbons, F. X., Wicklund, R. A., Fazio, R. H., & Hood, R. (1977). Self-focused attention and self-report validity. *Journal of Personality, 45*, 514-527.

Pryor, J. B., Kott, T. L., & Bovee, G. R. (1984). The influence of information redundancy upon the use of traits and persons as organizing categories. *Journal of Experimental Social Psychology, 20*, 246-262.

Romer, D., & Revelle, W. (1985). Personality traits: Fact or fiction? A critique of the Sweder and D'Andrade systematic distortion hypothesis. *Journal of Personality and Social Psychology, 47*, 1028-1042.

Rosenberg, S. & Sedlak, A. (1972). Structural representations of implicit personality theory. In L. Berkowitz (Ed.), *Advances in experimental social psychology* (Vol. 6). New York: Academic Press.

Runyan, W. M. (1983). Idiographic goals and methods in the study of lives. *Journal of Personality, 51*, 413-437.

Rushton, J. P., Jackson, D. N., & Paunonen, S. V. (1981). Personality: Nomothetic or idiographic? A response to Kenrick and Springfield. *Psychological Review, 88*, 582-589.

Sarason, I. G., Smith, R. E., & Diener, E. (1975). Personality research: Components of variance attributable to the person and the situation. *Journal of Personality and Social Psychology, 32*, 199-204.

Scheier, M. G., Buss, A. H., & Buss, D. M. (1978). Self-consciousness, self-report of aggressiveness, and aggression. *Journal of Research in Personality, 12*, 133-140.

Schneider, D. J., Hastorf, A.H., & Ellsworth, P. C. (1979). *Person perception*. Reading, MA: Addison-Wesley.

Sherman, S. J., & Fazio, R. H. (1983). Parallels between attitudes and traits as predictors of behavior. *Journal of Personality, 51*, 308-345.

Shweder, R. A., & D'Andrade, R. G. (1979). Accurate reflection or systematic distortion? A reply to Block, Weiss, and Thorne. *Journal of Personality and Social Psychology, 37*, 1075-1084.

Shweder, R. A., & D'Andrade, R. G. (1980). The systematic distortion hypothesis. In R. Shweder (Ed.), *New directions for methodology of social and behavioral science* (Vol. 4, pp. 37-58). San Francisco: Jossey-Bass.

Small, S., Zeldin, R. S., & Savin-Williams, R. C. (1983). In search of personality traits: A multimethod analysis of naturally occurring prosocial and dominance behavior. *Journal of Personality, 51*, 1-16.

Snyder, M. (1974). The self-monitoring of expressive behavior. *Journal of Personality and Social Psychology, 30*, 526-537.

Snyder, M. (1981). On the influence of individuals on situations. In N. Cantor & J. F. Kihlstrom (Eds.), *Personality, cognition, and social interaction*. Hillsdale, NJ: Erlbaum.

Snyder, M. (1983). The influence of individuals on situations: Implications for understanding the links between personality and social behavior. *Journal of Personality, 51*, 497-516.

Snyder, M., & Gangestad, S. (1982). Choosing social situations: Two investigations of self-monitoring processes. *Journal of Personality and Social Psychology, 43*, 123-135.

Snyder, M., & Ickes, W. (1985). Personality and social behavior. In G. Lindzey & E. Aronson (Eds.), *Handbook of social psychology*. New York: Random House.

Storms, M. D. (1973). Videotape and the attribution process: Revising actors' and observers' points of view. *Journal of Personality and Social Psychology, 27,* 165-175.

Sypher, H. E. (1980). Illusory correlation in communication research. *Human Communication Research, 7,* 83-87.

Tellegen, A., Kamp, J., & Watson, D. (1982). Recognizing individual differences in predictive structure. *Psychological Review, 89,* 95-105.

Underwood, B., & Moore, B. S. (1981). Sources of behavioral consistency. *Journal of Personality and Social Psychology, 40,* 780-785.

West, S. G. (1983). Personality and prediction: An introduction. *Journal of Personality, 51,* 275-285.

Wiggins, J. S. (1979). A psychological taxonomy of trait-descriptive terms: The interpersonal domain. *Journal of Personality and Social Psychology, 37,* 395-412.

Wiggins, J. S. (1980). Circumplex models of interpersonal behavior. In L. Wheeler (Ed.), *Review of personality and social psychology* (pp. 265-294). Beverly Hills, CA: Sage.

Wishner, J. (1960). Reanalysis of "Impressions of personality." *Psychological Review, 67,* 96-112.

Woodruff, C. (1984). The consistency of presented personality: Additional evidence from aggregation. *Journal of Personality, 52,* 308-317.

Wymer, W. E., & Penner, L. A. (1985). Moderator variables and different types of predictability: Do you have a match? *Journal of Personality and Social Psychology, 49,* 1002-1015.

Zuckerman, M. (1974). The sensation seeking motive. In B. Maher (Ed.), *Progress in experimental personality research* (pp. 79-148). New York: Academic Press.

Zuckerman, M. (1983). The distinction between trait and state scales is not arbitrary: Comments on Allen and Potkay's "On the arbitrary distinction between traits and states." *Journal of Personality and Social Psychology, 44,* 1083-1086.

# 2

# Personality and Communication
## Classical Approaches

## THOMAS M. STEINFATT

The variables discussed in this chapter are "classical" personality variables in the sense that communication research on these variables began a number of years earlier than on most of the personality variables discussed in the remaining chapters. For each variable, I have attempted to provide historical background as a context for understanding the communication research that has employed the variable.

The modern scientific study of individual differences among human beings began with the dismissal of Kinnebrook, the assistant to the royal astronomer Maskelyne, at Greenwich Observatory in 1796. Maskelyne observed that Kinnebrook had recorded the occurrence of stellar transits about a full second later than Maskelyne himself had recorded them, and fired him for his careless reporting. In 1816 the astronomer Bessel read of this incident and began recording differences in the measurements of the same event by different astronomers. He suggested that such differences were stable properties of individual persons and referred to these differences as "personal equations." This early work, together with an increased social concern for the welfare of the insane, led to attempts at developing standardized methods of discriminating among the sane, the insane, and the mentally retarded. It is interesting to note that the original tests developed by Esquirol (1838) primarily measured verbal abilities, as do most current mental tests, though verbal-based tests were out of favor for most of the latter part of the nineteenth century. Perhaps the first *personality* test was the Personal Data Sheet, a self-report checklist of neurotic symptoms developed during World War I by Woodworth to screen out men unfit for military service.

Much of the classical personality research related to communication began in the 1950s when the field of personality was dominated by research on the "3 A's": achievement, anxiety, and authoritarianism. Each led to strong lines of research in communication. Authoritarianism was preceded by rigidity, was closely related to the intolerance of ambiguity, and led to Rokeach's work on dogmatism and, to a lesser extent, to Christie's work on Machiavellianism. Achievement research was the principal moving force behind interest in each of the "need" variables and led to Infante's work on argumentativeness, discussed in a later chapter. Anxiety is represented in the communication literature principally through the communication apprehension studies of McCroskey (discussed in a later chapter), the affiliation studies of Schachter (1959), the fear appeals research in persuasion through the receptivity/yielding hypotheses of McGuire (1968, 1969), and through occasional citations in later work on communicator style (Norton, 1983, pp. 69, 137) and stress (Pease, 1981).

Each of the variables discussed in this chapter should be viewed as existing on a continuum, not as an either/or typology. While personality variables are often conceived as relatively enduring and consistent traits across situations, different situations can evoke different traits and different levels of the same trait within an individual. The score a person receives on a personality scale may thus be thought of as a probability—the likelihood of a particular trait being manifested in a situation relevant to that trait. An exceptionally high scorer on a variable should behave across many situations as would the ideal type, but not always with the same intensity and same set of behaviors. The person scoring lower on that scale should be less likely to evidence the behaviors characteristic of the trait across all situations in general but may engage in some of these behaviors far more intensely than would the high scorer in some situations where the situational cues trigger the type. I know that I can be very dogmatic in situations where politics is being discussed, disbelieving anything that a particular political party says on an issue, simply because they said it. Yet at the same time and in the same situation, I can be very open to other issues of love and life and people's problems. An understanding of the situational cues that trigger a personality type is important to the prediction and understanding of the communication behavior which may result from a person in a given situation.

This chapter occasionally refers to persons as *being* "high Machs" (from Machiavellianism) or "externals" (in terms of locus of control). This type of statement is a convenient fiction, much the same as referring to "the meaning of a word." Meanings exist only in people, not in words. And personality variables may reside more in the realm of behavioral scientific prediction than actually in the person. Scores on any given set of personality variables provide one way of cutting up the ebb and flow of events, but not the only way. There are many such sets of scores. To say that a person *is* a high dogmatic (dogmatism) means that the person *acts as though* he or she were in possession of a particular cognitive-affective-behavioral syndrome.

I like to think of personality variables as interacting with each other as well as with the situation, though little personality research has been so conceptualized. If a person is energized to behave as a high dogmatic in a particular discussion, does that not open the way for the person's manipulative side to show? Is not the person then also more willing to behave as a high Mach, willing to engage in manipulation, when energized to behave as a high dogmatic? It seems to me that this may be so, and that interactions among personality variables must enter into any complete theory of personality and communication. While the variables in this chapter, and in this book, are usually treated individually, some well-designed experiments of the future are sure to consider the effects that personality variables have on the probability of each other's manifestation in specific situations.

## AUTHORITARIANISM, DOGMATISM, RIGIDITY, AND INTOLERANCE OF AMBIGUITY

Four classical personality variables which are of interest to interpersonal communication have strong theoretical and historical interrelationships. Authoritarianism, dogmatism, rigidity, and intolerance of ambiguity all originated in the 20-year period from 1934 to 1954, a time of great social and economic upheaval in the world. Dogmatism in particular is of major importance to work in interpersonal communication.

### Authoritarianism

The reasons for the interest in these four variables can be traced to the rise of the Nazi and Fascist parties in the Europe of the 1920s, and specifically to the fall of the Weimar Republic in 1933, followed by the appointment of Hitler as Chancellor of Germany. While a substantial number of studies of fascist and authoritarian personality types were published prior to 1950 (Christie & Cook, 1958), the publication in that year of *The Authoritarian Personality* by Adorno, Frenkel-Brunswik, Levinson, and Sanford provided the focal point for much of the authoritarianism, dogmatism, rigidity, and intolerance of ambiguity research since that time. Only Rokeach's *The Open and Closed Mind* (1960) rivals *The Authoritarian Personality* for impact on authoritarianism, dogmatism, and rigidity research, and Rokeach's work has been more influential in communication research.

Prior to 1950, Stagner's (1936) study of fascist attitudes, Maslow's (1943) work on the authoritarian personality structure, and particularly Fromm's historical analysis of German character in *Escape from Freedom* (1941) provided important benchmarks in conceptualizing the authoritarian character. Reich (1933) was the first to develop the concept of authoritarianism, which he called "Charakterpanzer." In 1936 Fromm introduced a similar concept he called "sadomasochistische charakterstruktur." These early works by Reich and Fromm provide the first descriptions of the concept of authoritarianism. Fromm (1941) was the first to adopt the term "authoritarian" later used by both Maslow and Adorno et al. to relate their work to Fromm's (1941) historical analysis.

The problem addressed by Fromm, Maslow, Adorno et al., and other researchers of their time was the question of how the German people, living in a relatively modern technological society with a history of democratic political processes, could possibly accept and even cooperate with their government in the violent atrocities against Jewish people. Fromm argued that historical changes in religious experience since the Reformation, particularly Colonialism and Protestantism, produced a sense of greater individual freedom due to a loosening of the traditional moral authority of the church. Concurrent economic changes, particularly the rise of capitalism, created more potential freedom. Yet the freedom from moral authority, and the freedom to act as an independent economic entity, led to feelings of individual powerlessness and insignificance due to isolation and fear.

The character structure which resulted from these economic and religious forces idealized authority, according to Fromm, while at the same time fearing and submitting to it and exploiting it for personal gain. The authoritarian character, seen by Fromm as the basis for fascism, melted two seemingly opposed characteristics into one: the desire to dominate, and the desire to be dominated. The authoritarian wishes to give unquestioned emotional allegiance to those with power and authority. He or she wishes to avoid all moral choice, and thus any responsibility for the consequences of such a choice, by being told what to do and obeying unquestioningly. At the same time, the authoritarian expects the same unquestioned obedience from those below him or her in the hierarchy.

### The Authoritarianism Scale

The influence of the work of Adorno et al. may stem from their use of Americans as their object of study, while Stagner, Fromm, and

Maslow focused on Germans. Adorno et al. set out to study anti-Semitism. Could the Nazi experience happen here, or was it confined to something purely German, or at least European, in character? Supported by the Department of Scientific Research of the American Jewish Committee, Adorno et al. developed the A-S (anti-Semitism) scale, a 52-item paper and pencil measure with a 10-item short form, each with corrected split-half reliabilities of around .90. All items were worded such that agreement with the item was scored as an indication of prejudice. The upper and lower quartiles of scores on the A-S Scale were used as a working definition of anti-Semitism and lack of anti-Semitism, respectively. Subjects from these two groups were given a modified 10-picture TAT (see Atkinson, 1958; Steinfatt, 1987), were asked to respond to a set of projective questions, and were assessed through a clinical interview. Most subjects for these studies came from California and Oregon.

Expanding on their work in anti-Semitism, Adorno et al. developed the E scale to measure ethnocentrism, a more generalized prejudice against any identifiable social subgroup, including the mentally deficient, blacks, women, criminals, foreigners, and other out-groups. Correlations between the E scale and the A-S scale averaged around .70, and items on the E scale were all in the same direction. Convinced that both political and economic forces affected the nurturing of ethnocentric attitudes, a third scale measuring political-economic conservatism (the PEC scale) was constructed. It correlated around .30 with both the E and A-S scales, suggesting a relationship between conservative attitudes and prejudice.

While Adorno et al. considered the A-S and E scales good measures of ethnic prejudice, these scales used the names of the out-groups in the scale items: "Jews," "Negroes," and so on. Yet their goal was to develop an unobtrusive measure of generalized prejudice in order to disarm any hostility or resistance to the scale which might affect its validity. Believing prejudice to be a consequence of deep personality structure, the 30-item F scale was developed as a measure of the prefascist personality. In its classically administered form, subjects respond on a six-point scale from "strongly agree" to "strongly disagree." Corrected split-half reliabilities are around .90. While some item analysis techniques were used, a large set of items was never developed and statistically analyzed during construction of the F scale. All items are worded in the same direction. Most items were selected on the basis of TAT responses and clinical interviews with upper-quartile scorers from the E and A-S scales. In addition to Adorno et al. (1950), versions of the F scale may be found in Robinson and Shaver (1970, pp. 224-232) and in Appendix B of Rokeach (1960, pp. 416-417).

The items of the F scale and the trait of authoritarianism are composed of nine variables (Adorno et al., 1950, pp. 255-257):

(1) *Conventionalism:* Rigid adherence to conventional, middle-class values (sample item: "obedience and respect for authority are the most important virtues children should learn.")

(2) *Authoritarian submission:* Submissive, uncritical attitude toward idealized moral authorities of the ingroup (sample item: "What this county needs most, more than laws and political programs, is a few courageous, tireless, devoted leaders in whom the people can put their faith.")

(3) *Authoritarian aggression:* Tendency to be on the lookout for, and to condemn, reject, and punish people who violate conventional values (sample item: "Homosexuals are nothing but degenerates and ought to be severely punished.")

(4) *Anti-intraception:* Opposition to the subjective, the imaginative, the tender-minded (sample item: "When people have problems or worries, it is best not to think about them, but to keep busy with more cheerful things.")

(5) *Superstition and stereotypy:* The belief in mystical determinants of the individual's fate, combined with the disposition to think in rigid categories (sample item: "Some day it will probably be shown that astrology can explain a lot of things.")

(6) Power and toughness: Preoccupation with the dominance-submission, strong-weak, leader-follower dimension; identification with power figures; overemphasis upon the conventionalized attributes of the ego; exaggerated assertion of strength and toughness (sample item: "Most people don't realize how much our lives are controlled by plots hatched in secret places.")

(7) *Destructiveness and cynicism:* Generalized hostility; vilification of the human (sample item: "Human nature being what it is, there will always be war and conflict.")

(8) *Projectivity:* The disposition to believe that wild and dangerous things go on in the world; the projection outward of unconscious emotional impulses (sample item: "Nowadays when so many different kinds of people move around and mix together so much, a person has to be especially careful about catching an infection or disease from them.")

(9) *Sex:* Exaggerated concern with sexual "goings-on" (sample item: "Sex crimes, such as rape and attacks on children, deserve more than imprisonment; such criminals ought to be publicly whipped, or worse.").

In summary, the F scale as conceived by Adorno et al. measured authoritarianism by assessing an individual's position on nine interrelated variables. These variables were believed to be indicative of the prefascist personality, a personality type that could easily succumb to fascism and a fascist form of government. No particular set of criteria for the arousal of authoritarian attitudes is set forth by Adorno et al., though some of the research with rigidity suggests that situational requirements may affect authoritarian behavior (see Einstellung research).

## Methodological and Theoretical Criticisms of Authoritarianism

By 1954 serious questions were being raised about the concept of authoritarianism and the F scale used to measure it. Methodologically, there was the potential problem of an acquiescent response set as an alternative to authoritarianism, since each of the items was worded in the same direction (Christie, Havel, & Seidenberg, 1958). In addition, Adorno et al. (1950) believed that the best information could be obtained from subjects if interviewers were fully informed about the authoritarian tendencies of each subject. Thus data from these interviews are open to bias due to interviewers' prior expectations concerning interviewees' behavior. Third, only "American-born gentiles" were used as interviewers for subjects who scored highly on authoritarianism, in order to avoid a clash between a prefascist and the object of his or her prejudice. This produced a potential source of bias, since such interviewer screening was not practical for lower scoring subjects.

Samelson and Yates (1967) provide a good discussion of the issues surrounding the acquiescent response set and the F scale, and these issues are discussed at length in Kirscht and Dillehay (1967). Smith (1965) proposed an alternative to the F scale for the measurement of authoritarianism, but many of Smith's items include complex wording that might create problems of interpretation for less than well-educated subjects. In Germany, where Adorno headed the Frankfurt Institute of Social Research during the 1960s, a 13-item German version of the F scale was developed and administered to a cross section of the German population (von Freyhold, 1971). This scale differs substantially from the American versions (von Freyhold, 1985). Cherry and Byrne (1977) developed a "balanced" F scale which may be the most commonly used measure of authoritarianism in current research. A shorter balanced F scale may be found in Ray (1979).

In addition to the methodological shortcomings, the conception of authoritarianism itself was being questioned on a theoretical level. Shils (1954) first raised the issue of right-wing bias in the F scale, arguing that the domain of authoritarianism was not encompassed by the right half of the the political spectrum. Comparing communism and fascism, Shils argued strongly for the separation of content from style. A high score on the F scale, he argued, is capable of multiple interpretations. It could indicate an individual with right-wing sympathies, or someone high in authoritarianism, or both. Since Adorno et al. (1950) were not claiming that all right wingers were necessarily prefascist, what was the meaning of a score on the F scale, and how was it to be interpreted? The principal response to this criticism by adherents of authoritarianism has been that the goal of the Adorno group was to study the prefascist personality, which is exactly what they did (Dillehay, 1978). However, this response does not answer the principal theoretical question.

The concept of general authoritarianism was well stated by a West Coast longshoreman (Hoffer, 1951). Hoffer argued that mass movements are explainable through the psychology of the individual adherent, the true believer. While never referring to authoritarianism by name, and apparently unaware of the Adorno group just a stone's skip away at Berkeley, Hoffer set the stage for Shils and other academicians to attack the right-wing bias of the F scale.

> In pre-Hitlerian Germany, it was often a tossup whether a restless youth would join the Communists or the Nazis. In the overcrowded pale of Czarist Russia the simmering Jewish population was ripe both for revolution and Zionism. In the same family, one member would join the revolutionaries and the other the Zionists. (Hoffer, 1951, p. 25)

Hoffer's chapter on the interchangeability of mass movements for their principal adherents left an indelible impression on the future of authoritarianism research. Few who read it could again feel comfortable with a multidimensional concept compressed into a single score.

Perhaps the most damaging summary against the F scale and authoritarian personality research is given by Hyman and Sheatsley (1954). Adorno et al. (1950) used both clinical interviews and standardized questionnaires, as discussed earlier. The questionnaires were given first, followed by interviews conducted by interviewers fully informed as to the questionnaire results, so that they could look for predicted results. The interviews were then used as the validation criterion for the questionnaires, with a correlation between questionnaires and interviews almost guaranteed by the procedure. In addition, Adorno et al. placed greater importance on the results of the interviews than on the statistical questionnaire results in interpreting their findings. The evidence on the relationship of authoritarianism to childhood experiences is based almost exclusively on memories of times past. Of course, memory for past events is strongly colored by emotional factors and the simple passage of time (Robbins, 1963; Steinfatt, Gantz, Seibold, & Miller, 1973; Yarrow, 1963).

Despite these characteristics, the F scale and right-wing authoritarianism continue to be of use when the area of interest is prefascist behavior. The 1984 International Conference on Authoritarianism and Dogmatism hosted in Potsdam by the State University of New York produced renewed interest in the area. Well over half of the 100-plus papers at the conference concerned authoritarianism rather than generalized dogmatism. Moreover, Browning's (1983, 1985) work in relating Loevinger's (1957; Loevinger & Wessler, 1970) stages of ego development to clusters of authoritarian attitudes indicates a continued research interest in certain areas of authoritarianism. Rigby (1985) reviews a series of studies that relate authoritarianism to behavior using single-act and multiple-act criteria. Hanson (1968, 1975, 1980) has compiled bibliographies of the 533 doctoral dissertations on authoritarianism and dogmatism completed in the United States and Canada prior to 1975, and of the 446 master's theses on these two variables completed by 1978. These include 15 dissertations and 12 theses relating communication to authoritarianism and dogmatism.

## Dogmatism

In 1954, Rokeach published "The Nature and Meaning of Dogmatism," followed in 1960 by *The Open and Closed Mind*. In addition to the work of Hoffer (1951), Rokeach was influenced by Orwell's *1984*, also published in 1951, and *The God That Failed* (Crossman, 1949), a series of essays by American writers who had joined or been admirers of the Communist party and who had later become disillusioned. Rokeach introduced the term "dogmatism" both to indicate a connection to the work on authoritarianism and to make clear the demarcation between a dogmatic style and any given set of content. While Adorno et al. had set out to study the prefascist personality, Rokeach had a different goal: "to try to find a single set of concepts, a single language, that is equally appropriate to the analysis of personality, ideology, and cognitive behavior" (1960, p. 7).

### The Belief-Disbelief Dimension

Rokeach's fundamental concern in the development of the concept of dogmatism was the belief system of the individual. He refers to this as the belief-disbelief system, to emphasize that a person has a single set of beliefs organized into a belief subsystem, plus a number of disbelief subsystems. The belief subsystem is composed of all the statements a person believes to be true at any time, and the disbelief subsystems of all that a person believes to be false. All disbeliefs and all disbelief subsystems are conceived of as being arranged along a continuum of similarity with respect to the belief subsystem. The farther from the belief subsystem, the greater the degree of disbelief.

Following are three significant properties of the belief-disbelief dimension:

*Isolation.* Two belief-disbeliefs are said to be isolated if they are not "in communication" with each other. Indications of isolation are (1) the existence of logically contradictory beliefs within a single subsystem, (2) "the accentuation of differences and minimization of similarities between belief and disbelief systems," (3) the perception that logically relevant information is irrelevant to a belief or disbelief, and (4) the denial of a contradiction between elements of a subsystem when such a contradiction logically exists (Rokeach, 1960, pp. 36-37).

*Differentiation.* Differentiation refers to the degree of articulation or richness of a belief system. Operationally, it is the number of beliefs that exist in the various subsystems. Indications of differentiation are the relative amount of information in the system and "the perception of similarity between adjacent disbelief subsystems," such that greater perceived similarity indicates less differentiation.

*Comprehensiveness of the system.* Comprehensiveness is the range of the disbelief subsystems in a given system—that is, the breadth of the disbeliefs represented. One person may reject the theory of cognitive dissonance, while another person, with a less comprehensive belief system, may never have heard of the theory.

A major hypothesis of dogmatism is the notion that differentiations will decrease in disbelief subsystems as the subsystems become more removed from the belief subsystem. The greatest differentiation should occur in the belief subsystem itself, with progressively less differentiation as distance from the belief subsystem increases. Persons higher in dogmatism are conceived as having less differentiation both within and between disbelief subsystems than do low dogmatic persons.

## The Central-Peripheral Dimension

Rokeach conceived of beliefs and disbeliefs as ordered along a central-peripheral dimension. This conception has changed over time. In *The Open and Closed Mind,* it was conceived as having three regions: central, intermediate, and peripheral. By 1963, the central region had been expanded to include Type A and Type B beliefs. Type A beliefs receive unanimous support from everyone around the individual, about the nature of physical reality, social reality, and the self. Type B beliefs receive support from none: they include phobias and other beliefs highly resistant to change regardless of the outside messages that may involve them. Both A and B beliefs are central because no authority figures are needed to support them. Type C beliefs concern authority, both who is trusted and how they are trusted. It is in these beliefs that the major central-peripheral distinction between high and low dogmatics is found. All people, both high and low dogmatics, must depend on others for information about the world. But low dogmatics have a "rational, tentative" reliance on authority while high dogmatics have an "arbitrary, absolute" reliance. The higher the dogmatism, the greater the distinction that will be made between positive and negative authority figures.

High dogmatics are said to engage in *opinionated acceptance* of positive authorities and *opinionated rejection* of negative authorities. Opinionated acceptance is a qualified, tentative acceptance of both a belief and any person who agrees with the belief. Opinionated rejection is a complete rejection of both an idea and any person who accepts the idea (e.g., "Only an idiot would think that personality variables are important in interpersonal communication").

Type D and E beliefs are peripheral, the first derived from authority and the second involving arbitrary matters of taste. The more central a belief, the greater its resistance to change, and the greater its potential for influencing beliefs that are less central than it, if it should change. New information is seen as progressing through the central region outward to the more peripheral regions, where it is stored as a belief or disbelief. Peripheral beliefs and disbeliefs may be in communication with each other, as in a low dogmatic system, or they may be isolated, as in a high dogmatic system. Type D beliefs are seen as being in contact with the authority beliefs in the intermediate region that produced them. A "party-line" change is said to occur when a Type D belief changes as the result of a message from an authority figure, while other peripheral beliefs which are logically related to the Type D belief fail to change. A "genuine" change occurs when a message affecting one belief or disbelief "sets off a sequence of autonomous activity that changes other peripheral beliefs, thereby changing the internal organization of the peripheral region and, possibly, of the intermediate and primitive (central) regions as well" (Rokeach, 1960, p. 50).

The more closed the system, the more the new information in the message will be changed and the belief system left intact when a message opposed to current content is received. The more open the system, the more such a message will be "assimilated as is" and produce logical changes in the system. Of course, one such logical change could be the rejection of a message which challenges beliefs in an open system, resulting in no change in beliefs. But this rejection would occur after the message was assimilated and processed in an open system, while it would occur largely prior to assimilation in a closed system.

## The Time Perspective Dimension

A broad perspective of time, representing past, present, and future, is characteristic of a low dogmatic person. A narrow time perspective is characteristic of the high dogmatic, with a tendency to fixate only on the past, or the present, or the future. In practice, the dogmatism scale measures only future orientation in assessing narrowness of time perspective. Highly dogmatic individuals tend to live only for a cause rather than for love, people, relationships, or simple pleasures. Since the cause can never be realized until the future, past and present have little meaning except as they relate to the future. Portions of the labor movement in the early 20th century tried to distinguish their cause as one requiring action in the present from the Christian, future-oriented approach apparent in the Wobbly song, "There'll be pie in the sky when you die, yes there will, there'll be pie in the sky when you die."

## Relationship Between Dogmatism and Source/Content Discriminations

Rokeach conceived of dogmatism as far more than a measure of individual differences in authoritarianism. He regarded it principally as a measure of "the extent to which the total mind is an open or closed one" (1960, p. 397). While it is obvious from reading the preceding descriptions of authoritarianism and dogmatism that the latter is far more theoretically oriented to the notion of communication than authoritarianism, Rokeach (1960) made this orientation even more explicit in his conceptual definition of dogmatism:

> A basic characteristic that defines the extent to which a person's system is open or closed . . . [is] the extent to which the person can receive, evaluate, and act on relevant information received from the outside on its own intrinsic merits, unencumbered by irrelevant factors in the situation arising from within the person or from the outside. . . . The more closed the belief system, the more difficult should it be to distinguish between information received about the world and information received about the source. (pp. 57-58)

Thus the low dogmatic should, by definition, perceive the dual character of a message as giving information about both its source and its content. The high dogmatic, by definition, should be unable to discriminate readily between these two aspects. It is this theoretic orientation toward one aspect of communication, the ability to discriminate between source and content, which makes dogmatism a major communication variable in studies of source credibility (Steinfatt, 1977b, pp. 188-193).

## The Dogmatism Scale

Working from the theoretic perspective discussed here, Rokeach produced 57 items intended to measure the various definitional parts of the theory. The original pool was narrowed to 36 items by eliminating those with the poorest discrimination indices. Additional items with face validity were added to the pool and checked for discrimination, and the total scale was checked at each stage for reliability. These procedures produced the 66-item Form D and the 40-item Form E through further item analysis procedures (Rokeach, 1960, p. 89). Form E is the final form, though in much actual research a 20-item short form is employed which was developed by Troldahl and Powell (1965). Reliabilities for these scales are around .90 for Form D and average .78 for Form E (Rokeach, 1960, p. 90). Troldahl and Powell's short form correlated .94 and .95 with Form E in tests with 84 Lansing and 227 Boston respondents. Corrected reliabilities for the 20-item short form ranged from .73 to .84. As with authoritarianism, all items are in the same direction.

While Rokeach did not commit the range of methodological sins of the Adorno group, and while the dogmatism scale did not try to measure multiple concepts, political and psychological, with a single scale, the potentially confounding problem associated with an acquiescent response set was nevertheless present in the dogmatism scale. Rokeach (1960) rejected the response set as anything but a minor determinant of dogmatism scores (pp. 406-407), arguing on the basis of the wealth of confirmation of differences accurately predicted by the scale, and of Christie et al.'s (1958) conclusion that response set was only a minor determinant of scores on the F scale. The dogmatism scale may be found in Appendix A of Rokeach (1960, pp. 413-415). Robinson and Shaver (1970, pp. 334-352) provide the commonly used versions.

Dogmatism items include the following: (1) "Even though freedom of speech for all groups is a worthwhile goal, it is unfortunately necessary to restrict the freedom of certain political groups." (2) "In this complicated world of ours, the only way we can know what's going on is to rely on leaders or experts who can be trusted." (3) "I'd like it if

I could find someone who would tell me how to solve my personal problems." (4) "It is only when a person devotes himself to an ideal or cause that life becomes meaningful."

Rokeach's work has been extended by a number of researchers. The extensions of Deconchy (1984, 1985) seem to have had substantial international impact. Schmitz (1985) summarizes the demographic results of some large-sample administrations of the dogmatism scale in the United States and Germany, and Rigby (1985) discusses the behavioral implications of attitudes toward authority. Just as authoritarianism theory specifies no particular situational criteria for the arousal of authoritarian attitudes, dogmatism is conceived by Rokeach as a generalized way of thinking, applicable in any situation. The importance of dogmatism as a predictor in communication situations depends on the presence of authority figures, positive or negative, for the high dogmatic subjects, and on the perception that these authorities hold a specific position on the topic of interest.

## Rigidity

At about the same time that Fromm was completing *Escape From Freedom*, Kounin (1941) and Luchins (1942) were conducting a number of experimental studies of rigidity. Rigidity was conceived to be the resistance to change of a person's beliefs. Given a belief that X is correct, the rigid individual will cling to X across a spectrum of situations, regardless of the content of X, and regardless of its past, present, or future relationship to reality. After an exchange over the importance of abnormal versus subnormal rigidity between Werner (1946) and Kounin (1948), Cattell and Tiner (1949) and Luchins (1949) laid out the basic notions of rigidity as a characteristic trait observable in the *behavior* of many individuals. Rigidity was conceived as a generalized behavioral trait with no particular situational requirements for its arousal, but the Einstellung research (cited in the next section) indicates that situational variables related to stress, threat, and formality may affect rigidity.

### *Measuring Rigidity: Einstellung*

Prior to 1952, the principal measure of rigidity was the water-jar Einstellung test, first suggested for use as a measure of rigidity by Luchins (1942). The Einstellung test involved a task in which the subject needed to overcome a specific prior belief in order to engage in a task successfully. Subjects are presented with the following problem: You have 3 jugs that will hold 31 quarts (A), 61 quarts (B), and 4 quarts (C), respectively, and an unlimited supply of water. Explain how to get a jug filled with exactly 22 quarts of water. The solution is to fill B and then fill C from B, empty C, fill it again from B, and then fill A from B. This leaves 22 quarts in B.

*Einstellung research.* Rokeach (1948) presented college and junior high school subjects with two Einstellung problems that could be solved using only this type solution: biggest into middle once and into smallest twice. He then gave subjects 5-10 problems that could be solved by this method but that could also be solved by a more direct route. For example, given 49-, 23-, and 3-quart jugs, produce 20 quarts. Subjects who continued to use the indirect solution when a direct one was available were considered rigid. In the college sample, Rokeach found that high scorers on Adorno et al.'s (1950) E Scale produced a greater number of rigid solutions than did low scorers. All 10 problems with a direct solution produced a greater number of rigid solutions among high-E versus low-E junior high school students, but only four of the differences were statistically significant.

Frenkel-Brunswick (1949) suggested a similarity between Rokeach's (1948) findings and the behavior of children in her clinical interviews. But Luchins (1949) criticized the Rokeach study, contending that the E Scales used in both the college and junior high school groups were both invalid and unreliable, that the direct solution may not be more efficient than the indirect, that Rokeach's effect sizes were small, and that rigidity is a situational, not a personality, factor. Rokeach (1949) responded to most of these criticisms, pointing out that Luchins himself discussed rigidity as though it were a personality variable.

Brown (1953) attempted to replicate Rokeach's findings. When Einstellung problems were administered to several hundred University of Michigan undergraduates in psychology labs, no differences emerged between high- and low-scoring groups on the E Scale. Using 162 undergraduates from an English course, Brown wore a suit while administering the Einstellung problems in an aloof and serious manner to half of the group. For the other half, he dressed less formally and was casual and relaxed in his presentation. No relationship was found between scores on the F Scale and Einstellung-rigidity in the informal group ($r = .00$), but in the formal administration, F and Einstellung-rigidity correlated .40 ($p < .001$). The formal situation seemed to energize authoritarianism, producing a rigid response as an attempt to avoid failure in a formalized, more threatening success-failure situation. Applezweig (1954) found similar results in a stress situation but a negative relationship ($r = -.34$, $p < .01$) between E score and Einstellung-rigidity when no stress was involved. A series of other studies (French,

1955; Jackson, Messick, & Solley, 1957; Levitt, 1956; Levitt & Zelin, 1953, 1955) found mixed results in relating E and F scores to Einstellung-rigidity.

Levitt (1956) calculated the mean correlation across 18 analyses in nine studies between Einstellung and E or F scores as .04, suggesting that Einstellung problems are inappropriate for rigidity research for three reasons: (1) reliability is impossible to calculate, (2) many subjects are eliminated because they cannot complete the task, and (3) Einstellung scores are not normally distributed. While Levitt's third criticism can be answered, the lack of a reliability estimate, the elimination of half or more of the subjects from many Einstellung tasks for failure to finish and other problems, and the suggestion of Levitt and Zuckerman (1959) that Einstellung is measuring a form of intelligence rather than rigidity together ended the interest in Einstellung as a measure of rigidity. Goldstein and Blackman (1978) provide a more thorough review of the Einstellung water jug literature.

Yet these problems could be solved. An alternate-forms type of reliability estimate could be calculated for Einstellung problems, and a latency measure, or manipulated initial set, used to overcome subject mortality. By devising a series of Einstellung problems, a reliability estimate could be based on the solution to more than one such problem and on the subsequent effect on "direct" variants of each problem. The combinatorial solution to each problem would have to involve different sequences of arithmetic operations. If one accepts Rokeach, McGovney, and Denny's (1955) contention (see "Denny's Doodlebug problem") that analytic latency is a measure of rigidity and that synthetic latency is a measure of dogmatism, then analytic latency of Einstellung could provide reliability estimates, could make use of the failure-to-finish problem, and could be used together with a manipulation of initial solution type to provide a multimeasure assessment of rigidity. Rather than throw out nonfinishers, one could time them and give them a solution after a specific time lapse. One could give sufficient Einstellung problems to be sure that the proffered solution has "set" and then provide the direct problems. The criticism that Einstellung measures intelligence and not rigidity might be answered by pointing out that rigidity is a form of intelligence, and perhaps a more important form than the factor of intelligence currently measured by IQ tests (Rokeach, 1960, pp. 407-408).

While any Einstellung procedure takes more time than a paper and pencil measure, that additional time may be well spent. Research time, rather than Luchins's arguments, may have been the major factor in the demise of Einstellung. Still, far more studies on rigidity have used Einstellung than any other measure.

## Measuring Rigidity: Gough-Sanford, Wesley, RAPH, and Rehfisch

An unpublished but widely circulated manuscript which appeared in 1952 provided a commonly used measure of rigidity. Gough and Sanford proposed a 22-item rigidity scale. All 22 items are in the same direction, so agreement with the item indicates rigidity. In the California Psychological Inventory (see Anastasi, 1982, pp. 507-508) the Gough-Sanford scale is labeled "Flexibility," and the scoring for each item is reversed such that higher scores on flexibility indicate a movement away from rigidity. Reliabilities for the 22-item scale are normally around .78, and it is available as Appendix C of Rokeach (1960, pp. 418-419).

Gough-Sanford items include the following: (1) There is usually only one best way to solve most problems; (2) I usually check more than once to be sure that I have locked a door, put out the light, or something of the sort; (3) I have never done anything dangerous for the thrill of it; and (4) I always put on and take off my clothes in the same order.

Wesley (1953) published a 50-item rigidity scale that includes the 22 Gough-Sanford items plus 28 items rated by five clinical psychologists as showing high rigidity, several of which are worded in the reverse direction. Seventeen additional MMPI items (Minnesota Multiphasic Personality Inventory; see Anastasi, 1982, pp. 500-507) are suggested for use with the 50 items for disguise of the purpose of the test. No reliability data are available. A 41-item version of the scale without the 17 filler items is available in Robinson and Shaver (1970, pp. 313-316). Meresko, Rubin, Shontz, and Morrow (1954) constructed a 20-item Rigidity of Attitudes Regarding Personal Habits (RAPH) scale to measure both rigidity and intolerance of ambiguity. It is discussed by Robinson and Shaver (1970, pp. 309-312). Rehfisch (1958a) reports the construction of a 39-item scale intended to measure rigidity (see Robinson and Shaver, 1970, pp. 304-308). Rehfisch's definition of rigidity as (1) constriction and inhibition, (2) conservatism, (3) intolerance of disorder and ambiguity, (4) observational and perseverative tendencies, (5) social introversion, and (6) anxiety and guilt is markedly different from the definitions discussed earlier, and surely multidimensional. The scale correlates −.40 with a measure of verbal fluency, and 13 of its 39 items appear to be measures of communication apprehension rather than any form of rigidity. Goldstein and Blackman (1978) discuss other measures of rigidity and some of the statistical issues involved in them.

## Intolerance of Ambiguity

Else Frenkel-Brunswik published "Intolerance of Ambiguity as an Emotional and Perceptual Personality Variable" in 1949, during the time that work on *The Authoritarian Personality* (Adorno et al., 1950) was nearing completion. Frenkel-Brunswik's thinking was based in psychoanalysis. She saw a close correspondence between affect and cognition in producing behavior, especially as that behavior occurred within a social context. Freud's concept of emotional ambivalence is seen in psychoanalytic theory as a strong factor in personality development during childhood. All children experience emotional ambivalence toward parents as a result of dependence on the parents for wants and needs, contrasted with punishment for misdeeds. Since human beings are not consistent, a given set of parents varies in their permissiveness/punitiveness over time due to many factors such as fatigue and immediate past events.

Frenkel-Brunswik believed that to the extent that the child was not allowed to express ambivalent feelings about his or her parents, perhaps due to punishment by the parents for such expressions, the child tended to develop a three-part syndrome consisting of a generalized need for premature closure, a rigid view of the world, and a general intolerance of ambiguity. Two principal results of such a syndrome would be an inability to function effectively on the cognitive level and the holding of stereotyped attitudes toward out-groups. Some children seem to tolerate this emotional ambiguity better than others. For children with high intolerance of ambiguity, certain memories and experiences are removed from cognitive awareness to a far greater extent than for those with low intolerance of ambiguity. The child clings to existing attitudes regardless of new experiences. McCandless (1961) relates the toilet training research of Sears, Maccoby, and Levin (1957) to an intolerance of the anxiety presented by unclear situations. McCandless suggests that the child attempts to reduce this anxiety by forcing new evidence into clear, tight categories and rigid rules.

Once developed, intolerance of ambiguity was conceived as a generalized personality variable that would operate across situational contexts with no special conditions necessary for its arousal. Budner's (1962) conception, discussed in the next section, suggests that situations which are new, complex, or contradictory will be most likely to arouse intolerance of ambiguity.

## Measuring Intolerance of Ambiguity

A number of scales for the measurement of intolerance of ambiguity have been developed (Eysenck, 1954; Martin & Westie, 1959; O'Connor, 1952; Saunders, 1955; Siegel, 1954; Walk, 1950). Martin and Westie's eight-item scale was designed to measure Frenkel-Brunswik's original conception of intolerance of ambiguity and is reviewed by Robinson and Shaver (1970, pp. 322-324), but no reliability figures are available. Martin and Westie's items include the following: (1) A person is either 100% American or he isn't; (2) There are two kinds of women: the pure and the bad; and (3) There is only one right way to do anything.

Until 1962, most research on intolerance of ambiguity was concerned with its relationship to the authoritarian personality (Frenkel-Brunswik, 1949, 1954). In 1962, Budner published a modified version of his 1960 doctoral dissertation, done under Christie, which treated intolerance of ambiguity as a generalized personality variable where ambiguous situations are perceived as threatening and undesirable, as opposed to Frenkel-Brunswik's more Freudian conception discussed earlier. An ambiguous situation was defined as one that could not be "adequately structured or categorized by the individual because of the lack of sufficient cues" (Budner, 1962). Budner identifies three situations that might normally be ambiguous: new situations, complex situations, and contradictory situations. Threat was operationalized phenomenologically by repression, denial, anxiety, or discomfort, and behaviorally by destructive, reconstructive, or avoidance behavior.

Beginning with a pool of 33 items, each designed to tap at least one of the phenomenal or behavioral indicators of intolerance of ambiguity, Budner (1962) used a sample of 117 students in an item analysis to eliminate nonsignificant items from the pool. This left 8 negatively worded and 10 positively worded items. The two positive items that had the lowest item-total correlations were dropped in order to balance the scale on positive and negative items. Subjects responded to positive items from strongly agree (7) to strongly disagree (1) on a six-point scale with no neutral (4) point. Nonresponses to an item were scored as 4. Negative items reversed this scoring. Cronbach's alpha reliabilities averaged .48 over 813 subjects, but the two-week to two-month test-retest correlation for a small experimental group (n = 15) was .85. Validity was assessed by asking four judges to rank order brief biographies of 15 experimental subjects, given the definition and items of intolerance of ambiguity, and by two high school English classes where students selected others from the class who most preferred either rigid and uncomplicated or unfamiliar and complex situations. Validity coefficients were .48 and .34 for the experimental and high school samples, respectively.

Budner's items include the following: (1) An expert who doesn't come up with a definite answer probably doesn't know too much; (2) A good job is one where what is to be done and how it is to be done are always clear; and (3) Teachers or supervisors who hand out vague assignments give a chance for one to show initiative and originality [reversed item]. While Budner's scale is perhaps the most widely used measure of intolerance of ambiguity, Rydell and Rosen (1966) developed a 16-item true-false test for intolerance of ambiguity, later expanded to 20 items by MacDonald (1970), which is referred to as the AT-20. This test, along with Walk's A-Scale (1950) and Budner's IA scale, accounts for much of the research on intolerance of ambiguity. Of the scales available for the measurement of intolerance of ambiguity, these are currently the most used, and probably the most reliable and valid.

## *Research on Intolerance of Ambiguity*

Much of the research on intolerance of ambiguity has been summarized by Goldstein and Blackman (1978). Block and Block (1951) used Sherif's (1936) autokinetic effect as a measure of intolerance of ambiguity. A point source of light in a darkened room or box will appear to move after a few seconds of observation, even though the light actually remains stationary. Sixty-five male college students made estimates of the distance through which the light moved over a series of 100 trials. In the Sherif experiments, subjects observed the light until each came to an individual judgment of the extent of movement of the light, followed by overheard, unintentional communications which influenced subjects' judgments toward the norm of the overheard others. Montgomery, Hinkle, and Enzie (1976) found that high F scorers clung to the group-defined norms longer than low F scorers after confederates who established the norms were replaced. Block and Block (1951) used the number of trials to the establishment of an individual norm as a measure of intolerance of ambiguity and found that it correlated with E scale scores. Taft (1956) found similar results using a different measure of intolerance of ambiguity, as did Zacker (1973), who used F scale rather than E scale scores.

Millon (1957) also used F scores and the autokinetic effect in an experiment reminiscent of Brown's (1953) Einstellung versus E scale investigations. Millon found that high authoritarians required fewer trials to reach a norm but found no difference between informing subjects that the task required intelligence and ability and that the task was simply being considered for use in a later study. Millon incorrectly reports a significant relationship between a somewhat questionable autokinetic-based measure of rigidity and F scores, as Goldstein and Blackman (1978) point out. Davids (1955, 1956) also failed to confirm a Brown-type relationship between F scores and intolerance of ambiguity as measured both by number of suggested concepts on a Rorschach test which were rejected by the subject, and by the number of ideas recalled from a contradictory passage. Other studies (Jones, 1955; Nye, 1973; Siegel, 1954; Steiner, 1954; Steiner & Johnson, 1963) found small but significant relationships between various measures of intolerance of ambiguity, authoritarianism, or ethnocentrism.

## INTERRELATIONSHIPS AMONG AUTHORITARIANISM, DOGMATISM, RIGIDITY, AND INTOLERANCE OF AMBIGUITY

### Relationship of Rigidity, Intolerance of Ambiguity, and Authoritarianism

While rigidity and intolerance of ambiguity have different measures and experimental backgrounds, the distinctions between the two have often been blurred. This is especially true in the original intolerance of ambiguity work of Frenkel-Brunswik (1949), who defined rigid as "the various kinds of Intolerance of Ambiguity discussed" (p. 117). Goldstein and Blackman (1978) discuss other overlapping uses of the two terms and suggest that rigidity is best conceptualized as continued behavior that does not take situational changes into account, while intolerance of ambiguity is the attempt to structure an essentially unstructured situation. Rigidity then becomes a behaviorally defined variable, while intolerance of ambiguity is defined by cognitive style.

Both rigidity and intolerance of ambiguity predated and were closely related to authoritarianism as conceived by Adorno et al. (1950), cutting across the nine definitional categories. The prefascist personality was discussed as high in rigidity and high in intolerance of ambiguity, especially when clear cases of high authoritarianism were involved. Much of the literature relating authoritarianism to rigidity and intolerance of ambiguity has been reviewed here. The general finding is that authoritarianism is related to both rigidity and intolerance of ambiguity. Since intolerance of ambiguity and rigidity were often treated as the same variable in early research and conceptualizing, it would not be surprising to find a strong relationship between them. Yet data on the relationships between their various measures is scarce or nonexistent. Figure 2.1, discussed below, lists a correlation of zero between Budner's (1962) intolerance of ambiguity and Gough-Sanford's rigidity. I obtained this correlation for 43 Clarkson subjects, but the sample is small and the range on rigidity is considerably smaller than for the non-Clarkson scores, so any conclusions would be premature.

## Dogmatism and Intolerance of Ambiguity

Barker (1963) reported that high dogmatic subjects among 160 graduate students were significantly higher on intolerance of ambiguity, as measured by Siegel's (1954) TICA test, than were low dogmatic subjects. Day (1966) found a nonsignificant correlation between dogmatism and Budner's intolerance of ambiguity scale using only 26 students. Feather (1969, 1971) found significant correlations for these two variables, ranging from .20 to .50 among four larger groups. MacDonald (1970) found a correlation of .42 between dogmatism and the AT-20 among 698 undergraduates. Norton (1975) failed to find a significant correlation between Troldahl and Powell's (1965) 20-item short form of the dogmatism scale and two different measures of intolerance of ambiguity in a sample of 79 undergraduates. Chabassol and Thomas (1975) found a correlation of .37 between dogmatism and the AT-20 among 400 junior high school and high school students. Sanders (1977; cited in Goldstein and Blackman, 1978, p. 82) used two measures related to intolerance of ambiguity, lowered tendency to see reversals on a Necker cube, and the tendency to see alternating (as opposed to fused) images in binocular vision. Both intolerance of ambiguity measures correlated with dogmatism—.35 and .49, respectively—in a sample of 84 undergraduates. In *The Open and Closed Mind,* Rokeach (1960) refers to intolerance quite frequently, but always as generalized intolerance. Rokeach saw the concept of intolerance of ambiguity in the same way as he viewed authoritarianism: a specific manifestation of a more general, and more interesting, problem.

## Dogmatism and Authoritarianism

While authoritarianism began as the study of the prefascist personality, the concept of an "authoritarian" person does not necessarily connote right-wing political beliefs in either everyday or technical usage. Authoritarianism is defined in nine characteristics and the items of the F scale. Three of these characteristics—conventionalism, projectivity, and sex—have explicit belief content rather than structural formal content as their thrust. Dogmatism explicitly set out to be a measure of general intolerance and general authoritarianism, devoid of any investment for or against specific ideologies. Dogmatism is defined by the dogmatism scale operationally, and by the belief-disbelief, central-peripheral, and time perspective dimensions conceptually. While Adorno et al.'s (1950) central concern was with an attitude structure that would lead toward fascism, Rokeach's central concern was the processing of information by the belief system and the relationship of this processing to the view of the nature of authority that was operationalized within the individual's belief system.

Rokeach subsumed Frenkel-Brunswik's work on the intolerance of ambiguity and Adorno et al.'s work on authoritarianism within his concept of dogmatism, attempting to remove the right-wing bias from both the conceptual and operational definitions of authoritarianism, and moving the thrust from an understanding of prefascist behavior to an understanding of all human behavior. Did Rokeach succeed in removing right-wing bias? DiRenzo (1968, 1971) found evidence that high dogmatic subjects had a greater preference for more conservative presidential candidates. Parrott and Brown (1972) asked 48 undergraduates to classify the items on the dogmatism scale as left or right, finding two of 40 items biased left and 14 biased right. While Zippel and Norman (1966) found no effect for dogmatism scores on presidential preference, and Bettinghaus, Miller, and Steinfatt (1970) found both high and low dogmatics who favored or opposed the conflict in Vietnam in about equal numbers, there is some evidence of right-wing bias in the dogmatism scale.

## Dogmatism and Rigidity

Rokeach's work also subsumed the notion of rigidity, but considerable confusion still exists on the differences between a rigid and a closed-minded person, as is evident in the discussions of dogmatism in many basic communication texts. Rigidity is concerned with resistance to change in behavior and beliefs. If a person is rigid, he or she will prefer the known to the unknown and engage in fixed behavior patterns whenever possible. Item 22 of the Gough-Sanford scale is a good example: "I always put on and take off my clothes in the same order." Archie and Mike provide a wonderful illustration of rigidity in an *All in the Family* episode when Mike puts on a sock followed by a shoe on the same foot. Archie argues passionately for a "sock and a sock and a shoe and a shoe," while Mike argues equally passionately for a "sock and a shoe and a sock and a shoe."

The rigid person has great difficulty dealing with change. Resistance to change in beliefs, or to the formation of new beliefs, is extensive and occurs across a broad spectrum of beliefs. Dogmatic individuals, on the other hand, are rigid in their beliefs about authority. Positive authorities and negative authorities abound in their belief systems. Positive authorities do not err, and negative authorities do not speak the truth. While both rigid and dogmatic individuals have difficulty with "genuine" belief change, as discussed earlier, dogmatic individuals (but not rigid individuals) can engage in a "party line" change with ease. If one wishes to change the beliefs of a highly dogmatic individual, one needs only to convince the person that a positive authority figure has spoken in favor of the change, or possibly that a negative authority has spoken against it. No such mechanism is available for a rigid person. While "closed-minded" and "rigid" are often used synonymously, the closed-minded person is by no means rigid when it comes to belief change, nor is there evidence that high dogmatics are more rigid than lows in their behavior. For high dogmatics, it is as in Orwell's (1951) *1984*: When the Ministry of Education dictates a change in belief, the change occurs.

*Denny's Doodlebug problem.* Rokeach, McGovney, and Denny (1955) used "Denny's Doodlebug problem" to clarify this distinction. They suggest that the preservation of individual beliefs is the goal of the rigid person, while preservation of the total system and its relationship to authority should be the goal for the high dogmatic. Given a problem that demands analytic thinking to overcome specific beliefs which are counterproductive to finding a solution, followed by synthetic thinking to put together a workable solution, rigidity should block analysis but not synthesis. Dogmatism should pose little trouble to analysis given positive sources, nor to synthesis up to the point that the "outlines of another system that threatens [the] present belief system" begin to appear (Rokeach, 1960, p. 184). At that point synthesis may be affected. Thus rigid persons will have trouble analyzing a problem due to their inability to discard antiquated beliefs, but they will have no trouble synthesizing a solution once analysis is complete. Dogmatic individuals will have no trouble with analysis but will begin to show problems in synthesis as a solution counter to their belief system approaches.

Denny's Doodlebug problem may be summarized as follows: Joe Doodlebug has certain restrictions on his behavior, mainly that he must always face north, that once he jumps in a direction he must make four jumps in that direction before he can change directions, that he can only move by jumping, and that he can only move due north, south, east, or west, though he can jump any distance on any jump. Joe stops, facing north, when a pile of food is placed three feet directly west of him. Joe cannot reach the food in fewer than four jumps (see Rokeach, 1960, pp. 185-188, for a full description). Why? The answer must explain the condition in which Joe found himself when the food was put in place.

The analysis phase of the solution involves overcoming three beliefs about animal movement which are untrue for Joe Doodlebug (that he must face the food to eat it, that he can only jump forward, and that he is free to choose the direction of his movement). The synthesis of a solution involves recreating the situation in which Joe found himself when the food appeared. The solution is that Joe must have just completed his first jump to the east.

Rokeach et al. (1955) studied 60 subjects divided into four groups of 15: (1) high dog, high rigid; (2) high dog, low rigid; (3) low dog, low rigid; and (4) low dog, high rigid. High rigids were found to take significantly longer in analysis than low rigids, but no significant differences were found between high and low dogmatics. In the synthetic phase, rigids were not significantly different, but limited support for a difference between high and low dogmatics was found in that low dogmatics solved the problem significantly more quickly than high dogmatics after the second belief (forward jumping) had been overcome.

## Summary of the Concepts

Authoritarianism, dogmatism, rigidity, and intolerance of ambiguity are four interrelated but distinctly different variables. Authoritarianism is best invoked when interest is in prefascist attitudes and behavior. Dogmatism is a measure of general authoritarianism unfettered to a specific ideology. It is based on the notion of information processing by the receiver and is different from both rigidity and intolerance of ambiguity. Rigidity is generalized resistance to behavioral and belief change, while dogmatism is excessive reliance on authority beliefs resulting in an apparent inability to discriminate source from content, allowing for relatively easy change of non-authority beliefs.

Intolerance of ambiguity evolves from a psychoanalytic interpretation of emotional ambivalence toward authority where ambiguous situations are seen as threatening. It is often seen as *cognitive* intolerance as opposed to *behavioral* rigidity, though rigidity also applies to beliefs and belief change. Dogmatism deals with a generalized intolerance of persons, ideas, and situations that do not correspond to the world as promulgated by authority figures, while intolerance of ambiguity examines emotional personality development based on inconsistency in sanctioning behavior by parents.

These four variables have much in common, allowing for their aggregation into this section. But as conceived and employed in research, their differences are such that any one might be appropriate, depending on one's research purposes.

## Intercorrelations Among the Variables

Given the conceptual and historical relationships among these variables, it is interesting to examine their intercorrelation. Complicating this examination is the nature of the epistemic relationship between each of the variables conceptually and their operationalizations. Not only are there different measures of each to consider, but different forms of each measure, different administrative procedures, and a different range of the variable present in the measured group, all of which can substantially affect the correlation. Correlations in Figure 2.1 are noncorrected and come from a number of sources.

Many of the correlations are from data compiled between 1970 and 1985 in my classes on communication theory and persuasion taught at the University of Michigan, Queens College, Temple University, Auburn University, and Clarkson University. I routinely administer the 20-item short-form Dogmatism Scale (Troldahl & Powell, 1965), the 29-item California F-scale (Rokeach, 1960, pp. 416-417), and the 22-item Gough-Sanford Rigidity scale (Rokeach, 1960, pp. 418-419) to all students who enroll in either of these classes. Beginning at Auburn, I also administered the 20-item Mach IV scale as a part of these classes, and at Clarkson I began collecting data on both intolerance of ambiguity and locus of control. The Clarkson data are from management students, while the prior data are primarily from arts and sciences majors.

I use two nonstandard procedures in these administrations of which the reader should be aware. First, I administer the scales orally, early in the term, by reading each item twice slowly, with a seven-anchor "strongly agree" to "strongly disagree" scale printed on the blackboard. For each administration I change the order of the tests so that the average rank order of administration for each item is approximately equal across the total sample of students. While all of the items for each individual test are read together, students are not told when one scale ends and another begins until the scores have been collected.

The second nonstandard practice I use is scoring all items on a seven-point scale running from one (strongly disagree) to six (strongly agree) rather than the standard practice, apparently begun by Adorno et al., of

| | External Chance PowOth | Dog | Auth | Rigid | Mach |
|---|---|---|---|---|---|
| PowOth | .56 (S) (n = 246) <br> .59 (L) (factor r) | | | | |
| Dog | . 41 (S) –.02 (S) <br> (n = 246) | | | | |
| Auth | | .51 (S) <br> (n = 647) <br><br> $\overline{.65}$ (GB215) | | | |
| Rigid | .15 (S)   .01 (S) <br> (n = 246) | .48 (S) <br> (n = 687) <br><br> $\overline{.45}$ (R193) | .48 (S) <br> (n = 649) <br><br> .41m (SS) <br> (n = 147m) | | |
| Mach | .34 (S)   .36 (S) <br> (n = 246) <br> .43 (WC) <br> .39 (SB)   (n=170) <br> .41 (PB)   .09 (PB) <br> .45 (HGB)  .33 (HGB) <br> (n = 351) | .21 (S) <br> (n = 285) <br><br> .24 (HGB) <br> (n = 351) | .14 (S) <br> (n = 281) <br> "0" (G308) <br> –.20 (CG38) <br> (n = 1782) | –.13 (S) <br> (n = 282) <br><br> –.23 (CG48) <br> (factor r) | |
| I of A | .04 (S)       .06 (S) <br> (n = 246) | $\overline{.28}$ (F) <br><br> "0" (N) | $\overline{.32}$ (B41) <br> (n = 502) | "0" (S) <br> (n = 246) | –.$\overline{18}$ (B43) <br> (n = 502) <br><br> –.25 (CG51) |
| IQ | | –.02 (R190) | –.$\overline{40}$ (A282) | | $\overline{.00}$ (CG36) <br> (n = 446) |

**Figure 2.1: Some Intercorrelations among the Variables**

Note:   $\overline{.XX}$ = weighted average correlation          m = male sample
     HGB = Hunter, et al. (1982)                "0" = n.s.d. or actual near zero
        S = Steinfatt sample                        A = Adorno et al. (1950)
      GB = Goldstein and Blackman (1978)     F = Feather (1969, 1971)
       R = Rokeach (1960)                          N = Norton (1975)
      SS = Schroder and Streufert (1962)       B = Budner (1962)
      CG = Christie and Geis (1970)             SB = Solor and Bruehl (1971)
      WC = Wrightsman and Cook (1965)       PB = Prociuk and Breen (1976)
       L = Levenson (1974)

scoring the six responses on a seven-point scale by counting one, two, three, five, six, and seven. I have elaborated elsewhere on the psychometric reasons for this opposing method of scoring (Steinfatt, 1973, 1977). In Adorno et al.'s scoring procedure, subjects are presented with six choices, equally spaced on a piece of paper. If a subject moves between any two adjacent categories, it makes a difference of one unit on the scale, unless the subject moves between the two middle categories, in which case it is counted as a two-unit move. The rationale for this "magic" seems to be that there is a neutral point in between the two "slightly" categories. My point is that if this is true, why not present this neutral point to the subject and let the subject decide into which category to place his or her response? The use of a forced choice procedure for the elimination of social desirability does not require the addition of a phantom category which can substantially inflate the correlations obtained.

The effects of administering the scales orally does not appear to have a major impact on the scores. Six week test-retest correlations for a sample of 68 students who completed the dogmatism, authoritarianism, rigidity, and Machiavellianism scales—first in written form and then orally—produced correlations that were not significantly different from the reliability figures for each of the four tests. Scoring from one to six, rather than in the Adorno fashion, means that the correlations obtained will normally be smaller than those based on the same data if scored in the Adorno fashion.

The correlations reported in Figure 2.1 indicate that dogmatism and authoritarianism share about 25% to 40% of their variance in common, suggesting a strong relationship yet different concepts. Rigidity appears to account for around 20% of the variance in both dogmatism and authoritarianism. Intolerance of ambiguity appears far less strongly related to dogmatism, authoritarianism, and rigidity than these three are to each other. While intolerance of ambiguity is conceptually more similar to rigidity than to dogmatism or authoritarianism, common measures of intolerance of ambiguity and rigidity appear to be essentially independent of each other. The relationships of Machiavellianism and intelligence to the dogmatism-related variables in Figure 2.1, though often significant, are generally negligible. For example, Machiavellianism and dogmatism share only 4% of their variance in common. The only exception to this seems to be the relationship between intelligence and authoritarianism, which share 16% of their variance. Yet intelligence is uncorrelated with dogmatism.

## Communication Research on Authoritarianism,
## Dogmatism, Rigidity, and
## Intolerance of Ambiguity

Each of the four variables discussed in this section has been related to communication behavior, with most of the research in the area of cognitive functioning and message processing. An equally important area, message selection behavior, has received far less attention.

### Authoritarianism and Communication

While we can hypothesize that authoritarians should produce a greater number of more prejudiced messages over a greater variety of situations, little research beyond the clinical studies in *The Authoritarian Personality* (Adorno et al., 1950) exists to bear this out. A relationship between authoritarianism and certain forms of mass media has been discussed by Kelley (1985) and by Greendlinger (1985). Kelley found both male and female high authoritarians to have significantly more negative feelings about pornography as presented in sexually explicit slides depicting same-sex masturbation than did low authoritarians. Similarly, Greendlinger (1985) found that high authoritarians responded less positively to pornographic videotapes depicting homosexual rather than heterosexual activity, and that high authoritarianism was negatively correlated with attitudes toward masturbation (–.32), general attitude toward sexuality (–.28), and toward male (–.48) and female (–.52) homosexuals. It was positively correlated with sex guilt (+.27) and homophobia (+.49).

Though authoritarianism theory suggests that high authoritarians should be good at controlling others and successful as leaders (Christie, 1978, p. 111), Shils (1954) rejects this view on the grounds that people who are both suspicious of others and who project their own aggression onto others are unlikely to excel at leadership in an organization. Mann (1959) reviewed ten studies of authoritarianism and leadership and found that in each study, high authoritarians were rated lower on leadership than were low authoritarians.

As I discuss shortly under "Dogmatism and Communication," a strong interaction exists between dogmatism and source credibility such that high dogmatics are far more influenced by credibility than are low dogmatics. This type of interaction has been proposed for authoritarianism, but research has not supported this prediction. Johnson and Steiner (1967) cite Adorno et al. (1950) as the source for their hypothesis that high authoritarians will respond more to the source of a message, while low authoritarians will be more influenced by its content. Johnson,

Torcivia, and Poprick (1968) tested this hypothesis and found a significant interaction in the opposite direction, such that low authoritarians were more influenced by source differences than high authoritarians. They interpret these data as supporting McGuire's (1968) receptivity/ yielding theory. While dogmatism and authoritarianism are intercorrelated, it seems that high dogmatism, but not high authoritarianism, is related to source credibility. Low authoritarians may be more affected by credibility influence than high authoritarians, based on Johnson et al.'s (1968) findings, but until more research is done this must be considered at best a tentative finding.

## *Rigidity, Intolerance of Ambiguity, and Communication*

The message behavior of persons high in rigidity should show indications of that rigidity in message structure, content, and style; in the timing of messages; in the choice of channels appropriate for certain messages; and in the intended targets of those messages. Since rigidity is conceptualized and often measured as a behavioral variable, we might expect it to influence message selection behavior, and behavior which occurs as a result of message reception, more than the process of message reception itself. Yet rigidity affects analytic thinking, so we might also examine rigidity with respect to message processing variables which are more likely to reflect or be affected by analytic than synthetic processing. To date, little such research is available beyond the finding of Rokeach et al. (1955) that persons high in rigidity have increased latency during the analytic phase of Denny's Doodlebug problem.

Mortensen (1972, pp. 164-165) discusses the relationship between intolerance of ambiguity and Sherif and Sherif's (1967) notion of latitudes of acceptance such that increased ego involvement leads to reduced tolerance, which in turn affects latitudes of acceptance, rejection, and noncommitment (Sherif & Sherif, 1967; Sherif, Sherif, & Nebergall, 1965). Such a conception, treating intolerance of ambiguity as a function of involvement, allows intolerance of ambiguity to be viewed as a situationally influenced personality variable, dependent on one's level of intolerance of ambiguity, one's involvement in the situation, and one's tendency to become ego-involved in discussions and topics. Yet little research is available to bring to bear on these extensions. Most of the research that exists is in the area of intolerance of ambiguity rather than rigidity, though some of the literature still occasionally refers to intolerance of ambiguity as rigidity (e. g., Davis, 1975).

Smock (1955) used imprecise pictures to study intolerance of ambiguity. He found that persons high in intolerance of ambiguity tend to base judgments on first impressions formed prematurely, before all available information has been considered. Similarly, Martin and Westie (1959) describe persons high in intolerance of ambiguity as overlooking factors that do not fit neatly into rigidly held conceptions of reality, with a tendency to base judgments on first impressions. Teger (1970) found that subjects who had been duped by a confederate and who were high in intolerance of ambiguity tended to continue a conflict longer than persons low in intolerance of ambiguity.

Pilisuk (1963; Pilisuk, Potter, Rapoport, & Winter, 1965) discusses his own measure of intolerance of ambiguity. He found that persons low in intolerance of ambiguity were more open to new information than those high in intolerance of ambiguity, while the high scorers tended to change less than the lows after feedback from interpersonal interactions. Feldman and Rice (1965) found that persons high in intolerance of ambiguity were more threatened by specific than general feedback. While this may seem counter to the usual intolerance of ambiguity predictions, the specific feedback was of a form difficult to fit into previous cognitive patterns. The general feedback could be placed more easily into preexisting categories by leveling and sharpening processes.

The relationship of intolerance of ambiguity to the perception of threats has also been studied by Nardin (1968). He found that persons high in intolerance of ambiguity tended to interpret threats as indications of hostility by another person, while persons low in intolerance of ambiguity tended to interpret threats as signals intended to provide information relevant to a change in behavior. Illardo (1973) discusses the relationship between information theory and intolerance of ambiguity and the actions of the high intolerance of ambiguity communicator when faced with stress. He suggests that highs may avoid information overload by strategies such as avoiding interactions, aligning themselves with formal belief systems such as a religion or a political group, avoiding strong relationships with individuals which might require tolerance of ambiguity, and by the use of stereotypes and simplified conceptual categories.

Davis (1975) studied 184 highest and lowest scorers of 396 undergraduates who filled out Budner's intolerance of ambiguity scale. She divided them into three dyad types of high/high, high/low, and low/low scorers and asked them to complete a collective bargaining task, half with complete information and half where one person had complete information but the other did not. Davis found an interaction between the information condition and level of intolerance of ambiguity in effects on payoffs, time to complete negotiations, and postnegotiation attitudes. Specifically, high intolerance of ambiguity, together with incomplete information, produced increased divergence in payoffs and increased negotiation times. When compared to the other pairs, subjects in the high/low dyads also had increased divergence in payoffs and increased negotiation times.

Intolerance of ambiguity is not the same as intolerance of inconsistency. In an ambiguous situation one does not know exactly what is going on, or why, due to multiple possibilities. In an inconsistent situation some of the possibilities conflict. Ambiguity is inherent in an inconsistent situation, but the reverse is not necessarily true. Inconsistencies produce ambiguity, since one cannot know exactly which of the two or more apparent contradictions is the correct or preferable interpretation. While such reasoning could justify a discussion of the entire cognitive consistency literature under the heading of intolerance of ambiguity, I will resist this temptation. Steiner (1954), Steiner and Johnson (1963), Bieri (1961), and Rosen (1961) discuss correlations of intolerance of inconsistency with other personality and demographic measures. These studies are summarized by Glass (1967). Foulkes and Foulkes (1965) report a positive relationship between intolerance of inconsistency and dogmatism.

## Dogmatism and Communication

Though a wealth of studies is not available, sufficient studies of the relationship between source credibility and dogmatism have been conducted to warrant some clear generalizations. Perhaps most important is the observation that at least among published results, few negative or null findings have occurred. While the file-drawer problem must be considered, the lack of negative findings on this relationship is striking when compared to the reviews of most other variable relationships cited in this chapter. G. R. Miller (1977) and Goldstein and Blackman (1978, pp. 87-90) have each summarized portions of the literature relating dogmatism and communication, though only two studies (Bettinghaus et al., 1970; Powell, 1962) are cited in common by these reviewers.

*Dogmatism and source credibility.* The theoretic relationship between source credibility and dogmatism becomes clear through Rokeach's conceptual definition of closed-mindedness (1960, pp. 57-60), which treats dogmatism as the apparent inability of the high dogmatic to distinguish between the source and content of a message. That is, highly dogmatic individuals should treat message content as one with the source of the message and dominated by the source, while less dogmatic persons should better discriminate between judgments about a source and judgments about the truth value of the source's messages.

Vidulich and Kaiman (1961) operationalized source credibility as status. They used high- and low-status confederates, presented as a college professor or a high school student, respectively, to provide messages concerning judgments of movement in a Sherif-like auto-kinetic paradigm. Thirty high and low dogmatic females each made 30 judgments individually as to whether a light was moving left or right. The confederate then made 30 judgments, 80% of which were in the direction opposite to the majority of the subject's judgments, followed by 30 more judgments by the subject. High dogmatics were more influenced by confederates' judgments than lows, but only when the confederates were of high status. Harvey and Hays (1972) manipulated high and low credibility in the transcript of a speech on air pollution, finding a positive relationship between dogmatism and degree of influence by the prestige source among 80 female undergraduates.

During the 1960 election campaign, Powell (1962) asked 38 high and 38 low dogmatics to judge three statements each by Kennedy and Nixon on foreign and domestic policy and integration using 14 semantic differential scales. Mean source-message differences were used as a measure of ability to distinguish between source and content. These differences were twice as large for low dogmatics as for high dogmatics (38.32 versus 16.36 sd units), confirming the dogmatism predictions. Powell had half of his subjects rate the sources first, and the other half the content first, with no significant differences between these conditions. Thus Powell's findings showed that high dogmatic subjects will move their judgments of sources closer to previously judged messages, as well as moving judgments of messages closer to the sources.

Norris (1965), Hunt and Miller (1965), and Cronkhite and Goetz (1965) all report a greater willingness of high dogmatic subjects to endorse the opinions of authority figures, a willingness not shared by low dogmatics. However, Norris found that this tendency was not equally strong across all topics tested.

N. E. Miller (1965) studied the effects of dogmatism and of ego involvement in the issues of the message on attitude change. He found that while issue involvement reduced the effectiveness of belief-discrepant messages, dogmatism had a tendency, significant in only some conditions, to further reduce message effectiveness.

G. R. Miller and Roberts (1965) manipulated source credibility by using pictures of a black or white female as the source who guided readers through an information booklet on weather control. They argued that a black source (in 1965) would be of lower credibility than a white, and that this difference should be more pronounced for high than for low dogmatic subjects. In all, 36 high and 36 low dogmatic subjects completed a 10-item multiple choice test on information in the message, as well as five semantic differential-type scales on attitude toward the message content. Miller and Roberts found a significant interaction between dogmatism and communicator race on the retention of information. The mean retention score for high dogmatics in the black source condition was significantly lower than this score in the other three conditions. As predicted, they also found a main effect for race of source that was not attributable to the significant interaction: Information from white sources was retained significantly better than information from black sources. High dogmatic subjects in the black source condition also had the lowest opinion of the quality of the message content. These findings may also bear on the contention, discussed earlier, that right-wing bias has not been completely removed from the dogmatism scale. Yet the treatment of blacks in some leftist countries might argue that anti-black prejudice is not completely a right-wing phenomenon, and that these results do not necessarily suggest right-wing bias in the scale.

Mertz, Miller, and Ballance (1966) presented high and low dogmatic subjects with a message that was discrepant with the subject's beliefs and measured attitude change toward the source and the content. High dogmatic subjects changed little away from the source and greatly away from the content, while low dogmatic subjects changed more away from the source than away from the content, again indicating a greater reliance on source by high dogmatics.

Becker (1967) asked 150 undergraduates to make judgments about the degree of humor in six jokes attributed to different comedians. He found that both high and low dogmatic subjects were influenced by source credibility operationalized as the popularity of the comedian, while mid dogmatics were not. This finding does not conform to Rokeach's second definition predictions. G. R. Miller and Bacon (1971) report that high dogmatics tend to see less humor in cartoons depicting novel or unusual situations due to a more conventional and stereotyped approach to such situations than is the case with low dogmatics. Nevertheless, Becker's (1967) finding for low dogmatics still does not fit the pattern of the other studies reviewed here.

Rosenman (1967) found that high dogmatic subjects rated the movie *Dr. Strangelove* less favorably than low dogmatic subjects. While Rosenman argued that this was due to the attack on U.S. authority figures in the movie, Goldstein and Blackman (1978) suggest that a greater proportion of right than left high dogmatics in Rosenman's sample may better account for these results.

Siegel, Miller, and Wotring (1969) proposed the construct of credibility-proneness—the degree to which a person is sensitive to differences between sources—to account for some of the dogmatism findings. They found that this construct was related to Fiedler's (1960) psychological distance measures of assumed similarity between opposites (ASo), with low ASo's more influenced by credibility than high ASo's. However, the ASo measures did not correlate significantly with dogmatism.

Mouw (1969) found that dogmatism affected performance on a series of tasks as the task moved from dependence on authority to dependence on self. Low dogmatic subjects improved as the tasks changed from authority-dependent to self-dependent, while the performance of high dogmatic subjects on the non-authority-based tasks did not improve. A related finding is reported by Plax and Rosenfeld (1976), who found that high dogmatics were less likely to engage in risky decisions whether alone or in the presence of a group.

Bettinghaus, Miller, and Steinfatt (1970) asked 120 subjects to judge the validity of 16 syllogisms relating to the conflict in Vietnam. Half of the syllogisms were valid and half invalid, half with pro-war and half with anti-war conclusions. Half of the subjects were pro-war and half anti-war. Half of the syllogisms were presented as originating from positive and half from negative sources. High dogmatic subjects made fewer errors than low dogmatics when the valid syllogisms were presented by positive sources and the invalid syllogisms presented by negative sources. However, high dogmatics made more errors than low dogmatics with valid syllogisms and negative sources and with invalid syllogisms and positive sources. The high dogmatic subjects tended to respond that the conclusions to the syllogisms presented by positive sources were valid and those presented by negative sources invalid, while the low dogmatic subjects tended to attempt the task as presented to them, making judgments of the syllogism's validity more on the basis of agreement with content than agreement with source. Low dogmatic subjects essentially behaved as would be expected from research on syllogistic judgments, marking "valid" on conclusions with which they agree and "invalid" on conclusions with which they disagreed. High dogmatic subjects did not do this, however. An especially interesting finding of this study is that high dogmatic subjects will mark conclusions with which they agree as invalid when such conclusions are presented by a negative source. Similarly, high dogmatics will mark conclusions with which they disagree as valid when such conclusions are presented by a positive source. Low dogmatics are influenced more by content, while high dogmatics are influenced more by source.

Schultz and DiVesta (1972) provided a helpful and an unhelpful hint to subjects working on the Doodlebug problem. Experts were said to endorse either the helpful (new belief) or unhelpful (old belief) hint. High dogmatic subjects performed better than low dogmatics when the helpful hint was endorsed by experts but fared worse when the unhelpful hint received expert endorsement. Thus Schultz and DiVesta predicted and replicated the type of interaction found by Bettinghaus et al. (1970). McNeel and Thorsen (1985) also found a significant correlation between dogmatism and the tendency to rely on external authorities in making decisions among students at a Christian college.

*Dogmatism and communication in conflict games.* Additional research supporting the relationship between dogmatism and communication variables has been reported in gaming studies of conflict. Druckman (1967) asked subjects to play the role of either union or management in a simulated bargaining game somewhat similar to the one used by Davis (1975). In both role positions, Druckman found that high dogmatic subjects resolved fewer issues and had a greater resistance to compromise than did low dogmatic subjects. High dogmatic subjects also had a greater tendency to believe that a compromise was a loss.

Steinfatt (1972, 1973a) and Steinfatt, Seibold, and Frye (1974) report studies relating dogmatism to persuasive influence attempts in the context of Steinfatt's creative alternative game (see Figure 2.2). These studies are reviewed in part by Steinfatt and Miller (1974) and by Seibold and Steinfatt (1979). The game is a nonsymmetric game matrix where only one of two players (P) appears to have something to gain from changing a response pattern into which the players seem locked. In Steinfatt's (1973a) study, all player pairs were composed of equal status players who were previously acquainted only through attendance in the same class and presumed to be of approximately equal credibility to each other. Subjects were told neither that a creative solution of splitting the points from one cell of the game matrix existed nor that it would be allowed.

When both players were low dogmatics, influence attempts by the player (P) with something apparently to gain, suggesting that the gain could be split, were 50% effective in changing the choice behavior of the other (O). The player with apparently nothing to gain (O) served as the target of influence attempts by the player with something to gain. With high dogmatic subjects in the target (O) position, the effectiveness of the persuasive attempts dropped to near 30%. When high dogmatic subjects were in the source position (P), effectiveness dropped to near zero. The explanation for these findings may be rooted in the cognitive behavior of the highly dogmatic subjects. Steinfatt's (1973) highly dogmatic undergraduate subjects generally recognized the existence of the creative solution but did not think the authority figure (the experimenter) would allow them to implement it by splitting the points from one cell of the game matrix. In contrast, Steinfatt, Seibold, and Frye's (1974) high dogmatic prison subjects appear not to have recognized the existence of the creative solution. While Steinfatt et al. did not test for rigidity, it is possible that the highly dogmatic prison sample was more rigid than the highly dogmatic undergraduate sample, thus accounting for the analytic block of the prisoner high dogmatics as compared with the synthetic block of the undergraduate high dogmatics.

It would be interesting to test for this possibility with four groups of subjects divided into high rigid-high dogmatic, low rigid-high dogmatic, and so on, groups. The analytic error of the prisoner high dogmatic subjects and the synthetic error of the undergraduate high dogmatic subjects decreased the persuasive message attempts by both sets of high dogmatic subjects to near zero, thus reducing any chance of a persuasive effect. With the low dogmatic in the source position influence attempts were not reduced, but the explanation for the decrease in "creative" responses still appears to lie with the effect of dogmatism on cognitive functioning. High dogmatic subjects receiving influence attempts tended to reject the possibility that these solutions would be allowed by the experimenter more often than did low dogmatic subjects. This may have been due to the apparently neutral credibility of the source of the influence attempts, though the conditions of the experiment did not allow a test of this possibility. Hazelton's (1977) study of Machiavellianism in Steinfatt's creative alternative game is discussed later in the section on Machiavellianism.

*Dogmatism in interpersonal communication.* A series of studies have examined the relationship of dogmatism to interpersonal relationships. Byrne and Blaylock (1963) found a significant correlation between spouses in the dogmatism scores of 36 married couples. Lesser and Steininger (1975) found evidence that children of highly dogmatic parents have a greater tendency to be highly dogmatic themselves than do children whose parents are lower in dogmatism. This relationship is further discussed in Lesser (1985). Stefflre and Leafgren (1964) asked each of 40 counselor trainees to make sociometric choices among the other trainees. Three sets of choices were formed from these data: persons who mutually selected each other, persons who mutually rejected each other, and cases where only one person was selected by the other. Dogmatism score discrepancies between the pairs were not significantly different between the mutual rejection group and either of the other two groups. However, persons choosing each other were significantly closer to each other in dogmatism scores than were pairs of persons where only one person chose the other.

In a study of 215 graduate counselor trainees' skill in facilitative responding to clients, Carlozzi, Campbell, and Ward (1982) and Carlozzi (1985) report a significant negative relationship (–.47) between dogmatism scores and Carkhuff's (1969) "gross rating of facilitative interpersonal functioning" scale. Rosenfeld and Nauman (1969) observed interaction patterns for 10 weeks among freshman women living in the same dormitory. They found greater satisfaction in interpersonal interactions between pairs of persons similar in dogmatism than among persons whose dogmatism scores were highly dissimilar. Over the 10-week period, fewer and fewer contacts were initiated with high dogmatic subjects by others in the dormitory, and most contact initiation began with the high dogmatics. In addition, negative evaluations of high dogmatics by other residents increased over the 10 weeks.

A series of studies by Altman and his associates (Altman & Haythorn, 1965, 1967; Haythorn & Altman, 1967; Haythorn, Altman, & Myers, 1966), studied pairs of Navy recruits who were either under stress conditions, isolated in a small room together for 10 days performing both dyadic and monadic tasks, or performing these tasks under nonstress conditions in regular Navy facilities. Differences were found in and between these groups on willingness to self-disclose personal experiences and self-images, but these differences were unrelated to dogmatism. Similarly, dogmatism was unrelated to performance on any of the three tasks under nonstress conditions. However, dogmatism had a noticeable effect on task performance in the stress conditions. When subjects were isolated, pairs who differed little in dogmatism scores performed better than average on their tasks, while pairs with heterogeneous dogmatism scores did significantly worse.

Roloff and Barnicott (1978) found that dogmatism was positively related to the willingness of their 124 subjects to endorse Marwell and Schmitt's (1967) 16 compliance-gaining strategies. Highly dogmatic subjects said that in interpersonal situations they would be more likely to use compliance-gaining strategies—including prosocial, psychological force, and punishing activity techniques—than did low dogmatic subjects. In noninterpersonal situations, high dogmatics were significantly more likely to say they would use prosocial techniques than were low dogmatics, but no differences were found in claimed willingness to use psychological force and punishing activity techniques.

In studies with other than American subjects, Kremer-Hayon, Moore, and Nevat (1985) found a significant interaction between dogmatism and style of supervision affecting Israeli teacher trainees' ability to employ probing questions effectively in their classes. An open style of supervision was more effective in producing the desired probing style in low dogmatic student teachers, while the closed style was more effective with the high dogmatic group. The low dogmatic trainees reported significantly higher satisfaction with the open style of supervision than with the closed style, while the high dogmatic trainees were significantly more satisfied with the closed style than the open.

Shirali (1985) studied the middle-class Indian families of origin of 45 males who were students at Punjab University, including 84 parents. Nine TAT cards on three areas of interpersonal relationships, and form E of the dogmatism scale, were administered to the parents in their homes. It is not clear whether the TAT administrator was aware of the subject's dogmatism score. Given this restriction, the messages of high dogmatic parents were more limited in range, restricted, and stereotyped, and more dominant and coercive in conflict situations, than were the messages of low dogmatic parents. Highly dogmatic parents perceived their children as more submissive and obedient, expressed less love and concern for their children, and indicated less involvement with their marriage partner than did less dogmatic parents. Highly dogmatic fathers' stories had a higher proportion of pacifying-game, or *manana* motif characteristics in their stories, while the same was true for less dogmatic mothers.

*Dogmatism and linguistic features of messages.* An alternative approach to the study of dogmatism through the analysis of linguistic features of messages may be found in the work of Ertel. His thesis is that language usage and speech style signal the cognitive features which underlie the writer's or speaker's degree of ideological commitment. Ertel (1972) developed a linguistic indicator of cognitive closure based on lexemes, clear-cut linguistic units, and a DOTA (dogmatism text analysis) dictionary of 430 purely structural lexemes. These serve as the operationalization of six categories (alwaysness, allness, extremeness, certainty, exclusion, and necessity) narrowed from eight original categories through factor analysis. Each lexeme falls into one of the six categories and is either an A- or B-lexeme. A-lexemes denote extremes (e.g., always, none, must), while B-lexemes denote differential gradings (e.g., rarely, some, might). A DQ (dogmatism quotient) is formed by $A/(A + B)$ where A and B are the raw frequencies of A- and B-lexemes across the six categories.

Ertel (1985) reviews five of approximately 40 studies using his method and concludes that the DQ is a reliable indicator of individual and "group" cognitive states, that it is related to the openness and closedness of minds, and that interpretation of the DQ is dependent on both the topic and the intent of the communicator. Many of these studies were conducted in German on German social, political, and historic issues. For example, his analysis of the official platforms and other political literature of the six political parties of the Weimar Republic demonstrates a repeated finding with the DQ of a U-shaped curve when plotting DQ values against the positions of these parties on a political spectrum from left to right. The potential utility of Ertel's method may lie in its ability to analyze both mass media and interpersonal messages. While most personality measures require obtrusive measurement, such as the administration of a paper-and-pencil test, the DQ requires only a sample of message behavior with known topic, source, target, and intent. It can be applied without knowledge of these four factors, but with diminished predictive utility.

## Summary of Communication Research on Dogmatism-Related Variables

### Authoritarianism

A significant relationship appears to exist between authoritarianism and reactions to pornographic materials. High authoritarians have significantly stronger negative feelings about pornography than do low authoritarians. Studies of authoritarianism and leadership suggest that high authoritarians are consistently rated lower in leadership than low authoritarians. Suggestions of an interaction of source credibility with authoritarianism have generally not been supported in the direction of the predicted interaction. Indeed, one study found a significant interaction in the opposite direction such that low authoritarians were more influenced by source differences than were high authoritarians. The principal utility of authoritarianism in communication theory and research is in situations involving right-wing and prefascist persons, groups, and societies. Dogmatism, not authoritarianism, is the more appropriate variable for the study of general authoritarianism.

### Rigidity

Little actual research has been conducted relating communication and rigidity beyond the finding of greater message-processing latency under analytic than synthetic conditions. Yet rigidity would seem to have strong potential utility when used together with dogmatism and the differences between analytic and synthetic thinking to sort out individual differences in message-processing and message-selection behavior.

## *Intolerance of Ambiguity*

Research suggests that persons high in intolerance of ambiguity tend to base their judgments on first impressions formed before all available information is considered. High scorers who have been duped by a confederate tend to continue a conflict longer than low scorers. Persons low in intolerance of ambiguity are more open to new information than high scorers, while the high scorers tend to change less after feedback from interpersonal interactions. There is evidence to suggest that high scorers are more threatened by specific than by general feedback when the specific feedback is difficult to fit into previous cognitive patterns. High scorers seem to interpret threats as indications of hostility by the other person, while persons low in intolerance of ambiguity may interpret threats as signals that provide information relevant to a change in behavior. One study suggests that high scorers have greater divergence in payoffs and increased negotiation times under incomplete information conditions in negotiations. Pairs with dissimilar scores (high versus low) also have increased divergence in payoffs and increased negotiation times.

In much the same way as rigidity, intolerance of ambiguity should influence both the reception of messages and message-selection behavior. The research summarized earlier tends to show that persons who are intolerant of ambiguity tend to see inconsistencies as consistent and complexity as simple structure, and are more likely to smooth off rough edges in forming a simplified cognitive picture of the world than are persons more tolerant of ambiguity. This should affect the listening behavior of such persons in important ways. The common perceptual processes of leveling and sharpening should affect listeners intolerant of ambiguity differently than those more tolerant. The listener high in intolerance of ambiguity should fail to recall contradictions, details in general (complexity), and details that do not seem to fit their prior conception. In relaying a message, such listeners should show a higher proportion of loss of detail, contradiction, and complexity than persons more tolerant of ambiguity. The differential treatment of message details has great practical implications for the processing of messages. Research is needed to test such speculations and to clarify any differences in communication effects between rigidity and intolerance of ambiguity.

## Dogmatism

Highly dogmatic persons have great difficulty in separating the source and content of a message. They treat message content as one with the source of the message and as dominated by the source. Low dogmatics are better able to discriminate between judgments about a source and judgments about the truth value of the source's messages. Evidence suggests that information from highly credible sources is easier for highly dogmatic persons to retain. Twelve out of 14 studies support the proposition that high dogmatics are influenced by authority to a greater extent than are low dogmatics. High dogmatic receivers have greater difficulty distinguishing between and evaluating messages and their sources than do low dogmatic receivers. They are also more influenced by source credibility while low dogmatic receivers are more influenced by message content.

The dogmatism of the receiver is an important mediator of the function of source credibility in communication. In conflict games, high scorers resolve fewer issues and have greater resistance to compromise than low scorers. They also have a greater tendency to regard compromise as loss. Among low dogmatic subjects in conflict games, influence attempts are about 50% effective in changing the choice behavior of the other. With high scorers, the point of view from their position in the situation (game matrix) appears to influence the effectiveness of their persuasive attempts. Compared with low scorers high scorers *receiving* influence attempts tend to reject more often the possibility that these solutions will be allowed by the authority figure.

In interpersonal communication situations, persons choosing each other sociometrically tend to be significantly more similar in dogmatism scores than pairs of persons where only one person chooses the other. Greater satisfaction in interpersonal interactions also appears to occur between pairs of persons similar in dogmatism than between persons whose dogmatism scores are highly dissimilar, and similar pairs perform significantly better on tasks, while dissimilar pairs perform significantly worse. Fewer contacts are initiated toward highly dogmatic persons, and negative evaluations of high dogmatics seem to increase over extended interactions.

A possible situational constraint on dogmatism is suggested by the finding that dogmatism has a noticeable effect on task performance under stress (but not nonstress) conditions. An open style of supervision seems more effective in producing a probing questioning style among low scorers, while a closed style appears more effective with high scorers. Low scorers report significantly higher satisfaction with open style supervision, while high scorers appear significantly more satisfied with a closed style. Messages of highly dogmatic parents seem more limited, restricted, stereotyped, dominant, and coercive than messages of less dogmatic parents. Highly dogmatic parents may perceive their children as more submissive and obedient, may express less love and concern for their children, and may indicate less involvement with their spouse than do less dogmatic parents. Dogmatism is the personality variable of choice when research and theory is concerned with the differential influence of levels of source credibility on specific receivers.

It is fitting to conclude this section on communication research in dogmatism-related variables by suggesting that in addition to the traditional dogmatism scale approach, the rigidity relationship and the analytic-synthetic distinction made possible by measuring dogmatism through Denny's Doodlebug problem, and Ertel's DQ method of textual analysis, seem fertile ground on which to begin a renewed interest in the study of dogmatism and communication.

## MACHIAVELLIANISM AND LOCUS OF CONTROL

### Machiavellianism

Machiavellianism takes its name from the Italian statesman and political philosopher Niccolo Machiavelli, author of *The Prince* published in the year 1513. In *The Prince*, Machiavelli argued that it was the duty of a person with power to use it to gain more in order to retain power and achieve one's goals. Machiavelli has come to represent the ruthless use of power to achieve ends at any cost. A person high in Machiavellianism is one who believes that people are manipulable, and who is both willing and able to manipulate others toward his or her own ends. Christie and Geis (1968) discuss the origins of Machiavellianism and in 1970 published the most complete work on the subject. Geis (1978a) provides a good summary of the research conducted on Machiavellianism in psychology to 1978, though she does not discuss the Machiavellianism research published in journals outside of her field. Hanson and Vleeming (1981) have compiled a bibliography of 333 publications on Machiavellianism which is quite complete through 1980.

### *The Machiavellianism Scales*

Christie's earlier work in authoritarianism, together with influences from Hoffer (1951), Shils (1954), and Lasswell (1954), led him to consider the methods by which those in positions of power and authority had achieved that authority: Are persons in power positions more likely to practice Machiavellian tactics than the powerless? Drawing on the writings of Machiavelli, Christie developed 71 statements describing human nature and various tactics used to deal with people. A number of the items were then reversed to form the original version of the scale. The items were administered to 1196 students at three colleges. Fifty of the 71 items discriminated significantly in an item analysis using *phi* coefficients for item-whole correlations. Ten Machiavellian-worded and 10 reversed-worded items were selected from the 50-item pool. These items form Mach IV, the most commonly used version of the Machiavellianism scale, which has a split-half reliability of .79 and correlates −.40 with Edwards's social desirability scale (Robinson & Shaver, 1970, p. 506). A forced choice version of the Machiavellianism scale was also developed, Mach V, which reduces the possible influence of social desirability responses. Reliabilities for Mach V fall in the .60s. Mach V correlates −.40 with an internal measure of social desirability (Robinson & Shaver, 1970, p. 507) but does not correlate with the Crowne-Marlowe or the Edwards social desirability scales.

Mach IV items include the following: (1) Never tell anyone the real reason you did something unless it is useful to do so, (2) The best way to handle people is to tell them what they want to hear, (3) The biggest difference between most criminals and other people is that the criminals are stupid enough to get caught, and (4) Most men forget more easily the death of their father than the loss of their property.

### Characteristics of Machiavellians

Four theoretical characteristics are listed by Christie (1970c, pp. 3-4) as important to Machiavellianism: depressed affect in interpersonal relationships, a lack of concern with conventional morality, a lack of gross psychopathology, and low ideological commitment. Observation of the behavior of high and low scorers on Mach IV and Mach V suggests that three factors characterize the empirical differences between them. The principal difference found between high and low scorers is the concentration of high Machs on the task and on their own *private goals* in the situation, versus the concentration of low Machs on other *persons as individuals* and seeing the situation from the other's point of view: "High Machs . . . [were] involved in the *game*; lows . . . [were] more involved with other *players*" (Geis, 1978a, p. 325). Low Machs are better at predicting the characteristics of other persons, while high Machs are better at predicting what is relevant to winning within the situation (Geis, 1978a; Saling, 1973). Low Machs are better at seeing how a person differs from other people in general, while high Machs are better at seeing how a person differs from themselves (Geis & Levy, 1970). The differential abilities of high and low Machs in person-versus-situation orientation are not usually apparent to others. For example, Downs (1985) studied the relationship of level of Machiavellianism of the subject to another person's perception of the subject's communication competence, social style, and immediacy. She found no relationship between one person's Machiavellianism and the other's perceptions of the person on these three variables.

According to the theory, high Machs think first and then act. Low Machs act first, according to the interpersonal requirements of the situation, often without consideration for the task or their personal goals, and reconcile their cognitions with their actions later. High Machs change their strategy as the situation changes, while low Machs change their strategies with changes in people, from one person to another, or with changes within a person. High Machs manipulate when the manipulatee cannot retaliate. When retaliation is possible, or when manipulative attempts would be visible and might work to their disadvantage, high Machs do not attempt manipulation. Low Machs occasionally attempt manipulation when it works to their disadvantage by being visible, and they are liked less because of it. Similarly, high Machs appear to be concerned with others but in fact use others' concerns to their own ends. "High Machs are the ones who get others to help them win in such a way that the others feel grateful for the opportunity" (Geis, 1978a, p. 354).

Another theoretical difference is that high Machs *resist social influence*, while low Machs are more likely to do something simply because another wishes them to do so. Both will change their beliefs given effective rational persuasive attempts, but high Machs are far less likely to change simply due to social pressure or to please someone else.

A final difference involves the *structure* of the social situation in which action occurs. Christie and Geis (1970, p. 351) diagram an expected difference in behavior based on an interaction between Machiavellianism and the degree of structure in a situation. In highly structured situations, both high and low Machs should work within the given system, with high Machs performing perfunctorily and low Machs making a serious effort to do well. In more loosely structured situations, high Machs should engage in limits testing, attempt to initiate and then control the structure of the situation, and exploit the resources available in the situation for their own instrumental purposes. Low Machs faced with loose structure should implicitly assume unstated limits, accept structures provided by others, and concentrate on people to the detriment of tasks and goals. Thus the major differences between high and low Machs should occur in loosely structured situations.

Geis and Christie (1970, pp. 285-288), Geis (1978a), and Christie (1978) summarize these structural situational variables affecting Machiavellianism as follows: High Machs tend to win and to achieve their goals more than low Machs. However, this is not true in all situations. Only when interpersonal manipulation can influence the outcome, when the high Mach can use the cognitions and behaviors of others to personal advantage, does the high Mach tend to win. In situations where winning strategies do not involve interpersonal manipulation, highs win no more than lows. Geis and Christie (1970) label this criterion ''latitude for improvisation,'' stating, ''Latitude for Improvisation implies both that subjects must improvise and that improvisation can influence outcomes'' (p. 287). I refer to this criterion throughout as *interpersonal manipulation* affecting outcomes to the high Mach's advantage. Second, high Machs tend to ignore *irrelevant affect* in the situation and concentrate on winning, while low Machs are more easily distracted from their goals. High Machs win no more debates than low Machs when the content is trivial, but when both high and low Machs are defending personal convictions on a meaningful topic, low Machs get more involved in the affect of the content than do highs and consequently do less well. A measure of irrelevant affect is seriousness, defined as ''the importance of values at stake in the situation with consequences extending beyond it'' (Geis & Christie, 1970, p. 288). Third, a *face-to-face* situation seems necessary for high Machs to win, since high Machs do not perform better on private tasks.

Burgoon (1971) found that high Machiavellians received better grades in certain types of communication courses. When the course was structured such that face-to-face communication with other persons was a determinant of the course grade, high Machiavellians received better grades than low Machiavellians. But this was not true in courses such as public speaking, where face-to-face dyadic interaction did not affect course grades. Geis (1978a) offers two reasons for this type of finding: First, high Machs succeed by manipulating others' cognitions and commitments; second, the interpersonal presence of others with whom one must interact is more distracting to low Machs than to high Machs.

One might expect Machiavellians to have other characteristics: to be high in both the need for power and the need for achievement, for example. Christie (1970a, p. 43) argues that such relationships should not be expected to occur with Machiavellianism, since it is concerned with the manner by which goals are achieved, not with the desire to achieve them. He reports correlations of .27 and −.03 between

Machiavellianism and two nonstandard measures of the need for achievement (Christie, 1970a, pp. 43-44). Mach IV correlates about .40 with anxiety, while in Mach V this correlation is reduced to near zero (Christie, 1970a, pp. 44-45). Wrightsman and Cook (1965) report eight of 78 measures tested which correlated above .40 with Machiavellianism. At least five of these eight are forms of hostility.

## Subscales of Machiavellianism

Christie and Lehmann (1970) report the results of an extensive factor analysis of Mach IV, Mach V, a counterbalanced revision of Srole's anomia scale (1956; Rosnow & Robinson, 1967, pp. 172-174), and a counterbalanced authoritarianism scale (Christie et al., 1958). Williams, Hazelton, and Renshaw (1975) factor analyzed the Mach IV and Mach V scores of 246 subjects and found evidence of multidimensionality in both scales and a correlation of .58 between them. While finding a substantially different factor structure than that reported by Williams et al., Hunter, Gerbing, and Boster (1982) question the unidimensional view of Machiavellianism proposed by Christie and Geis (1970) and explicated in most of the research on Machiavellianism. Hunter et al.'s test of two causal models, based on data from 351 subjects, suggests that Machiavellianism is not a unidimensional trait composed of a set of weaker subtraits, but rather a set of strong subtraits where each correlates more highly with other relevant variables than does their composite score, labeled Machiavellianism. Machiavellianism is discussed as the arbitrary sum of the willingness to endorse two types of tactics—*deceit* and *flattery*—and two views, one of *cynicism* and the other of the essential *immorality* of other persons. Christie (1970b, pp. 11-13) classified each of the 71 original Mach I items into categories of tactics, views, or morality which either support or reject Machiavellian views.

Kuo and Marsella (1977) factor analyzed the Mach IV scores of Chinese and American college students and found additional evidence of this tactics/views distinction. Hunter et al. (1982) argue that Machiavellianism weakens the predictive power of the four traits when it is used as their composite surrogate. While Mach IV scores show weak correlations with many traits, the subscales of Machiavellianism show strong correlations with a few traits. Holding their second-order Machiavellianism factor constant, Hunter et al. report partial correlations of −.71 and .93 of deceit and cynicism, respectively, with dogmatism. Similar partials for flattery and immorality, respectively, were .58 and −.55 with the control-by-powerful-others subscale of locus of control, and .84 and −.64, respectively, with competitiveness. The relationship of

Machiavellianism and locus of control is discussed in greater detail in the section entitled "Locus of Control and Machiavellianism."

Mach IV correlations are significantly lower than the corrected partials for most traits with which Machiavellianism would be expected to correlate. Hunter et al. (1982) conclude,

> The entire existing literature on the relationship of Machiavellian thought to social action should be regarded as misleading. At present that literature suggests that Machiavellian thought is weakly and rather haphazardly related to many traits and attitudes. This is the blurring effect of using a meaningless composite score as the primary research tool. (p. 1304)

While Hunter et al. may be correct, there is a theoretical coherence, if not a correlational coherence, to Machiavellianism. Hunter et al.'s results were obtained in a situation devoid of the three criteria of Machiavellianism detailed earlier. It is not entirely clear that the inter-correlations among responses to a series of personality items obtained in a noninterpersonal, nonaffective, nonmanipulative-by-the-subject environment are capable of modeling the causal relationships that exist when such an environment is present. Such intercorrelations do not explain the consistently strong findings for Machiavellianism when the situational criteria for it have been met. The review of the Machiavellianism literature presented here will need reinterpretation in terms of deceit, flattery, immorality, and cynicism if Hunter et al. are correct. Since little research is currently available demonstrating that the Machiavellianism subscales are better predictors of behavior than Machiavellianism in situations of interest to Machiavellianism theory, a "classical" interpretation of the research on Machiavellianism and communication is presented here.

## Machiavellianism and Communication

A number of communication-related predictions are implicit in the classical discussion of Machiavellianism presented by Christie and Geis (1970). If actions follow cognitions for high Machs, then high Machs should be more disposed toward particular behaviors after changes in cognition than should low Machs. A persuasive message that changes such cognitions equally for high Machs and low Machs should have more effect on the *behavior* of the high Machs. If cognitions follow actions for low Machs, then dissonance results such as counterattitudinal advocacy should be more pronounced among low Machs than among high Machs. High Machs should be more willing to use manipulative persuasive strategies that show promise of producing results than should low Machs, and high Machs should be more willing and able to engage in successful persuasive communication. Each of these predictions is contingent on the presence of the three conditions inducing Machiavellianism.

*Game studies.* Geis (1970a) reports the results of a con game that could be won by the willingness and ability to talk another player into joining into a coalition against a third player, by gaining an uneven split of the points awarded to the coalition through bargaining with one's coalition partner, and by willingness to desert one coalition for a more favorable one. High Machs won far more points than low Machs (47 versus 22, where 33 is the expected value), and points won correlated .71 with scores on Mach IV. Geis (1970b) analyzes the tactics used by players in the con game. Under high ambiguity conditions where statements made by the players about their resources could not be verified, high Machs won by a significantly wider margin than under low ambiguity conditions, where all their statements were subject to objective verification. High Machs initiated and controlled the structure of the bargaining communication in their group and concentrated on a cognitive-probabilistic approach, generally ignoring the personal and ethical concerns of others.

Oskenberg (1968) studied 124 males in 24 groups which were either heterogeneous or homogeneous in Machiavellianism. Groups worked on Shure, Rogers, Larsen, and Tassone's (1962) group problem-solving task involving information sending and retrieval, where an efficient solution could be obtained through establishing a communication network. No differences occurred in the time needed to establish a network between heterogeneous and homogeneous groups. Hazelton (1976, 1977) also employed a game to study Machiavellianism (see the section entitled "Failures to Predict"; see also Steinfatt & Miller, 1974, for a review of communication game studies).

*Situational effects.* Braginski (1970) found that high Mach fifth graders were more adept at persuading their peers to eat bitter crackers than were low Machs when the persuader was paid 5 cents for every cracker eaten by the persuadee. Geis, Weinheimer, and Berger (1970) asked subjects to debate either emotional or trivial issues "in Congress" for a payoff in votes if their bill was passed and another defeated. While the low Machs did as well as the high Machs in the trivial issues condition, high Machs did significantly better than low Machs when debating emotional issues. The explanation for these results appears to be the ability of the high Machs, not shared by the low Machs, to discuss and debate an issue without becoming emotionally involved in it.

Similarly, Novielli (1968) studied 64 debates between high Machs and low Machs—32 in which the debaters actually believed in the side they were defending, and 32 in which they did not. High Machs won significantly more of the emotionally involving "sincere" debates but about an equal number of the debates in which the subjects argued against their own position. Apparently it is easier for high Machs than low Machs to make the truth sound convincing (Geis, 1978a, p. 329).

*Group discussions.* Geis and Berger (1965) studied 32 male subjects in groups of four or five who were asked to engage in a 10-minute discussion on whether one should tell people the truth or what they want to hear, and attempt to reach a consensus. Low Machs significantly changed their initial opinion on the issue, while high Machs did not. High Machs were rated higher than lows on five task performance measures, including effective presentations, listening, idea quality, leadership, and overall contribution but were not preferred sociometrically over the lows. Bochner, DiSalvo, and Jonas (1972) report that high Machs engaged in a group discussion contributed more to that discussion during phases of the discussion which significantly affected its outcome than in other phases. These contributions were usually composed of task-relevant information. The influence of the high Machs was related to their ability to saturate the discussion with task information. Bochner and Bochner (1972) found that low Mach groups tended to use socio-emotional information and to be more accepting of each other's views, while high Mach groups used task information and were less accepting of differing viewpoints in completing a task. Similarly, Hacker and Gaitz (1970) found that high Machs made more contributions to a group discussion, asked for more information, and provided their own orientation more often that low Machs.

*Interpersonal variables.* Durkin (1970) discusses two types of interpersonal communication—*encountering,* and the *cognitive exchange.* The encounter involves spontaneous self-disclosure, unpremeditated and without a goal, though a goal may emerge from the conversation, while the cognitive exchange has a predefined goal, a specific topic or agenda, and messages are filtered for relevance to that goal and agenda. In a face-to-face coordination task between two persons, high Machs' behavior tended to be that of the cognitive exchange, while low Machs' behavior followed the pattern of an encounter. It would be interesting to test Durkin's notion in other communication contexts.

Novgorodoff (1974) studied interpersonal sensitivity training groups composed of six men and six women, with half of the males and half of the females high Machs and the other half low Machs. After interacting with each of the six opposite-sex members, and regardless of the level of

Machiavellianism, all of the men expressed a preference for low Mach women on a romantic attraction scale. This preference was significantly stronger among the low Mach males, who demonstrated again the low Machs' apparent ability to discriminate better among people, while the high Mach is better able to discriminate among situations. Thus low Mach women should have more first-choice romantic relationships than high Mach women, since they are universally more preferred. While high Mach women prefer high Mach men, low Mach women (the most preferred women) prefer low Mach men, who also prefer them. On this basis it would seem that both low Mach men and women would establish more of their preferred romantic relationships, and that these would be with each other. Yet as Geis (1978a) points out, "The low Machs' advantage of being the first choice of those they prefer may be only an unrealized potentiality if high Machs are quicker to translate interest into action" (p. 344).

*Attitude change.* Harris (1966) found that among 76 male subjects, low Machs changed their attitudes on traits of characters in *Waiting for Godot* toward that of their partner more than did highs. Among 36 males, low Machs changed significantly more than highs on counterattitudinal refutational messages on McGuire's truisms when fake public opinion poll data were used to create a bandwagon effect, but not under factual refutational conditions (see McGuire, 1964; Pryor & Steinfatt, 1978, on refutational message conditions).

Bogart, Geis, Levy, and Zimbardo (1970) gave favorable personality information and either high- or low-status information about a confederate to a subject who was to interact with the confederate in completing a human relations problem test containing very difficult problems. The high-status confederates were made even more attractive by stating that they had performed well on a personality test, while the low-status confederates were said to have some psychological weaknesses. Part of the way through the test, the confederate "discovered" the answer key on the experimenter's desk and used it to complete his test. The confederate explained his behavior as not wanting to look "stupid" and offered the key to the subject on repeated occasions. About half of both the high Machs and low Machs cheated, but the high Machs cheated almost exclusively with the high-status partner while the low Machs cheated with high- and low-status partners about equally. This manipulation created the defining conditions for cognitive dissonance. Bogart et al. then administered Mach IV a second time as a measure of increased acceptance of cheating behavior. The high Machs' Machiavellianism scores did not change, nor did those of the low Machs in the attractive partner condition. These low Machs presumably had ample justification for their counterattitudinal behavior in the status and attractiveness of their partners. However, the scores of low Machs who had cheated with an unattractive partner increased significantly on Mach IV, by an average of eight points, conforming to an insufficient justification prediction (see Steinfatt, 1977b, pp. 212-218, for a more detailed discussion of justification). Additional studies supporting their results are discussed by Bogart et al. (1970, pp. 248-250).

Burgoon, Miller, and Tubbs (1972) found that when high Machiavellians are placed in a game situation with high stakes, the high Machiavellian has little difficulty advocating a position which he previously rejected, while the low Machiavellian is significantly less likely to engage in such counterattitudinal advocacy. Yet if the low Mach is induced to perform such counterattitudinal communication behavior, the evidence suggests that it is performed just as competently as by a high Mach, given that the topic is not emotionally involving for the low Mach (Novielli, 1968).

*Cognitive complexity.* Delia and O'Keefe (1976) suggest that low Machs should employ more complex interpersonal construct systems than high Machs due to the low Machs' greater involvement with others. They report correlations of −.54 and −.49 between Machiavellianism and Crockett's measure of cognitive complexity. But Mulligan (1979) and Sypher, Nightingale, Vielhaber, and Sypher (1981) both failed to replicate these results, with correlations in the Sypher et al. study near zero (+.05 and +.06).

## Failures to Predict

Several studies have questioned the predictive validity of Machiavellianism in communication situations. Hazelton (1976, 1977) studied the effects of Machiavellianism in the creative alternative game (see Figure 2.2). Using conditions of real rewards and full communication, he found a greater number of creative solutions when the high Mach player was in the O or target position than when a high Mach was in the P position. This finding seems to run counter to the theory of high Machs as defining the situation and influencing as opposed to being influenced. Hazelton's study may be a negative finding for Machiavellian theory predictions. Alternatively, the following reasoning, admittedly post hoc, may serve as a context for his results. While the P player is apparently in a more powerful position than O in the CA game, due to his greater potential winnings, this apparent power is illusory since P can do nothing without the full cooperation of O. O is actually the controlling person in the game since P, unlike O, is motivated toward the creative solution by the situation, the game matrix itself, once he recognizes the existence of this solution. Dogmatism, not Machiavellianism, was found to be related to whether P perceives the existence of the creative solution (Steinfatt, 1973a; Seibold & Steinfatt, 1979), and there is a relatively low (.21) correlation between dogmatism and Machiavellianism, though no current data exist on whether Machiavellianism influences the perception of the creative solution. Thus low dogmatic high and low Machs should both perceive the existence of the creative solution when in the P position and attempt to influence O to go along. But P has no real power, aside from the possibility of reneging on a deal with O, well after any creative solutions have been achieved. O has the power to give P points, and we might expect a high Mach to use communication more skillfully in employing this power than a low Mach. This is exactly what Hazelton found.

Roloff (1981, p. 52) discusses the orientations of two interacting persons about how rewards ought to be exchanged as a "dispositional matrix" in conceptualizing interpersonal communication through a game-theoretic viewpoint. He suggests that Machiavellianism may be related to the way in which participants transform this matrix in terms of its alternatives and outcomes. Roloff and Barnicott (1978) asked high and low Machiavellian subjects to judge the extent to which they would be likely to use 16 compliance-gaining strategies representing prosocial, psychological force, and punishing techniques in interpersonal and non-interpersonal situations. In interpersonal situations, they found high Machs to be significantly more likely to lay claim to the employment of psychological force techniques and punishing activity techniques than low Machs, while in noninterpersonal situations high Machs were significantly more likely to say they would employ psychological force techniques and prosocial techniques than were low Machs. No difference in willingness to use punishing activity techniques was found between high and low Machs when predicting what their behavior was likely to be in noninterpersonal situations. This result is interpreted by Roloff and Barnicott (1978) as counter to the expectations generated by Machiavellianism theory. Indeed, Christie (1970a) states that "Machiavellians . . . are more likely to admit to socially undesirable statements about themselves" (p. 49).

The most likely explanations for Roloff and Barnicott's (1978) findings are (1) the difference between one's behavior and the predictions one makes about one's behavior, and (2) the failure to meet the three situational criteria of Machiavellianism. The first explanation would seem to hinge on the extent to which Roloff and Barnicott's subjects, particularly the high Machs, saw the "rate how likely you are to do

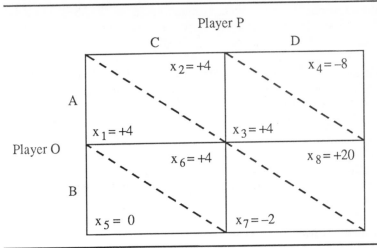

Figure 2.2 Steinfatt's Creative Alternative Game

this'' instructions as indicative of a situation in which they might be judged and would have something to lose, or in which manipulation for personal gain was possible. The situation of the experiment (filling out a rating form individually) would clearly seem to preclude finding strong Machiavellianism effects of any type. The second explanation would suggest that rather than running counter to the theory, these findings occurred under experimental conditions in which all three situational criteria for Machiavellianism of (1) interpersonal manipulation affecting the outcome to the high Mach's advantage, (2) irrelevant affect, and (3) a face-to-face situation did not occur. Thus no Machiavellian effects should have been expected in this study. While the behavior versus predictions argument would still hold, the need for power, might be more predictive of the generalized use of power tactics than would Machiavellianism. Machiavellians should use power only when it is the best alternative available in helping them win.

Roloff and Barnicott (1978) anticipated the first criticism, that their study involved intentions rather than behaviors. They cite Fishbein and Ajzen's (1975, pp. 368-381) theory as support for intentions as the best predictors of behavior. However, the pages cited refer to *single-act criteria*, while Roloff and Barnicott's intended behaviors clearly fall under what Fishbein and Ajzen would call *repeated observations criteria*, since target, situation, and time are unspecified in the Fishbein and Ajzen sense: ''a directly observable response to a certain target, in a given situation, at a given point in time" (1975, pp. 352-353; Fishbein, 1973). While Fishbein and Ajzen would also support intentions as predictive of repeated observations criteria, the relationship between intentions and such criteria is more complex than for single-act criteria. To summarize: Given the item content of Mach IV, if Machiavellianism predicts an intent, it should be an intent to achieve one's own private goals, however such manipulation might best be accomplished, not the likelihood of use of a generalized type of behavior in an unspecified interpersonal or noninterpersonal situation without knowing anything about the probabilities of success or of exposure as a manipulator which are related to those strategies. It does not seem surprising that studies which ask persons to predict their own behavior find different results from studies in which the behaviors themselves are observed in a face-to-face situation, with both irrelevant affect and improvisation for personal gain available to the subjects.

Exline, Thibaut, Hickey, and Gumpert (1970) found that among 48 subjects, both male and female high Machs were more likely than low Machs to look the experimenter in the eye while denying cheating that had actually occurred. While this finding supports Machiavellianism theory, and while DePaulo, Zuckerman, and Rosenthal (1980a, p. 134) report high Machs as quite successful in perpetrating lies, Zuckerman, DePaulo, and Rosenthal (1981, p. 35) report that "subsequent work (Knapp et al., 1974; O'Hair, Cody, & McLaughlin, 1981) failed to replicate these findings." Unfortunately, this statement by Zuckerman et al. is misleading. Knapp, Hart, and Dennis (1974) obtained Mach IV scores for 38 subjects who were all veterans and videotaped them in two 1-minute interactions with two confederates. Subjects in the deception condition were introduced with an alias to the confederates, who were posing as interviewers, and were instructed to lie about their prior military status to the interviewers. Out of a set of 32 possible verbal and nonverbal variables observed, Knapp et al. found only three significant differences between high and low Machs.

O'Hair et al. (1981) studied 44 high quartile and 44 low quartile Mach IV scorers, half of whom, in the guise of serving as a confederate, were asked to lie to an equal status interviewer about their grade point average. This manipulation served as the prepared lie condition. Subjects were not told that the interviewer would ask them if the grade point average they had just reported was a "rough estimate, averaged up a little?" Subjects' responses to this question served as data for the spontaneous lie condition. Responses to both the prepared and the spontaneous lie condition occurred in the middle of a list of interview questions. While low Mach liars differed from low Mach truthtellers on two of 11 variables, no significant differences were observed between high and low Machs for any condition.

The problem with Zuckerman et al.'s (1981) statement that Knapp et al. (1974) and O'Hair et al. (1981) failed to replicate Exline et al.'s (1970) findings is that neither Knapp et al. nor O'Hair et al. even came close to replicating the Machiavellianism conditions of Exline et al. As in the case of Roloff and Barnicott (1978), Knapp et al. and O'Hair et al. failed to meet the three situational criteria for Machiavellianism of (1) interpersonal manipulation capable of affecting the outcome to the high Mach's advantage, (2) irrelevant affect, and (3) a face-to-face situation.

Both Knapp et al. and O'Hair et al. provided their subjects with a face-to-face situation. The degree of irrelevant affect is clearly far higher in Exline et al. than in Knapp et al. Exline et al.'s subjects fully believed that they were co-conspirators in a plot to gain money by deceiving the experimenter, justified only by the deceitful behavior of another apparent subject. These subjects were actually *accused of lying* and were interrogated on this accusation by the experimenter. Knapp et al.'s subjects knew that they had the official blessing of the experimenter to lie and were introduced to the interviewer with an alias, thus further reducing irrelevant affect by suggesting that it was not "really" the subject who was lying but someone with another name. Since the interviewer was associated with the experimenter, subjects may well have believed that the interviewer understood on some level that they were expected to behave deceptively. The subjects in O'Hair et al. were in an affective position slightly stronger than those in Knapp et al. but far weaker than that of subjects in Exline et al. The experimenter in O'Hair et al. (1981) provided clear justification to the subjects for their deceptive behavior by stating, "We want you to be a confederate for this study. We want you to look better than your partner. We want to see the consequences this has" (p. 331). Subjects in O'Hair et al. were not provided with an alias, and it seems likely that they believed that their partner thought they were lying.

It is unclear whether subjects in Knapp et al. were provided with a chance to use interpersonal manipulation to influence situational outcomes to their advantage. Knapp et al. (1974) refer to an "additional compensation system (contingent upon performance in both conditions) up to 25 dollars" (p. 27) but provide no explanation of the type of performance to be rewarded, nor of the contingencies of reward distribution that subjects believed would be used. The subjects in O'Hair et al. (1981) clearly had no chance to use interpersonal manipulation to influence situational outcomes to their advantage. They were simply instructed to lie and given a clear justification for doing so.

While it would be interesting to find differences of the type sought for Machiavellianism in Knapp et al. and O'Hair et al., neither study provides a setting for Machiavellian manipulation attempts that would justify expecting such findings based on the overview of experimental research prior to 1970 presented by Geis and Christie (1970, pp. 285-313). In a review of all available studies to that date, Geis and Christie found only one study out of 14 in which all three situational criteria were present where the expected Machiavellianism effects did not occur. In the case of that study (Geis & Leventhal, 1966), Geis and Christie may have erred in applying their criterion judgments, since seriousness is lacking under irrelevant affect, and the improvisation available could not be used to the subject's advantage (i.e., the subject could not gain personally by doing better in the experiment). In reviewing the published research on Machiavellianism in psychology and communication journals since 1970, I have found no study meeting the three situational criteria in which the Machiavellianism predictions failed to be fulfilled.

Some studies which have not fully met the three Machiavellianism criteria have nevertheless found a significant effect for Machiavellianism—for example, Geis, Christie, and Nelson (1970), who found significant verbal effects but nonsignificant nonverbal effects under these conditions, and DePaulo and Rosenthal (1979). Geis and Christie (1970, p. 294) report that 12 out of 36 studies not meeting all criteria have found Machiavellian effects, and each of the 12 had at least one of the situational criteria present. In all 11 cases where all three criteria were lacking, there were no findings of high Machs outperforming lows. Thus, in all but perhaps one study in which the three key situational components were in place, support for Machiavellianism theory has been found. And in each of the studies finding mixed or negative results, at least one of these crucial components is lacking—often the opportunity to use interpersonal manipulation for personal gain.

*Lying.* Geis, Christie, et al. (1970) asked 27 male subjects to administer a personality test to another subject after taking this test themselves and being mildly deceived on their performance by an equal-status test administrator. High mach subjects told more lies than lows, devised a greater number of innovative lies, and generally made more comments that could be scored as manipulative.

Zuckerman et al. (1981, p. 35) discuss six studies where the ability to lie without detection, clearly an attribute to be expected of a high-Mach in a Machiavellian situation, was studied together with Machiavellianism. Averaging across the six studies, without regard for type of

Machiavellianism conditions, Zuckerman et al. report a combined Z statistic of −1.63 (p = .11) in the direction of high Mach deceivers being less detectable than low Mach deceivers. While this finding is interesting, the failure to sort studies by experimental conditions decreases the meaning that can be associated with the results. Again, the study most supportive of low detectability for high Machs is that by Geis and Moon (1980), which most closely meets the three Machiavellianism criteria. This is confounded with the fact that it is also the study conducted by researchers most closely involved with the promulgation of Machiavellianism theory.

*Lie detection.* In a similar review of five studies relating ability to detect lies with Machiavellianism, Zuckerman et al. (1981, p. 35) report a combined Z for the studies of 1.20 in the direction of high Machs being better able to detect lies than low Machs. While the theoretical rationale for high Machs as good liars in a Machiavellian-type situation seems clear, the rationale concerning why high Machs should be good as detectors of lies seem tenuous at best.

Geis and Leventhal (1966) were the first to study Machiavellianism as a predictor of lie detection ability. Their study was exploratory in this area rather than predicting that such an ability should occur on the basis of Machiavellianism theory. Subsequent studies have not provided a rationale beyond suggesting that the ability to detect lies by others would surely be an advantage if one were to engage in manipulative behavior. There are many such potentially advantageous abilities, but no single one should be expected to be characteristic of high Machs. High Machs are improvisers who use whatever is available in the situation. Kraut and Poe (1980) studied the lie detection behavior of customs inspectors and lay judges and concluded that the behavior of the observed person, rather than the characteristics of the observer, determines perceptions of lying:

> Deception judgments . . . are stimulus driven. What a liar does and the motivational context in which a lie occurs compel most observers to agree about whether he or she is lying. . . . The manner in which different observers use cues to form a deception judgment is very consistent across judges. (Kraut, 1980, p. 214)

Current evidence suggests that no observer characteristic, Machiavellianism included, is a good predictor of ability as a lie detector, though DePaulo, Zuckerman, and Rosenthal (1980b) believe that some fairly small correlations may exist. The Z of 1.20 is best regarded as a chance finding in an area where there was no clear reason to expect Machiavellianism, or any observer-bound variable, to predict results.

## Locus of Control

The concept of locus of control developed from Rotter's social learning theory (1954; Rotter, Chance, & Phares, 1972), which holds that behavior is a joint function of expected reinforcement, the value of that reinforcement, and the situation as perceived by the individual. The expectations of reinforcement are dependent on the person's past experience with situations that are regarded by the person as similar to the situation in question. Consider a person applying for a job in the training department of a power company. If the person has never previously applied for such a job, then some situation the person regards as similar—perhaps applying for other jobs with that company, in the power industry, or high school teaching jobs—will be used to form expectations. The greater the number of specific similar experiences, the less that generalized expectancies, such as those formed from applying for jobs in general, will influence the person's expectations. In the absence of specific similar experiences, the generalized expectancies will have greater weight.

Locus of control is a generalized expectancy about the nature of the relationship between one's behavior and the reinforcing consequences that result from this behavior. Thus the notion of locus of control is directly related to the interpretation of reinforcement theory. From the viewpoint of locus of control, reinforcement is a necessary but not sufficient condition for learning. If the individual does not perceive a causal relationship between behavior and reinforcement, locus of control theory would hold that reinforcement contingencies will not influence learning. When the occurrence of a potentially reinforcing event is attributed to luck, chance, fate, powerful others, or the general complexity and unpredictability of events, this is an attribution of *external control*. "If the person perceives that the event is contingent upon his own behavior or his own relatively permanent characteristics, we have termed this a belief in *internal control*" (Rotter, 1966, p. 1). Since locus of control is a generalized expectancy, it is clearly a situationally specific variable, most important in situations where the individual's prior experience with the specific situation is minimal. Phares (1978, pp. 267-271) discusses the relationship of the situation to locus of control in more detail.

The notion of locus of control arose from a clinical case rather than from theoretical considerations. A male psychotherapy patient was being treated for a severe lack of social skills. Treatment took the form of social skills training and discussions with the patient about how to find a job, become successful with women, and become better educated. The training and discussions led to reasonable success for the patient in these areas, but the successes did not appear to enhance learning. He was no more likely to perform the skilled behaviors after they led to success, nor did he associate their application with his successes. Rather, he attributed success to luck or other factors he could not control.

## Measuring Locus of Control

The I-E scale, internal versus external control, was published by Rotter in 1966. It consists of 23 forced-choice locus of control items and six irrelevant items for disguise purposes. Test-retest reliabilities were around .75 for three-month intervals but decreased to about .25 over nine months. Thus, to the extent that it is measured by the I-E scale, locus of control is a personality variable quite capable of varying over time within an individual, as well as across persons. Phares (1976) reviews a number of measures of locus of control, including the I-E scale. Levenson (1974) suggests that there are two types of externals—those who believe that events affecting them are controlled by fate, chance, or luck, as suggested by Rotter, and those who believe that their fate is controlled by powerful others. She has developed an I-E scale (Levenson, 1976) composed of three subscales—one of internal control and two of external control, powerful others, and chance or fate. Phares (1978, pp. 271-276) discusses a number of methodological and interpretive issues concerning I-E scales.

I-E scale items include the following (1) Much of what happens to me is probably a matter of luck, (2) I control my own fate (reversed item), (3) When I am right I can convince others (reversed item), and (4) Most students would be amazed at how much grades are determined by capricious events.

## Locus of Control and Machiavellianism

Wrightsman and Cook (1965) report a correlation of .43 between Machiavellianism and locus of control. Solar and Bruehl (1971) investigated the relationship between Mach IV and Rotter's I-E scale and found significant correlations of .44, .41, and .33 between external control and Machiavellianism in groups of 67, 42, and 61 subjects, respectively. They interpret this in terms of the externals' feelings of powerlessness in a world ruled by fate and luck; their rejection of traditional values such as truth, honesty, and hard work in producing results; and their belief that it is important to know the right people. According to Solar and Bruehl (1971), the willingness to manipulate others, Machiavellianism, becomes a necessary defense for externals. Yet the correlations between Machiavellianism and external locus of control are not as high as such an explanation might suggest.

Prociuk and Breen (1976) used Levenson's (1974) distinction between powerful-others externals and chance externals to suggest that only powerful-others externals should show high Machiavellianism, since neither internals nor chance externals would need (or believe in) the effectiveness of manipulation of others. For the 32 males in their sample, Prociuk and Breen report a correlation of .37 between Rotter's I-E scale and Mach V but correlations of .41 between Mach V and P (powerful others; Levenson, 1976) and .09 between Mach V and C (chance; Levenson, 1976). These latter two correlations are significantly different from each other. For 65 female subjects there was no relationship between Mach V and I-E, P, C, or I (internal; Levenson, 1976).

Hunter, Gerbing, and Boster (1982) found correlations of .45 and .33, respectively, between P and C with Mach IV. They suggest that these relationships are due almost entirely to the flattery (with P) and cynicism (with C) subscales of Mach IV (see the section, "Subscales of Machiavellianism"). Holding their second-order Machiavellianism factor constant, Hunter et al. report higher partial correlations for flattery and immorality with P than for deceit and cynicism. Deceit and cynicism have higher partials with C than do flattery and immorality. None of the four Machiavellianism components correlates highly with I, and Mach IV correlations are significantly lower than the corrected partials of the Mach subscales with P, C, and I.

While is seems clear that certain subscales of Machiavellianism and of locus of control have a strong conceptual relationship and correlate more strongly with each other than do the main scales, the exact nature of that relationship is still in doubt. As expected, flattery correlates highly with P, but the partial of immorality with P is not significantly different from the partial for flattery with P. And while the partial of cynicism with C is high, as expected, it is not significantly different from the partial of deceit with C. It would seem to make more conceptual sense if deceit rather than immorality correlated with P, and it is difficult to explain why deceit or honesty should be related to C, the belief that events are governed by chance and fate. Prociuk and Breen's (1976) finding of a sex difference for the Machiavellianism/locus of control relationship is also difficult to explain, since no such difference is report by Solar and Bruehl (1971) nor by Hunter et al. (1982).

## Locus of Control and Communication

The studies reported here used Rotter's I-E scale as a measure of locus of control. Ritchie and Phares (1969) found a relationship between locus of control, source credibility, and persuasibility. Internals changed less than externals, and externals changed more from a highly credible source than from a less credible source. This source influence was not present in the internals. Ryckman, Rodda, and Sherman (1972) and McGinnes and Ward (1974) found support for these results. Sherman (1973) found greater attitude change in internals subjected to a passive persuasive manipulation (reading a message), while externals were more susceptible to an active persuasive condition (writing a counterattitudinal message). Hjelle (1970) found greater persuasibility in externals in response to a number of persuasive communications. Snyder and Larson (1972) found externals more willing than internals to accept interpretations of their personality. And Stewart, Kearney and Plax (1986) found externals perceived more influence attempts by teachers than did internals.

Crowne and Liverant (1963) found that internals were more likely to resist group pressures toward conformity in Asch-type situations than were externals, and Tolor (1971) found externals more likely to experience the autokinetic effect in Sherif-type situations. Gore (1962, 1963) used no influence, subtle influence, or overt influence in attempting to control the length of the stories subjects produced in response to TAT cards. No differences occurred in the no and overt conditions, but internals in the subtle condition reacted negatively to the influence attempts and responded with story lengths moving in the opposite direction from the influence attempts. Biondo and MacDonald (1971) also found greater resistance by internals but failed to replicate Gore's interaction-with-subtlety results. Strickland (1970) found that internals were more likely to deny having been influenced by verbal reinforcers than were externals, were actually less likely to have been influenced, and were even less likely to change when they were aware of the existence of the reinforcing contingency. Getter (1966) also found that the greatest response to verbal reinforcement occurred in externals. Based on these results, internals seem more likely to resist persuasive attempts, while externals seem more susceptible to them.

The relationship is not quite that simple, however. James, Woodruff, and Werner (1965) found that male smokers who quit following the surgeon general's report on cancer and smoking had higher internal scores than others who believed the report but did not quit smoking. Similarly, Platt (1969) found greater change in the smoking behavior of internals than externals in response to doctor/patient role-playing on cancer and smoking. A study by Lefcourt, Lewis, and Silverman (1968) may explain the difference in results between these two studies of smoking behavior and the several studies cited earlier. Lefcourt et al. found that internals were less likely than externals to accept directions that stressed chance factors but more likely to accept directions that stressed skill. When the influence attempt involves an area perceived by the subject to be within his locus of control, internals seem more likely than externals to respond to such messages. When the influence attempt does not involve factors seen as being under internal control, externals are more likely to respond to it than internals. Smoking is seen by internals as being under internal control. The influence attempts in the studies cited in the previous paragraph are generally concerned with external factors.

Lefcourt (1972, p. 7) suggests that internals respond more to reasoned argument, messages that agree with their own perceptions, and respond more to any message or procedure that produces internal self- directives. He further suggests that externals seem more influenced by source credibility than message content, are generally more persuasible, and evidence a greater degree of dependence and need for affiliation than do internals. It would be interesting to study the relationship between dogmatism and locus of control in terms of their interaction with source credibility, given Lefcourt's interpretation of the literature.

Several studies have linked locus of control to verbal and nonverbal expressive styles. Rosenthal and DePaulo (1979) have argued that the human voice is a major channel for the leakage of unintended information about a person's attitudes, anxieties, and hidden self. Bugental, Henker, and Whalen (1976) have related voice leakage to locus of control. Counselor trainees were tape recorded during spontaneous conversation and while role-playing a supervisor. A written transcript and an electronically filtered, content-masked version of each of the recordings were rated for assertiveness. Internals were rated as more assertive in voice quality than in words, while externals were more assertive in words than voice quality in the conversation condition. Bugental et al. (1976) suggest that this is because externals will leak their low expectations of the expected influence of their messages through their voice, while internals will similarly leak their high expectations of the effects of their messages. Bugental, Caporael, and Shennum (1980) also found a relationship between locus of control and vocal assertiveness among women who were attempting to control an uncooperative child, but externals displayed higher vocal assertiveness than internals on neutral messages.

Hall, Mroz, and Braunwald (1983) asked subjects to explain CPR techniques to confederates over the telephone. Using Bugental et al.'s transcript/filtered speech method, their results were closer to those of Bugental et al.'s 1980 study rather than the 1976 study, since externals displayed higher vocal assertiveness. Hall et al. pointed out that leakage may not always occur through the nonverbal channel—since their externals leaked through verbals—and that channel discrepancy does not necessarily imply the "truth" of either channel over the other. The area of verbal/nonverbal comparisons using Bugental et al.'s technique would seem a fertile area for further research, both with locus of control and other personality style measures.

## Summary of Communication Research on Machiavellianism and Locus of Control

### *Machiavellianism*

In group discussions, high Machiavellians are more willing and able to talk another player into joining a coalition against a third player when it is to their advantage to do so. Under high ambiguity conditions, where statements made by the players about their resources are difficult to verify, high Machs win by a significantly wider margin. High Machs initiate and control the structure of bargaining communication, use a cognitive-probabilistic approach in their messages, and ignore the personal and ethical concerns of others. High Machs appear to be better persuaders and do significantly better than low Machs when debating emotional issues in which they believe. High Machs seem less persuasible than lows and are rated higher on five task performance measures, including effective presentations, listening, idea quality, leadership, and overall contribution, but are not preferred sociometrically over lows. In a group discussion, high Machs are more influential than lows, apparently because they contribute more task-relevant information during phases of the discussion that significantly affect its outcome. Low Machs tend to use socioemotional information and to be more accepting of each other's views, while high Machs use task information and are less accepting of differing viewpoints.

In the area of interpersonal communication, low Machs tend to engage in unpremeditated, spontaneous self-disclosure without a goal, while high Machs tend to have a predefined goal, a specific topic or agenda, and to filter messages for relevance to their agenda. Males in general are more attracted to low than to high Mach women. This preference is significantly stronger among low Mach males. Low Machs appear better able to discriminate among people, while high Machs are better able to discriminate among situations. High Machs seem more willing to lie and better able to devise a greater number of innovative lies, especially when supported by a high-status partner, while neither statement is true of low Machs. The Machiavellianism scores of low Machs, but not high Machs, who lie when supported by an unattractive partner, increase significantly, providing some evidence that low Machs seem more susceptible to cognitive dissonance effects than highs. If a low Mach is induced to state a counterattitudinal position, this act is performed as competently as by a high Mach, given that the topic is not emotionally involving for the low Mach. High Machs appear more likely than low Machs to look the experimenter in the eye while lying, though disagreement exists on this point, as discussed earlier. High Mach liars seem somewhat less detectable than low Mach liars.

Each of the statements in this summary must be understood in the context of situations that meet all three Machiavellianism criteria. Rather than being unduly restrictive of the domain of Machiavellian theory, these criteria specify interpersonal communication situations with consequences important to and under the volitional control of the actors as the primary arena for Machiavellian-type effects.

Overall, Machiavellianism has a strong track record in predicting the behavioral effects of actors in communication situations involving the three Machiavellian criteria. The studies finding mixed and negative results have generally failed to meet the three criteria necessary for a Machiavellian to be effective. Studies employing all three criteria are strongly supportive of Machiavellianism. Techniques such as gaming studies of communication similar to those conducted by Hazelton (1976, 1977) could be used to allow for the creation of the criterial conditions through the creative alternative game. The results of Hunter et al. (1982) suggest the need for a careful consideration of the role of deceit, flattery, immorality, and cynicism and their interrelationships in situations where Machiavellianism has been a variable of interest. Their results also indicate a need to study causal models based on data obtained in situations where the phenomenon in question would theoretically be expected to occur.

## Machiavellianism and Locus of Control

These variables appear to be related largely through the feelings of powerlessness of powerful-others externals, their rejection of traditional values, and their belief that it is important to know the right people. Machiavellianism—the willingness to manipulate others—may become a necessary defense for such externals. The flattery (with P) and cynicism (with C) subscales of Mach IV may account for this relationship, but the exact mechanism needs further study.

## *Locus of Control*

There is evidence for a relationship between locus of control, source credibility, and persuasibility. Internals have been found to change less than externals when influence is attempted, especially if they are aware of the attempt. Persuasibility may be more pronounced for internals when the influence attempt is passive (reading), and for externals when the attempt is active (writing). Externals seem to be more affected by the credibility of the source than internals, though the evidence is not as massive as for the same effect among high dogmatics. Though internals seem more resistant to change in general, they may simply be responding to different types of appeals. Internals appear to respond more than externals to reasoned argument, to directions that stress skill over chance, and to directions that are perceived as being within the individual's locus of control. Internals are more likely than externals to change when receiving such directions. When chance or other external factors are stressed, externals are more likely to change than internals. Thus the finding of greater change among externals may be an artifact of the external factors used in the influence attempts of the studies finding such changes. Externals show some evidence of a greater dependence and need for affiliation than is found among internals. Some evidence exists that internals may be more assertive in voice quality than externals, but the results are mixed and more research is needed.

Studies of communication and locus of control have generally used Rotter's I-E scale as a measure of the latter concept. Since a major relationship of locus of control to communication is through persuasibility and resistance to persuasion, it would make conceptual sense to use Levenson's (1976) P, C, and I scales to replicate and extend many of these studies. The assumed differences in cognitive processing between a P and a C external lead to a number of interesting propositions. Specifically, (1) P should be related to dogmatism, as well as to the flattery subscale of Machiavellianism; (2) the type of messages which are persuasive to an internal should be very different from those persuasive to a P or a C external; (3) internals should respond more to messages which provide evidence that action on their part will be rewarded; (4) P externals should respond more to messages that powerful others desire them to act in a particular fashion and will reward them if they do; and (5) C externals should respond to messages arguing that an event is "due" to occur, in the same fallacious probabilistic sense of a batter being "due" in baseball, or to messages claiming knowledge of a predictive pattern—or the ability to predict a pattern—of fate. Thus the messages of fortune tellers and the astrology charts printed by otherwise reputable newspapers should be of higher credibility to a C external than to an internal or P external.

Future research in these areas would be interesting. The importance of locus of control in communication theory and research should appear in any research situation involving differential reinforcement contingencies and differences in volitional versus external control. In fact, a strong potential message effect difference exists between internals and externals based in the stress on internal or external factors in the message.

## SUMMARY

Each of the personality variables reviewed in this chapter has been studied in relation to communication behavior. Dogmatism and Machiavellianism seem to have the clearest theoretical relationships to communication behavior and the most empirical support. Locus of control would seem to come in as a high third. Yet each of the variables is related to communication to a greater or lesser extent, and none has been tapped to its heuristic limits. The communication relationships suggested for the variables of this chapter are: *authoritarianism*, through its prediction of sexual content differences in media preferences, the greater production of prejudiced messages by high authoritarians, and its relationship to dogmatism; *dogmatism*, through the apparent inability of high dogmatics to discriminate between the source and content of a message, as a synthetic block in cognitive functioning, through its relationship to communication satisfaction, performance under stress, style of supervision, and family communication patterns, and through Ertel's relationship of dogmatism to linguistic content patterns; *rigidity* as an analytic block in cognitive functioning; *intolerance of ambiguity*, through listening, through latitudes of acceptance and ego involvement, through threat, conflict, and stress situations, and through openness to information; *Machiavellianism*, through attitude-behavior relationships, nonverbal communication, effectiveness as a persuader, emotional involvement in the topic, differential information use, encountering versus cognitive exchange interpersonal styles, romantic preference, conformity to dissonance predictions, and ease of engaging in counter-attitudinal advocacy; and *locus of control*, through persuasibility, responses to internal versus external persuasive attempts, vocal assertiveness, and verbal and nonverbal expressive styles as they relate to the leaking of emotions.

Several common themes run among the variables of this chapter. For example, the *attenuation-sharpening of source effects* is important in dogmatism, Machiavellianism, and locus of control. In this regard, I have commented extensively on the relationship of dogmatism to source credibility. Machiavellianism is related through the finding that high Machs are more willing to lie with a high-status than a low-status confederate. Locus of control is also related through findings suggesting that externals seem more influenced by source credibility than internals.

*Persuasibility* is related to several variables: to dogmatism through the greater persuasibility of high dogmatics under authoritative source conditions; to Machiavellianism through the greater persuasibility of low Machs; and to locus of control through the greater persuasibility of externals and the interaction of persuasibility with internal-external message emphasis. The *situation-person* dimension is particularly important to Machiavellianism, while *interpersonal attraction* is related to authoritarianism and dogmatism, in that high scorers on these variables tend to be disliked. Such attraction is also related to Machiavellianism since high scorers under some conditions (games) and low scorers under others (romantic attraction) tend to be liked.

The distinction between *analytic/synthetic thinking* and its implications for message processing and message selection is related to dogmatism and rigidity. *Openness to information* is related to intolerance of ambiguity, rigidity, and dogmatism, with the latter relationship mediated by attitude toward the source. *Stress, anxiety, or threat* has been related to increases in the effects of authoritarianism, dogmatism, rigidity, and intolerance of ambiguity.

A final comment on the role of situation in personality effects is in order. Ignoring major features of the situation seems endemic to studies and reviews in the area of personality. This is especially true in the case of Machiavellianism theory, as detailed earlier. Even in cases where the role of the situation is carefully explicated (e.g., Terhune, 1970, pp. 195-198) and carefully considered for one set of variables (Terhune, 1970, p. 205), it seems to be ignored just as carefully when summarizing the results of studies by other researchers using other personality variables (e.g., Terhune, 1970, pp. 199-201). Future research should be especially self-conscious of its failure or success in meeting the situational requirements relevant to a given variable, and of the effects of such failure or success on the interpretation of results.

## REFERENCES

Adorno, T. W., Frenkel-Brunswik, E., Levinson, D. J., & Sanford, R. N. (1950). *The authoritarian personality*. New York: Harper & Row.

Altman, I., & Haythorn, W. (1965). Interpersonal exchange in isolation. *Sociometry, 28*, 411-426.

Altman, I., & Haythorn, W. (1967). The ecology of isolated groups. *Behavioral Science, 12*, 169-182.

Anastasi, A. (1982). *Psychological testing* (5th ed.). New York: Macmillan.

Applezweig, D. G. (1954). Some determinants of behavioral rigidity. *Journal of Abnormal and Social Psychology, 49*, 224-228.

Atkinson, J. W. (Ed.). *Motives in fantasy, action, and society*. Princeton, NJ: Von Nostrand.

Barker, E. N. (1963). Authoritarianism of the political right, center, and left. *Journal of Social Issues, 19*, 63-74.

Becker, G. (1967). Ability to differentiate message from source as a curvilinear function of scores on Rokeach's Dogmatism Scale. *Journal of Social Psychology, 72*, 265-273.

Bettinghaus, E., Miller, G., & Steinfatt, T. (1970). Source evaluation, syllogistic content, and judgments of logical validity by high- and low-dogmatic persons. *Journal of Personality and Social Psychology, 16*, 238-244.

Bieri, J. (1961). Complexity-simplicity as a personality variable in cognitive and preferential behavior. In D. W. Fiske & S. R. Maddi (Eds.), *Functions of varied experience* (pp. 355-379). Homewood, IL: Dorsey.

Biondo, J., & MacDonald, A. P. (1971). Internal-external locus of control and response to influence attempts. *Journal of Personality, 39*, 407-419.

Block, J., & Block, J. (1951). An investigation of the relationship between intolerance of ambiguity and ethnocentrism. *Journal of Personality, 19*, 303-311.

Bochner, A. P., & Bochner, B. A. (1972). A multivariate investigation of Machiavellianism and task structure in four-man groups. *Speech Monographs, 4*, 277-285.

Bochner, A. P., Disalvo, V., & Jonas, T. (1972). *How they control group structure: A words computerized content analysis of Machiavellian message strategies*. Paper presented at the annual meeting of the Speech Communication Association, Chicago.

Bogart, K., Geis, F. L., Levy, M., & Zimbardo, P. (1970). No dissonance for Machiavellians. In R. Christie & F. L. Geis (Eds), *Studies in Machiavellianism* (pp. 236-259). New York: Academic Press.

Borgatta, E. F., & Lambert, W. W. (Eds.). (1968). *Handbook of personality theory and research*. Chicago: Rand McNally.

Braginski, D. D. (1970). Machiavellianism and manipulative interpersonal behavior in children. *Journal of Experimental Social Psychology, 6*, 77-99.

Brown, R. W. (1953). A determinant of the relationship between rigidity and authoritarianism. *Journal of Abnormal Psychology, 48*, 469-476.

Browning, D. L. (1983). Aspects of authoritarian attitudes in ego development. *Journal of Personality and Social Psychology, 45*, 137-144.

Browning, D. L. (1985). Development aspects of authoritarian attitudes and sex role conceptions in men and women. *High School Journal, 68*, 177-182.

Budner, S. (1962). Intolerance of ambiguity as a personality variable. *Journal of Personality, 30*, 29-50.

Bugental, D. B., Caporael, L., & Shennum, W. A. (1980). Experimentally produced child uncontrollability: Effects on the potency of adult communication patterns. *Child Development, 51*, 520-528.

Bugental, D. B., Henker, B., & Whalen, C. K. (1976). Attributional antecedents of verbal and vocal assertiveness. *Journal of Personality and Social Psychology, 34*, 405-411.

Burgoon, M. (1971). The relationship between willingness to manipulate others and success in two different types of basic speech communication courses. *The Speech Teacher, 20*, 178-183.

Burgoon, M., Miller, G. R., & Tubbs, S. L. (1972). Machiavellianism, justification, and attitude change following counterattitudinal advocacy. *Journal of Personality and Social Psychology, 22*, 366-371.

Byrne, D., & Blaylock, B. (1963). Similarity and assumed similarity of attitudes between husbands and wives. *Journal of Abnormal and Social Psychology, 67*, 636-640.

Carkhuff, R. R. (1969). *Helping and human relations: A primer for lay and professional helpers.* New York: Holt, Rinehart & Winston.

Carlozzi, A. F. (1985). Dogmatism and the person of the counselor. *High School Journal, 68*, 147-153.

Carlozzi, A. F., Campbell, N. J., & Ward, G. R. (1982). Dogmatism and externality in locus of control as related to counselor trainee skill in facilitative responding. *Counselor Education and Supervision, 21*, 227-236.

Cattell, R. B. (1983). *Structured personality-learning theory: A wholistic multivariate research approach.* New York: Praeger.

Cattell, R. B., & Tiner, L. G. (1949). The varieties of structural rigidity. *Journal of Personality, 17*, 321-341.

Chabassol, D. J., & Thomas, D. (1975). Needs for structure, tolerance of ambiguity and dogmatism in adolescents. *Psychological Reports, 37*, 507-510.

Cherry, F., & Byrne, D. (1977). Authoritarianism. In T. Blass (Ed.), *Personality variables in social behavior* (pp. 109-133). Hillsdale, NJ: Erlbaum.

Christie, R. (1970a). Relationships between Machiavellianism and measures of ability, opinion, and personality. In R. Christie, & F. L. Geis (Eds.), *Studies in Machiavellianism* (pp. 35-52). New York: Academic Press.

Christie, R. (1970b). Scale construction. In R. Christie & F. L. Geis (Eds.), *Studies in Machiavellianism* (pp. 10-34). New York: Academic Press.

Christie, R. (1970c). Why Machiavelli? In R. Christie & F. L. Geis (Eds.), *Studies in Machiavellianism* (pp. 1-9). New York: Academic Press.

Christie, R. (1978). The person in the person × situation paradigm: Reflections on the (p)erson in Lewin's B=f(P,E). In H. London (Ed.), *Personality: A new look at metatheories* (pp. 97-121). New York: John Wiley.

Christie, R., & Cook, P. (1958). A guide to published literature relating to the authoritarian personality through 1956. *Journal of Psychology, 45*, 171-199.

Christie, R., & Geis, F. L. (1968). Some consequences of taking Machiavelli seriously. In E. F. Borgatta & W. W. Lambert (Eds.), *Handbook of personality theory and research* (pp. 959-973). Chicago: Rand McNally.

Christie, R., & Geis, F. L. (Eds). (1970). *Studies in Machiavellianism*. New York: Academic Press.

Christie, R., Havel, J., & Seidenberg, B. (1958). Is the F scale irreversible? *Journal of Abnormal Social Psychology, 56*, 143-159.

Christie, R., & Jahoda, M. (Eds.). (1954). *Studies in the scope and method of "The authoritarian personality."* Glencoe, IL: Free Press.

Christie, R., & Lehmann, S. (1970). The structure of Machiavellian orientations. In R. Christie & F. L. Geis (Eds.), *Studies in Machiavellianism* (pp. 359-387). New York: Academic Press.

Cronkhite, G., & Goetz, E. (1965). *Dogmatism, persuasibility, and attitude instability*. Paper presented at the annual meeting of the Speech Association of America, New York.

Crossman, R. (Ed.). (1949). *The god that failed*. New York: Harper.

Crowne, D. P., & Liverant, S. (1963). Conformity under varying conditions of personal commitment. *Journal of Abnormal and Social Psychology, 66*, 547-555.

Davids, A. (1955). Some personality and intellectual correlates of intolerance of ambiguity. *Journal of Abnormal and Social Psychology, 51*, 415-420.

Davids, A. (1956). The influence of ego-involvement on relations between authoritarianism and intolerance of ambiguity. *Journal of Consulting Psychology, 20*, 179-184.

Davis, L. J. (1975). *An experimental investigation of tolerance of ambiguity and information in interpersonal bargaining*. Unpublished doctoral dissertation, University of Texas.

Day, H. (1966). Looking time as a function of stimulus variables and individual differences. *Perceptual and Motor Skills, 22*, 423-428.

Deconchy, J. P. (1984). Rationality and social control in orthodox systems. In H. Tajfel (Ed.), *The social dimension: European developments in social psychology* (pp. 425-445). Cambridge: Cambridge University Press.

Deconchy, J. P. (1985). From the construct of dogmatism to the construct of orthodoxy: The articulation of the subject and the group within the ideological field. *High School Journal, 68*, 327-334.

Delia, J. G., & O'Keefe, B. J. (1976). The interpersonal constructs of Machiavellians. *British Journal of Social and Clinical Psychology, 15*, 435-436.

DePaulo, B. M., & Rosenthal, R. (1979). Telling lies. *Journal of Personality and Social Psychology, 37*, 1713-1722.

DePaulo, B. M., Zuckerman, M., & Rosenthal, R. (1980a). Humans as lie detectors. *Journal of Communication, 30*, 129-139.

DePaulo, B. M., Zuckerman, M., & Rosenthal, R. (1980b). The deceptions of everyday life. *Journal of Communication, 30*, 216-218.

Dillehay, R. C. (1978). Authoritarianism. In H. London and J. Exner (Eds.), *Dimensions of personality* (pp. 85-127). New York: John Wiley.

DiRenzo, G. J. (1968). Dogmatism and presidential preferences in the 1964 elections. *Psychological Reports, 22,* 1197-1202.

DiRenzo, G. J. (1971). Dogmatism and presidential preferences: A 1968 replication. *Psychological Reports, 29,* 109-110.

Downs, V. C. (1985). *Personality variables as predictors of an individual's perceived communication competence.* Unpublished master's thesis, West Virginia University.

Druckman, D. (1967). Dogmatism, prenegotiation experience, and simulated group representation as determinants of dyadic behavior in a bargaining situation. *Journal of Personality and Social Psychology, 6,* 279-290.

DuBois, P. H. (1970). *A history of psychological testing.* Boston: Allyn & Bacon.

Dunnette, M. (1976). *Handbook of industrial psychology.* Chicago: Rand McNally.

Durkin, J. E. (1970). Encountering: What low machs do. In R. Christie & F. L. Geis (Eds.), *Studies in Machiavellianism* (pp. 260-284). New York: Academic Press.

Edwards, A. L. (1970). *The measurement of personality traits by scales and inventories.* New York: Holt, Rinehart & Winston.

Ehrlich, D. (1958). *Determinants of verbal commonality and influencibility.* Unpublished doctoral dissertation, University of Minnesota.

Endler, N. S., (1981). Persons, situations, and their interactions. In A. I. Rabin et al. (Eds.), *Further explorations in personality* (pp. 114-151). New York: John Wiley.

Endler, N. S., & Magnusson, D. (Eds.). (1976). *Interactional psychology and personality.* New York: John Wiley.

Ertel, S. (1972). Erkenntnis und Dogmatismus. *Psychologische Rundschau, 23,* 241-269.

Ertel, S. (1985). Content analysis: An alternative approach to open and closed minds. *High School Journal, 68,* 229-240.

Esquirol, J.E.D. (1838). *Des maladies mentales considerees sous les rapports medical, hygienique, et medico-legal.* Paris: Bailliere.

Exline, R. B., Thibaut, J., Hickey, C. B., & Gumpert, P. (1970). Visual interaction in relation to Machiavellianism and an unethical act. In R. Christie & F. L. Geis (Eds.), *Studies in Machiavellianism* (pp. 53-75). New York: Academic Press.

Eysenck, H. J. (1954). *The psychology of politics.* London: Routledge & Kegan Paul.

Eysenck, H. J. (Ed.). (1976) *The measurement of personality.* Baltimore: University Park Press.

Feather, N. T. (1969). Preference for information in relation to consistency, novelty, intolerance of ambiguity, and dogmatism. *Australian Journal of Psychology, 21,* 235-249.

Feather, N. T. (1971). Value difference in relation to ethnocentrism, intolerance of ambiguity, and dogmatism. *Personality, 2,* 349-366.

Feldman, S., & Rice, J. K. (1965). Tolerance for unambiguous feedback. *Journal of Personality and Social Psychology, 2,* 341-347.

Feldman, S. (1966). *Cognitive consistency*. New York: Academic Press.

Fiedler, F. E. (1960). The leader's psychological distance and group effectiveness. In D. Cartwright & A. Zander (Eds.), *Group Dynamics* (2nd ed., pp. 586-606). Evanston, IL: Row Peterson.

Fishbein, M. (1973). The prediction of behavior from attitudinal variables. In C. D. Mortensen & K. K. Sereno (Eds.), *Advances in communication research* (pp. 3-31). New York: Harper & Row.

Fishbein, M., & Ajzen, I. (1975). *Belief, attitude, intention, and behavior: An introduction to theory and research*. Reading, MA: Addison-Wesley.

Foulkes, D., & Foulkes, S. (1965). Self-concept, dogmatism, and tolerance of trait inconsistency. *Journal of Personality and Social Psychology, 2*, 104-110.

French, E. G. (1955). Interrelation among some measures of rigidity under stress and nonstress conditions. *Journal of Abnormal and Social Psychology, 51*, 114-118.

French, E. G. (1956). Motivation as a variable in work-partner selection. *Journal of Abnormal and Social Psychology, 53*, 96-99.

Frenkel-Brunswik, E. (1949). Intolerance of ambiguity as an emotional and perceptual personality variable. *Journal of Personality, 18*, 108-143.

Frenkel-Brunswik, E. (1954). Further explorations by a contributor to The Authoritarian Personality. In R. Christie & M. Jahoda (Eds.), *Studies in the scope and method of The Authoritarian Personality* (pp. 226-275). New York: Free Press.

Fromm, E. (1936). A social psychological approach to authority and family. In M. Horkheimer (Ed.), *Studien über Authoritat und Familie*. Paris: Librairie Felix Alcan.

Fromm, E. (1941). *Escape from freedom*. New York: Farrar & Rinehart.

Geis, F. L. (1970a). The con game. In R. Christie & F. L. Geis (Eds.), *Studies in Machiavellianism* (pp. 106-129). New York: Academic Press.

Geis, F. L. (1970b). Bargaining tactics in the con game. In R. Christie & F. L. Geis (Eds.), *Studies in Machiavellianism* (pp. 130-160). New York: Academic Press.

Geis, F. L. (1978a). Machiavellianism. In H. London & J. Exner (Eds.), *Dimensions of personality* (pp. 305-363). New York: John Wiley.

Geis, F. L. (1978b). The psychological situation and personality traits in behavior. In H. London (Ed.), *Personality: A new look at metatheories* (pp. 123-152). New York: John Wiley.

Geis, F. L., & Berger, D. (1965). *Taking over in group discussion*. Unpublished manuscript, New York University.

Geis, F. L., & Christie, R. (1970). An overview of experimental research. In R. Christie & F. L. Geis (Eds.), *Studies in Machiavellianism* (pp. 285-313). New York: Academic Press.

Geis, F. L., Christie, R., & Nelson, C. (1970). In search of the Machiavel. In R. Christie & F. L. Geis (Eds.), *Studies in Machiavellianism* (pp. 76-95). New York: Academic Press.

Geis, F. L., & Leventhal, E. (1965). *Attempting to deceive and detecting deception*. Unpublished manuscript, New York University.

Geis, F. L., & Levy, M. (1970). The eye of the beholder. In R. Christie & F. L. Geis (Eds.), *Studies in Machiavellianism* (pp. 210-235). New York: Academic Press.

Geis, F. L., & Moon, T. H. (1980). *Machiavellianism and deception.* Unpublished manuscript, University of Delaware.

Geis, F. L., Weinheimer, S., & Berger, D. (1970). Playing legislature: Cool heads and hot issues. In R. Christie & F. L. Geis (Eds.), *Studies in Machiavellianism* (pp. 190-209). New York: Academic Press.

Getter, H. (1966). A personality determinant of verbal conditioning. *Journal of Personality, 34*, 397-405.

Glass, D. (1967). Theories of consistency and the study of personality. In E. F. Borgatta & W. W. Lambert (Eds.), *Handbook of personality theory and research.* Chicago: Rand-McNally.

Goldstein, K. M., & Blackman, S. (1978). *Cognitive style.* New York: John Wiley.

Gore, P. (1962). *Individual differences in the prediction of subject compliance to experimenter bias.* Unpublished doctoral dissertation, Ohio State University.

Gore, P. (1963). Individual differences in the prediction of subject compliance to experimenter bias. *Dissertation Abstracts, 24 (1)*, 390.

Gough, H. G., & Sanford, R. N. (1952). *Rigidity as a psychological variable.* Unpublished manuscript, University of California, Institute of Personality Assessment and Research.

Greendlinger, V. (1985). Authoritarianism as a predictor of response to heterosexual and homosexual erotica. *High School Journal, 68*, 183-186.

Guilford, J. P. (1967). *The nature of human intelligence.* New York: McGraw-Hill.

Hacker, S., & Gaitz, C. M. (1970). Interaction and performance correlates of Machiavellianism. *Sociological Quarterly, 2*, 94-102.

Hall, J. A., Mroz, B. J., & Braunwald, K. G. (1983). Locus of control. *Journal of Personality and Social Psychology, 45*, 156-162.

Hanson, D. J. (1968). *Dogmatism and authoritarianism: A bibliography of master's theses.* Unpublished manuscript, SUNY Potsdam, Department of Sociology.

Hanson, D. J. (1975). Dogmatism and authoritarianism: A bibliography of doctoral dissertations. *Catalog of Selected Documents in Psychology*, Manuscript No. 1100, *5*, 329.

Hanson, D. J. (1980). Dogmatism and authoritarianism: A bibliography of master's theses. *Catalog of Selected Documents in Psychology,* Manuscript No. 2113, *10*, 87.

Hanson, D. J., & Vleeming, R. G. (1981). *Machiavellianism: A bibliography.* Unpublished manuscript, SUNY Potsdam, Department of Sociology.

Harris, T. M. (1966). *Machiavellianism, judgment independence, and attitudes toward teammate in a cooperative judgment task.* Unpublished doctoral dissertation, Columbia University.

Harvey, J., & Hays, D. G. (1972). Effect of dogmatism and authority of the source of communication upon persuasion. *Psychological Reports, 30,* 119-122.

Haythorn, W. W., & Altman, I. (1967). Personality factors in isolated environments. In M. H. Appley & R. Trumbull (Eds.), *Psychological stress.* New York: Appleton-Century-Crofts.

Haythorn, W. W., Altman, I., & Myers, T. I. (1966). Emotional symptomatology and subjective stress in isolated pairs of men. *Journal of Experimental Research in Personality, 1,* 290-305.

Hazelton, V., Jr. (1976). *Syntax and the distribution of speech behaviors in cooperative and uncooperative dyads.* Paper presented at the annual meeting of the Speech Communication Association, San Francisco.

Hazelton, V., Jr. (1977). *Machiavellianism, power, and language choice in the creative alternative game.* Unpublished doctoral dissertation, University of Oklahoma.

Hjelle, L. A. (1970). *Susceptibility to attitude change as a function of internal-external control.* Paper presented at the annual meeting of the Eastern Psychological Association, Atlantic City, NJ.

Hoffer, E. (1951). *The true believer.* New York: Mentor.

Hunt, M., & Miller, G. R. (1965). *Open- and closed-mindedness, belief discrepant communication behavior, and tolerance for dissonance.* Paper presented at the annual meeting of the Speech Association of America, New York.

Hunter, J., Gerbing, D., & Boster, F. (1982). Machiavellian beliefs and personality: Construct invalidity of the Machiavellianism dimension. *Journal of Personality and Social Psychology, 43,* 1293-1305.

Hyman, H. H., & Sheatsley, P. B. (1954). The authoritarian personality—a methodological critique. In R. Christie & M. Jahoda (Eds.), *Studies in the scope and method of the authoritarian personality.* New York: Free Press.

Illardo, J. A. (1973). Ambiguity tolerance and disordered communication: Therapeutic aspects. *Journal of Communication, 23,* 371-391.

Jackson, D. N., Messick, S. J., & Solley, C. M. (1957). How rigid is the authoritarian? *Journal of Abnormal and Social Psychology, 54,* 137-140.

James, W. H., Woodruff, A. B., & Werner, W. (1965). Effect of internal and external control upon changes in smoking behavior. *Journal of Consulting Psychology, 29,* 127-129.

Johnson, H. H., & Steiner, I. D. (1967). Some effects of discrepancy level on relationships between authoritarianism and conformity. *Journal of Social Psychology, 73,* 199-204.

Johnson, H. H., Torcivia, J. M., & Poprick, M. A. (1968). Effects of source credibility on the relationship between authoritarianism and attitude change. *Journal of Personality and Social Psychology, 9,* 179-183.

Jones, M. B. (1955). Authoritarianism and intolerance of fluctuation. *Journal of Abnormal and Social Psychology, 40,* 125-126.

Kelley, K. (1985). Sexuality and hostility of authoritarians. *High School Journal, 69,* 173-176.

Kirscht, J. P., & Dillehay, R. C. (1967). *Dimensions of authoritarianism.* Lexington: University of Kentucky Press.

Knapp, M. L., Hart, R. P., & Dennis, H. S. (1974). An exploration of deception as a communication construct. *Human Communication Research, 1*, 15-29.

Kounin, J. S. (1941). Experimental studies of rigidity, I and II. *Character and Personality, 9*, 251-272; 273-282.

Kounin, J. S. (1948). The meaning of rigidity: A reply to Heinz Werner. *Psychology Review, 55*, 157-166.

Krauss, R. M., Geller, V., & Olson, C. (1976). *Modalities and cues in the detection of deception.* Paper presented at the annual meeting of the American Psychological Association, Washington, D.C.

Kraut, R. E. (1978a). Verbal and nonverbal cues in the perception of lying. *Journal of Personality and Social Psychology, 36*, 380-391.

Kraut, R. E. (1978b). *Verbal and nonverbal cues in the perception of lying: A replication.* Unpublished manuscript, Cornell University.

Kraut, R. E. (1980). Humans as lie detectors: Some second thoughts. *Journal of Communication, 30*, 209-216.

Kraut, R. E., & Poe, D. (1980). Behavioral roots of person perception: The deception judgments of customs inspectors and laymen. *Journal of Personality and Social Psychology, 39*, 784-798.

Kremer-Hayon, L., Moore, M., & Nevat, R. (1985). Dogmatism in teacher education practices. *High School Journal, 68*, 154-157.

Kuo, H. K., & Marsella, A. J. (1977). The meaning and measurement of Machiavellianism in Chinese and American college students. *Journal of Social Psychology, 101*, 165-173.

Lamiell, J. T. (1982). The case for an idiothetic psychology of personality: A conceptual and empirical foundation. In B. A. Maher & W. B. Maher (Eds.), *Progress in experimental personality research* (Vol. 11). New York: Academic Press.

Lasswell, H. (1954). The selective effect of personality on political participation. In R. Christie & M. Jahoda (Eds.), *Studies in the scope and method of The Authoritarian Personality.* New York: Free Press.

Lefcourt, H. M. (1972). Recent developments in the study of locus of control. In B. A. Maher (Ed.), *Progress in experimental personality research* (Vol. 6). New York: Academic Press.

Lefcourt, H. M. (1976). *Locus of control: Current trends in theory and research.* New York: John Wiley.

Lefcourt, H. M., Lewis L., & Silverman, W. W. (1968). Internal versus external control of reinforcement and attention in a decision making task. *Journal of Personality, 36*, 663-682.

Lesser, H. (1985). The socialization of authoritarianism in children. *High School Journal, 68*, 162-166.

Lesser, H., & Steininger, M. (1975). Family patterns in dogmatism. *Journal of Genetic Psychology, 126*, 155-156.

Levenson, H. (1974). Activism and powerful others: Distinctions within the concept of internal-external control. *Journal of Personality Assessment, 38,* 377-383.

Levenson, H. (1976). Multidimensional locus of control in sociopolitical activists of conservative and liberal ideologies. *Journal of Personality and Social Psychology, 33,* 199-208.

Levitt, E. E. (1954). Studies in intolerance of ambiguity, I: The decision location test with grade schoolchildren. *Child Development, 24,* 263-268.

Levitt, E. E. (1956). The water-jar Einstellung test as a measure of rigidity. *Psychological Bulletin, 53,* 347-370.

Levitt, E. E., & Zelen, S. L. (1953). The validity of the Einstellung test as a measure of rigidity. *Journal of Abnormal and Social Psychology, 48,* 573-580.

Levitt, E. E., & Zelen, S. L. (1955). An investigation of the water-jar Einstellung problem as a measure of rigidity. *Psychological Reports, 1,* 331-334.

Levitt, E. E., & Zuckerman, M. (1959). The water-jar test revisited: The replication of a review. *Psychological Reports, 5,* 365-380.

Linton, H., & Graham, E. (1959). Personality correlates of persuasibility. In I. L. Janis & C. I. Hovland (Eds.), *Personality and persuasibility* (pp. 69-101). New Haven, CT: Yale University Press.

Loevinger, J. (1957). Objective tests as instruments of psychological theory. *Psychological Reports, 3,* 635-694.

Loevinger, J., & Wessler, R. (1970). *Measuring ego development,* 1 and 2. San Francisco: Jossey-Bass.

Luchins, A. S. (1942). Mechanization in problem solving—the effect of Einstellung. *Psychological Monographs, 54* No. 6 (whole No. 248).

Luchins, A. S. (1949). Rigidity and ethnocentrism: A critique. *Journal of Personality, 17,* 449-466.

MacDonald, A. P., Jr. (1970). Revised scale for ambiguity tolerance: Reliability and validity. *Psychological Reports, 26,* 791-798.

Machiavelli, N. (1940). *The prince: The discourses.* New York: Modern Library.

Mandler, G., & Sarason, S. B. (1952). A study of anxiety and learning. *Journal of Abnormal and Social Psychology, 47,* 166-173.

Mann, R. D. (1959). A review of the relationships between personality and performance in small groups. *Psychological Bulletin, 56,* 241-270.

Marlowe, D., & Gergen, K. J. (1969). Personality and social interaction. In G. Lindzey & E. Aronson (Eds.), *The handbook of social psychology* (2nd ed., pp. 590-665). Reading, MA: Addison-Wesley.

Martin, J. G., & Westie, F. R. (1959). The tolerant personality. *American Sociological Review, 24,* 521-528.

Marwell, G., & Schmitt, D. (1967). Dimensions of compliance-gaining behavior: An empirical analysis. *Sociometry, 30,* 350-364.

Maslow, A. H. (1943). The authoritarian character structure. *Journal of Social Psychology, 18,* 401-411.

McCandless, B. R. (1961). *Children and adolescents.* New York: Holt, Rinehart & Winston.

McClelland, D. C. (1981). Is personality consistent? In A. I. Rabin et al. (Eds.), *Further explorations in personality* (pp. 87-113). New York: John Wiley.

McGinnes, E., & Ward, C. D. (1974). Persuasibility as a function of source credibility and locus of control: Five cross cultural experiments. *Journal of Personality, 42*, 360-371.

McGuire, W. J. (1964). Inducing resistance to persuasion. In L. Berkowitz (Ed.), *Advances in experimental social psychology* (Vol. 1, pp. 191-229). New York: Academic Press.

McGuire, W. J. (1966). Attitudes and opinions. *Annual Review of Psychology, 17*, 484.

McGuire, W. J. (1968). Personality and susceptibility to social influence. In E. F. Borgatta & W. W. Lambert (Eds.), *Handbook of personality theory and research* (pp. 1130-1187). Chicago: Rand McNally.

McGuire, W. J. (1969). The nature of attitudes and attitude change. In G. Lindzey & E. Aronson (Eds.), *The handbook of social psychology* (2nd ed., pp. 136-314). Reading, MA: Addison-Wesley.

McNeel, S. P., & Thorsen, Philip L. (1985). A developmental perspective on Christian faith and dogmatism. *High School Journal, 68*, 211-220.

Meresko, R., Rubin, M., Shontz, F. C., & Morrow, W. R. (1954). Rigidity of attitudes regarding personal habits and its ideological correlates. *Journal of Abnormal and Social Psychology, 49*, 89-93.

Mertz, R. J., Miller, G. R., & Ballance, L. (1966). Open- and closed-mindedness and cognitive conflict. *Journalism Quarterly, 43*, 429-433.

Miller, G. R. (1977). *Dogmatism and message effects: Some prior findings and a few thoughts about future research.* Paper presented at the annual meeting of the Speech Communication Association, Washington, D.C.

Miller, G. R., & Bacon, P. (1971). Open- and closed-mindedness and recognition of visual humor. *Journal of Communication, 21*, 150-159.

Miller, G. R., Boster, F., Roloff, M., & Seibold, D. (1977). Compliance-gaining message strategies: A typology and some findings concerning effects of situational differences. *Communication Monographs, 44*, 37-51.

Miller, G. R., & Roberts, K. (1965). Communicator race, open- and closed-mindedness, and response to informative communications. *AV Communication Review, 13*, 259-269.

Miller, N. E. (1965). Involvement and dogmatism as inhibitors of attitude change. *Journal of Experimental Social Psychology, 1*, 121-132.

Millon, T. (1957). Authoritarianism, intolerance of ambiguity, and rigidity under ego- and task-involving conditions. *Journal of Abnormal and Social Psychology, 55*, 29-33.

Mischel, W. (1968). *Personality and assessment.* New York: John Wiley.

Montgomery, R. L., Hinkle, S. W., & Enzie, R. F. (1976). Arbitrary norms and social change in high- and low-authoritarian societies. *Journal of Personality and Social Psychology, 33*, 698-708.

Mortensen, C. D. (1972). *Communication: The study of human interaction.* New York: McGraw-Hill.

Mouw, J. T. (1969). Effect of dogmatism on levels of cognitive processes. *Journal of Educational Psychology, 60*, 363-369.

Mulligan, M. (1979). *A critique and reconceptualization of self-disclosure: Theoretical elaboration and empirical evidence.* Unpublished doctoral dissertation, University of Michigan, Ann Arbor.

Murphy, G., Murphy, L. B., & Newcomb, T. M. (1937). *Experimental social psychology.* New York: Harper & Row.

Nardin, T. (1968). Communication and effects of threats. *Peace Research Society (International) Papers, 9*, 69-86.

Norris, E. (1965). Attitude change as a function of open- or closed-mindedness. *Journalism Quarterly, 42*, 571-575.

Norton, R. W. (1975). Measurement of ambiguity tolerance. *Journal of Personality Assessment, 39*, 607-619.

Norton, R. W. (1983). *Communicator style.* Beverly Hills, CA: Sage.

Novgorodoff, B. D. (1974). *Boy meets girl: Machiavellianism and romantic attraction.* Unpublished master's thesis, University of Delaware.

Novielli, J. (1968). *Who persuades whom?* Unpublished master's thesis, University of Delaware.

Nye, R. D. (1973). Authoritarianism and the formation and change of impressions. *JSAS Catalog of Selected Documents in Psychology, 3*, 11 (Ms. No. 301).

O'Connor, P. (1952). Ethnocentrism, intolerance of ambiguity, and abstract reasoning ability. *Journal of Abnormal and Social Psychology, 47*, 526-530.

O'Hair, H. D., Cody, M. J., & McLaughlin, M. L. (1981). Prepared lies, spontaneous lies, Machiavellianism, and nonverbal communication. *Human Communication Research, 7*, 325-339.

Orwell, G. (1951). *1984.* New York: New American Library.

Oskenberg, L. (1968). *Machiavellianism and organization in five-man task oriented groups.* Unpublished doctoral dissertation, Columbia University.

Parrott, G. (1971). Dogmatism and rigidity: A factor analysis. *Psychological Reports, 29*, 135-140.

Parrott, G., & Brown, L. (1972). Political bias in the Rokeach dogmatism scale. *Psychological Reports, 30*, 805-806.

Pease, V. (1981). *Anxiety into energy.* New York: Elsevier-Dutton.

Peele, S. (1983). *The science of experience.* Lexington, MA: D. C. Heath.

Phares, E. J. (1976). *Locus of control in personality.* Morristown, NJ: General Learning Press.

Phares, E. J. (1978). Locus of control. In H. London & J. Exner (Eds.), *Dimensions of personality* (pp. 263-304). New York: John Wiley.

Pilisuk, M. (1963). Anxiety, self acceptance, and open mindedness. *Journal of Clinical Psychology, 19*, 386-391.

Pilisuk, M., Potter, P., Rapoport, A., & Winter, J. A. (1965). Warhawks and peace doves: Alternative resolutions of experimental conflicts. *Journal of Conflict Resolution, 9*, 491-508.

Platt, E. S. (1969). *Internal-external control and changes in expected utility as predictors of the change in cigarette smoking following role playing.* Paper presented at the annual meeting of the Eastern Psychological Association, Philadelphia.

Plax, T. G., & Rosenfeld, L. B. (1976). Dogmatism and decisions involving risk. *Southern Speech Communication Journal, 41*, 266-277.

Powell, F. A. (1962). Open- and closed-mindedness and the ability to differentiate message from source. *Journal of Abnormal and Social Psychology, 65*, 61-64.

Prociuk, T., & Breen, L. (1976). Machiavellianism and locus of control. *Journal of Social Psychology, 98*, 141-142.

Pryor, B., & Steinfatt, T. M. (1978). The effects of initial belief level on innoculation theory and its proposed mechanisms. *Human Communication Research, 4*, 217-230.

Ramsay, R. W. (1966). Personality and speech. *Journal of Personality and Social Psychology, 4*, 116-118.

Ray, J. J. (1979). A short balanced F scale. *Journal of Social Psychology, 109*, 309-310.

Rehfisch, J. M. (1958a). A scale for personality rigidity. *Journal of Consulting Psychology, 22*, 10-15.

Rehfisch, J. M. (1958b). Some scale and test correlates of a personality rigidity scale. *Journal of Consulting Psychology, 22*, 372-374.

Reich, W. (1933). Massenpsychologie. In M. Horkheimer (Ed.), *Studien über Autorität und Familie*. Paris: Librairie Felix Alcan.

Rigby, K. (1985). Are there behavioral implications for attitudes to authority? *High School Journal, 68*, 365-373.

Ritchie, E., & Phares, E. J. (1969). Attitude change as a function of internal-external control and communicator status. *Journal of Personality, 37*, 429-443.

Robbins, L. C. (1963). The accuracy of parental recall of aspects of child development and of child-rearing practices. *Journal of Abnormal and Social Psychology, 66*, 261-270.

Robinson, J., & Shaver, P. (1970). *Measures of social psychological attitudes*. Ann Arbor, MI: Institute for Social Research.

Rokeach, M. (1948). Generalized mental rigidity as a factor in ethnocentrism. *Journal of Abnormal and Social Psychology, 43*, 259-278.

Rokeach, M. (1949). Rigidity and ethnocentrism: A rejoinder. *Journal of Personality, 17*, 467-474.

Rokeach, M (1954). The nature and meaning of dogmatism. *Psychological Review, 61*, 194-204.

Rokeach, M. (1960). *The open and closed mind*. New York: Basic Books.

Rokeach, M., McGovney, W. C., & Denny, M. R. (1955). A distinction between dogmatic and rigid thinking. *Journal of Abnormal and Social Psychology, 51*, 87-93.

Roloff, M. E. (1981). *Interpersonal communication: The social exchange approach*. Beverly Hills, CA: Sage.

Roloff, M. E., & Barnicott, E. F., Jr. (1978). The situational use of pro- and anti-social compliance-gaining strategies by high and low Machiavellians. In

B. Rubin (Ed.), *Communication Yearbook II* (pp. 193-208). New Brunswick, NJ: Transaction.

Rosen, S. (1961). Postdecision affinity for incompatible information. *Journal of Abnormal and Social Psychology, 63*, 188-190.

Rosenfeld, H. M. (1966). Instrumental affiliative functions of facial and gestural expressions. *Journal of Personality and Social Psychology, 4*, 65-72.

Rosenfeld, H. M., & Nauman, D. (1969). Effects of dogmatism on the development of informal relationships among women. *Journal of Personality, 37*, 497-511.

Rosenman, M. F. (1967). Dogmatism and the movie *Dr. Strangelove*. *Psychological Reports, 20*, 942.

Rosenthal, R., & DePaulo, B. M. (1979). Sex differences in accommodation. In R. Rosenthal (Ed.), *Skill in nonverbal communication: Individual differences*. Cambridge, MA: Oelgeschlager, Gunn & Hain.

Rosnow, R. L., & Robinson, E. J. (1967). *Experiments in persuasion*. New York: Academic Press.

Rotter, J. B. (1954). *Social learning and clinical psychology*. Englewood Cliffs, NJ: Prentice-Hall.

Rotter, J. B. (1966). Generalized expectancies for internal versus external control of reinforcement. *Psychological Monographs, 80* (whole No. 609).

Rotter, J. B., Chance, J. E., & Phares, E. J. (Eds.). (1972). *Applications of a social learning theory of personality*. New York: Holt, Rinehart & Winston.

Rump, E. E. (1985). Personality ramifications of attitude to authority: Studies in Australia and Italy. *High School Journal, 68*, 287-292.

Ryckman, R. M., Rodda, W. C., & Sherman, M. F. (1972). Locus of control and expertise relevance as determinants of changes in opinion about student activism. *Journal of Social Psychology, 88*, 107-114.

Rydell, S. T., & Rosen, E. (1966). Measurement and some correlates of need-cognition. *Psychological Reports, 19*, 139-165.

Saling, N. (1973). *An investigation of the effects of competition and cooperation on the accuracy and congruency of communication in cooriented dyads*. Unpublished master's thesis, University of Kentucky, Department of Speech.

Samelson, F., & Yates, J. F. (1967). Acquiescence and the F scale: Old assumptions and new data. *Psychological Bulletin, 68*, 91-103.

Saunders, D. H. (1955). *Some preliminary interpretive material for the PRI*. Research memorandum 55-15, Educational Testing Service.

Schachter, S. (1959). *The psychology of affiliation*. Stanford, CA: Stanford University Press.

Schmitz, P. G. (1985). Sociocultural and personality differences in the dimension of the open and closed mind. *High School Journal, 68*, 348-354.

Schroder, H. M., & Streufert, S. (1962). *The measurement of four systems of personality structure varying in level of abstractness (sentence completion method)*. Technical Rep. 11, ONR. Princeton, NJ: Princeton University Press.

Schultz, C. B., & DiVesta, F. J. (1972). Effects of expert endorsement of beliefs on problem-solving behavior of high and low dogmatics. *Journal of Educational Psychology, 63*, 194-201.

Sears, R. R., Maccoby, E. E., & Levin, H. (1957). *Patterns of child-rearing.* Evanston, IL: Row, Peterson.

Seibold, D., & Steinfatt, T. M. (1979). The creative alternative game: Exploring interpersonal influence processes. *Simulation and Games, 10,* 429-457.

Sherif, M. (1936). *The psychology of social norms.* New York: Harper.

Sherif, C. W., & Sherif, M. (1967). *Attitude, ego involvement, and change.* New York: John Wiley.

Sherif, C. W., Sherif, M., & Nebergall, R. E. (1965). *Attitude and attitude change.* Philadelphia: Saunders.

Sherman, S. J. (1973). Internal-external control and its relationship to attitude change under different social influence techniques. *Journal of Personality and Social Psychology, 23,* 23-29.

Shils, E. A. (1954). Authoritarianism: "Right" and "left." In R. Christie & M. Jahoda (Eds.), *Studies in the scope and method of The Authoritarian Personality.* New York: Free Press.

Shirali, K. A. (1985). The interiors of North Indian families: Interpersonal relations and power games in TAT stories of mothers and fathers of open and closed minded sons. *High School Journal, 68,* 311-315.

Shure, G. H., Rogers, M. S., Larsen, I. M., & Tassone, J. (1962). Group planning and task effectiveness. *Sociometry, 25,* 263-282.

Siegel, E. R., Miller, G. R., & Wotring, C. E. (1969). Source credibility and credibility proneness: A new relationship. *Speech Monographs, 36,* 118-125.

Siegel, S. (1954). Certain determinants and correlates of authoritarianism. *Genetic Psychology Monographs, 49,* 187-230.

Smith, M. B. (1965). An analysis of two measures of authoritarianism among Peace Corps teachers. *Journal of Personality, 33,* 513-535.

Smock, C. D. (1955). The influence of psychological stress on the intolerance of ambiguity. *Journal of Abnormal and Social Psychology, 50,* 177-182.

Snider, J. G., & Osgood, C. E. (1969). *Semantic differential technique.* Chicago: Aldine.

Snyder, C. R., & Larson, G. R. (1972). A further look at student acceptance of general personality interpretations. *Journal of Consulting and Clinical Psychology, 38,* 384-388.

Solar, D., & Bruehl, D. (1971). Machiavellianism and locus of control: Two conceptions of interpersonal power. *Psychological Reports, 29,* 1079-1082.

Srole, L. (1956). Social integration and certain corollaries: An exploratory study. *American Sociological Review, 21,* 709-716.

Stagner, R. (1936). Fascist attitudes: An exploratory study. *Journal of Social Psychology, 7,* 309-319.

Stefflre, B., & Leafgren, F. (1964). Mirror, mirror on the wall . . . : A study of preferences for counselors. *Personnel Guidance Journal, 42,* 459-462.

Steiner, I. D. (1954). Ethnocentrism and tolerance of trait inconsistency. *Journal of Abnormal and Social Psychology, 49,* 349-354.

Steiner, I. D., & Johnson, H. H. (1963). Authoritarianism and tolerance of trait inconsistency. *Journal of Abnormal and Social Psychology, 67,* 388-391.

Steinfatt, T. M. (1972). Communication in the prisoner's dilemma and in a crea-
tive alternative game. *Proceedings: National Gaming Council's Eleventh
Annual Symposium,* Report #143 (pp. 221-224). Baltimore: Johns Hopkins
University, Center for Social Organization of Schools.

Steinfatt, T. M. (1973a). The prisoner's dilemma and a creative alternative
game: The effects of communication under conditions of real reward. *Simulation and Games, 4,* 389-409.

Steinfatt, T. M. (1973b). *A critique of the top three papers in interpersonal and
small group communication.* Paper presented at the annual meeting of the
Speech Communication Association, New York.

Steinfatt, T. M. (1977a). Measurement, transformation, and the real world: Do
the numbers represent the concept? *Et cetera, 34,* 277-289.

Steinfatt, T. M. (1977b). *Human communication.* Indianapolis: Bobbs-Merrill.

Steinfatt, T. M. (1987). *Communication and personality needs.* Unpublished
monograph, University of Miami.

Steinfatt, T. M., Gantz, W., Seibold, D. R., & Miller, L. D. (1973). News dif-
fusion of the George Wallace shooting: The apparent lack of interpersonal
communication as an artifact of delayed measurement. *Quarterly Journal of
Speech, 59,* 401-412.

Steinfatt, T. M., & Miller, G. R. (1974). Communication in game theoretic
models of conflict. In G. Miller & H. Simons (Eds.), *Perspectives on communication in social conflict* (pp. 14-75). Englewood Cliffs, NJ: Prentice-
Hall.

Steinfatt, T. M., & Ray, A. (1981). Why Cleveland is funny: An experimental
study of the use of plosive consonants in punch lines. *Proceedings of the
Western Humor and Irony Meeting* (pp. 291-292). Phoenix: Arizona State
University Press.

Steinfatt, T. M., Seibold, D., & Frye, J. (1974). Communication in game simulated conflicts: Two experiments. *Speech Monographs, 41,* 24-35.

Stewart, R. A., Kearney, P. & Plax, T. G. (1986). Locus of control as a
mediator: A study of college students' reactions to teachers' attempts to gain
compliance. In M. McLaughlin, (Ed.), *Communication Yearbook 9* (pp. 691-
703). Newbury Park, CA: Sage.

Strickland, B. R. (1970). Individual differences in verbal conditioning extinction
and awareness. *Journal of Personality, 38,* 364-378.

Sypher, H. E., Nightingale, J. P., Vielhaber, M. E., & Sypher, B. D. (1981). The
interpersonal constructs of Machiavellians: A reconsideration. *British Journal
of Social Psychology, 20,* 219-220.

Taft, R. (1956). Intolerance of ambiguity and ethnocentrism. *Journal of Consulting Psychology, 20,* 153-154.

Taylor, J. A. (1953). A personality scale of manifest anxiety. *Journal of Abnormal and Social Psychology, 48,* 285-290.

Teger, A. I. (1970). The effect of early cooperation on the escalation of conflict.
*Journal of Experimental Social Psychology, 6,* 187-204.

Terhune, K. W. (1968). Motives, situation, and interpersonal conflict within prisoner's dilemma. *Journal of Personality and Social Psychology, 8(3)*, Part 2 (monograph supplement).

Terhune, K. W. (1970). The effects of personality in cooperation and conflict. In P. Swingle (Ed.), *The structure of conflict* (pp. 193-234). New York: Academic Press.

Terhune, K. W., & Firestone, J. M. (1967). *Psychological studies in social interaction and motives (SIAM), phase 2: Group motives in an international relations game*. CAL Report VX-2018-G-2, Cornell Aeronautical Laboratory, Buffalo, NY.

Tolor, A. (1971). Are the alienated more suggestible? *Journal of Clinical Psychology, 27*, 441-442.

Troldahl, V. C., & Powell, F. A. (1965). A short-form dogmatism scale for use in field studies. *Social Forces, 44*, 211-214.

Vidulich, R. N., & Kaiman, I. P. (1961). The effects of information source status and dogmatism upon conformity behavior. *Journal of Abnormal and Social Psychology, 63*, 639-642.

von Freyhold, M. (1971). *Authoritarismus und politische Apathie: Analyze einer Skala zur Ermittlung autoritätsgebundener Verhaltensweisen*. Unpublished paper, Frankfurt/Main.

von Freyhold, M. (1985). Old and new dimensions of authoritarianism and its opposite. *High School Journal, 68*, 241-246.

Waid, W. M., & Orne, M. T. (1981). Cognitive, social, and personality processes in the physiological detection of deception. In L. Berkowitz (Ed.), *Advances in experimental social psychology* (Vol. 14, pp. 61-106). New York: Academic Press.

Walk, R. D. (1950). *Perception and personality: A pretest*. Unpublished manuscript, Harvard University, Social Relations Library.

Werner, H. (1946). Abnormal and subnormal rigidity. *Journal of Abnormal and Social Psychology, 41*, 15-24.

Wesley, E. (1953). Perseverative behavior, manifest anxiety, and rigidity. *Journal of Abnormal and Social Psychology, 48*, 129-134.

Willerman, L. (1979). *The psychology of individual and group differences*. San Francisco: W.H. Freeman.

Williams, M., Hazelton, V., & Renshaw, S. (1975). The measurement of Machiavellianism: A factor analytic and correlational study of Mach IV and Mach V. *Speech Monographs, 42*, 151-159.

Wrightsman, L. (1959). *The effects of small-group membership on level of concern*. Unpublished doctoral dissertation, University of Minnesota.

Wrightsman, L. S., Jr., & Cook, S. W. (1965). Factor analysis and attitude change. *Peabody Papers in Human Development, 3*, No. 2.

Yarrow, M. R. (1963). Problems of methods in parent-child research. *Child Development, 34*, 215-226.

Zacker, J. (1973). Authoritarian avoidance of ambiguity. *Psychological Reports, 33*, 901-902.

Zippel, B., & Norman, R. D. (1966). Party switching, authoritarianism, and dogmatism in the 1964 election. *Psychological Reports, 19*, 667-670.

Zuckerman, M., DePaulo, B. M., & Rosenthal, R. (1981). Verbal and nonverbal communication of deception. In L. Berkowitz (Ed.), *Advances in experimental social psychology* (Vol. 14, pp. 1-59). New York: Academic Press.

# Part II
# COMMUNICATION ORIENTATIONS

# 3

# Willingness to Communicate

## JAMES C. McCROSKEY
## VIRGINIA P. RICHMOND

Although talk is a vital component in interpersonal communication and the development of interpersonal relationships, people differ dramatically in the degree to which they actually do talk. Some people tend to speak only when spoken to—and sometimes not even then. Others tend to verbalize almost constantly. Many people talk more in some contexts than in others. Most people talk more to some receivers than they do to others. This variability in talking behavior is rooted in a personality variable that we call "willingness to communicate" (McCroskey & Baer, 1985). This variable—its nature, its causes, and its effects on interpersonal communication—is the focus of this chapter.

## WILLINGNESS TO COMMUNICATE AS A PERSONALITY CONSTRUCT

Whether a person is willing to communicate with another person in a given interpersonal encounter is certainly affected by situational constraints. Many situational variables can have an impact. How the person feels that day, what communication the person has had with others recently, who the other person is, what that person looks like, what might be gained or lost through communicating, and the demands of time can all have a major impact, as can a wide variety of other elements not enumerated here.

Willingness to communicate, then, is probably to a major (though as yet undetermined) degree situationally dependent. Nevertheless, individuals exhibit regular willingness-to-communicate tendencies across situations. Indeed, consistent behavioral tendencies with regard to frequency and amount of talk have been noted in the research literature for decades (Borgatta & Bales, 1953; Chapple & Arensberg, 1940; Goldman-Eisler, 1951). Such regularity in communication behavior across interpersonal communication contexts suggests the existence of the personality variable, willingness to communicate. It is this personality orientation which explains why one person will talk and another will not under identical, or virtually identical, situational constraints.

## FOUNDATIONS OF THE WILLINGNESS-TO-COMMUNICATE CONSTRUCT

The present willingness-to-communicate (WTC) construct has evolved from the earlier work of Burgoon (1976) on unwillingness to communicate; from Mortensen, Arnston, and Lustig (1977) on predispositions toward verbal behavior; and from McCroskey and Richmond (1982) on shyness. All of these writings center on a presumed traitlike predisposition toward communication.

### Unwillingness to Communicate

Burgoon (1976) originated the first construct in this area. She labeled her construct "unwillingness to communicate" and described this predisposition as a "chronic tendency to avoid and/or devalue oral communication." To argue the existence of such a predisposition, Burgoon drew upon work in the areas of anomie and alienation, introversion, self-esteem, and communication apprehension. All of these areas of research (which we discuss at greater length later) indicate variability in people's willingness to speak in various communication settings.

A self-report measure, the unwillingness-to-communicate scale (UCS), was developed as an operational definition of the construct. The measure was found to include two factors. One factor was labeled "approach-avoidance" and subsequently was found to be so highly correlated (> .80) with a measure of communication apprehension as to be virtually interchangeable with such a measure. The other factor was labeled "reward." This factor was not correlated with a measure of communication apprehension (r = .01).

Data reported by Burgoon (1976), while pointing to the potential usefulness of the UCS, also demonstrated that it was not a valid operationalization of the construct which had been advanced. The scores on the approach-avoidance (or communication apprehension) factor were found to be correlated with a measure of communication apprehension, total participation in a small group, and the amount of information-giving and information-seeking in a small group. The reward factor was uncorrelated with any of these criterion measures. In contrast, scores on the reward factor were correlated with satisfaction with a group, attraction to group members, and perceived coordination in a group, while scores on the approach-avoidance factor were uncorrelated with these criterion measures.

These results were discouraging because the behavioral measures of communication, which could be taken as validating a willingness or unwillingness to communicate predisposition, were only correlated with the approach-avoidance, or communication apprehension, factor scores. Thus the results did not provide support for a general predisposition of unwillingness to communicate. Rather, they indicated only that people who are fearful or anxious about communication are likely to engage in less communication than others—a finding observed many times before and since this investigation.

The results of the validation research for the UCS, then, suggest that the measure is not a valid operationalization of the construct of a global predisposition to be willing or unwilling to communicate. However, the results do not deny the possible existence of such a predisposition. In fact, they provide additional evidence that some regularity in the amount a person communicates may exist.

### Predispositions Toward Verbal Behavior

Mortensen et al. (1977) argue that "the more global features of speech tend to be consistent from one class of social situations to another." Although they recognize the importance of variance in situational characteristics in determining how much a person will communicate, they note findings from over 25 years of research which indicate consistency in the amount of an individual's communication across communication situations. They also suggest that there is a characteristic predisposition to say a given amount and that such a predisposition operates within the constraints of individual situations. They label this phenomenon "predispositions toward verbal behavior."

Unlike Burgoon (1976), these authors do not explore the possible causes of the global predisposition. Rather, they simply argue that it exists and provide a self-report scale that is designed to measure it. This measure is known as the Predispositions Toward Verbal Behavior (PVB) Scale. It is a 25-item, Likert-type scale employing a seven-step response option.

On the basis of the data reported by Mortensen el al. (1977), the PVB appears to be a unidimensional scale, although they indicate that an interpretable multiple-factor solution can be forced. Only one of the five factors interpreted centered on a general disinclination to engage in communication. The remaining factors appeared to measure dominance in communication, initiating and maintaining interpersonal communication, frequency and duration of communication, and anxiety about communication.

Data on validity indicated the ability of the PVB to significantly predict both the number of words spoken and the duration of talk in interpersonal interactions. This is a positive indication of validity of the scale. However, since only five of the 25 items focus directly on a general willingness or unwillingness to communicate (the communication disinclination factor), the reason for the obtained predictive validity is in considerable doubt. The predictive power of the instrument suggests that it is a valid measure of something, but whether that something is a general willingness to communicate is very questionable.

A reported high correlation of the PVB with a measure of communication apprehension ($r = .67$) increases this doubt. As we noted previously, considerable research prior and subsequent to the development of the PVB has found communication apprehension to be predictive of the amount a person says in various settings. Communication apprehension measures are not presumed to be direct measures of a global predisposition to approach or avoid communication. Rather, they are presumed to be indicants of the amount of fear˙ or anxiety an individual is likely to experience about communication. Such fear or anxiety, however, is likely to be one of the antecedents of general predispositions to be willing or unwilling to communicate.

The PVB, therefore, does not appear to be a valid operationalization of a general predisposition to be willing or unwilling to communicate. As was the case with the UCS, however, the research results based on the PVB provide additional indications that some regularity exists in the amount that an individual communicates.

### Shyness

"Shyness" is a term which has been used by many researchers when investigating traitlike predispositions toward communication. Unfortunately, some researchers fail to provide any definition of the term, and those who do are far from universal agreement. Leary (1981), basing his efforts on earlier work on shyness, has generated a construct he calls "social anxiety." He notes two components in his construct—an internally experienced discomfort and externally observable behavior. Some writers in the area of shyness have focused on the internal experience. Their work has paralleled work in the area of communication apprehension. Others have focused on shyness as reduced communication behavior. This approach appears to be consistent with a concern for a predisposition toward willingness to communicate.

The work of McCroskey and Richmond (1982) falls in the latter category. They define shyness as "the tendency to be timed, reserved, and most specifically, talk less." They note that communication apprehension is one of possibly numerous elements which may impact that tendency but that the two predispositions are conceptually distinct.

In earlier work, McCroskey attempted to develop a simplified version of a measure of communication apprehension for use in a study with preliterate children (McCroskey, Andersen, Richmond, & Wheeless, 1981). As a serendipitous artifact of that work, he developed a self-report scale which was factorally distinct from, yet substantially correlated with, a measure of communication apprehension. The items on the scale centered on the amount of talking that people report they do. He initially labeled the new instrument the Verbal Activity Scale (VAS) but changed the name to the Shyness Scale (SS) in later reports of its use. We will refer to it here by its original name to avoid confusion of this measure with a large number of other available measures also called shyness scales which focus on anxiety about communication rather than communication behavior.

In the belief that measures of communication apprehension and the VAS were tapping distinctly different, although related, constructs, McCroskey and Richmond (1982) attempted to validate both by examining their factorial independence and their relationships with reports of communication behavior taken from untrained observers who were friends of the subjects completing the measures. Employing both college student and older adult samples, they found that the measures were factorially distinct, as McCroskey had found in previous work, and that they were significant predictors of observer reports of communication behavior. The validity coefficient for the VAS and the observer reports of behavior was .53.

While these results suggest that the VAS is a valid measure of something, it is not certain that "something" is a predisposition to be willing or unwilling to communicate. The VAS is a self-report of the amount of talk in which one typically engages. The data reported by McCroskey and Richmond (1982) suggest that the scores generated are valid predictors of the amount of talk in which observers *believe* the individual engages. Even if we grant the validity of observer reports as quality indicants of actual behavior, this simply means that the VAS is a valid report of behavioral tendencies in communication. It does not validate the existence of a personality-based predisposition to be willing or unwilling to communicate. That a person can with some accuracy self-report whether he or she talks a lot or a little does not necessarily demonstrate that the behavior being reported is consistent with a predispositional desire, much less produced by such a predisposition.

As was the case with the research involving the UCS and PVB noted above, the research involving the VAS lends additional support for the argument that some regularity exists in the amount an individual communicates. Unfortunately, it is not clear that the VAS is a measure of a personality-based predisposition to be willing or unwilling to communicate, even though it may be a valid measure of a behavioral tendency to communicate more or less.

## Willingness to Communicate

As of this writing, there has been no instrument reported in the literature which has been positively demonstrated to be valid measure of our construct of a personality-based predisposition which we have labeled "willingness to communicate." However, abundant evidence exists to support the argument that people exhibit differential behavioral tendencies to communicate more or less across communication situations. To presume that such a personality orientation exists, then, seems reasonable in spite of the lack of availability of a demonstrably valid measure of it.

A recently developed self-report instrument, known as the Willingness to Communicate (WTC) Scale (see Figure 3.1), may provide a valid operationalization of the construct. It has strong content validity and there is some support for its construct validity. We briefly describe its development.

Underlying the construct of willingness to communicate is the assumption that this is a personality-based, traitlike predisposition which is relatively consistent across a variety of communication contexts and types of receivers. For us to argue that the predisposition is traitlike, it is necessary that the level of a person's willingness to communicate in one communication context (like small group interaction) is correlated with the person's willingness in other contexts (such as public speaking, talking in meetings, and talking in dyads). Further, it is necessary that the level of a person's willingness to communicate with one type of receiver (like acquaintances) is correlated with the person's willingness to communicate with other types of receivers (such as friends and strangers).

This assumption does not mandate that a person be equally willing to communicate in all contexts or with all receivers—only that the level of

*Directions:* Below are 20 situations in which a person might choose to communicate or not to communicate. Presume that you have *completely free choice*. Indicate the percentage of time you would choose *to communicate* in each type of situation. Indicate in the space at the left what percent of the time you would choose to communicate. 0 = never, 100 = always.

_____ 1. *Talk with a service station attendant.
_____ 2. *Talk with a physician.
_____ 3. Present a talk to a group of strangers.
_____ 4. Talk with an acquaintance while standing in line.
_____ 5. *Talk with a salesperson in a store.
_____ 6. Talk in a large meeting of friends.
_____ 7. *Talk with a policeman/policewoman.
_____ 8. Talk in a small group of strangers.
_____ 9. Talk with a friend while standing in line.
_____ 10. *Talk with a waiter/waitress in a restaurant.
_____ 11. Talk in a large meeting of acquaintances.
_____ 12. Talk with a stranger while standing in line.
_____ 13. *Talk with a secretary.
_____ 14. Present a talk to a group of friends.
_____ 15. Talk in a small group of acquaintances.
_____ 16. *Talk with a garbage collector.
_____ 17. Talk in a large meeting of strangers.
_____ 18. *Talk with a spouse (or girl/boyfriend).
_____ 19. Talk in a small group of friends.
_____ 20. Present a talk to a group of acquaintances.

*Filler item

---

*Scoring:* To compute the subscores, add the percentages for the items indicated and divide the total by the number indicated below.
*Public:* 3 + 14 + 20; divide by 3.
*Meeting:* 6 + 11 + 17; divide by 3.
*Group:* 8 + 15 + 19; divide by 3.
*Dyad:* 4 + 9 + 12; divide by 3.
*Stranger:* 3 + 8 + 12 + 17; divide by 4.
*Acquaintance:* 4 + 11 + 15 + 20; divide by 4.
*Friend:* 6 + 9 + 14 + 19; divide by 4.

To compute the total WTC score, add the subscores for Stranger, Acquaintance, and Friend. Then divide that total by 3.

---

**Figure 3.1 Willingness to Communicate Scale (*continued*)**

*(continued)*

Normative means, standard deviations, and internal reliability estimates for the scores, based on a sample of 428 college students, are as follows:

| Score | Mean | Standard Deviation | Reliability |
|-------|------|--------------------|-------------|
| Total WTC | 67.3 | 15.2 | .92 |
| Public | 56.1 | 22.2 | .76 |
| Meeting | 60.0 | 20.9 | .70 |
| Group | 73.4 | 15.8 | .65 |
| Dyad | 79.5 | 15.0 | .69 |
| Stranger | 41.3 | 22.5 | .82 |
| Acquaintance | 75.0 | 17.9 | .74 |
| Friend | 85.5 | 13.8 | .74 |

**Figure 3.1 Willingness to Communicate Scale**

willingness in various contexts and with various receivers be correlated. Thus, if Person A is much more willing to communicate in small groups than in a public speaking context, the underlying assumption is not necessarily violated. However, if Person A is more willing to communicate than Person B in one context, it is assumed that Person A will be more willing to communicate than Person B in other contexts as well. If no such regularity exists when data are aggregated for a large number of people, willingness to communicate in one context will not be predictive of willingness to communicate in another context, and willingness to communicate with one type of receiver will not be predictive of willingness to communicate with another type of receiver. In this event, the data would invalidate the assumption of traitlike predisposition and necessitate that we redirect our attention to predispositions that are context-based and/or receiver-based. Alternatively, we could forego the predispositional approach in favor of a purely situational explanation of willingness to communicate.

The WTC scale includes items related to four communication contexts—public speaking, talking in meetings. talking in small groups, and talking in dyads—and three types of receivers—strangers, acquaintances, and friends. The scale includes 12 scored items and 8 filler items. In addition to an overall WTC score, presumably representing the general personality orientation of willingness to communicate, 7 subscores may be generated. These represent the four types of communication contexts and three types of receivers.

Available data on the instrument are very promising (McCroskey & Baer, 1985). The internal reliability of the total WTC score is .92. Internal reliabilities for the subscores for communication context range from .65 to .76. Internal reliabilities for the subscores for types of receivers range from .74 to .82. The mean correlation among context subscores is .58, which is also the mean correlation among receiver-type subscores. After correction for attenuation, the mean correlation among context subscores is .88; among receiver-type subscores it is .82. Factor analysis indicates that all 12 scored items load most highly on the first unrotated factor, indicating that the scale is unidimensional. No interpretable multidimensional structure could be obtained through forced rotations in McCroskey and Baer's (1985) study.

The preceding correlations and reliabilities suggest that an individual's willingness to communicate in one context or with one receiver type is closely related to his or her willingness to communicate in other contexts and with other receiver types. This does not mean, however, that individuals are equally willing to communicate in all contexts and with all types of receivers. In fact, major mean differences were observed across the sample of subjects studied on the basis of receiver type. The observed mean percentage of time that people would be willing to communicate with friends was 85.5. For acquaintances and strangers the percentages were 75.0 and 41.3, respectively. Contexts produced less dramatic differences in willingness. The percentages for the contexts were as follows: dyad, 79.5; group, 73.4; meeting, 60.0; and public, 56.1. In general, the larger the number of receivers and the more distant the relationship of the individual with the receiver(s), the less willing the individual is to communicate.

The data generated by the WTC scale suggest the validity of our construct of a general predisposition toward being willing (or unwilling) to communicate. The scale also appears to be valid. The items clearly represent the construct as we have outlined it, and the subscore correlations suggest that the instrument is measuring a broadly based predisposition rather than a series of independent predispositions. Whether the WTC scale can be used a valid predictor of actual communication behavior is another question, one that remains to be answered by future research. People conducting that research must take care that the behavior to be observed be under conditions where the subjects truly have free choice of whether to communicate or not. Other observational data would be only marginally related to the validity of the WTC scale.

## ANTECEDENTS OF WILLINGNESS TO COMMUNICATE

That there is regularity in the amount of communication behavior of an individual across situations has been clearly established in many research studies. We have posited a personality-based mediational variable as the immediate cause of that regularity—willingness to communicate. The question that we now address is why people vary in this predispositional orientation. We refer to the variables that we believe lead to differences in willingness to communicate as "antecedents." It is likely that many of these antecedents develop concurrently with the willingness-to-communicate predisposition. Hence it cannot be clearly established that the antecedents are the causes of variability in the willingness to communicate. It is more likely that these variables may be involved in mutual causality with each other, and even more likely that both the antecedents and the willingness to communicate are produced in common by other causal elements.

The antecedents that we consider here are variables that have received considerable attention from scholars in communication and/or psychology. Each of them is of interest to scholars for a variety of reasons, only one of which is a possible relationship with willingness to communicate. The variables we consider are introversion, anomie and alienation, self-esteem, cultural divergence, communication skill level, and communication apprehension.

### Introversion

The construct of extroversion-introversion has received considerable attention from scholars in psychology for several decades (Eysenck, 1970, 1971). The construct postulates a continuum between extreme extroversion and extreme introversion. The nearer the individual is to the extroversion extreme, the more "people-oriented" the person is likely to be. The more introverted the individual, the less need the individual feels for communication and the less value the person places on communicating. Introverts tend to be inner-directed and introspective. They also tend to be less sociable and less dependent on others' evaluations than more extroverted people.

Introverts are often characterized as quiet, timid, and shy. Other things being equal, they prefer to withdraw from communication. This may stem in part from anxiety about communication. However, the relationship between introversion and communication apprehension is only modest ($r = .33$; Huntley, 1969). Numerous studies have indicated a relationship between introversion and communication behaviors characteristic of people presumed to have a low willingness to communicate. For example, Carment, Miles, and Cervin (1965) found that introverts participated in a small group discussion significantly less than extroverts and tended to speak only when spoken to rather than initiating inter- action. Similarly, Borg and Tupes (1958) found that introverts were significantly less likely than extroverts to engage in the communication behaviors necessary to exercise leadership in small groups.

## Anomie and Alienation

Anomie refers to a state in which an individual's normative standards are severely reduced or lost. Anomics are normless; they have failed to internalize society's norms and values, including a value for communication. They often feel alone and socially isolated (Bloom, 1970; Dean, 1961; Elmore, 1965). Alienation, an extreme manifestation of anomie, is a feeling of estrangement, of being apart and separate from other human beings and from society in general.

Alienation has been found to be directly related to withdrawal from communication (Giffin, 1970; Giffin & Groginsky, 1970). Anomie- alienation have also been found to be associated with negative attitudes toward communication and reduced interaction with peers, parents, teachers, and administrators (Heston & Andersen, 1972). In short, anomie and alienation appear to generate behavior characteristic of people presumed to have a low willingness to communicate.

## Self-Esteem

A person's self-esteem is that person's evaluation of his or her own worth. Since self-esteem is discussed at length in Chapter 7, we will not elaborate on the construct here.

A person with low self-esteem might be expected to be less willing to communicate because of a feeling that he or she has little of value to offer. Similarly, a person with low self-esteem may be less willing to communicate because he or she believes that others will respond negatively to what might be said. Although we believe there is good reason to consider self-esteem to be an antecedent of willingness to communicate, little research support is available that directly bears on this issue.

In an unpublished study, we found self-esteem to be significantly related to the number of times people talked in a small group setting— the higher the self-esteem, the more times they talked. However, we also found that if the variance attributable to communication apprehension was removed, self-esteem accounted for no significant variance in the times talked. Thus it may be that self-esteem is related to the willingness to communicate, but only as a function of the relationship between self-esteem and anxiety about communication, a relationship that has been found to be quite strong (McCroskey, Daly, Richmond, & Falcione, 1977).

## Cultural Divergence

Although communication exists in all human cultures and subcultures, communication norms are highly variable as a function of culture. Thus one's communication norms and competencies are culture-bound. In a few countries, like Japan, a single culture is almost universally dominant. In other countries, like the United States, there is a majority culture and many subcultures. These subcultures exist both as a function of geographic region and ethnicity. People from Texas and people from Maine have differing communication norms. So too do Mexican Americans, Black Americans, Japanese Americans, Native Americans, and so forth.

Whenever people find themselves in an environment in which their own subculture is in a minority position compared to other people with whom they must communicate, such a group may be described as culturally divergent. It is incumbent on the divergent individual to adapt to the larger group's communication norms in order to be effective in communication in that environment. As anyone who has traveled extensively can testify, particularly if that travel has taken one to another country, such adaptation can be difficult or even impossible to achieve.

Culturally divergent individuals are very similar to people who have deficient communication skills (whom we discuss shortly). Because they do not know how to communicate effectively, they tend to be much less willing to communicate at all for fear of failure and possible negative consequences. The difference between the culturally divergent and the skill-deficient is that the culturally divergent individual may have excellent communication skills for one culture but not for the other. Cultural divergence, then, is seen as being closely related to a traitlike willingness to communicate if a person regularly resides in a culture different from his or her own. On the other hand, if the person communicates primarily in one culture and only occasionally must do so in another culture, the impact will be only on situational willingness.

## Communication Skills

Work in the area of reticence (Phillips, 1968, 1977, 1984) leads us to believe that a major reason that some people are less willing to communicate than others is deficient communication skills. To be reticent is to avoid social interaction, to be reserved, to say little. In this sense, it is to behave exactly opposite to how one would expect a person to behave who is willing to communicate.

Early work in the area of reticence focused on behavior as a function of anxiety about communication and was essentially similar to the work to be discussed here related to communication apprehension. The original definition of a reticent individual advanced by Phillips (1968, p. 40) was "a person for whom anxiety about participation in oral communication outweighs his projection of gain from the situation."

More recent work in this area has moved away from anxiety and chosen to focus on communication skills. Although Phillips and others working with the reticence construct do not deny that many people engage in reduced communication because they are apprehensive about communicating, they choose to focus their attention on people who may or may not be anxious but who are definitely deficient in their communication skills.

Case studies drawn from work on communication skills training with reticent individuals indicate that when skills are increased, the willingness to communicate in contexts related to the training also increases. This reinforces our belief that for some people, willingness to communicate in some contexts and/or with some receivers is reduced as a function of not knowing how to communicate. The relationship between communication skills and a general predisposition to be willing to communicate is unknown at this time. Most likely, small skill deficits would have little relationship. However, the perception of one's own skill level may be more important than the actual skill level. Hence people with low self-esteem may see their skills as deficient—even if their skills in reality are quite satisfactory—and be reticent as a result.

The relationship between skills and willingness is a complex one. Low skills, as noted earlier, may lead to lowered willingness. Conversely, low willingness may result in decreased experience in communication and, hence, reduced skills. In addition, such things as low self-esteem and high communication apprehension may lead to reduced levels of both skills and willingness. For all these reasons, however, it is reasonable to believe that skill level and willingness level should be related.

### Communication Apprehension

Communication apprehension (CA) is "an individual's level of fear or anxiety associated with either real or anticipated communication with another person or persons'' (McCroskey, 1977, 1984). An individual's level of CA is probably the single best predictor of his or her willingness to communicate. The higher the CA level, the lower the level of the willingness to communicate.

Although most of the work related to CA has been done under the CA label (Daly & McCroskey, 1984; McCroskey, 1970, 1977), similar work has also been done under other labels. Some of these include "stage fright" (Clevenger, 1959), the early work on "reticence" (Phillips, 1968), "unwillingness to communicate" (Burgoon, 1976), "social anxiety" (Leary, 1983), "audience anxiety" (Buss, 1980), and "shyness" (Buss, 1980; Zimbardo, 1977).

Although there are some meaningful differences in the conceptualizations advanced under these various labels, the main differences involve the operational measures employed. Both subjective examination of the measures and correlational analyses (Daly, 1978) indicate that the measures are highly related and are probably all tapping into the same global construct.

Regardless of the operationalization of the construct, research overwhelmingly indicates that people who experience high levels of fear or anxiety about speaking tend to avoid and withdraw from communication. Although not measured directly, these research results strongly suggest that CA directly affects an individual's willingness to communicate. Because we believe that CA is the most potent of the antecedents of willingness to communicate, we examine this construct in greater detail in the next section.

## THE COMMUNICATION APPREHENSION CONSTRUCT

In the following section we outline the essential components of the CA construct. In particular, we discuss the types of CA, its causes, effects, and measurement.

### Types of CA

Our concern with CA views the construct as a traitlike, personality-type variable. Over the almost two decades in which research on CA has been conducted, most of the attention it has received has centered on this view. However, the overall conceptualization of CA extends beyond the traitlike predisposition and identifies four types of CA which extend from the traitlike to the purely situational. The four types are referred to as traitlike, context-based, receiver-based, and situational. We consider each in turn.

*Traitlike CA* is viewed as *a relatively enduring, personality-type orientation toward a given mode of communication across a wide variety of contexts.* Our concern here is with oral communication. However, traitlike apprehension about other modes of communication has also been studied under the labels of writing apprehension (Daly & Miller, 1975) and singing apprehension (Andersen, Andersen, & Garrison, 1978).

Traitlike CA is presumed to be a relatively stable predisposition toward experiencing fear and/or anxiety in a variety of communication contexts. While an individual's level of traitlike CA is presumed to be subject to change over time as a function of differing communication experiences or treatment interventions, it is also presumed to be relatively consistent over extended time periods in the absence of major traumatic experiences or systematic interventions. In short, it is imbedded in the total personality of the individual.

*Context-based CA* is viewed as *a relatively enduring, personality-type orientation toward communication in a given type of context.* Apprehension about public speaking, commonly known as "speech fright" or "stage fright," is an example of this type of CA. Whereas traitlike CA is presumed to generalize across communication contexts, context-based CA is presumed to be restricted to a single type of context. For example, a person could have consistently high CA with regard to communication in public but experience little CA in dyadic or small group interactions. Similarly, a person could have consistently high CA with regard to interpersonal communication but experience little CA when presenting a public speech or talking in a large meeting. As was the case with traitlike CA, context-based CA is presumed to be stable over extended periods of time.

*Receiver-based CA* is viewed as *a relatively enduring orientation toward communication with a given person or group of people or a given type of person or group of persons.* This type of CA is viewed as personality-based and/or a response to consistent situational constraints generated by a given person or group of people. Receiver-based CA that centers on a certain type of person or group of persons (strangers, acquaintances, or friends) is presumed to be rooted in personality. However, that which centers on a particular person or group of persons (the boss, the teacher, or one's colleagues) may be a function of both personality and situational constraints generated by the other person or group. If one is apprehensive about all bosses, this probably stems from a personality orientation and would likely be quite stable over time. If, however, the person is usually not bothered by bosses, but is bothered by one particular boss, this probably stems from situational constraints generated by that boss. This would be much more subject to change as a function of the boss generating different situational constraints.

People can differ greatly in the level of receiver-based CA. For example, a teacher might experience very little CA when talking to a student but a great deal when talking to the principal. Similarly, a speaker may experience a great deal of CA when talking to a group of strangers but very little when talking to a group of friends.

Length of acquaintance may be expected to have a major impact on the degree to which receiver-based CA is affected by personality as opposed to situational constraints generated by a given receiver or group of receivers. The shorter the acquaintance period, the more we should expect personality to be a factor (Richmond, 1978).

*Situational CA* is viewed as *a transitory orientation toward communication with a given person or group of people.* This type of CA should be expected to fluctuate substantially as a function of changed constraints introduced by the environment in which the communication takes place and the behavior of the other person or people in the communication encounter

Receiver-based, context-based, and traitlike CA should be expected to be predictive of situational CA considered across relevant situations. However, they should not be expected to be equally predictive. Receiver- and context-based CA should be expected to be more predictive than traitlike because they relate more directly and restrictively to elements present in given situations. However, traitlike CA is also presumed to be predictive of CA experienced across a wide variety of situations. It will be most predictive of the average situational CA experienced when a variety of types of context and types of receivers are considered together.

## Causes of CA

The two primary explanations provided for the development of personality in human beings center on heredity and environment. In short, one can be born with it or learn it. Explanations for the development of CA have focused on these two factors.

Researchers in the area of social biology have established that significant social traits can be measured in infants shortly after birth, and that infants differ sharply from each other on these traits. One of these traits is referred to as "sociability," which is believed to be a predisposition directly related to adult sociability—the degree to which one reaches out to other people and responds positively to contact with other people.

Research with identical and fraternal twins of the same sex reinforces the theoretical role of heredity in personality development. Identical twins are biologically identical, whereas fraternal twins are not. Thus, if differences between twins raised in the same environment are found to exist, biology (heredity) can be discounted as a cause in one case but not in the other. Research has indicated that biologically identical twins are much more similar in sociability than are fraternal twins. This research is particularly important because it was conducted with a large sample of adult twins who had the opportunity to have many different and varied social experiences (Buss, 1980).

This research strongly suggests that heredity may have an important bearing on an individual's willingness to communicate. Whether such hereditary influence passes through CA to affect the willingness to communicate, however, remains an unknown. No hereditary research to date has involved the measurement of CA, so the question of the impact of heredity on CA must remain open. At this point we doubt that a substantial impact exists. Research on the treatment methods for reducing high CA (McCroskey, 1972; McCroskey, Ralph, & Barrick, 1970) suggests that methods based on learning models are highly effective and require relatively brief time periods to implement. It strikes us as unlikely that such would be the case if CA were biologically based. Thus, at present we believe any substantial impact of heredity on the willingness to communicate more than likely passes through some other antecedent of this predisposition. The one we consider most likely is extroversion-introversion. In any event, in the absence of directly relevant research, any presumed relationship must rest on pure speculation.

We believe that CA is a learned phenomenon. More specifically, traitlike CA represents an accumulation of state anxiety experiences (McCroskey & Beatty, 1984). An explanation of this process centers on work in expectancy learning, particularly that concerning learned helplessness (Seligman, 1975).

People develop expectations with regard to other people and with regard to situations. Expectations are also developed concerning the probable outcomes of engaging in specific behaviors (such as talking). To the extent that such expectations are found to be accurate, the individual develops confidence. When expectations are found to be inaccurate, the individual is confronted with the need to develop new expectations. When this continually recurs, the individual may develop a lack of confidence. When no appropriate expectations can be developed, anxiety is produced. When expectations are produced that entail negative outcomes seen as difficult or impossible to avoid, fear is produced.

When applied to communication behavior, these last two cases are the foundation of CA.

Reinforcement is a vital component of expectancy learning. Organisms form expectations on the basis of attempting behaviors and being reinforced for some and either not reinforced or punished for others. The most gestalt expectancy is that there is regularity in the environment. This forms the basis for the development of other, more specific expectations. When no regularity can be discovered in a given type of situation, either because none exists or there is too little exposure to that type of situation to obtain sufficient observation and reinforcement, the organism is unable to develop a regular behavioral response pattern for that situation that will maximize rewards and minimize punishments. Anxiety is the cognitive response to such situations, and the behavior is unpredictable to a large extent. However, nonbehavior such as avoidance or withdrawal is probable, since even though this does not increase the probability of obtaining a reward, in many instances it decreases the probability of receiving punishment. The organism essentially becomes helpless.

In the early animal research concerning helplessness, dogs were placed in a environment in which rewards and punishments were administered on a random schedule. After attempting behaviors to adapt to this environment but receiving no regular response from the environment, the dogs retreated to a corner and virtually stopped behaving. They became helpless, and some actually died (Seligman, 1975). Although a major portion of the research supporting the learned helplessness construct has been conducted with animals, Feinberg, Miller, and Weiss (1983) have demonstrated its applicability to the learning of communication behavior by humans.

We learn our communicative behavior by trying various behaviors in our environment and receiving various rewards and punishments (or the absence of rewards or punishments) for our efforts. Over time and situations,we develop expectations concerning the likely outcomes of various behaviors within and across situations. Three things can occur from this process, all of which can occur for the same individual, and all of which are environmentally controlled. However, they may occur to greatly different degrees for different individuals. The three things that can occur are positive expectations, negative expectations, and helplessness. Let us consider each.

When we engage in communication behaviors that work (that is, are reinforced by the achievement of some desired goal), we develop positive expectations for those behaviors and they become a regular part of our communicative repertoire. In the early childhood years, much of this occurs through trial and error; during later stages of development, cognition becomes more important. We may think through a situation and choose communication behaviors that our previous experience suggests should be successful. Formal instruction in communication adds to our cognitive capacity to develop such expectations and choose appropriate behaviors. To the extent that our behaviors continue to be reinforced, we develop stronger positive expectations and our communication behavior becomes more regularly predictable. In addition, we develop confidence in our ability to communicate effectively. Neither anxiety nor fear—the core elements of CA—is associated with such positive expectations.

The development of negative expectations follows much the same pattern as that of positive expectations. We discover that some communication behaviors regularly result in punishment or a lack of reward and tend to reduce those behaviors. During later stages of development, we may make cognitive choices between behaviors for which we have positive and negative expectations, the former being chosen and the latter rejected. However, we may also find situations for which we have no behaviors with positive expectations for success. If we can avoid or withdraw from such situations, this is a reasonable choice. However, if participation is unavoidable, we may have only behaviors with negative expectations available. A fearful response is the natural outcome. Consider, for example, the person who has attempted several public speeches. In each case, the attempt resulted in punishment or lack of reward. When confronted with another situation that requires the individual to give a public speech, the person will fear that situation. The person knows what to expect, and the expectation is negative.

The development of helplessness occurs when regularity of expectations, either positive or negative, is not present. Helplessness may be either spontaneously learned or developed over time. Spontaneous helplessness occurs in new situations. If the person has never confronted the situation before, he or she may be unable to determine any behavioral options. While this is much more common for young children, adults may also confront such situations. For example, visiting a foreign country where one does not understand the language may place one in a helpless condition. Similarly, some people who are divorced after many years of marriage report that they find themselves helpless when it comes to communication in the "singles scene." Such spontaneous helplessness may generate strong anxiety feelings, and the behavior of people experiencing such feeling is often seen by others in the environment as highly aberrant.

Helplessness that is learned over time is produced by the inconsistent receipt of reward and punishment. Such inconsistency may be a function of either true inconsistency in the environment or the inability of the individual to discriminate among situational constraints in the environment that produce differential outcomes. For example, a child may develop helplessness if the parent reinforces the child's talking at the dinner table on some days and punishes it on other days. If the child is unable to determine why the parent behaves differently from day to day, the child is helpless to control the punishments and rewards. Similarly, the child may be rewarded for giving an answer in school but punished for talking to another child in the classroom. If the child is unable to see the differences in these situations, the child may learn to be helpless. When helplessness is learned, it is accompanied by strong anxiety feelings.

Learned helplessness and learned negative expectations are the foundational components of CA. The broader the helplessness or negative expectations, the more traitlike the CA. Inversely, the more situationally specific the helplessness or negative expectatious, the more situational the CA. It should be stressed that helplessness and negative expectation (as well as positive expectations) are the product of an interaction between the individual's behaviors and the responses of other individuals in the environment. The development of the cognitive responses of the person, then, may be heavily dependent on his or her behavioral skills, partly dependent on those skills and partly dependent on the responsiveness of the environment, or almost entirely a result of the environment. Thus any hereditary component which may exist may only have an impact through its interaction with the environment.

## Internal Effects of CA

The effects of traitlike CA have been the focus of extensive research, much of which has been summarized elsewhere (McCroskey, 1977). Unfortunately, much of this work has centered on the impact of CA on communication behaviors. This research is not completely compatible with the conceptualization of CA as a cognitively based variable. Although CA may indeed be linked with communication behavior, current theory suggests that traitlike CA is a precursor of CA in a given situation which may have, but not necessarily *will* have, an impact on situational willingness to communicate (McCroskey & Beatty, 1984).

As has been noted elsewhere (McCroskey, 1984), *the only effect of CA that is predicted to be universal across both individuals and types of CA is an internally experienced feeling of discomfort.* As CA is heightened, feelings of discomfort increase and willingness to communicate is predicted to decline.

The importance of this conceptualization of CA must be emphasized. Since CA is experienced internally, the only potentially valid indicant of CA is the individual's report of that experience. Thus self-reports of individuals, whether obtained by paper-and-pencil measures or careful interviews, or under circumstances where the individual has nothing to gain or lose by lying, provide the only potentially valid measures of CA. Measures of physiological activation and observations of behavior can provide, at best, only indirect evidence of traitlike CA and thus are inherently inferior approaches to measuring CA. Physiological and behavioral instruments intended to measure CA must be validated with self-report measures, not the other way around. To the extent that such measures are not related to self-report measures, they must be judged invalid. Currently available data indicate that such physiological measures and behavioral observation procedures generally have low validity as measures of traitlike CA but may be somewhat more valid for measuring situational CA (Behnke & Beatty, 1981; Clevenger, 1959).

## External Effects of CA

As noted earlier, there is no single behavior that is predicted to be a universal product of varying levels of traitlike CA. Any impact of CA on behavior must be mediated by willingness to communicate in interaction with situational constraints. Nevertheless, there are some externally observable behaviors that are either more or less likely to occur as a function of varying levels of CA. Behavioral prediction from traitlike CA should be assumed to be correct only when considering aggregate behavioral indicants of the individual across time, contexts, and receivers.

Three patterns of behavioral response to high traitlike CA may be predicted to be generally applicable: communication avoidance, communication withdrawal, and communication disruption. A fourth pattern is atypical but sometimes does occur—excessive communication. We now consider each of these patterns.

When people are confronted with a circumstance that they anticipate will make them uncomfortable, and they have a choice of whether or not to confront it, they may decide either to confront it and make the best of it or to avoid it and thus avoid the discomfort. Some refer to this as the choice between "fight" and "flight." Research in the area of CA indicates that the latter choice should be expected in most cases. In order to avoid having to experience high CA, people may become less willing to communicate and therefore select occupations that involve low communication responsibilities, pick housing units that reduce incidental contact with other people, choose seats in classrooms or in meetings that are less conspicuous, and even avoid social settings. Avoidance, then, is a common behavioral response to high CA.

Avoidance of communication is not always possible, no matter how high a person's level of traitlike CA or low the willingness to communicate. People can find themselves in a situation that demands communication with no advance warning. Under such circumstances, withdrawal from communication is the behavioral pattern to be expected. This withdrawal may be complete (absolute silence) or partial (talking only as much as absolutely required). In a public speaking setting, this response may be represented by the very short speech. In a meeting, class, or small group discussion, it may be represented by talking only when called upon. In a dyadic interaction, it may represented by answering questions briefly or supplying agreeing responses with no initiation of discussion.

Generally, then, verbal communication is substantially reduced when a person wishes to withdraw from communication. Nonverbal communication, on the other hand, may not be reduced, but the nonverbal messages sent may be primarily of one type. That type is referred to as "nonimmediate." Nonimmediate messages include such things as frowns, standing or sitting away from other people, avoiding eye contact, and standing with arms folded. These messages signal others that a person is not interested in communicating and tend to reduce communication initiation attempts from others.

Communication disruption is the third typical behavioral pattern associated with high CA. The person may have disfluencies in verbal presentation or unnatural nonverbal behaviors. Equally likely are poor choices of communicative strategies. It is important to note, however, that such behaviors may also be produced by inadequate communication skills, anomie-alienation, and cultural divergence. Thus inferring the existence of high CA from observations of such behavior is often inappropriate.

Overcommunication as a response to high traitlike CA is believed to be uncommon (McCroskey, 1984), but this pattern is exhibited by at least some people. This behavior may exhibit overcompensation for a person's high level of apprehension and a low level of willingness to communicate. It also might represent a circumstance where a person has a high need and willingness to communicate but also has high apprehension. Willingness and apprehension are presumed to be substantially, but not perfectly, correlated. Thus this may represent the "fight" response, an attempt to communicate in spite of the presence of high apprehension. The person who elects to take a public speaking course in spite of his or her extreme stage fright is a classic example. Less easily recognizable is the individual with high CA who attempts to dominate social situations. Most of the time people who employ this behavioral option are seen as poor communicators but are not recognized as having high CA. In fact, they may be seen as people with very low CA.

## Measurement of CA

As we noted previously, since CA is an internally experienced phenomenon, it must be measured by means of self-report by the person who experiences it. The most commonly employed instrument for measuring traitlike CA is the Personal Report of Communication Apprehension (PRCA). The original 20-item instrument (PRCA-20; McCroskey, 1970), as well as two later versions (PRCA-10, PRCA-25; McCroskey, 1978), were dominated by items related to public speaking. This led to questions as to whether the instrument actually measured traitlike CA or was only measuring one form of context-based CA.

Although a strong case was built for the validity of the earlier forms of the instrument (McCroskey, 1978), a new form was generated which included a balanced number of items for each of four contexts (PRCA-24; McCroskey, 1982): public speaking, speaking in large meetings, speaking in small groups, and speaking in dyads. In addition to providing more face validity for the instrument as a traitlike measure, this version provided a method by which subscores could be generated for the four general communication contexts included.

The latest version of the instrument, known as the PRCA-24B (McCroskey, 1986), permits the generation of subscores not only for types of communication context but also for types of receivers—strangers, acquaintances, and friends. The PRCA-24B correlates very highly with the PRCA-24 (McCroskey & Baer, 1985), but since it permits generation of scores related to receiver types, it may be more useful for some purposes than others. Since all forms of this instrument are highly intercorrelated, they all have concurrent validity. However, the PRCA-24 and PRCA-24B have more face validity and provide greater flexibility in use. Hence, these are the forms that we would recommend for use.

## EFFECTS OF WILLINGNESS TO COMMUNICATE
## ON INTERPERSONAL COMMUNICATION

Research relating to the impact of willingness to communicate on interpersonal communication has been conducted under a variety of constructs—CA, shyness, unwillingness to communicate, predisposition toward verbal behavior, talkativeness, reticence, quietness, and social anxiety, to name a few. Such research has been reported in the literature of psychology and communication for over four decades. The three basic research models that have been employed are (1) direct observation of amount of communication with assessment of outcomes; (2) measurement of a predisposition (such as CA) which is presumed to be related to the willingness to communicate, allowing communication to occur, and assessing outcomes; and (3) simulation of talkativeness variation with assessment of outcomes.

Regardless of the model employed, the results of this research have been remarkably consistent. The general conclusion that can be drawn from this immense body of research is that reduced willingness to communicate results in an individual being less effective in communication and generating negative perceptions of himself or herself in the minds of others involved in the communication.

Since this research has been thoroughly summarized (Daly & Stafford, 1984) and interpreted (Richmond, 1984) previously, we will not take the space here to repeat those efforts. Instead, we will simply draw from that work some of the conclusions that appear most obvious from the research results.

Interpersonal communication occurs primarily within three general environments—school environments, organizational environments, and social environments. While these three environments are neither mutually exclusive nor exhaustive of all environments in which interpersonal communication can occur, they will suffice for our purposes here.

In the school environment, students with a high level of willingness to communicate characteristically have all the advantages, even though they may be reprimanded occasionally for communicating when they are not supposed to. Teachers have positive expectations for students who are highly willing to communicate and negative ones for those less willing. Student achievement, as measured by teacher-made tests, teacher-assigned grades, and standardized tests, is consistent with these expectations—in spite of the fact that intellectual ability has not been found to be associated with communication orientations.

Students who are less willing to communicate are also seen in negative ways by their peers. Such negative perceptions have been observed all the way from the lower elementary level through graduate school. In contrast, students who are willing to communicate have more friends and report being more satisfied with their school experience. With both academic achievement and social support on the side of the student who is willing to communicate, it should not be surprising that such students are more likely to remain in school and graduate than those who are less willing.

The impact of willingness to communicate within the organizational environment is no less than that in the school. People who are highly willing to communicate receive preference in the hiring process and are more likely to be promoted to positions of importance in the organization. People who are less willing to communicate tend to self-select themselves in occupational roles that ensure themselves lower social status and lower economic standing. People who report a higher willingness to communicate also report being more satisfied with their employment and are much more likely to remain with an organization. People with lower willingness to communicate tend to generate negative perceptions in the minds of their co-workers. They are seen as neither task-attractive nor credible and are rejected for leadership positions.

On the social level, the picture is very similar. People with a high willingness to communicate have more friends and are less likely to be lonely. They are likely to have more dates and to date more people than those who are less willing to communicate. The latter are more likely to engage in exclusive dating and to marry immediately after completing their schooling. People who are highly willing to communicate are seen as more socially and physically attractive by others, which may explain some of the effects noted earlier.

## CONCLUSION

The general conclusion that we draw from the research and theory summarized here is that a global, personality-type orientation toward willingness to communicate exists which has a major impact on interpersonal communication in a wide variety of environments. While willingness to communicate in a given situation can be affected by situational constraints, traitlike willingness to communicate has a potential impact in all communication settings. High willingness is associated with increased frequency and amount of communication, which in turn are associated with a variety of positive communication outcomes. Low willingness is associated with decreased frequency and amount of communication, which in turn are associated with a variety of negative communication outcomes.

While not denying the existence or importance of other personality variables in interpersonal communication, we believe that willingness to communicate plays the central role in determining an individual's communicative impact on others. Thus willingness to communicate deserves to receive a high degree of attention from scholars concerned with individual differences in communication.

## REFERENCES

Andersen, P.A., Andersen, J.F., & Garrison, J.P. (1978). Singing apprehension and talking apprehension: The development of two constructs. *Sign Language Studies, 19,* 155-186.

Behnke, R. R., & Beatty, M.J. (1981). A cognitive-physiological model of speech anxiety. *Communication Monographs, 48,* 158-163.

Bloom, R. (1970). Dimensions of mental health in adolescent boys. *Journal of Clinical Psychology, 26,* 35-38.

Borg, W. R., & Tupes, E. C. (1958). Personality characteristics related to leadership behavior in two types of small group situational problems. *Journal of Applied Psychology, 42,* 252-256.

Borgatta, E. F., & Bales R. F. (1953). Interaction of individuals in reconstituted groups. *Sociometry, 16,* 302- 320.

Burgoon, J. K. (1976). The unwillingness-to-communicate scale: Development and validation. *Communication Monographs, 43,* 60-69.

Buss, A. H. (1980). *Self-consciousness and social anxiety.* San Francisco: W. H. Freeman.

Carment, D. W., Miles, C. G., & Cervin, V. B. (1965). Persuasiveness and persuasibility as related to intelligence and extraversion. *British Journal of Social and Clinical Psychology, 4,* 1-7.

Chapple, E. D., & Arensberg, C. M. (1940). Measuring human relations: An introduction to the study of the interaction of individuals. *Genetic Psychology Monographs, 22,* 3-147.

Clevenger, T., Jr. (1959). A synthesis of experimental research in stage fright. *Quarterly Journal of Speech, 45,* 134-145.

Daly, J. A. (1978). The assessment of social-communicative anxiety via self-reports: A comparison of measures. *Communication Monographs, 45,* 204-218.

Daly, J. A., & McCroskey, J. C. (1984). *Avoiding communication: Shyness, reticence, and communication apprehension.* Beverly Hills, CA: Sage.

Daly, J. A., & Miller, M. D. (1975). The empirical development of an instrument to measure writing apprehension. *Research in the Teaching of English, 9,* 242-249.

Daly, J. A., & Stafford, L. (1984). Correlates and consequences of social-communicative anxiety. In J. A. Daly & J. C. McCroskey (Eds.), *Avoiding communication: Shyness, reticence, and communication apprehension.* Beverly Hills, CA: Sage.

Dean, D. G. (1961). Alienation: Its meaning and measurement. *American Sociological Review, 26,* 735-758.

Elmore, T. M. (1965). The development of a scale to measure psychological anomie and its implications for counseling psychology. *Proceedings of the 73rd Annual Convention of the American Psychological Association,* 359-360.

Eysenck, H. J. (1970). *Readings in extraversion-introversion* (Vol. I). New York: Wiley-Interscience.

Eysenck, H. J. (1971). *Readings in extraversion-introversion* (Vol. II). New York: Wiley-Interscience.

Feinberg, R. A., Miller, F. G., & Weiss, R. F. (1983). Verbal learned helplessness. *Representative Research in Social Psychology, 13,* 34-45.

Giffin, K. (1970). Social alienation by communication denial. Research Report 32, University of Kansas.

Giffin, K., & Groginsky, B. (1970). A study of the relationship between communication denial and social alienation. Research report No. 31, University of Kansas.

Goldman-Eisler, F. (1951). The measurement of time sequences in conversational behavior. *British Journal of Psychology, 42, 355-362.*

Heston, J. K., & Andersen, P. (1972, November). *Anomia-alienation and restrained communication among high school students.* Paper presented at the annual convention of the Western Speech Communication Association, Honolulu.

Huntley, J. R. (1969). *An investigation of the relationships between personality and types of instructor criticism in the beginning speech-communication course.* Unpublished doctoral dissertation, Michigan State University.

Leary, M. R. (1983). *Understanding social anxiety: Social, personality, and clinical perspectives.* Beverly Hills, CA: Sage.

McCroskey, J. C. (1970). Measures of communication-bound anxiety. *Speech Monographs, 37,* 269-277.

McCroskey, J. C. (1972). The implementation of a large-scale program of systematic desensitization for communication apprehension. *Speech Teacher, 21,* 255-264.

McCroskey, J. C. (1977). Oral communication apprehension: A summary of recent theory and research. *Human Communication Research, 4,* 78-96.

McCroskey, J. C. (1978). Validity of the PRCA as an index of oral communication apprehension. *Communication Monographs, 45,* 192-203.

McCroskey, J. C. (1982). *An introduction to rhetorical communication* (4th ed.). Englewood Cliffs, NJ: Prentice-Hall.

McCroskey, J. C. (1984). The communication apprehension perspective. In J. A. Daly & J. C. McCroskey (Eds.). *Avoiding communication: Shyness, reticence, and communication apprehension.* Beverly Hills, CA: Sage.

McCroskey, J. C. (1986). *An introduction to rhetorical communication* (5th ed.). Englewood Cliffs, NJ: Prentice-Hall.

McCroskey, J. C., Andersen, J. F., Richmond, V. P., & Wheeless, L. R. (1981). Communication apprehension of elementary and secondary students and teachers. *Communication Education, 30,* 122-132.

McCroskey, J. C., & Baer, J. E. (1985, November). *Willingness to communicate: The construct and its measurement.* Paper presented at the annual convention of the Speech Communication Association, Denver.

McCroskey, J. C., & Beatty, M. J. (1984). Communication apprehension and accumulated communication state anxiety experiences: A research note. *Communication Monographs, 51,* 79-84.

McCroskey, J. C., Daly, J. A., Richmond, V. P., & Falcione, R. L. (1977). Studies of the relationship between communication apprehension and self-esteem. *Human Communication Research, 3,* 264-277.

McCroskey, J. C., Ralph, D. C., & Barrick, J. E. (1970). The effect of systematic desensitization on speech anxiety. *Speech Teacher, 19,* 32-36.

McCroskey, J. C., & Richmond, V. P. (1982). Communication apprehension and shyness: Conceptual and operational distinctions. *Central States Speech Journal, 33,* 458-468.

Mortensen, D. C., Arnston, P. H., & Lustig, M. (1977). The measurement of verbal predispositions: Scale development and application. *Human Communication Research, 3,* 146-158.

Phillips, G. M. (1968). Reticence: Pathology of the normal speaker. *Speech Monographs, 35,* 39-49.

Phillips, G. M. (1977). Rhetoritherapy versus the medical model: Dealing with reticence. *Communication Education, 26,* 34-43.

Phillips, G. M. (1984). Reticence: A perspective on social withdrawal. In J. A. Daly & J. C. McCroskey (Eds.), *Avoiding communication: Shyness, reticence, and communication apprehension.* Beverly Hills, CA: Sage.

Richmond, V. P. (1978). The relationship between trait and state communication apprehension and interpersonal perception during acquaintance stages. *Human Communication Research, 4,* 338-349.

Richmond, V. P. (1984). Implications of quietness: Some facts and speculations. In J. A. Daly & J. C. McCroskey (Eds.), *Avoiding communication: Shyness, reticence, and communication apprehension.* Beverly Hills, CA: Sage.

Seligman, M. E. (1975). *Helplessness: On depression, development, and death.* San Francisco: W. H. Freeman.

Zimbardo, P. G. (1977). *Shyness: What it is and what to do about it.* Reading, MA: Addison-Wesley.

# 4

# Aggressiveness

## DOMINIC A. INFANTE

Our interest in this chapter is with various kinds of behavior in interpersonal communication: A person feels that an acquaintance is taking advantage of her by asking for favors relentlessly. She decides to end this dependency by confronting the person on the issue. A husband and wife begin a discussion by disagreeing over how to solve their financial problems and end by the husband slapping and then punching the wife. One person accidentally breaks a second person's valuable vase. The second person says, "You stupid, clumsy fool! That vase meant so much to me, and you broke it!"

These behaviors share common elements which distinguish them from other types of interpersonal communication behaviors. At least one person applies force to another person. The individuals probably have greater than normal arousal, with elevated heart rates and blood pressure. They are very alert and may experience anger. Attack-and-defend cognitive orientations are assumed. The behaviors are decidedly active as opposed to passive, attention-getting rather than common place and dull, and have the potential to provoke further aggressive action. They differ from more usual interpersonal behaviors such as two friends trying to decide when they will spend the evening, or two classmates discussing an impending examination. Certainly, the greater proportion of interpersonal communication involves individuals talking with normal levels of arousal, calmly, with low levels of stress, and dealing with topics that are not always important. Our focus will be on understanding the smaller proportion of interpersonal behaviors, those which involve attack, and which therefore may be termed aggressive. While not as common in interpersonal communication, these behaviors require attention because, as we maintain in this chapter, they have extremely important interpersonal consequences.

Buss's (1961) definition of aggression as a response which delivers pain to another person has been widely accepted, as evidenced by subsequent definitions reflecting his basic idea. Berkowitz's (1962) definition of aggression as "behavior aimed at injury of some object" (p. 1) is broader in that it includes behavior directed at nonhuman objects. There are also several definitional issues which researchers have attempted to resolve (Geen, 1976). For instance, is intent necessary for an act to be considered aggressive? If an act is justified, is it aggressive? Can a lack of response in a situation be considered aggression? Does defense constitute aggression? Are there different kinds of aggression, and do the differences matter?

Tedeschi (1983) has pointed out that "aggression" is a word from the vernacular language that researchers have attempted to use scientifically. The problem is that the word applies to a wide variety of behaviors varying along numerous dimensions. For example, Buss (1971) proposes three dimensions: physical-verbal, active-passive, and direct-indirect. Moyer (1968) identified eight kinds of aggression: predatory, intermale, fear-induced, irritable, territorial, maternal, instrumental, and sex-related. Tedeschi (1983) has argued that the term "aggression" leads to conceptual confusion and should be abandoned as a scientific term. He proposed to redefine what is studied in terms of the concept "coercive power." Coercion was conceived as a form of social influence that uses force.

A different approach to the seemingly insurmountable problems in defining aggression has been taken by Kaminski, Whaley, Whaley, and Flaster (1984), who proposed a dynamic rather than a fixed definition. According to Kaminski et al., whether a given act is aggressive depends on the behavioral norms for the situation and whether or not the act is justified. They termed an act violent if it exceeded behavioral norms and was unjustified (e.g., punching someone who steps on your lawn). Interestingly, an act which falls below behavioral and justification norms in a situation is also aggressive (e.g., watching passively when someone needs help).

Mindful of the history of definitional problems, a definition of aggression in interpersonal communication was formulated for the purposes of the present chapter using several ideas from previous writers. An interpersonal behavior may be considered aggressive if it applies force physically and/or symbolically in order, minimally, to dominate and perhaps damage or, maximally, to defeat and perhaps destroy the locus of attack. The locus of attack in interpersonal communication can be a person's body, material possessions, self-concept, position on topics of communication, or behavior.

This definition probably does not resolve many of the definitional issues for aggression identified by Tedeschi (1983) and others (Feshbach, 1971; Geen, 1976; Zillmann, 1979). However, if does fulfill the need here to provide a beginning for conceptualizing aggression in interpersonal relationships. If a definition is able to provide a reasonably clear initial conception, we can then rely on the ensuing discussion to explicate detailed meanings.

Aggression in interpersonal relationships has not been ignored in the extensive research and vast literature on aggression (for summaries and analyses, see Bandura, 1973a; Berkowitz, 1962; Buss, 1961; Feshbach & Singer, 1971; Geen & Donnerstein, 1983a, 1983b; Zillmann, 1979). However, aggression is usually treated in a generic sense, and little attention is given to the meaning of aggression in interpersonal communication. It is apparent that these writers are interested in aggression in interpersonal relations. Yet their primary concern seems to be to provide an explanation for aggression in general, the assumption being that a broad theory would have application in specific contexts, such as interpersonal communication. This literature reveals three approaches to the study of aggression—instinct theory, frustration-aggression theory, and social learning theory—and provides a good deal of knowledge that can be applied to understanding aggression in interpersonal relations.

According to instinct theory (Freud, 1957, 1959; Lorenz, 1966), aggression is the result of an instinctive biological drive. Freud contended that the aggression drive was a manifestation of a death drive, the tendency for a person to be driven to return to an inorganic state. Thus aggression is a means for one's self-destruction. Lorenz (1966) took a different view of instincts. He asserted that aggression exists because it has survival value in terms of evolution. The most aggressive and hence dominant male mates the most, thus ensuring the survival of his genes. Aggression over territory ensures that the species is spread over the available living space, thus increasing the chance that it will survive if part of the living space is destroyed.

Frustration-aggression theory was formulated by Dollard, Doob, Miller, Mower, and Sears (1939) and refined by Berkowitz (1962, 1983). Miller (1941) argued that frustration is a necessary but not a sufficient condition for aggression. Thus frustrations instigate various responses, one of which is aggression. However, since frustration leads to many behaviors, it is not clear when it instigates aggression (Zillmann, 1979, p. 138). Frustration-aggression theory predicts that a cathartic effect should follow the expression of aggression. Releasing aggressive tensions should make a person less aggressive. Also, by observing the aggressive behavior of others (e.g., violence on television), the individual experiences aggression vicariously and thus the aggressive drive is purged.

Social learning theory (Bandura, 1973a, 1973b, 1978, 1983) maintains that aggression is only one of several responses to frustration. The theory emphasizes that people are influenced by the consequences of their behavior and that they do not even have to experience consequences directly in order to learn and repeat a behavior. A person can learn a response from a model (e.g., a character in a television program), and this can be as effective as direct reinforcement for a behavior. While frustration-aggression theory predicts a cathartic effect of aggressive behavior, social learning theory predicts a continuation or even an increase in aggressive behavior if the behavior is reinforced. Research does not provide much support for catharsis through emotional expression (Bandura, 1978; Feshbach, 1984; Quanty, 1976). Lack of support for the cathartic effect calls into question those forms of therapy which encourage the patient to express hostility, to ventilate frustrations and anger. In fact, encouraging patients to express aggression may make them more, not less, aggressive (Quanty, 1976).

## A PERSONALITY APPROACH TO AGGRESSION

A personality approach to understanding aggression in interpersonal communication will be taken in this chapter for several reasons. First, a personality approach accommodates instinct, frustration, and learning explanations of aggressive behavior. Behavior which originates for any of these three reasons is not incompatible with the notion of personality. According to Shontz (1965), the study of personality "is identified by its concern for inferred mediational processes that account for organization in the behavior of the individual" (p. 7). These mediational processes can have their genesis in instinct; can entail anger, cognitive readiness, and the related mechanisms of frustration; or can be cognitive structures of the perceived consequences of aggressive responses acquired through direct or vicarious reinforcement.

Second, the idea that personality involves mediational processes which account for the organization of behavior provides a central reason for a personality approach to aggression in interpersonal relations. Personality traits may be used to explain patterns in an individual's behavior. This does not mean that all behavior is controlled by personality traits or that factors in the immediate situation exert little influence. Berkowitz (1962) stipulates that to have a trait means to be sensitive to a certain class of stimuli. He emphasizes that a trait is learned and then aroused in situations by cues reminiscent of the learning context. Thus, whether a trait energizes behavior depends on its interaction with factors in the particular situation. This idea will be emphasized here. Personality, therefore, need not preclude a situational explanation of behavior, and the two approaches may best be served by a complementary rather than an antagonistic relationship.

A third reason for a personality approach is that although an aggressive personality trait has been posited and studied as an explanation for aggressive behavior (e.g., Berkowitz, 1962; Buss & Durkee, 1957; Edmunds & Kendrick, 1980), a comprehensive and unified conception of aggressiveness as a personality trait has not been developed. Instead of treating aggressiveness as a unidimensional trait, as it has been treated in much of the earlier research, or dealing only with socially undesirable behaviors, I propose a multidimensional conception that suggests four core aggressive personality traits. The goal will be to produce a clearer and more comprehensive understanding of the structure of socially desirable along with socially undesirable aggressive behavior patterns in interpersonal communication.

Finally, a personality approach is a valid way of studying aggression in particular and communication in general. The validity argument is quite strong, having developed considerable strength in recent years by means of the controversy over cross-situational consistency. This issue involved the idea that personality is overwhelmed by the situation, so that behavior across various situations is not consistent and hence not predicted well by personality traits (Bem & Allen, 1974; Mischel, 1968, 1969, 1973). This position, in essence, denies the concept of personality and replaces it with a situational account of behavior. This, of course, is contrary to common experience, which tells us that people have characteristic ways of behaving—patterns in their behavior which lead us to expect certain responses in certain situations. However, some research has supported the situationist position (for a good synthesis, see Bem & Allen, 1974).

On a very fundamental level, the cross-situational consistency argument is based on the "straw man" fallacy in logic and is therefore invalid. The structure of this form of specious reasoning is that a position which is the object of attack is made to seem more extreme and radical in order to make it easier to refute (i.e., in reality no one actually holds such a position). The argument about cross-situational consistency is a straw man because people with normal personalities, the implicit referent for the issue, are not extremely consistent from one situation to the next, whereas individuals with abnormal personalities, especially those with neurotic disorders involving obsessive compulsive symptoms, are very consistent. Thus a person who is neurotic regarding cleanliness will be remarkably clean across situations, while a normal person who also values cleanliness greatly will not always be clean. The predictability of normal personality is pale indeed when compared to the compulsive personality. Of course, no one actually holds the position that "normal equals abnormal"—hence the straw man fallacy.

Berkowitz (1962, p. 299) clarified the issue more than twenty years ago in discussing the aggressive personality. He explained that having a trait means being extremely sensitive to a class of stimuli, and not that a person will exhibit a behavior incessantly. There are several reasons why a person who has a strong aggressiveness trait will not always behave aggressively, and why cross-situational consistency will not be especially high: (1) aggressive cues may be absent in some situations or present but weak and thus not very salient, (2) aggression inhibitors such as punishment for hostile action are present in some situations more than others, (3) needs which are incompatible with aggressive behavior such as affiliation and dependency are especially important in some situations, and (4) there may be a desire to perform a given hostile act, but the person may doubt his or her ability to perform the act successfully.

The position maintained in this chapter is that a personality approach is a valuable and valid way of understanding aggression in interpersonal relationships. However, as Berkowitz (1962, 1983) has emphasized, aggressiveness interacts with the situation. An aggressive response is a function not only of the person's traits but also of the degree of anger stimulated, the strength of association between aggression cues and the source of anger, and the aggression inhibitors in the situation (Berkowitz, 1962, p. 299). Thus our approach is decidedly, but not exclusively, from a trait perspective, as situational influences are both acknowledged and included in theoretical statements.

## TYPES OF AGGRESSION IN INTERPERSONAL RELATIONS

An idea which will be treated as axiomatic in our discussion of aggression is that a constructive-destructive distinction is meaningful when considering aggression in interpersonal relations. Although this would usually evoke no objection, the implied value premise might be considered inappropriate in a discussion of research. However, following Feshbach (1971), I believe it would be extremely superficial to treat the "how" and "what" of aggression without placing this knowledge within the context of the human values involved. These values can be made explicit by stating what will be considered constructive or destructive.

We will view aggressive behavior as constructive if it facilitates interpersonal communication satisfaction and generally enhances a dyadic relationship by increasing understanding, empathy, and intimacy. On the other hand, aggressive behavior will be considered destructive if it produces dissatisfaction, if at least one person in a dyad feels less favorable about himself or herself, and if the quality of the relationship is reduced.

Several ideas may help clarify this position. Constructive or destructive outcomes can refer to immediate and/or long-term interpersonal effects (i.e., a temporal dimension is meaningful). Also, it should be noted that some aggressive acts can be both constructive and destructive. For example, a husband telling his wife he is not sexually attracted to her could enhance interpersonal understanding while harming the wife's self-concept. Finally, whether an act is constructive or destructive may be determined at least four ways: when one person in a dyad feels that the act is constructive or destructive; when both persons in the dyad agree upon the constructive or destructive nature of the act; when an observer of the dyad judges the act to be constructive or destructive; or when the act is consistent with societal standards for determining what is constructive or destructive. Thus the meaning assigned to a given aggressive act may vary according to the perspective from which the act is viewed.

Consistent with Buss (1971), we also make a distinction here in terms of physical and verbal aggression. Aggression in interpersonal relationships occurs both in physical and symbolic forms. Physical aggression, according to the definition of aggression presented earlier, involves using one's body or extensions of the body (e.g., a gun) to apply force to another person's body in order, minimally, to dominate and perhaps damage or, maximally, to defeat and perhaps destroy the locus of attack. The predominantly constructive types of physical aggression in interpersonal relationships are social and task. Social physical aggression includes sports, games, and playfulness involving mock assaults, while task aggression entails completing a job or project with another person aggressively—that is, taking control of a job, pushing a person to the point of exhaustion, and/or destroying physical impediments to task completion. Of course, these types of aggression can be destructive if, for example, a sport such as tennis is used to humiliate another person, or if a person being pushed on a job develops feelings of inadequacy.

Types of physical aggression that are usually destructive include violence against persons (e.g., wife-beating) and against objects (e.g., throwing a dish). Although it is difficult to imagine, these types can be constructive under certain circumstances. For example, a husband and wife slapping each other as the culmination of a long period of suspicion, resentment, and bitterness could shock both into seeking a marriage counselor, which eventually could result in a better marriage (i.e., the physical aggression could have therapeutic value).

Symbolic aggression involves using verbal and nonverbal communication channels in order, minimally, to dominate and perhaps damage or, maximally, to defeat and perhaps destroy another person's position on topics of communication and/or the person's self-concept. Types of symbolic aggressiveness in interpersonal relations which are mainly constructive are assertiveness and argumentativeness. Assertiveness may be viewed as a general tendency to be interpersonally dominant, ascendant, and forceful. This broad conception is derived from Costa and McCrae's (1980) trait model of personality, which will be explained in the next section. In line with this broad conception, assertiveness may also be viewed as a multidimensional trait. Lorr and More (1980) have identified four dimensions of assertive behavior: directiveness, independence, social, and the defense of rights and interests.

Argumentativeness is the tendency to recognize controversial issues in communication situations, to present and defend positions on the issues, and to attack the positions that other people take (Infante & Rancer, 1982). Argumentativeness may be considered a subset of assertiveness, in that all arguing is assertive, but not all assertiveness involves arguing.

Although the literature suggests that assertiveness (Alberti & Emmons, 1974; Eisler, Miller, & Hersen, 1973; Hedquist & Weinhold, 1970) and argumentativeness (Infante, 1981, 1982; Infante, Trebing, Shepherd, & Seeds, 1984; Infante, Wall, Leap, & Danielson, 1984; Johnson & Johnson, 1979) are constructive forms of communication, destructive applications are possible. For example, one might act assertively in order to make another person feel foolish. Alternatively, one might argue to make an adversary appear incompetent.

The destructive types of symbolic aggressiveness are hostility and verbal aggressiveness. Costa and McCrae (1980) conceive of hostility as a generalization of the affect of anger. Consistent with this is Buss and Durkee's (1957) multidimensional conception of hostility as a trait that involves the use of symbols to express irritability, negativism, resentment, and suspicion. Here, too, the distinction between a broad and more specific trait is meaningful. Verbal aggressiveness—defined as the tendency to attack the self-concepts of individuals instead of, or in addition to, their positions on topics of communication (Infante & Wigley, 1986)—is a subset of hostility, in that all verbal aggression is hostile, but not all hostility involves attacking the self-concepts of other people.

Although hostility and verbal aggressiveness are almost always destructive forms of interpersonal communication, constructive occurrences are conceiveable. For instance, attacking the character of a person engaged in unlawful deceit could prevent an observer from becoming a victim. As explained earlier, whether an act is seen as constructive or destructive can vary according to whether the vantage point for the judgment is the individual, the dyad, an observer, or society.

The focus of this chapter is on symbolic aggression, especially the four personality traits that are viewed as constituting the basic structure of the aggressive personality. Our interest in physical aggressiveness is mainly in terms of its relationship to symbolic aggression, where the attention is on verbal aggressiveness and the implications for reducing violence in interpersonal communication.

An idea that serves as a premise for the remainder of the chapter is that although personality is generally stable, it is possible to enhance portions of the structure through training. Research from more than four decades ago found that communication courses had a favorable impact on personality (Gilkinson, 1941; Moore, 1935; Rose, 1940). Later research (Infante, 1982) discovered that participation in curricular and extracurricular communication activities was related to increased trait argumentativeness. This presents the possibility that training in communication may reduce destructive aggression by enhancing the personality so that rational discourse becomes a preferred mode of social influence (Infante, Trebing, et al., 1984). Rational discourse, from an argumentation theory framework (e.g., Freeley, 1966; Jensen, 1981; Mills, 1968; Rieke & Sillars, 1984; Windes & Hastings, 1965), may be considered discourse which advances claims based on valid data and reasoning. This is discourse that does not use specious forms of reasoning and does not arouse emotions that are unwarranted in view of established facts. Of course, whether discourse is perceived as rational or not can vary according to the source of judgment. Along the line reasoned earlier, for whether an act is seen as constructive or not, the vantage points for judgments of rationality in interpersonal communication can be the individual, the dyad, observers, or society.

## Assertiveness

According to our model of trait aggressiveness in interpersonal communication, assertiveness is a person's general tendency to be interpersonally dominant, ascendant, and forceful. In line with previous research (e.g., Eisler et al., 1973; Hedquist & Weinhold, 1970), this will be viewed in the present chapter as a generally constructive form of symbolic aggression. The conception has its foundation in the trait model of personality by Costa and McCrae (1980). Before explicating that foundation, however, it is worth noting that the term assertiveness is commonly associated with the assertiveness training movement which was very popular in the 1970s.

Assertiveness training was developed to treat behavioral disorders stemming from extreme passivity and inhibition (Wolpe, 1958; Wolpe & Lazarus, 1966). It has been used successfully to treat a range of disorders having to do with interpersonal relationships. Wolpe and Lazarus (1966) considered assertive behaviors to include "all socially acceptable expressions of personal rights and feelings" (p. 39). Alberti and Emmons (1974), who were very influential in popularizing assertiveness training, said that assertiveness involved people acting in their own best interests, defending their rights without undue anxiety, expressing honest feelings comfortably, and exercising their rights without denying others' rights (p. 2). Norton and Warnich (1976) synthesized the ideas of several assertiveness researchers, saying, "The behaviors included refusal of unreasonable requests, initiation of requests, insistence on fair treatment of self, spontaneous expression of one's feelings, outgoingness and willingness to take the initiative in social situations, and active . . . disagreement" (pp. 62-63).

It is apparent that the spectrum of relevant behaviors is indeed wide—so expansive, in fact, that one wonders if assertiveness is not just another term for expressiveness. However, other issues have emerged. Who judges whether rights are violated? Is intent necessary for an act to be assertive? Can no response in a situation be assertive? Is the domain represented best by the term "assertiveness"? Tucker, Weaver, and Redden (1983) conclude that the choice of term was unfortunate for, among other reasons, assertiveness is associated with negative meanings. They advocate the use of terms such as "interpersonal competence" or "social skills."

The diffuse nature of the assertiveness training movement's focus and the attendant definitional problems are of only tangential interest to the present chapter. Our concern is not with the clinical techniques adapted for popular use in order to "liberate" individuals who are extremely inhibited, compliant, and socially inept. The focus here is on assertiveness as a personality trait. The conception of assertiveness as the trait of being interpersonally dominant, ascendant, and forceful is derived from Costa and McCrae's (1980) trait model of personality. They analyzed the traits posited by a variety of personality models and instruments and concluded that personality is structured around three major dimensions, each having six facets: neuroticism, extroversion, and openness. Assertiveness is one of the six facets of extroversion, along with attachment, gregariousness, excitement-seeking, positive emotions, and activity.

Hostility is a facet in the neuroticism dimension, in addition to anxiety, depression, self-consciousness, vulnerability, and impulsiveness. (Extremes on these traits define the abnormal personality; normals are more intermediate.) There is no necessary relationship between the neuroticism and extroversion dimensions. Thus assertiveness and hostility, as subconstructs, also might be independent. A study by Galassi and Galassi (1975) supports this idea. They found that assertiveness shared little variance with the eight subscales of Buss and Durkee's (1957) measure of hostility. Other research also supports this idea (e.g., Lorr & More, 1980).

The openness dimension is not directly relevant to our present purposes. It consists of six facets: phantasy, esthetics, feelings, actions, ideas, and values. The openness dimension primarily represents having an openness to experience, which results in an eventful life and a wide range of positive and negative experiences (Costa & McCrae, 1980).

Although assertiveness is not a hostile trait, it does involve using symbols aggressively. It should be noted that hostility and aggression have been used interchangeably at times (e.g., Berkowitz, 1962; Zillmann, 1979). However, while the connotative meanings of hostility are mostly negative, aggressiveness has many positive associations, such as being aggressive in solving a problem or providing leadership aggressively. Tucker et al. (1983) found that observers rated assertive individuals as aggressive. They also found that shyness had a strong negative correlation with assertiveness and aggressiveness. This study, along with Galassi and Galassi's (1975) investigation, align with assumptions made in the present chapter about assertiveness being aggressive but constructive. Other research also suggests that assertiveness is constructive (e.g., Eisler et al., 1973; Hedquist & Weinhold, 1970).

Researchers have developed a number of instruments for measuring assertiveness. Two of the most widely used scales are the College Self-Expression Scale (Galassi, DeLo, Galassi, & Bastien, 1974) and the Rathus Assertiveness Schedule (Rathus, 1973). However, Gambrill and Richey's (1975) Assertion Inventory, the Constriction Scale developed by Bates and Zimmerman (1971), and Lorr and More's (1980) multi-dimensional scale also appear to be valid and worthy of consideration by communication researchers. A relatively small amount of research has been conducted with these scales by researchers in the communication field.

In one study, Bell and Daly (1984) found that the four dimensions of assertiveness measured by Lorr and More's (1980) instrument were related to affinity-seeking (i.e., the strategies that people use to induce others to like them). Generally, they found that the assertiveness dimensions of directiveness, defense of rights, and independence were positively related to active affinity-seeking strategies (e.g., assuming control) and negatively related to passive strategies (e.g., conceding control). In another study, Bell and Daly (1985) discovered that the four dimensions of assertiveness were inversely related to loneliness. This could be viewed as research supportive of the idea that assertiveness is constructive, since the more assertive people experienced less loneliness.

A study of Beatty, Plax, Kearney, and McCroskey (1984) examined the wide range of communication behaviors specified on the Rathus Assertiveness Schedule (Rathus, 1973) to determine if they could be predicted by a measure of communication apprehension. Their factor analysis of the Rathus instrument yielded a four-factor solution. Since Nevid and Rathus (1979) found eight factors for females and nine for males, the Beatty et al. (1984) study may be viewed as indicating the instability of the factor structure of the instrument. Treating the scale as unidimensional is probably more reliable than relying on factor scores, which seem to vary according to the sample features and sex of respondents. In analyzing the total score using the Rathus scale as the criterion and four dimensions of communication apprehension as the predictors, Beatty et al. (1984) obtained a multiple correlation of .71. This result supported the cross-situational consistency of the communication apprehension construct and provides further evidence on the broader issue of the validity of a trait approach to the study of communication.

Norton and Warnick (1976) used both the College and Self-Expression Scale (Galassi et al., 1974) and the Rathus (1973) Assertiveness Schedule to identify the communicator style variables that are characteristic of assertive individuals. A cluster analysis of combined items from the two assertiveness measures revealed four clusters: openness in expressing feelings, low anxiety in interpersonal situations, contentiousness over personal rights, and refusal to be intimidated. A cluster analysis was then performed on these four assertiveness variables and the communicator style variables. The style variables of contentiousness, precision, impression-leaving, and dominance were related to assertiveness, along with three dispositions toward verbal behavior, verbal dominance, verbal intensity, and frequency of speech.

This research by Bell and Daly (1984, 1985), Beatty et al. (1984), and Norton and Warnick (1976) provides some understanding of the communication traits associated with assertiveness. From a knowledge of these traits we can speculate on the specific communication behaviors which characterize the assertive individual. Some research has revealed what some of those behavioral differences might be.

A study by Eisler et al. (1973) involved 30 male psychiatric patients role-playing 14 assertiveness situations which were videotaped and later coded to assess numerous communication variables. Subjects were not selected on the basis of diagnostic classification; however, patients with symptoms of acute psychosis or organic brain syndrome were excluded from the sample. A female role model was employed to act in various situations as a salesclerk, cashier, shopper, waitress, and wife. The results, summed across the 14 situations, were that highly assertive individuals, when compared to less assertive persons, responded more quickly to the situations (i.e., less latency of response), with more volume, and with more pitch variety. Assertive persons were more likely to resist the role-playing partner's position (i.e., were less compliant) and were more intent on changing the partner's behavior. There were no differences between assertive and less assertive individuals in their duration of eye contact, frequency of smiles, duration of reply, or speech fluency.

Eisler, Hersen, Miller, and Blanchard (1975) extended the Eisler et al. (1973) study by including role-playing situations that required commendatory assertive behavior. The earlier study examined situations requiring more hostile assertiveness. The situational context was also varied so that individuals responded to male and female role-playing partners who were either familiar or relatively unfamiliar to the subject. As with the first study, the behavior was videotaped and coded for communication variables by two trained judges. The subjects were 60 male hospitalized psychiatric patients. As in the previous study, patients with acute psychotic symptoms and organic brain syndrome were excluded.

The researchers found that the situational context had several effects on communication behavior. The negative scenes, in comparison to the positive scenes, were characterized by longer replies, more eye contact, more pitch variety, greater vocal volume, and greater response latency, while there was more smiling in the positive scenes. The sex of the role-playing partner was influential in that subjects talked longer and smiled more when the partner was female but had more speech disturbances when the partner was male. Also, negative content was expressed more with male partners. However, subjects were more assertive when the partners were female, asking them to change their behavior more frequently than they asked the male partners. The familiarity of the other person also influenced communicative behavior. Generally, subjects were more assertive with unfamiliar, compared with familiar, persons. Familiarity was defined as "having recurrent interactions with the dyad member." This factor was manipulated in the descriptions of the situations.

An interesting but unexpected result was that highly assertive individuals evidenced more speech disturbances than less assertive persons. The authors speculated that assertive persons may take greater risks in expressing themselves. This may produce more emotional arousal, which in turn provokes more speech disturbances.

This study also observed several interaction effects. For example, speech disturbances were highest when talking with a male in a negative context but about equal in the female-positive, female-negative, and male-positive conditions. This same pattern emerged for the latency-of-response variable. More smiles were directed at familiar persons in a positive context than at unfamiliar individuals in either context, or at familiar persons in a negative context.

These are only a portion of the results observed in Eisler et al.'s (1975) study, suggesting rather clearly that assertiveness involves a good deal of behavioral complexity. In order to act assertively, Eisler et al. concluded, "requires the coordinated delivery of numerous verbal and nonverbal responses" (p. 339). Such a complex problem of coordination might be a primary obstacle in inducing less assertive persons to behave more assertively. They may be stimulated to want to deliver an assertive message rather easily in comparison to actually acquiring an effective delivery system.

## Argumentativeness

As posited earlier, argumentativeness is a subset of assertiveness, since all arguing involves being assertive, but not all assertive behavior involves arguing. In terms of the trait model of personality (Costa & McCrae, 1980), while assertiveness is a facet of the extroversion dimension, argumentativeness is a side of assertiveness and therefore also an aspect of extroversion. We might speculate further, based on the research of Beatty et al. (1984) and Norton and Warnick (1976), that other sides or aspects of assertiveness are low communication apprehension, communication dominance, precision, and impression-leaving, and that these communication traits also pertain to extroversion.

Infante and Rancer (1982) conceived of argumentativeness as a predisposition to defend positions on controversial issues while attempting to refute others' positions. Earlier researchers identified variables termed argumentativeness (Hovland & Janis, 1959) and contentiousness (Norton, 1978). However, these researchers did not advance theoretical models. Infante and Rancer (1982) developed a model of argumentativeness based on Atkinson's (1957, 1966; Atkinson & Raynor, 1974) value-expectancy theory of achievement motivation. Atkinson maintained that excitation-inhibition conflict is experienced by individuals in situations where evaluation of their performance on some task is anticipated. This represents an approach-avoidance motivational conflict. The tendency to achieve success at a task and the tendency to avoid failure at the task interact, determining the individual's resultant motivation for the task. The tendency to avoid failure was viewed by Atkinson as a debilitating factor, with the anxiety associated with failure dampening the tendency to achieve success. The two tendencies are composed of traits and also perceptions of the particular situation. This inclusion of both trait and situational determinants of behavior by Atkinson was insightful and represents an early attempt to formalize the idea that personality interacts with situation to produce behavior that is unique but that has continuity over time.

According to Atkinson, the tendency to achieve success at a particular task is a multiplicative function of a person's motivation to achieve success (i.e., traits) and perceptions of both the incentive of success and the subjective probability of succeeding (i.e., perceptions influenced by the situation). In a parallel fashion, the tendency to avoid failure at a task is conceived as a function of the motive to avoid failure and perceptions of both the probability and incentive of failure.

Along these lines, then, Infante and Rancer (1982) conceptualized argumentativeness as a personality trait formed by two competing motivational tendencies: motivation to approach argumentative situations, $ARG_{ap}$, and motivation to avoid such situations, $ARG_{av}$. The person's general trait to be argumentative, $ARG_{gt}$, is thus viewed as an excitation-inhibition or approach-avoidance conflict:

$$ARG_{gt} = ARG_{ap} - ARG_{av}$$

An approach-avoidance model is assumed to be appropriate because, as with achievement behavior (Atkinson, 1957, 1966; Atkinson & Raynor, 1974), evaluation is typically expected when we argue. Possible sources of evaluation are the adversary and any observers of the argument. In accord with Atkinson's model, it is assumed that the competing motivational tendencies are independent. This assumption was supported in three factor-analytic studies (Infante & Rancer, 1982). Thus, how argumentative an individual is cannot be predicted accurately from only motivation to approach arguments; motivation to *avoid* arguments must also be considered.

According to this conception, the highly argumentative person is high on $ARG_{ap}$ and low on $ARG_{av}$. This person perceives arguing as an exciting intellectual challenge, a competitive event involving "winning points." Feelings of excitement and favorable anticipation are experienced when an argument is expected. Following an argument, the person feels invigorated, satisfied, and experiences a sense of accomplishment, even if the argument was not won (i.e., participating in the process produces pleasure).

The person who is low in argumentativeness is low in $ARG_{ap}$ and high in $ARG_{av}$. This individual also recognizes the potential for controversy in social situations. However, he or she tries to manipulate the situation to keep arguments from happening and feels relieved when arguments are avoided. When induced to argue, this person has unpleasant feelings before, during, and after the argument.

The moderate $ARG_{gt}$ is located between these two extremes and is represented by $ARG_{ap} = ARG_{av}$. This could occur for people who are low on both approach and avoidance or high on both, suggesting at least two types of moderates. The "apathetic moderate" is low on both $ARG_{ap}$ and $ARG_{av}$; arguing is not liked, but it is not disliked either. This person's argumentative behavior is probably controlled more by incentive variables in the particular situation (i.e., the person argues when a significant gain is possible). The "conflicting feelings moderate" is high on both; the person wants to argue but is afraid of the process. Such an individual is probably also influenced by situational variables such as arguing more when the probability of winning is high even though the incentive is low.

Rancer, Baukus, and Infante (1985) discovered that high, moderate, and low argumentatives have different belief structures about arguing. As would be expected, highs had more positive beliefs about arguing while lows had more negative beliefs. However, the content of the beliefs also varied greatly. High $ARG_{gt}$ individuals had beliefs about arguing being enjoyable, providing social power, enhancing one's self-concept, increasing learning, and developing rhetorical skills. Low argumentatives had belief systems that regarded arguing as leading to anger and creating interpersonal tensions, and changing someone's viewpoint as being nonproductive.

The argumentativeness scale was developed to measure $ARG_{gt}$ (Infante & Rancer, 1982). The scale contains 20 items, 10 for measuring $ARG_{ap}$ and 10 for assessing $ARG_{av}$. Research has indicated that the scale is reliable in terms of internal consistency and stability over time

(Infante & Rancer, 1982). Research has also supported the scale's predictive, concurrent, and construct validity (Infante, 1981; Infante & Rancer, 1982; Rancer & Infante, 1985).

Infante and Rancer (1982) proposed a state component of argumentative behavior in a given situation, since high $ARG_{gt}$ persons do not always argue, and low $ARG_{gt}$ people do not always avoid argument. Along the lines of Atkinson's (1957, 1966; Atkinson & Raynor, 1974) model, the state component was conceived as perceptions of the probability and importance of success and failure in the situation. Success is relative and can represent a wide range of outcomes (e.g., winning the argument, influencing observers, or appearing dynamic and attractive).

The tendency to approach a particular argument, $T_{ap}$, was viewed as a multiplicative function of motivation for approaching arguments in general and both the perceived probability of success and the importance of success for the particular argument. This was expressed as:

$$T_{ap} = ARG_{ap} \times P_s \times I_s$$

Similarly, a person's tendency to avoid a given argument, $T_{av}$, was conceived as a multiplicative function of motivation for avoiding arguments and both the perceived probability of failure and the importance of failure. Thus:

$$T_{av} = ARG_{av} \times P_f \times I_f$$

The individual's resultant motivation for being argumentative in a particular situation, $RM_{arg}$, was seen as an interaction of the tendency to approach the argument and the tendency to avoid the argument. The tendency to avoid an argument is debilitating, weakening the tendency to approach the argument. Hence:

$$RM_{arg} = T_{ap} - T_{av}$$

Although this conceptualization of argumentative communication emphasizes a personality trait, it does not exclude the impact of the situation on behavior. The idea that has evolved from Berkowitz (1962) and others is that personality interacts with situation to product behavior. Accounting for variables in the situation should improve the prediction of behavior from a trait alone. This speculation was supported in one study (Infante & Rancer, 1982) and replicated in another (Infante, in press). In these studies, the index for $RM_{arg}$, when compared to the trait alone, ARG$_{gt}$, correlated significantly higher with a measure of motivation for engaging in a particular argument.

In the model of symbolic aggressiveness presented here, argumentativeness was conceived as a constructive trait. On a more global level this was posited because arguing is an essential form of communication in the executive, legislative, and judicial branches of our government and is vital in the selection phase of the evolution of ideas (Cronkhite, 1976).

Arguing also appears to have constructive outcomes for the individual. Johnson and Johnson (1979) reviewed more than 100 studies and concluded that arguing is an important way to stimulate learning in instructional situations. Their review revealed several constructive effects: (1) Arguing stimulates curiosity about the topics of controversy. This increases learning because we seek more information about the topics we have argued for or against. (2) Egocentric thinking is reduced by arguing since the topics of argument must be examined from multiple vantage points. This discourages the individual from relating a topic only to the self. (3) Arguing improves social perspective-taking, a skill vital to communication effectiveness and social intelligence, because the act of refutation requires understanding the adversary's implied warrants for the claims presented. (4) Creativity is stimulated by an argument because of the heightened arousal experienced. (5) The quality of decision making and problem solving in groups is enhanced by argument.

Research has discovered that the communicative behavior of high argumentatives is perceived differently than that of lows by observers of an argument (Infante, 1981). When both types discussed controversial issues with same-sex moderate argumentatives, high argumentatives were perceived as more set in their positions, interested in the discussion, verbose, willing to attack and defend positions, expert in the topic of communication, dynamic in presentation, and skilled in arguing. College grade-point average was positively related to argumentativeness in another study (Infante, 1982). That study also found that being argumentative did not appear to have a negative effect on interpersonal relations. That is, high argumentatives did not differ from others in terms of satisfaction with interpersonal relations and how well they said they could relate to peers.

Some research has examined argumentativeness and verbal aggression in interpersonal relationships. Infante, Trebing, et al. (1984) found that highly argumentative individuals were not as easily provoked into the use of verbal aggression when the adversary was obstinate. Another study (Infante, Wall, Leap, & Danielson, 1984) discovered that in an interpersonal conflict situation, where the adversaries were of the same sex, males preferred more verbal aggression with more argumentative adversaries. Females preferred verbal aggression less and did not differentiate its use according to the opponent's argumentativeness. Subsequent research (Infante, 1985) suggests that highly argumentative individuals can influence whether or not they will be the recipients of verbal aggression. When high argumentatives used argument, as compared to both verbal aggression and argument, the amount of verbal aggression in males' responses was significantly reduced. Females were not provoked to reciprocate the use of verbal aggression and preferred argument as a response to verbal aggression, perhaps indicating a tendency for females to counter aggression with rational discourse.

An extensive series of studies of married couples by Gottman (1979) demonstrated the importance of arguing in marriages. On the basis of observations of the couples' communicative behavior in arguments, he concluded that unhappily married couples argued in a destructive manner, while those who were happily married argued constructively. Some of the destructive patterns identified by Gottman appear to involve verbal aggression (e.g., attribution of motives to a partner which serve to criticize the person). The constructive patterns involve principles typically taught in interpersonal communication courses (e.g., "validation sequences," or giving feedback to the speaker to show you are listening).

Recent investigations of argumentativeness in organizations also indicate that arguing has some constructive outcomes. In one study, supervisors who were more argumentative had more favorable job outcomes, such as higher salaries and more career satisfaction (Infante & Gorden, 1985b). In another study, the more subordinates perceived their superiors to be high in argumentativeness and low in verbal aggressiveness, the more the subordinates were satisfied with their job and supervisor (Infante & Gorden, 1985a).

A sex difference in argumentativeness has also been observed (Infante, 1982). Males were higher on the trait in comparison to females. This is consistent with the general finding that males are more aggressive than females (Maccoby & Jacklin, 1974). According to the cultural sex-role expectations model, arguing, an aggressive form of communication, is compatible with expectations for male behavior but incompatible with expectations for female behavior. This notion was refined in a study by Rancer and Dierks-Stewart (1985) who found, from a psychological sex-role framework, that traditional males were significantly more argumentative compared with traditional females or with androgynous or undifferentiated individuals.

In light of research which suggests that arguing has constructive outcomes, it would seem necessary to specify the components of argumentative competence. This would clarify what is involved in arguing constructively. What it takes to argue in an effective, constructive manner has been explicated in numerous books in the communication discipline (e.g., Freeley, 1966; Jensen, 1981; Mills, 1968; Rieke & Sillars, 1984; Windes & Hastings, 1965). Briefly, the major components of argumentative competence appear to be the ability to state a controversy in propositional form, determining the major issues of contention, developing a unified position on the proposition, discovering arguments to support the position, refuting other positions, and delivering arguments effectively. These components are just as relevant to casual interpersonal disagreements as they are to formal debate. However, in interpersonal communication, an additional competency is important, suggesting that a highly proficient debater may not always succeed in interpersonal conflict situations.

The additional component involves being able to manage interpersonal relations during an argument. The major concern here is to avoid damaging the adversary's self-concept while attacking the individual's position. There are numerous skills that are relevant to this task. Johnson and Johnson (1979), for instance, report on the effectiveness of reaffirming the adversary's sense of competence during an argument (e.g., "You made a real good point . . . but I do have something I would like to add"). Argumentative competence involves damaging the adversary's position on the proposition being discussed but leaving that person's self-concept intact or even enhanced. This feat is accomplished by proficient arguers and requires a finesse reminiscent of William Tell's prowess with the crossbow.

## Hostility

Continuing our analysis of the organization of the aggressive personality based on Costa and McCrae's (1980) model, while assertiveness is a facet of extroversion, hostility is a facet of neuroticism. Verbal aggressiveness, our topic in the next section, is a side or aspect of hostility, a structure that parallels our earlier specifications for assertiveness and argumentativeness. Costa and McCrae (1980) conceive of hostility as a "generalized conceptualization of the affect of anger" (p. 93). Moreover, "Individuals high in this trait tend to be irritable, quick to take offense, and hot-tempered. Interpersonally, they tend toward suspicion, aggression, and perhaps paranoia" (p. 93).

Buss and Durkee (1957) conceptualized hostility as a complex, multi-dimensional trait. They criticized previous unidimensional conceptions of hostility as ambiguous and misleading. For instance, two individuals might have the same score on a unidimensional hostility scale, yet one person might be assaultive and nonsuspicious while the other person could be non-assaultive and suspicious. Thus two very different manifestations of hostility would be quantitatively characterized as the same.

Buss and Durkee's (1957) analysis yielded seven subclasses of the hostile personality: (1) assault (pertaining to physical violence against other people); (2) indirect hostility (including malicious gossip, practical jokes, and undirected aggression such as rage directed as objects, as in slamming a door); (3) irritability (involving a quick temper in response to the slightest provocation, grouchiness, showing exasperation, and rudeness); (4) negativism (refusing to cooperate, antagonism toward authority, rules, and conventions); (5) resentment (jealousy, hatred, feelings of anger about real or imagined mistreatment); (6) suspicion (being wary of people, distrustful, believing that others are planning harm); and (7) verbal hostility (including negative affects expressed in the style and content of speech). The verbal hostility subclass corresponds to verbal aggressiveness, which will be discussed in the next section. The assault subclass pertains to the physical aggressiveness part of the model outlined in the early part of this chapter.

With the exception of the assault dimension, then, the subclasses of the hostile personality identified by Buss and Durkee may be used to conceptualize destructive symbolic aggressiveness in interpersonal communication. Accordingly, hostility may be expressed symbolically at least six ways in interpersonal communication: indirectness, irritability, negativism, resentment, suspicion, and verbalization. Our trait conception of aggressiveness in interpersonal communication suggests that each of these six types of expression is a product of the interaction of personality with the immediate situation.

As explained for argumentativeness in the previous section, the individual's perceptions of a particular situation can modify the behavior that would be predicted from traits alone. Thus individuals who score high, for instance, on the negativism subscale of the Buss-Durkee Hostility-Guilt Inventory (Buss & Durkee, 1957) might express no antagonism toward an authority in a situation and comply with myriad rules which had been formulated for the situation. On the other hand, a person who scores extremely low on this trait might curse the authority and refuse to abide by the rules. According to the ideas explained earlier, especially those of Berkowitz (1962), such an occurrence would not be unexpected. In the former case the individual might have, for example, a strong need for affiliation with people in the situation, which is given precedence over fulfilling aggressive urges because aggressive behavior would obstruct satisfaction of the affiliation need. In the case of the latter individual, the person may have a salient desire for revenge because the authority figure, it is believed, betrayed him or her, and expressing antagonism and refusing to legitimize the situation by following the rules is viewed as a way to retaliate against the authority figure (i.e., aggressive cues are especially salient). Although the trait of negativism would not accurately predict a given behavior in this situation, in terms of the theory and research discussed previously on the continuity of personality, we would expect that over a large number of situations our first individual would display more negativistic behaviors in comparison to the second person.

The analysis of the hostile personality by Berkowitz (1962) is particularly incisive and insightful. He emphasized that the highly aggressive person is not one who is chronically angry, but rather one who has a learned disposition to behave aggressively, which is latent until anger is aroused. The person has learned to categorize a large portion of his or her world as threatening, causing frustration. In a given situation, Berkowitz (1962) explains, anger is aroused when someone or something is categorized as frustrating according to the relevant cues and stimuli in the situation. Further, "In many instances the anger seems to become 'short-circuited' with continued repetition of the sequence so that the initial thought responses alone elicit hostile behavior" (pp. 258-259). Categorizing a portion of the world as threatening means treating many people and objects as functionally equivalent. Just the realization that the person or object is a member of the category may be sufficient to stimulate anger that will manifest itself, given the necessary conditions in the situation, as hostile behavior.

Essentially, Berkowitz (1962) posited that the aggressive individual has firmly learned habits of responding aggressively to aggressive cues. These habits can be acquired at an early age and might persist throughout the individual's life. Frustrations produce aggression, and if a child experiences a consistent pattern of thwartings, an expectation of future frustration can be established. Even ambiguous situations might then be interpreted as frustrations. Stimulus generalization may result in many people and objects being associated with the anger instigators. Hostile behavior in response to stimuli associated with anger instigators, if it is rewarded or if it produces personal satisfaction, is learned and becomes habitual the more the pattern of reinforcement is repeated.

The child's learning of hostile habits is influenced by the parents' disciplinary methods (Berkowitz, 1962, p. 29). More punitive methods (e.g., physical punishment) are associated with more aggressiveness, while nonpunitive methods (e.g., praise) develop internalized restraints for less desirable behavior. This suggests that the child learns from parents whether to behave aggressively in attempting to influence others. If a child is given physical punishment because he or she behaved one way rather than another, and if the child then changes the behavior, he or she may conclude, for instance, "Hitting someone must be a good method for getting your way; it sure worked on me."

Berkowitz (1973) also posits that some people are "brooders"; they think of previous insults, mull over injuries, and ponder previous attacks, all of which stimulates anger. Such brooding can keep the individual at a high level of arousal, and this can create further tension if the person has learned to be anxious about his or her aggressiveness. Brooding may be encouraged in children if parents remind children of past unpleasant experiences or encourage children to ventilate frustrations. Contrary to the notion from "expressive therapy" of getting over a hostile urge by talking about it, Berkowitz (1973) raises the possibility that encouraging people to express aggression only leads to further aggression. This idea is rather clearly established in light of the research that has failed to find much support for the catharsis hypothesis, which states that expressing aggression reduces the aggressive drive (Quanty, 1976). This research suggests caution in the teaching of interpersonal communication. Encouraging students to talk about sources of anger in interpersonal relations may increase the likelihood of aggressive action. A needed area of research may be to investigate whether focusing on "what is bothering you" is sound pedagogy in interpersonal communication.

Numerous scales and measurement techniques have been developed for measuring human aggressiveness. Projective techniques have met with mixed success. A Thematic Apperception Test developed to measure aggressiveness has been found to be related to aggression in some studies (e.g., Scodel & Lipetz, 1957) but unrelated in others (e.g., Purcell, 1956). Similar conflicting findings have been the case for the Rorschach Inkblot Test (e.g., Siegel, 1956; Wolf, 1957). A projective technique with sufficient evidence concerning validity would be of great interest to aggression researchers. Since the behaviors in question are often socially undesirable, subjects' attempts to portray themselves in a socially desirable manner create a source of measurement error. Projective techniques would largely avoid the social desirablility problem, because the purpose of assessment is not apparent to the subject.

Questionnaires have been the most common source of data on aggressiveness (for a good review of the various scales, see Edmunds & Kendrich, 1980). Of the many scales developed, probably the Hostility-Guilt Inventory (Buss & Durkee, 1957), the Need Aggression Scale from Edwards's (1959) Preference Schedule, and aggression scales developed from the Minnesota Multiphasic Personality Inventory (e.g., Cook & Medley, 1954; Siegel, 1956) have been used most in research.

A very popular method in the field of psychology for measuring aggressiveness in laboratory situations has been to use an apparatus for leading subjects in experiments to believe they are administering shocks to another subject (actually a confederate of the experimenter). The measure of aggression typically has been either the number of shocks administered or the intensity of the shock as determined by a bogus control dial (for a review of studies employing this method, see Berkowitz, 1962).

The research on aggressiveness has found that a sex difference appears quite consistently (Maccoby & Jacklin, 1974). Males are generally more aggressive than females. It could be expected, then, that males will also be higher on traits that have an aggressive component. In line with this thinking, research has found that males are more argumentative (Infante, 1982) and more verbally aggressive (Infante & Wigley, 1986).

## Verbal Aggressiveness

Verbal aggressiveness is an aspect of hostility. Since hostility is a facet of neuroticism (Costa & McCrae, 1980), verbal aggressiveness is also a part of the neuroticism dimension of personality.

It is not unusual for people to have very negative feelings about arguing (Rancer et al. 1985). Many feel that arguments signify imminent interpersonal difficulties, that personal suffering is a frequent outcome, and generally that the desire to argue represents a human frailty. A possible reason for this negative attitude is that genuine argument is sometimes confused with verbal aggression (Infante, Trebing, et al., 1984). Argument and verbal aggression are both aggressive, attacking forms of communication. However, they can be distinguished according to the locus of attack, the other person's position on an issue, in the case of arguing, and the person's self-concept for verbal aggression (Infante & Wigley, 1986). If this difference is not realized, or if the two forms of communication persistently occur in the same context for the individual, it is not surprising to find that some people dislike arguing.

Such a dislike is not trivial in interpersonal relationships, for as Terman, Buttenwieser, Ferguson, Johnson, and Wilson (1938) report in their extensive study of marriages, unhappiness in a marriage was indicated most when spouses differed in their liking of argument. A recent study found that when individuals were highly argumentative, their motivation to discuss a controversial issue was greatest when they were led to believe that the other person was also highly argumentative (Rancer & Infante, 1985). This suggests that homophily-heterophily (McCroskey, Richmond, & Daly, 1975) regarding aggressive personality traits may be especially important in interpersonal relationships.

Since verbal aggression is defined as attacking the person's self-concept instead of, or in addition to, the person's position on a topic of communication, it may considered, in terms of argumentation theory, an instance of the *argumentum ad hominem* fallacy. As such it is considered a barrier to rational discourse (Remland, 1982). According to how verbal aggression is conceived in this chapter, *ad hominem* is verbal aggression only when the person whose self-concept is under attack receives the message directly (i.e., verbal aggression is a dyadic phenomenon). Thus, if a speaker tries to convince an audience to reject a proposal because the proposal's sponsor cannot be trusted, verbal aggression has not occurred—nor has a fallacy, for that matter, if the claim is valid.

Whether or not a given message in interpersonal communication will be perceived as verbally aggressive is not always clear. As maintained earlier for the notions of constructive aggression and rational discourse, the major vantage points for judgment are the individual, the dyad, observers, and society. Examples of noncorrespondent perceptions would be when a message is meant by a source to be verbally aggressive but the receiver does not perceive an attack on himself or herself, a dyad observer believes that verbal aggression has occurred but the dyad members have no perception that a message was meant to do psychological harm, or when one person says he or she was verbally provoked into an act of violence against property but society (e.g., a court) disagrees.

Focusing on verbal aggression as an interpersonal construct seems especially important since theorists such as Berkowitz (1962, p. 118) have explained that impulsive aggression often begins with verbal aggression. Rage is then aroused and mounts, culminating with physical aggression. Other researchers support this interpretation (Patterson & Cobb, 1973; Toch, 1969); Zillmann (1979, p. 301), for example, points out that murders are commonly preceded by verbal aggression.

Although verbal aggression has not been ignored in the vast literature on aggression, as explained earlier, aggression is usually treated in the generic sense, with little attention given to verbal aggression as a form of interpersonal communication. However, verbal aggression is a type of communication worthy of study in its own right, especially in light of its possible role in instigating physical aggression in interpersonal relations. Certainly verbal aggression occurs in other communication contexts.

However, interpersonal communication may be considered the fundamental unit in the span of human communication contexts, and thus a knowledge of verbal aggression between individuals may be considered essential to achieving an understanding, for example, of verbal aggression between nations.

The Verbal Aggressiveness Scale was developed to measure verbal aggressiveness as a personality trait (Infante & Wigley, 1986). It was necessary to develop the scale because scales developed earlier confounded verbal aggression with argument and usually did not differentiate between verbal and physical aggression. For example, even the otherwise excellent set of hostility scales by Buss and Durkee (1957) included some argumentativeness items in their verbal aggressiveness subscale (e.g., item 74, "I would rather concede a point than get into an argument about it").

As explained earlier, verbal aggressiveness is a side of hostility which is further a facet in the neuroticism dimension of personality. Argumentativeness is located in another dimension—extroversion—as a side of assertiveness. Since verbal aggressiveness and argumentativeness each represent a different dimension of the trait structure of personality, it could be expected that they are statistically independent. This assumption was supported in two factor analytic studies (Infante & Rancer, 1982) and also in another set of studies (Infante & Wigley, 1986).

Theoretically, argumentativeness and verbal aggressiveness should be independent, because people discriminate among potential objects of attack. Liking to attack one type of object, such as positions taken on controversial issues, does not mean that one must also like attacking other classes of objects, such as the self-concepts of people (Infante & Rancer, 1982). If both argumentativeness and verbal aggressiveness were motivated by hostility, then it could be expected that the two traits would be related. However, research suggests that verbal aggressiveness has a hostility component but that argumentativeness shares no variability with hostility (Infante & Wigley, 1986). This also supports the constructive-destructive distinction made for the two traits.

Verbally aggressive messages attack an individual's self-concept in an attempt to make the person feel less favorably about himself or herself. In the vernacular, this is sometimes called a "put-down." There are many types of verbally aggressive messages: character attacks, competence attacks, insults, maledictions, teasing, ridicule, profanity, threats, and nonverbal indicators. The nonverbal channels are particularly effective in reinforcing an aggressive verbal message. For instance, a competence attack—"Do you really believe that?"—can be intensified by manipulating paralinguistics (e.g., elevating vocal pitch on "really") and facial expression (e.g., a look of shock and disbelief). However, a nonverbal expression can constitute an aggressive message even without recourse to words (e.g., rolling your eyes while someone is expressing an opinion). Thus, some nonverbal "emblems" (Ekman & Friesen, 1969) stand by themselves as instances of verbal aggression.

These verbally aggressive messages can produce a variety of effects in interpersonal communication (Infante, Trebing, et al. 1984). Damaged self-concepts are the most fundamental effect. The damage thus produced can be even more harmful and lasting than some forms of physical aggression (Buss, 1971, p. 7). A person could recover from a broken nose in a month or two, but if a disparaging remark is made, for instance, about a child's physical appearance (e.g., "You have a pig's nose"), the effect can endure for a lifetime and have an enormous impact on the amount of unhappiness experienced. All of the following effects stem, to some degree, from self-concept damage. Some effects are more temporal in nature: hurt feelings, anger, irritation, embarrassment. Others pertain more to interpersonal relations: relationship deterioration or termination. Probably the most serious effect from both a personal and societal perspective is that verbal aggression sometimes escalates into physical aggression. A good deal of research suggests that verbal aggression is a major cause of violence (see, e.g., Toch, 1969).

There appear to be at least four causes of verbal aggression (Infante, Trebing, et al., 1984). Two are clearly suggested from the frustration-aggression and the social learning theory approaches to aggression reviewed at the beginning of this chapter. In terms of the former, verbal aggression is behavior aroused and energized by frustration. In interpersonal communication, two common sources of frustration are having to deal with a disdained other and having the achievement of a goal blocked by another person. According to the latter approach, verbal aggression is learned by reinforcement and by modeling, where vicarious experience of consequences of the model's behavior produces a learned response.

The social learning approach may be used to explain a result commonly observed—that males are more verbally aggressive than females (Infante, Trebing, et al., 1984; Infante, Wall, et al, 1984; Roloff & Greenberg, 1979; Whaley, 1982). As with the argumentativeness sex difference (Infante, 1982), it could be maintained that females avoid verbal aggression because culture has taught them that such message behavior is not compatible with sex-role expectations. Of course, females do at times use verbal aggression. A recent study clarified this observation by demonstrating that females are more discriminating in the use of verbal aggression and resort to it mainly in extreme cases when an adversary is especially obstinate (Infante, Trebing, et al., 1984). Males, on the other hand, are relatively indiscriminant in using verbal aggression, employing it even when the opponent is easy to persuade.

Two additional causes of verbal aggression may be posited (Infante, Trebing, et al., 1984). A psychopathological basis for verbal aggression involves *transference*; a person attacks with verbally aggressive messages those people who symbolize unresolved conflict existing, perhaps, at the subconscious level. For example, a person may have been a victim of prejudice at an early age, was deeply hurt by it, but was unable to retaliate. The person might attempt to retaliate later in life by attacking the source of that hurt. To create a target for retaliation, the person projects the undesirable characteristics of the person or persons from the past on to individuals in the present who remind the person of the source of the hurt. This attribution, combined with the unresolved conflict, is experienced as justification for vicious verbal behavior.

Another cause is that verbal aggression sometimes results from an argumentative skill deficiency. According to this conception, the individuals in an argument assume attack-and-defend cognitive orientations. This is an indication of strongly experienced needs to attack and defend. The person who is unskilled argumentatively soon exhausts his or her store of arguments and is thus unable to refute the adversary's position. However, the need to attack is still experienced and, moreover, people in the situation expect the person to attack. Unable to attack the opponent's position, the unskilled person satisfies the need to act by attacking the closest object to the adversary's position—the person espousing the position.

The unskilled arguer similarly corrupts the need to defend. When the opponent attacks this person's position, he or she wants to defend the position but does not know how to refute an argument or rebuild a case. To satisfy the need to defend, a defense is set up around the object closest to the position—the self. An adversary's legitimate position attacks are then viewed by the unskilled arguer as personal attacks (i.e., the individual takes the arguments "personally"). The argumentatively inept person then feels justified in introducing verbal aggression, thinking that he or she is merely reciprocating.

This idea of an argumentative skill deficiency as a cause of verbal aggression is consistent with the analyses of Bandura (1973b) and Toch (1969), both of whom have concluded that violent persons do not have the verbal skills for dealing with normal frustrations and thus feel that violence is their only alternative. They respond to a frustration, for example, with an insult, and this increases the likelihood of physical aggression.

According to Infante, Trebing, et al. (1984), an argumentative skill deficiency might be responsible for a sizable portion of the verbal aggression that exists in society. If their analysis is correct, a remedy would be to teach unskilled disputants to argue more effectively so they would have less recourse to verbal aggression. The pedagogy for this has been developed and refined by the communication discipline over the past several centuries. In addition to delivering argumentation instruction on a large scale, especially to the public schools, it has been suggested (Infante, Wall, et al., 1984) that a unit on verbal aggression might be warranted in the communication curriculum. This would entail various forms of verbal aggression, effects on individuals and interpersonal relationships, causes of verbal aggression, and methods for dealing with verbally aggressive behavior.

## CONCLUSION

The purpose of this chapter was to provide a framework for understanding aggressive behavior in interpersonal communication. To this end, a personality approach was taken. Probably the most fundamental reason for taking such an approach is that it seems self-evident that people have a core of characteristic traits which are self-defining in that we can depend on people to exhibit certain patterns of behavior. However, this idea was not viewed as axiomatic by researchers who espoused a situationist position and who claimed that the seemingly apparent consistency is behavior was an illusion created out of the desire for predictability. This issue of cross-situational consistency and of the validity of the concept of personality traits in the field of psychology served a good purpose because it stimulated some excellent research and analysis that seems to have settled the issue beyond a reasonable doubt. The issue no longer appears to be the stability of behavior but rather the meaningful patterns of behavior, how the patterns are related, and what accounts for consistency in behavior, or for inconsistency when it occurs. When does personality change, and how can personality be enhanced so that it produces more personal satisfaction? What principles explain seemingly unique behavior in particular situations? How do traits interact with aspects of a situation to produce behavior?

The general context of the framework developed in this chapter was the trait model of personality developed by Costa and McCrae (1980), who posited three major dimensions of personality: neuroticism, extroversion, and openness, with facets of each dimension. The aggressive traits discussed in this chapter were located in the neuroticism and extroversion dimensions. This produced speculations about relations among traits, all of which seem to be supported by previous research.

The model of aggressiveness in interpersonal communication developed in this chapter conceives of aggression as attacking behavior, physical or symbolic, which is constructive or destructive to interpersonal relationships and can be distinguished as either global or more specific. Aggressiveness is viewed, then, as a core of four personality traits: assertiveness, argumentativeness, hostility, and verbal aggressiveness. Aggression in an interpersonal relationship was explained as being due to a latent learned disposition aroused by cues in the situation and directed by particular perceptions of the situation. This idea is formalized most clearly in the model of argumentativeness (i.e., the $RM_{arg}$ formula).

This chapter began with a brief description of several interpersonal communication situations and the statement that the interest was in understanding them better. For each situation a trait component, as it interacts with the situation, could be used to explain the aggressive behavior. For instance, in analyzing the second situation, where the husband slaps and then punches the wife, knowing the nature of the hostility facet of his neuroticism dimension of personality should help clarify why the behavior occurred. We are not contending that personality is the only thing that needs to be understood in order to comprehend this situation. The disinhibiting effects of alcohol, for example, at times contribute to explanations of behavior. However, while personality is not a sufficient basis for analysis, the contention here has been that personality is a necessary factor in attempting to understand aggressiveness in interpersonal communication.

The continuity of personality has some fairly important implications for interpersonal communication, some of which are ignored or denied by participants in the initial interaction stage. For instance, a woman who has just begun dating a man might realize that he is verbally aggressive but ignore this trait because he has never attacked her. However, a prediction based on the present ideas would be that he has not been verbally aggressive with her because other needs were more salient, and that with the passage of time, along with weakening of the aggression inhibitors, she will assume a place in his pattern of verbally aggressive behavior.

Although this chapter has stressed the continuity of personality, the claim was not one of inevitability. Personality can change. However, like improving the shape of the body through body building, changes in personality involve a great and sustained effort. The speculation was presented, based on a limited amount of research evidence, that training in communication skills may provide a means for enhancing personality. This could have important implications for the discipline of communication, especially if it should be determined that individuals' destructive aggressive traits are reduced by acquiring a stronger tendency to utilize rational discourse as the primary means for resolving social conflict.

## REFERENCES

Alberti, R. E., & Emmons, M.L. (1974). *Your perfect right: A guide to assertive behavior* (2nd ed.). San Luis Obispo, CA: Impact.

Atkinson, J. W. (1957). Motivational determinants of risk-taking behavior. *Psychological Review, 64*, 359-372.

Atkinson, J. W. (1966). *An introduction to motivation.* New York: Van Nostrand.

Atkinson, J. W., & Raynor, J. O. (1974). *Motivation and achievement.* New York: John Wiley.

Bandura, A. (1973a). *Aggression: A social learning analysis.* Englewood Cliffs, NJ: Prentice-Hall.

Bandura, A. (1973b). Social learning theory of aggression. In J. F. Knutson (Ed.), *The control of aggression: Implications from basic research* (pp. 201-250). Chicago: Aldine.

Bandura, A. (1978). Social learning theory of aggression. *Journal of Communication, 28*, 12-29.

Bandura, A. (1983). Psychological mechanisms of aggression. In R. G. Geen & E. I. Donnerstein (Eds.), *Aggression: Theoretical and empirical reviews* (Vol. 1, pp. 1-40). New York: Academic Press.

Bates, H. D., & Zimmerman, S. F. (1971). Toward the development of a screening scale for assertive training. *Psychological Reports, 28*, 99-107.

Beatty, M. J., Plax, T. G, Kearney, P., & McCroskey, J. C. (1984, November). *Communication apprehension and assertiveness: A test of cross-situational consistency.* Paper presented at the annual convention of the Speech Communication Association, Chicago.

Bell, R. A., & Daly, J. A. (1984). The affinity-seeking function of communication. *Communication Monographs, 51*, 91-115.

Bell, R. A., & Daly, J. A. (1985). Some communicator correlates of loneliness. *Southern Speech Communication Journal, 50*, 121-142.

Bem, D. J., & Allen, A. (1974). On predicting some of the people some of the time: The search for cross-situational consistencies in behavior. *Psychological Review, 81*, 506-520.

Berkowitz, L. (1962). *Aggression: A social psychological analysis.* New York: McGraw-Hill.

Berkowitz, L. (1973). Words and symbols as stimuli to aggressive responses. In J. F. Knutson (Ed.), *The control of aggression: Implications from basic research* (pp. 113-143). Chicago: Aldine.

Berkowitz, L. (1983). The experience of anger as a parallel process in the display of impulsive, "angry" aggression. In R. G. Geen and E. I. Connerstein (Eds.), *Aggression: Theoretical and empirical reviews* (Vol. 1, pp. 103-133). New York: Academic Press.

Buss, A. H. (1961). *The psychology of aggression.* New York: John Wiley.

Buss, A. H. (1971). Aggression pays. In J. L. Singer (Ed.), *The control of aggression and violence: Cognitive and physiological factors* (pp. 7-18). New York: Academic Press.

Buss, A. H., & Durkee, A. (1957). An inventory for assessing different kinds of hostility. *Journal of Consulting Psychology, 21*, 343-349.

Buss, A. H., Durkee, A., & Baer, M. B. (1956). The measurement of hostility in clinical situations. *Journal of Abnormal and Social Psychology, 52*, 84-86.

Cook, W. W., & Medley, D. M. (1954). Proposed hostility and pharisaic-virtue scales for the MMPI. *Journal of Applied Psychology, 38*, 414-418.

Costa, P. T., & McCrae, R. R (1980). Still stable after all these years: Personality as a key to some issues in adulthood and old age. In P. B. Baltes & O. G. Brim (Eds.), *Life-span development and behavior* (Vol. 3, pp. 65-102). New York: Academic Press.

Cronkhite, G. (1976). *Communication and awareness.* Menlo Park, CA: Cummings.

Dollard, J., Doob, L., Miller, N., Mower, O., & Sears, R. (1939). *Frustration and aggression.* New Haven, CT: Yale University Press.

Edmunds, G., & Kenrick, D. C. (1980). *The measurement of human aggression.* Chichester, Eng.: Ellis Horwood.

Edwards, A. L. (1959). *Edwards Personal Preference Schedule: Manual.* New York: Psychological Corporation.

Eisler, R. M., Hersen, M., Miller, P. M., & Blanchard, E. B. (1975). Situational determinants of assertive behaviors. *Journal of Consulting and Clinical Psychology, 43*, 330-340.

Eisler, R. M., Miller, P. M., & Hersen, M. (1973). Components of assertive behavior. *Journal of Clinical Psychology, 29*, 295-299.

Ekman, P., & Friesen, W. (1969). The repertoire of nonverbal behavior: Categories, origins, usage, and coding. *Semiotica, 1*, 49-98.

Feshbach, S. (1971). Dynamics and morality of violence and aggression: Some psychological considerations. *American Psychologist, 26*, 281-292.

Feshbach, S. (1984). The catharsis hypothesis, aggressive drive, and the reduction of aggression. *Aggressive Behavior, 10*, 91-101.

Feshbach, S., & Singer, R. D. (1971). *Television and aggression.* San Francisco: Jossey-Bass.

Freeley, A. J. (1966). *Argumentation and debate: Rational decision making* (2nd ed.). Belmont, CA: Wadsworth.

Freud, S. (1957). *Civilization and its discontents* (2nd ed.). London: Hogarth Press.

Freud, S. (1959). *Beyond the pleasure principle*. New York: Bantam.

Galassi, J. P., DeLo, J. S., Galassi, M. D., & Bastien, S. (1974). The college self-expression scale: A measure of assertiveness. *Behavior Therapy, 5*, 165-171.

Galassi, J. P., & Galassi, M. D. (1975). Relationship between assertiveness and aggressiveness. *Psychological Reports, 36*, 352-354.

Gambrill, E. D., & Richey, C. A. (1975). An assertion inventory for use in assessment and research. *Behavior Therapy, 6*, 550-561.

Geen, R. G. (1976). The study of aggression. In R. G. Geen & E. C. O'Neal (Eds.), *Perspectives on aggression* (pp. 1-10). New York: Academic Press.

Geen, R. G., & Donnerstein, E. I. (Eds.). (1983a). *Aggression: Theoretical and empirical reviews* (Vol. 1). New York: Academic Press.

Geen, R. G., & Donnerstein, E. I. (Eds.). (1983b). *Aggression: Theoretical and empirical reviews* (Vol. 2). New York: Academic Press.

Gilkinson, H. (1941). Indexes of change in attitudes and behavior among students enrolled in general speech courses. *Speech Monographs, 8*, 23-33.

Gottman, J. M. (1979). *Marital interaction: Experimental investigations*. New York: Academic Press.

Hedquist, F. J., & Weinhold, B. W. (1970). Behavioral group counseling with socially anxious and unassertive college students. *Journal of Counseling Psychology, 17*, 237-241.

Hovland, C. I., & Janis, I. L. (Eds.). (1959). *Personality and persuasibility*. New Haven, CT: Yale University Press.

Infante, D. A. (1981). Trait argumentativeness as a predictor of communicative behavior in situations requiring argument. *Central States Speech Journal, 32*, 265-272.

Infante, D. A. (1982). The argumentative student in speech communication classroom: An investigation and implications. *Communication Education, 31*, 141-148.

Infante, D. A. (1985, November). *Response to high argumentatives: Message and sex differences*. Paper presented at the annual convention of the Speech Communication Association, Denver.

Infante, D. A. (in press). Enhancing the prediction of response to a communication situation from communication traits. *Communication Quarterly*.

Infante, D. A., & Gorden, W. I. (1985a). Superiors' argumentativeness and verbal aggressiveness as predictors of subordinates' satisfaction. *Human Communication Research, 12*, 117-125.

Infante, D. A., & Gorden, W. I. (1985b). Benefits versus bias: An investigation of argumentativeness, gender, and organizational communication outcomes. *Communication Research Reports, 2*, 196-201.

Infante, D. A. & Rancer, A. S. (1982). A conceptualization and measure of argumentativeness. *Journal of Personality Assessment, 46*, 72-80.

Infante, D. A., Trebing, J. D., Shepherd, P. E, & Seeds, D. E (1984). The relationship of argumentativeness to verbal aggression. *Southern Speech Communication Journal, 50*, 67-77.

Infante, D. A., Wall, C. H., Leap, C. J., & Danielson, K. (1984). Verbal aggression as a function of the receiver's argumentativeness. *Communication Research Reports, 1*, 33-37.

Infante, D. A. & Wigley, C. J. (1986). Verbal aggressiveness: An interpersonal model and measure. *Communication Monographs, 53*, 61-69.

Jensen, J. V. (1981). *Argumentation: Reasoning in communication.* New York: Van Nostrand.

Johnson, D. W. & Johnson, R. T. (1979). Conflict in the classroom: Controversy and learning. *Review of Educational Research, 49*, 51-70.

Kaminski, E. P., Whaley, A. B., Whaley, M. A., & Flaster, M. L. (1984, November). *In defense of a dynamic definition of aggression.* Paper presented at the annual convention of the Speech Communication Association, Chicago.

Lorenz, K. (1966). *On aggression.* New York: Harcourt, Brace.

Lorr, M., & More, W. W. (1980). Four dimensions of assertiveness. *Multivariate Behavioral Research, 2*, 127-138.

Maccoby, E. M., & Jacklin, C. N. (1974). *The psychology of sex differences.* Stanford, CA: Stanford University Press.

McCroskey, J. C., Richmond, V. P., & Daly, J. A. (1975). The development of a measure of perceived homophily in interpersonal communication. *Human Communication Research, 1*, 323-332.

Miller, N. E. (1941). The frustration-aggression hypothesis. *Psychological Review, 48*, 337-342.

Mills, G. E. (1968). *Reason in controversy* (2nd ed.). Boston: Allyn & Bacon.

Mischel, W. (1968). *Personality and assessment.* New York: John Wiley.

Mischel, W. (1969). Continuity and change in personality. *American Psychologist, 24*, 1012-1018.

Mischel, W. (1973). Toward a cognitive social learning reconceptualization of personality. *Psychological Review, 80*, 252-283.

Moore, G. E. (1935). Personality changes resulting from training in speech fundamentals. *Speech Monographs, 2*, 56-59.

Moyer, K. E. (1968). Kinds of aggression and their physiological basis. *Communications in Behavioral Biology, 2*, 65-87.

Murray, E. (1937). *The speech personality.* New York: J. B. Lippincott.

Nevid, J. S., & Rathus, S. A. (1979). Factor analysis of the Rathus Assertiveness Schedule with a college population. *Journal of Behavior Therapy and Experimental Psychiatry, 10*, 21-24.

Norton, R. W. (1978). Foundations of a communicator style construct. *Human Communication Research, 4*, 99-112.

Norton, R., & Warnick, B. (1976). Assertiveness as a communication construct. *Human Communication Research, 3*, 62-66.

Patterson, G. R., & Cobb, J. A. (1973). Stimulus control for classes of noxious behaviors. In J. F. Knutson (Ed.), *The control of aggression: Implications from basic research* (pp. 145-199). Chicago: Aldine.

Purcell, K. (1956). The T.A.T. and antisocial behaviour. *Journal of Consulting Psychology, 20*, 448-456.

Quanty, M. B. (1976). Aggression catharsis: Experimental investigations and implications. In R. G. Geen & E. C. O'Neal (Eds.), *Perspectives on aggression* (pp. 99-132). New York: Academic Press.

Rancer, A. S., Baukus, R. A., & Infante, D. A. (1985). Relations between argumentativeness and belief structures about arguing. *Communication Education, 34,* 37-47.

Rancer, A. S. & Dierks-Stewart, K. (1985). The influence of sex and sex-role orientation on trait argumentativeness. *Journal of Personality Assessment, 49,* 69-70.

Rancer, A. S., & Infante, D. A. (1985). Relations between motivation to argue and the argumentativeness of adversaries. *Communication Quarterly, 33,* 209-218.

Rathus, S. A. (1973). A 30-item schedule for assessing assertive behavior. *Behavior Therapy, 4,* 398-406.

Remland, M. (1982). The implicit *ad hominem* fallacy: Nonverbal displays of status in argumentative discourse. *Journal of the American Forensic Association, 19,* 79-86.

Rieke, R. D., & Sillars, M. O. (1984). *Argumentation and the decision making process* (2nd ed.). Glenview, IL: Scott, Foresman.

Roloff, M. E., & Greenberg, B. S. (1979). Sex differences in choice of modes in conflict resolution in real-life and television. *Communication Quarterly, 27,* 3-12.

Rose, A. H. (1940). Training in speech and changes in personality. *Quarterly Journal of Speech, 26,* 193-196.

Scodel, A., & Lipetz, M. E. (1957). T.A.T. hostility and psychopathology. *Journal of Projective Techniques, 21,* 161-165.

Shontz, E. C. (1965). *Research methods in personality.* New York: Appleton.

Siegel, S. M. (1956). The relationship of hostility to authoritarianism. *Journal of Abnormal and Social Psychology, 52,* 368-372.

Tedeschi, J. T. (1983). Social influence theory and aggression. In R. G. Geen & E. I. Donnerstein (Eds.), *Aggression: Theoretical and empirical reviews.* (Vol. 1, pp. 135-162) New York: Academic Press.

Terman, L. M., Buttenwieser, P., Ferguson, L. W., Johnson, W. B., & Wilson, D. P. (1938). *Psychological factors in marital happiness.* New York: McGraw-Hill.

Toch, H. (1969). *Violent men.* Chicago: Aldine.

Tucker, R. K., Weaver, R. L., & Redden, E. M. (1983). Differentiating assertiveness, aggressiveness, and shyness: A factor analysis. *Psychological Reports, 53,* 607-611.

Weigel, R. H., & Newman, L. S. (1976). Increasing attitude-behavior correspondence by broadening the scope of the behavioral measure. *Journal of Personality and Social Psychology, 33,* 793-802.

Whaley, A. B. (1982). Televised violence and related variables as predictors of self-reported verbal aggression. *Central States Speech Journal, 33,* 490-497.

Windes, R. R., & Hastings, A. (1965). *Argumentation and advocacy.* New York: Random House.

Wolf, I. (1957). Hostile acting out and Rorschach test content. *Journal of Projective Techniques, 21*, 414-419.

Wolpe, J. (1958). *Psychotherapy by reciprocal inhibition.* Stanford, CA: Stanford University Press.

Wolpe, J., & Lazarus, A. A. (1966). *Behavior therapy techniques.* New York: Pergamon.

Zillmann, D. (1979). *Hostility and aggression.* Hillsdale, NJ: Erlbaum.

# Part III
# SOCIAL ORIENTATIONS

# 5

# Social Involvement

## ROBERT A. BELL

We all know individuals who characteristically are very active communicators. They seem by nature to be talkative, animated in gesture and expression, attentive, and responsive. These individuals are likely to be perceived as interested and enthused interactants. Our language provides numerous traitlike labels for these people. We may, for instance, describe them as intense, sociable, gregarious, outgoing, dynamic, extroverted, or charismatic. We have come to expect a high level of social involvement from such individuals.

Most of us are also acquainted with people who are typically passive in their social encounters. They may provide us with little feedback on our comments, make few conversational contributions of their own, communicate unemotionally, and remain relatively still. At times we may wonder if these individuals are directing any of their attention our way. We may describe them as listless, restrained, "laid back," languid, or detached. We have come to expect low levels of social involvement from these people.

Without question, involvement is a central dimension of interpersonal communication. Wish and his colleagues have carried out an extensive research program designed to uncover the dimensions underlying interpersonal communication and human relationships (Wish, 1976; Wish, D'Andrade, & Goodnow, 1980; Wish, Deutsch, & Kaplan, 1976; Wish & Kaplan, 1976). This research has consistently identified a dimension of *intensity* versus *superficiality* in communication. Levy (1981) has concluded that involvement is one of three fundamental "classes" of behavior; the other two classes are intelligence/achievement and attitude. She defines involvement in terms of the amount of cognitive, affective, or instrumental contact an individual has with an object. Levinger (1977) identifies involvement as one of three components of interpersonal relationships. There is thus a recognition that involvement is an integral aspect of communication. By extension, involvement can be considered

a central feature of the *dispositional* behavior of individual communicators.

Social involvement may also be a fundamental interpersonal need.
Schutz (1960) has proposed a multidimensional theory of interpersonal
behavior that identifies three basic needs: inclusion, control, and affec-
tion. The need for inclusion refers to the establishment and maintenance
of satisfactory relationships with respect to social involvement—namely,
association and frequency of interaction. Individuals with unmet
inclusion/involvement needs have been shown to suffer from a number
of personal turmoils.

This chapter reviews the extant literature on social involvement and
interpersonal communication. The initial section briefly examines
several theories of social involvement as an *interaction specific*
concept—that is, as a feature of specific conversations. This research
provides insight into a fundamental question: How do "involved"
people communicate? Subsequent sections examine several dispositional
conceptualizations closely related to social involvement. These include
interaction involvement, empathic responding, self-monitoring, rhetorical
sensitivity, and loneliness. The chief concern here is with the correlates
and consequences of these dispositions.

## INTERACTION-SPECIFIC CONCEPTUALIZATIONS
## OF SOCIAL INVOLVEMENT

Although our primary concern is with individual differences in social
involvement, the large body of research on involvement as a feature of
interactions serves as a useful starting point. Most of this research has
focused on mutual influence in communication—that is, on the tendency
for people to adapt the form and substance of their communication to
converge with or diverge from the involvement level of their conversational partners.

Mutual influence takes two forms: *matching* (reciprocity) and
*compensation* (Cappella, 1982). Matching occurs when one person
responds to an increase in another's level of involvement by becoming
more involved, or when he or she responds to a decrease in the other's
involvement by becoming less involved. Compensation is demonstrated
when an individual responds to an increase in another's level of
involvement by becoming less involved, or when he or she responds to a
decrease in the partner's involvement by becoming more involved.
Increases in involvement are considered by Cappella (1982) to be
*approaching* responses regardless of whether these compensate or match

another's level of involvement, while decreases in involvement are considered *avoidance* responses.

Investigators have examined matching and compensation on numerous communication behaviors, including characteristics of speech, kinesic actions, and verbalizations. Reviews of various aspects of this literature are available (Cappella, 1982; Edinger & Patterson, 1983; Feldstein & Welkowitz, 1978; Giles & Smith, 1979; Jaffe & Anderson, 1979; Patterson, 1982, 1983a,b; Street & Giles, 1982). Four general theories of mutual influence have been advanced: Argyle and Dean's equilibrium theory, Patterson's arousal-labeling theory, Cappella and Greene's discrepancy-arousal-affect model, and Patterson's (1982) sequential functional model of nonverbal exchange. Each is described briefly to provide a proper context for the subsequent sections. More extensive reviews of these models are provided by Patterson (1983a, 1983b, 1985).

## Equilibrium Theory

Argyle and Dean's (1965) equilibrium theory of intimacy is one of the most heuristic models of nonverbal interaction ever formulated. The model posits that there is an optimal level of intimacy in any interaction, defined by the workings of psychological approach and avoidance forces. Since affiliation produces both rewards and costs, individuals are simultaneously motivated to increase and decrease their involvement with others. Intimacy is a function of such behaviors as eye contact, physical proximity, topic intimacy, and smiling. The equilibrium level of an encounter is dependent upon numerous individual, situational, and relational factors. Since these factors can change over the course of an encounter, the equilibrium level within an interaction may also fluctuate (Argyle & Cook, 1976). If intimacy rises above or falls below the equilibrium level, participants in an encounter will experience anxiety-arousal. An attempt will then be made to restore equilibrium by decreasing or increasing intimacy via changes in the frequency, rate, or intensity of affiliative behaviors.

While most scholars pay respect to equilibrium theory, few accept it as an adequate account of involvement in interaction. First, the model was designed to explain compensation in interaction. While most studies have found compensation in lieu of matching, scholars cannot ignore the reality of matching (e.g., Chapman, 1975). Equilibrium theory cannot explain matching responses. Second, Argyle and Dean unjustifiably equate specific behaviors with affiliation and intimacy. As Cappella (1982) has noted, "identifying kinesic . . . and paralinguistic . . . signs with various interpersonal attitudes is not useful and is even misleading. Rather, they signal a degree of involvement in the situation and involvement with the other person whose emotional tone depends on situational factors, relationship stage, and individual differences'' (p. 117). In fairness to Argyle and Dean, it should be noted that other scholars have also made the assumption that certain behaviors are inherently tied to specific interpersonal attitudes. For instance, Mehrabian (1969) notes that verbal and nonverbal immediacy cues indicate liking and a desire for affiliation. He even defined immediacy as ''the extent to which communication behaviors enhance closeness to and nonverbal interaction [involvement] with another'' (p. 203).

Patterson's work on nonverbal involvement has also been motivated, in part, by a desire to disassociate specific behaviors from the concept of intimacy. He observes that gaze, touch, and other behaviors can signal sentiments other than intimacy. Patterson (1983) offers the following as a tentative list of involvement behaviors: interpersonal distance, gaze, touch, body orientation, facial expressiveness, speech duration, postural openness, interruptions, relational gestures, head nods, and various paralinguistic cues such as intonation, speech rate, and volume. These behaviors are considered nonverbal involvement behaviors because they ''operationally define (in some as yet unweighted fashion) the degree of involvement manifested between individuals in a social setting'' (Patterson, 1982, p. 233). On the basis of Cappella's (1982) discussion, we may add several other behaviors to this list: talkativeness, self-disclosure, topic intimacy, speech latency, and laughing. Following the lead of Patterson and Cappella, ''involvement'' will be used throughout this chapter because it does not imply an inherent connection between involvement behaviors and intimacy.

### Arousal-Labeling Model

Patterson (1976) has developed a theory of greater scope than equilibrium theory to explain compensatory and reciprocal responses to the involvement of others. His arousal-labeling model, which was originally proposed as a model of intimacy and later generalized to a model of involvement (Patterson, 1983), proposes that an individual's response to another's level of involvement is mediated by arousal change and emotional labeling. The model suggests that when person A changes his or her level of involvement, person B may or may not experience a change in arousal. If A's shift in involvement is not large enough to result in a change in B's level of arousal, B will make no effort to label his or her emotional state and will make no adjustment in involvement.

However, if A's change in involvement is large enough to lead to an arousal change in B that is noticeable to B, then B will respond by labeling this arousal change as a positive or negative emotion. If the arousal change is labeled negatively (e.g., anxiety, discomfort, or embarrassment), B will respond in a compensatory manner. If the arousal change is interpreted as a positive emotion (e.g., liking, love, or relief), then B will reciprocate A's change in involvement. Factors influencing B's emotional labeling include his or her past experiences with A and the characteristics of the situation.

Although arousal-labeling theory offers greater explanatory power than equilibrium theory, Patterson's approach has not gone unchallenged. Cappella and Greene (1982), for instance, observe that the model fails to specify conditions likely to produce positive or negative labeling, ascribes centrality to the labeling of emotional states which is inconsistent with empirical research, cannot account for infant-adult interaction, and cannot explain cyclical patterns of reciprocity and compensation.

## Discrepancy-Arousal-Affect Model

Cappella and Greene (1982), in attempting to overcome the limitations of the arousal-labeling approach, have formulated a discrepancy-arousal-affect model of mutual influence based on Stern's (1974, 1977) discrepancy arousal theory of adult-infant interaction. Although Stern's theory was constructed to explain the ebb and flow of involvement within infant-adult interactions, Cappella and Greene (1982) suggest that the model could be broadened to explain a wide range of expressive behaviors. Such a model would, in contrast to Patterson's approach, explain mutual influence without unnecessary (and perhaps unjustifiable) reference to cognitive labeling. Second, the model could explain involvement within both infant-adult and adult-adult interactions (Cappella & Greene, 1982).

The discrepancy-arousal-affect model integrates four central components: expectations, discrepancy, arousal, and affect. An expectation is a relatively stable standard of the anticipated involvement that each person in an interaction holds for another's behavior. The term "discrepancy" denotes the degree to which the other's level of involvement departs from the expected level. "Affect" refers to the amount of pleasantness, the sentiment, and the reward/punishment value experienced. "Arousal" is defined as the neural excitation of the cortex.

The model posits three basic linkages between these four variables. The behavior-arousal linkage predicts that when person A's involvement falls above or below person B's expectation for that involvement, the resulting discrepancy will produce arousal. The arousal-affect relationship is hypothesized to take the form of an inverted U, with high amounts of arousal experienced as aversive and small-to-moderate amounts experienced as neutral or positive. It is at this point that the discrepancy-arousal-affect model differs considerably from the arousal-labeling model, for Cappella and Greene replace Patterson's labeling step with a rather automatic arousal-affect response. In arousal-labeling theory, cognitions *mediate* arousal and affect. In the discrepancy-arousal-affect model, cognitions *precede* the arousal-affect linkage in the form of expectations for another's involvement. Thus the amount of arousal determines the affective response of an individual, and subsequently the nature of his or her involvement adjustment. Little or no arousal will be affectively neutral, requiring no behavioral adjustment; moderate arousal will be affectively positive, leading to matching; high arousal will be affectively negative, leading to compensation.

## A Sequential Functional Model

Patterson (1983) has reviewed the equilibrium, arousal-labeling, and discrepancy-arousal-affect models and found all three wanting. His primary criticism is that none of them gives formal consideration to the social functions served by involvement and to the antecedent factors that shape mutual influence. Patterson has advanced a sequential functional model of nonverbal exchange in an attempt to overcome these limitations. The theory identifies five functions of nonverbal involvement: providing information, regulating interaction, expressing intimacy, exercising social control, and facilitating service or task goals. This theory also goes beyond modeling interaction sequences as solely reactive behavioral adjustments to preceding acts by examining how involvement within an interaction is controlled by proactive factors. Patterson gives special attention to antecedent factors such as social scripts and personality which affect people's level of involvement.

In the sections that follow, several conceptualizations of social involvement as an individual difference are examined. These constructs include interaction involvement, empathic response, self-monitoring, rhetorical sensitivity, and loneliness.

## INTERACTION INVOLVEMENT

Cegala (1981) has advanced what may be the most comprehensive treatment of social involvement as an individual difference in his work on *interaction involvement*, which is considered a central dimension of communication competence. Interaction involvement is defined as "the extent to which an individual partakes in a social environment" (p. 112)—namely, interpersonal communication situations. Cegala grounds his explication of the interaction involvement construct in Goffman's (1967) dramaturgical perspective. Competence is defined by Cegala (1981) as "an individual's ability to advance interpersonal goals without resulting in loss of face to self or others" (p. 111). In Goffman's terminology, communication competence is effective "face-work," constituted by "the actions taken by a person to make whatever he is doing consistent with face. Face-work serves to counteract 'incidents'—that is, events whose effective symbolic implications threaten face" (p. 110).

According to Goffman, effective face-work requires *perceptiveness* and *attentiveness*. Perceptive communicators are aware of how others interpret their acts and how they should interpret others' acts. In Cegala's words, perceptiveness "involves the integration of meanings of self in relation to another" (1981, p. 111). Perceptiveness presupposes attentiveness, which is a selective directing of one's senses toward sources of information relevant to the ongoing interaction. The attentive person keeps his or her mind on the conversation and listens closely to other interactants.

Cegala (1981) has developed a self-report measure of people's dispositional levels of interaction involvement. The Interaction Involvement Scale (IIS) is composed of 18 items constructed to be consistent with Goffman's (1976) discussion of perceptiveness and attentiveness (examples: "I am keenly aware of how others perceive me during my conversations" and "My mind wanders during conversations and I often miss parts of what is going on"). Respondents report the extent to which each item is an accurate self-description on 7-point scales. A factor analysis of the responses of almost seven hundred individuals to the IIS resulted in three factors: perceptiveness, other-oriented perceptiveness, and attentiveness.

Cegala, Savage, Brunner, and Conrad (1982) have reexamined the factor structure of the IIS. These scholars combined data from Cegala's initial study with the responses of over one thousand other people. While a three-factor solution was once again obtained, Cegala et al. labeled the factors *perceptiveness, attentiveness,* and *responsiveness.* Responsiveness, the "new" factor, refers to the "tendency to react mentally to one's social circumstances and adapt by knowing what to say and when to say it" (p. 233). The responsive person is able to find appropriate lines to extend another's comments and has awareness of his or her role in an interaction. Cegala and his colleagues consider perceptiveness and attentiveness to be primarily cognitive constructs, while responsiveness is assumed to have both cognitive and behavioral components.

Given its recent development, the interaction involvement construct has received very little attention. In his initial report, Cegala (1981) explored the relationship between scores on the IIS and communication competence within dyadic encounters. He found considerable differences in the abilities of dispositionally high-involved and low-involved people to obtain personal information from their conversational partners. Involved people were more likely to elicit disclosures on one of four personal topics using indirect, and presumably more competent, information-seeking strategies.

Cegala et al. (1982) examined the relationship of the three components of interaction involvement to other personality traits within a sample of college students. Responsiveness was inversely related to neuroticism, social anxiety, and communication apprehension in groups, meetings, and dyads but positively related to sociability, behavioral flexibility, interaction management (females only), affiliation/supportiveness, and social relaxation. Perceptiveness was inversely related to social anxiety, group communication apprehension, meeting communication apprehension (males only), dyadic communication apprehension, and public speaking apprehension (males only). It was positively correlated with private self-consciousness (males only), public self-consciousness (females only), behavioral flexibility, impression management, affiliation/supportiveness, empathy, and social relaxation. Attentiveness was inversely related to neuroticism, impulsiveness (males only), private self-consciousness (females only), and social anxiety (males only) but positively correlated with interaction management, affiliation/supportiveness (males only), and empathy (males only). These results support the concurrent validity of the IIS.

Cegala et al. (1982) also report an investigation of nonverbal manifestations of interaction involvement within 20 dyadic interactions involving college students. The specific behaviors examined were object-focused gesturing; body-focused gesturing; posture changes; shoulder, leg, and foot movements; and eye gaze. Responsiveness scores correlated inversely with body-focused gesturing while speaking and with nongesture body movements. Perceptiveness was inversely related to body-focused gesturing while speaking but correlated positively with eye gaze while speaking. Attentiveness was also correlated with eye gaze while speaking. Unfortunately, Cegala et al. do not provide a theoretical justification for their selection of nonverbal behaviors. As a result, the importance of these correlations is not easily assessed. Indeed, many of the nonverbal signs examined, including body-focused gesturing and body movements, are considered by Patterson (1983, p. 6) to be theoretically irrelevant to nonverbal involvement.

Bell and Daly (1984) have examined the relationship of interaction involvement and affinity-seeking competence. "Affinity-seeking" refers to the communication strategies people use to get others to like them and to feel positive about them. They asked college students to generate lists of behaviors that could be used to generate affinity with a hypothetical other within a specified situation. Dispositional responsiveness had a small but significant association with the ability to generate descriptions of affinity-seeking behaviors, with the latter representing a wide range of affinity-seeking strategies. In another study, Bell and Daly (1984) asked undergraduates to report how likely they would be to use each of 25 affinity-seeking strategies. All three subscales were significantly related to some of the strategies. Responsiveness, for instance, was inversely related to the likelihood ratings for strategies labeled "concede control" and "supportiveness," while attentiveness and perceptiveness were positively correlated with "listening."

In a later study, Bell and Daly (1985) administered the IIS and a measure of loneliness to a sample of college students. Loneliness was inversely related to responsiveness and attentiveness. No significant association was found between perceptiveness and loneliness.

Cegala (in press) has examined the relationship of interaction involvement to cognitive and affective domains of experience within social interaction. Dyads composed of high-involved or low-involved college students engaged in casual, unstructured conversations and then role-played an encounter between lawyers attempting to reach an out-of-court settlement in a hypothetical legal case. After each communication event, subjects completed measures of mood state, ego strength, and recall. Consistent with the interaction involvement construct, high-involved individuals felt more positive and had greater ego strength than did low-involved subjects during both interactions. High-involved subjects also recalled significantly more details of their unstructured conversations.

To be sure, Cegala and his colleagues are not the only behavioral scientists to give attention to the topic of responsiveness. Many other scholars have advanced conceptualizations of responsiveness to others. Most central to present concerns are the constructs *empathic responding, self-monitoring,* and *rhetorical sensitivity.*

## EMPATHIC RESPONDING

Ever since Carl Rogers (1957) described empathy as a "necessary and sufficient condition" for personality change, the topic has received considerable attention by behavioral scientists. Though "empathy" has been used in numerous and sometimes inconsistent ways, there is consensus that the construct is multifaceted, including cognitive, affective, and communicative components. Cognitively, the empathic person takes the perspective of another person, and in doing so strives to see the world from the other's point of view. Affectively, the empathic person experiences the emotions of another; he or she *feels* the other's experiences. Communicatively, the empathic individual signals understanding and concern through verbal and nonverbal cues. These three aspects of empathy have been integrated by Barrett-Lennard (1981) in his five-step model of the empathy cycle. He proposes that empathy involves the recurrent sequencing of various processes that can be outlined as follows: (1) A attends with an empathic set to B, who is communicating his or her own experiences; (2) B's expressed experiences become "experientially alive" to A (empathic resonation); (3) A communicates to B "a quality of felt awareness of B's experiencing" (expressed empathy); (4) B attends to A's empathic response (received empathy); and (5) B continues to communicate.

The concern of this section is with the communication dimension of empathy, *empathic responding*, which is often discussed under such labels as "faciliative responding," "empathic communication," "caring manner," "overt sensitivity," "emotional responsiveness," and (in the case of Barrett-Lennard) "expressed empathy." Empathic responding functions within an interaction to signal one's emotional involvement with another. The present assumption is that such responding is a trait on which individuals may vary considerably. This is not to suggest that people cannot be taught to demonstrate empathy. Indeed, considerable evidence suggests that empathic responding is a communication skill open to improvement (Crabb, Moracco, & Bender, 1983; Epstein & Jackson, 1978; Goldfarb, 1978; Hodge, Payne, & Wheeler, 1978; Therrien, 1979).

In comparison to perspective-taking, empathic responding has been a neglected topic of research. Most of the extant literature comes from clinical and counseling psychology and is primarily concerned with the relationship of empathic responding to counselor effectiveness and treatment outcomes. Though the relevance of the clinical literature to less structured, everyday dyadic encounters is not readily clear, it has been suggested that "the same variables which predict the effectiveness

of counseling will hold true in unplanned therapeutic transactions''
(Shapiro, Krauss, & Truax, 1969, p. 290).

A primary concern has been with the identification of verbal and nonverbal correlates of perceived empathy. The available research suggests
that empathic responding is signaled by numerous behaviors, most of
which are considered cues of involvement. These include facial grimaces
of distress or anxiety, body gestures, smiles, laughter, forward leaning,
eye contact, vocal intonation and quality, facial expressiveness, open
arm and leg positioning, nonverbal mirror-imaging, head nods, closed
body orientation, vocal back-channels, touch, references to the here and
now, topic centrality, and vivid/metaphorical language (see, e.g.,
DeWever, 1977; Elliott, Filipovich, Harrigan, Gaynor, Reimschuessel, &
Zapadka, 1982; Haase & Tepper, 1972; Maurer & Tindall, 1983; Smith-
Hanen, 1977; Tepper & Haase, 1978; Young, 1980; Zahn-Waxler, Friedman, & Mark, 1983). Research by Haase and Tepper (1972; Tepper &
Haase, 1978) suggests that nonverbal behaviors account for twice as
much variance in perceived empathy as verbal behaviors. It is important
to note that studies have not invariably found these behaviors to be
related to perceived empathy (e.g., Gaushell, Fretz, Corn, & Tuemmler,
1979) and that ratings of empathy by clients, supervisors, and observers
do not always converge (e.g., Burstein & Carkhuff, 1968; Caracena &
Vicory, 1969; Gurman, 1973; Hansen, Moore, & Carkhuff, 1968;
McWhirter, 1973; McWhirter & Marks, 1972). Perceptions of empathy
may also be influenced by factors other than verbal and nonverbal
behaviors. A study by Young (1980), for example, indicates that the
major influence on an individual's perceptions of another's empathy
may be his or her global impression of, and attitudes toward, that person.

While the effects of empathic responding have received little
attention, some consequences are known. Adams, Schvaneveldt, and
Jenson (1979) found empathic responding related to social competence.
Harrigan and Rosenthal's (1983) findings suggest that physicians who
behave empathically may have better rapport with their patients. Shapiro
et al. (1969) have demonstrated that people are more likely to
selfdisclose to their parents and friends when they are perceived as
empathic. Murphy and Rowe (1977) found faciliative interviewees
within a counseling analogue better able to induce suggestibility than
nonfaciliative interviewees. Woodall and Hill (1982), however, found no
relationship between perceived empathy and the degree to which
subjects took a task-oriented (versus a relationship-oriented) leadership
style within small college classes. More research is needed before the
correlates and effects of empathic responding are understood. The more

fundamental issue of how empathic responding relates to other aspects of empathy also needs clarification.

The predominant concern of the discussion up to this point has been with quantitative aspects of individuals' responses. However, people's responses to others also vary qualitatively. Of particular importance is the extent to which people adjust their mode of responding to fulfill situational and interpersonal demands. At least two constructs have been proposed to account for individual differences in communication adaptation: Snyder's *self-monitoring construct* and Hart and Burks's *rhetorical sensitivity* construct.

## SELF-MONITORING

Snyder (1974, 1979) proposes that people vary in their tendencies to monitor their verbal and nonverbal behaviors and to adapt these behaviors to the requirements of social situations. The high self-monitor asks, "Who does this situation want me to be and how can I be that person?" (Snyder, 1979). To such an individual, all the world is a stage and he or she is merely a player. As such, self-monitoring individuals carefully, deliberately, and strategically construct images consistent with and appropriate to the contexts in which they find themselves. Thus high self-monitors are extremely sensitive to situational cues, their presentation of self, and the behavior of others. Low self-monitors, on the other hand, ask, "Who am I and how can I be me in this situation?" (Snyder, 1979). These individuals have less developed self-presentation skills. Their behavior is controlled primarily by internal factors such as their values, attitudes, and beliefs. In short, they "tell it like it is," or at least like they think it is (Buss & Briggs, 1984).

Snyder (1974) has developed a self-monitoring scale for assessing these individual differences. The instrument consists of 25 items which address the extent to which people engage in, and are effective at, impression management within social situations. Examples of scale items include, "I can look anyone in the eye and tell a lie (if for a right end)" and "In different situations and with different people, I often act like very different persons." Recent analyses of the psychometric properties of the self-monitoring scale indicate that it is not unifactorial. Briggs, Cheek, and Buss (1980) found the scale to be decomposable into three factors: *acting, extroversion,* and *other-directedness.* Gabrenya and Arkin (1980) obtained a four-factor solution in their analysis of the instrument. These factors were: *theatrical acting ability, sociability/ social anxiety, other-directedness,* and *speaking ability.* Taken together, the results of these two investigations suggest that Snyder's self-monitoring scale assesses at least three components of response adaptation: acting abilities, other-directedness, and social activity.

Research is generally supportive of the proposition that the social behavior of high self-monitors is guided by situational cues, while the behavior of low self-monitors is directed by internal dispositions, attitudes, values, and beliefs. Several investigators have found, for example, that correlations between attitudes and behavior are much stronger for low self-monitors than for high self-monitors (Ajzen, Timko, & White, 1982; Bercherer & Richard, 1978; Snyder & Swann, 1976; Snyder & Tanke, 1976). Other studies have also demonstrated the importance of situation to high self-monitors. For example, the human tendency to link one's own behavior to situational cues and other people's behavior to their personalities is much stronger for high self-monitors than for low self-monitors. High self-monitors also show less consistency in their behavior across situations (Snyder & Monson, 1975). It is probably not surprising, then, that the personalities of high self-monitors are not judged as consistently by others as the personalities of low self-monitors (Lippo & Mash, 1981).

Norms of reciprocal responding may also be more strongly endorsed by high self-monitors. Shaffer, Smith, and Tomarelli (1982) found that high self-monitors are much more likely to reciprocate the intimacy, emotionality, and descriptive content levels of a confederate's self-disclosures than are low self-monitors. High self-monitors also report that their conversational behavior is guided by their partners' behavior more so than low self-monitors, and the former may be more concerned about behaving in a socially appropriate manner. For instance, they are more likely to modify their messages to be consistent with the attitudes held by their auditors (McCann & Hancock, 1983) and may be more strongly influenced by social consensus (Kulik & Tayler, 1981; Rarick, Soldow, & Geizer, 1976). Even more basic is the preference of high self-monitors for social situations with clearly defined, "readable" characteristics. In contrast, low self-monitors prefer social situations consistent with their personalities (Snyder & Gangestad, 1982).

The need of high self-monitors to adapt to situational constraints is also demonstrated by their pursuit of social knowledge. High self-monitors, relative to low self-monitors, tend to recall more information about individuals with whom they anticipate interaction (Berscheid, Graziano, Monson, & Dermer, 1976; but see Douglas, 1983), will make greater use of information obtained in their conversations when selecting responses to others' communications (Douglas, 1983), are more likely to make use of available social comparison information (Snyder, 1974), are more aware of the impressions they make on others (Lippa, 1978; Tobey & Tunnell, 1981), and are more inclined to purchase information about another individual at personal cost when preparing a fabrication (Elliott, 1979). High and low self-monitors may also differ in the kinds of social information they find useful when anticipating interaction with another individual. Berger and Douglas (1981) had individuals evaluate the informativeness of pictures of a target person with whom they either did or did not anticipate interaction. High self-monitors had a preference for pictures showing the individual in informal situations, while low self-monitors found slides of the target within formal situations more informative. If informal situations provide more useful information for predicting others' behavior, as Berger and Douglas suggest, then high self-monitors' preferences reflect a greater level of social perceptiveness.

Evidence also suggests that high self-monitors are more socially competent than low self-monitors. They have broader communication response repertoires (Douglas, 1983), are better able to generate communication responses likely to facilitate friendly interaction (Douglas, 1984), have more sophisticated scripts for initial interactions (Douglas, 1984), and possess richer cognitive constructs for prototypic examples of various personality traits (Snyder & Cantor, 1980). Self-monitoring is also positively related to knowledge of communication strategies for generating liking, and to the likelihood of using such strategies (Bell & Daly, 1984). Self-monitoring may also be positively related to the ability to deceive others without detection (Elliott, 1979; but see Kraut & Poe, 1980), especially when given the opportunity to rehearse these deceptions (Miller, deTurck, & Kalbfleisch, 1983), and to the ability to detect the deceptions of others (Brandt, Miller, & Hocking, 1980; Geizer & Rarick, 1977).

Studies have also shown that high self-monitors, relative to low self-monitors, exhibit higher rates of the involvement behaviors discussed earlier. Dabbs, Evans, Hopper, and Purvis (1980), for instance, found that conversations between high self-monitors moved at a faster pace than conversations between low self-monitors. Dyads composed of high self-monitors exhibited shorter speaking turns and more interruptive simultaneous speech. Such dyads did not, however, engage in more eye contact or have a higher congruence of vocal behaviors in comparison to low self-monitoring dyads. In a second study, Dabbs et al. found that high self-monitors talked more than low self-monitors. The authors suggest that the conversational role of low self-monitors is usually that of listener, while high self-monitors may enact a speaker role. Ickes and Barnes (1977) found high self-monitors more likely to initiate conversation sequences and to be perceived as having a greater need to talk and to be directive.

Danheiser and Graziano (1982) examined motives for prosocial behavior in conjunction with self-monitoring. They found high self-monitors more cooperative in a prisoner's dilemma game when they believed that future contact with their opponent would occur. In contrast, the level of cooperation of low self-monitors did not vary as a function of beliefs about the possibility of future contact with opponents. The authors suggest that cooperation may be motivated by altruism for low self-monitors and by selfishness for high self-monitors.

High self-monitors are also more expressive and have greater control over their expressive behavior. Lippa (1976, 1978) found high self-monitors more expressive than low self-monitors. They used more eye contact, talked for longer periods of time, and were judged by others as more friendly, outgoing, extroverted, and relaxed than their low self-monitoring counterparts. Snyder (1974) found self-monitoring to be related to people's acting abilities. High self-monitors, in comparison to low self-monitors, were better able to encode specific emotional states. Indeed, Snyder found that professional stage actors scored considerably higher on the self-monitoring scale than nonactors.

Studies examining the relationship of self-monitoring to other dispositions have found it to be associated with constructs indicative of high levels of social activity and social sensitivity. Self-monitoring correlates positively with extroversion, sociability, public self-consciousness, and nonshyness (Pilkonis, 1977) and is inversely related to depression (Rahaim, Waid, Kennelly, & Stricklin, 1980). Briggs et al. (1980) examined the correlations between three factors of the self-monitoring scale (acting, extroversion, and other-directedness) and measures of sociability, shyness, self-esteem, public self-consciousness, and private self-consciousness. Extroversion was most strongly related to nonshyness, sociability, and self-esteem. Other-directedness correlated most strongly with self-esteem and nonshyness. Acting was not strongly related to any of these other measures.

Snyder and Simpson (1984) examined the relationship of self-monitoring to aspects of people's relational involvement. High self-monitors were found to be more willing to terminate current dating relationships than low self-monitors in favor of other potential partners and less likely to engage in exclusive dating with one person. Taken together, the results suggest that self-monitoring tendencies are inversely related to relational longevity.

Several investigations of the social consequences of self-monitoring have been undertaken. Furnham (1981) found that low self-monitors attributed more self-monitoring to liked individuals than to themselves, while high self-monitors attributed less self-monitoring to liked individuals than to themselves. Thus the effects of self-monitoring on interpersonal attraction may depend on one's own level of self-monitoring. Sypher and Sypher (1983) examined the relationship of self-monitoring to self-perceived communication effectiveness, job level, and self-perceptions of persuasive abilities in a sample of insurance company employees. Self-monitoring had small to moderate correlations with all three variables. In further analyses, these scholars found the extroversion and acting factors of the self-monitoring scale to be strongly related to these three outcome measures; the acting factor had only a weak relationship with job level. Finally, Bell and Daly (1985) have found a strong correlation between the extroversion factor of the self-monitoring scale and a measure of loneliness.

## RHETORICAL SENSITIVITY

Hart and Burks (1972) have recognized the importance of response adaptability in advancing the construct of rhetorical sensitivity. The prototypical rhetorically sensitive person cherishes a "rhetorical style of thought" that "champions tentativeness over rigidity" (Hart, Carlson, & Eadie, 1980). Such an individual is able and willing to be "an undulating, fluctuating entity, always unsure, always guessing, continually weighing" communicative alternatives (Hart & Burks, 1972, p. 91). Hart and Burks outline five central characteristics of rhetorically sensitive people. First, rhetorical sensitives accept their personal complexity by recognizing that they embody a number of social selves, only a subset of which deserve "social visibility" at any particular time. Second, rhetorical sensitives avoid communication rigidity; they do not value consistency for its own sake. Third, such individuals are interaction-conscious, as opposed to self- or other-focused. Fourth, rhetorical sensitives have a sense for the communicability of ideas. Thy realize that "not all ideas and feelings are grist for our interpersonal mills" (Hart et al., 1980, p. 2) and that "some ideas (no matter how phrased) are situationally bereft of rhetorical impact" (Hart & Burks, 1972, p. 85). Fifth, rhetorical sensitives tolerate inventional searching by the self and others. In recognizing that ideas and feelings are distinct from the manner in which they are expressed, they appreciate the fact that "there are probably as many ways of making an idea clear as there are people" (Hart & Burks, 1972, p. 88).

Darnell and Brockriede (1976) have extended the rhetorical sensitivity construct by identifying two types of rhetorical *in*sensitivity. *Noble selves* are individuals who "see any variation from their personal norms as hypocritical, as a denial of integrity, as a cardinal sin," while *rhetorical reflectors* "have no selves to call their own. For each person and for each situation they present a new self" (Darnell & Brockriede, 1976, pp. 176, 178).

It is useful to contrast rhetorical sensitivity with self-monitoring. The two constructs converge in that both pay tribute to the value of flexibility and strategy in social interaction. The constructs diverge at several points. Most notably, the rhetorical sensitivity construct is primarily concerned with people's verbal behavior while the self-monitoring construct gives attention to both verbal and nonverbal behaviors. Thus the self-monitor is an impression manager while the rhetorically sensitive individual is, more narrowly, a message manager. Second, the constructs endorse different (indeed, competing) behaviors as "social competence." Snyder's writings indicate a view of competence in which the socially skilled person is one who "becomes" what situations require and tells others what they want to hear. As such, the high self-monitor is most like the rhetorical reflector, at least at the conceptual level. The low self-monitor is most akin to the noble self; both "tell it like it is." In contrast, Hart and his colleagues seem to prefer a view of competence in which the socially skilled individual is one who is "constantly walking an interpersonal tightrope" (Hart et al., 1980, p. 2) by carefully balancing the needs of the self and others and the requirements of the situation. Empirically, self-monitoring has little relationship with rhetorical sensitivity, noble selfness, or rhetorical reflectiveness (Hart et al., 1980).

In 1980, Hart et al. reported the results of a program of research designed to develop a self-report measure of rhetorical sensitivity and insensitivity. The final product of these investigations was a 40-item instrument dubbed the RHETSEN. Each item on the RHETSEN makes a statement about the desirability of self-expression (e.g., "It is best to hide one's true feelings in order to avoid hurting others," "When conversing, you should tell others what they want to hear," and "A person who speaks his or her gut feelings is to be admired"). Respondents indicate how often each statement is true (response options: Almost always true, frequently true, sometimes true, infrequently true, and almost never true). The rhetorically sensitive response is assumed to be "sometimes true." Other responses indicate varying degrees of rhetorical sensitivity, rhetorical reflectiveness, and noble selfness. Most items are keyed in three different ways to derive scores for each of the three constructs. Though the reliability and validity of the RHETSEN has not been extensively examined, findings to date suggest validity. Hart et al. (1980), for instance, found the abilities of nursing students to correlate positively with rhetorically sensitive attitudes. These scholars also administered the RHETSEN with a battery of other measures to assess discriminant validity. All correlations with the RHETSEN were small, suggesting that the construct is not redundant with existing constructs. In particular, the correlation between rhetorical sensitivity and self-monitoring, while significant, was trivial (.15). The conceptual implications of this low correlation deserve elaboration in future research.

Hart et al. (1980) undertook a national survey of rhetorical sensitivity to derive an understanding of the "sociology of interpersonal communication." Results suggest that rhetorical sensitivity is higher among males, academically competitive people, the financially well-to-do, those from the professional (as opposed to labor) class, and those low in ethnic identification. Noble selves were more likely to be single, Democratic in political affiliation, and "humanistic." They were also more likely to come from the eastern United States, cities, large families, poorer families, ethnic groups, and nonmainstream Protestant religions. Rhetorical reflectors were more likely to be female, non-Jewish, over 21, nonsingle, academically noncompetitive, conservative Protestants, well acculturated, and churchgoers. Rhetorical reflectors were usually not from the eastern part of the United States, the labor class, or ethnic groups.

Cahn and Shulman (1980) examined the relationship of rhetorical sensitivity to leadership effectiveness and rank within a sample of U.S. National Guard officers, sergeants, and enlisted men. Rhetorical sensitivity was unrelated to leadership effectiveness but positively related to rank. The latter finding was assumed to reflect the greater role complexity found at higher levels of organizational hierarchies.

Eadie and Paulson (1984) examined the relationship of communicator style and communication competence to rhetorical sensitivity, noble selfness, and rhetorical reflectors. They found that noble selves were perceived as more impression-leaving, dominant, and unfriendly than rhetorically sensitive people and rhetorical reflectors. Noble selves were perceived as competent communicators only in a one-up communication situation. They scored considerably lower in communication competence than both rhetorically sensitive subjects and rhetorical reflectors in symmetrical and one-down situations. This pattern of results was interpreted in terms of noble selves' need to exert control over others and their lack of empathy. Ironically, the results also suggest that noble selves may be more rhetorically creative in situations of a nonintimate nature. In addition, Eadie and Paulson found rhetorical sensitives and reflectors to be distinguishable on several communication styles. Rhetorical reflectors were perceived as more precise and impression-leaving than rhetorical sensitives but less dominant, open, and friendly. Reflectors were also found, in a manner consistent with theory, to be most competent in one-down communication situations. Rhetorically sensitive people were perceived as quite competent in one-up, one-down, and symmetrical situations. This finding should be expected given the "interaction consciousness" of rhetorical sensitives. Moreover, rhetorical sensitives were more competent than noble selves and rhetorical reflectors in symmetrical communication situations.

As this review suggests, the rhetorical sensitivity construct has received considerable theoretical development but little empirical investigation. The number of published studies on this topic is very small indeed.

## LONELINESS

The topic of loneliness, while certainly not isomorphic with social involvement, is nonetheless relevant to it. Scholars frequently suggest that the experience of loneliness signifies deficient levels of social involvement. Young (1982, p. 380), for example, defines loneliness as "a response to the absence of important social reinforcements." Gordon (1976, p. 26) believes that loneliness is "a feeling of deprivation caused by the lack of certain kinds of human contact." Flanders (1982, p. 170) considers loneliness to be "an adaptive feedback mechanism for bringing the individual from a current lack stress state to a more optimal range of human contact in quantity or form." Moreover, clinicians often prescribe increased involvement as a potent antidote to loneliness. Rook and Peplau (1982), for example, give attention to intervention strategies designed to help lonely clients develop relationships and expand their social networks.

Without question, loneliness is a ubiquitous and detrimental societal problem. Surveys indicate that 10-20% of the general public is frequently and severely lonely (Asher, Hymel, & Renshaw, 1984; Bradburn, 1969; Brennan & Auslander, 1979; Cutrona, 1982; Ostrov & Offer, 1980; Rubenstein & Shaver, 1980; Tunstall, 1967). The effects of loneliness can be considerable. The condition is defined by psychological distress that takes the form of a painful yearning for other people (Hartog, 1980). Loneliness is associated with depression and anxiety (Anderson, Horowitz, & French, 1983; Baum, 1982; Gerson & Perlman,

1979; Hojat, 1982; Russell, Cutrona, Rose, & Yurko, 1984; Russell, Peplau, & Cutrona, 1980; Russell, Peplau, & Ferguson, 1978; Weeks, Michela, Peplau, & Bragg, 1980), low self-esteem (Goswick & Jones, 1981; Jones, Freemon, & Goswick, 1981; Russell et al., 1980), general emotional health (Baum, 1982), various dimensions of psychopathology (Corty & Young, 1981; Goswick & Jones, 1981; Hojat, 1982), and feelings of abandonment, emptiness, hopelessness, isolation, self-enclosement, life dissatisfaction, unhappiness, awkwardness, restlessness, and boredom (Russell et al., 1980; Russell et al., 1978). Researchers have linked loneliness to adolescent truancy and behavior problems (Brennan & Auslander, 1979), susceptibility to illness (Lynch, 1977), poor health and stress (Rubenstein & Shaver, 1980), dropping out of college (Lamont, 1979), alcoholism/drug abuse (Bell, 1956; Lamont, 1979; Newman, 1971), and suicide (Lamont, 1979; Newman, 1971; Sermat, 1980; Wenz, 1977).

## The Nature of Loneliness

Perlman and Peplau (1982) have discerned eight theoretical approaches to loneliness in the literature. Although each perspective focuses on different aspects of the problem of loneliness, several important points of convergence can be found among these approaches. First, loneliness is assumed to be an outcome of deficiencies in an individual's relationships with others. These deficiencies, which are experienced as aversive states such as unhappiness and dissatisfaction, may be of a social and/or emotional nature (Jong-Gierveld & Raadschelders, 1982; Russell et al., 1984; Weiss, 1973). Second, there is agreement that loneliness cannot be equated with social isolation. As Peplau and Perlman (1982) succinctly state, "people can be alone without being lonely, or lonely in a crowd" (p. 3). Third, the experience of loneliness is influenced by a number of cognitive factors. For example, there is some support for the proposition that loneliness begins when an individual perceives a discrepancy between the kinds of soical relationships he or she has and the kinds of relationships he or she desires (Cutrona & Peplau, 1979; Paloutzian, Janigian, & Van Mouwerik, 1982; Sermat, 1978). Lonely and nonlonely people may also differ in attributional style. The lonely may be more likely to ascribe interpersonal failure to character defects, as opposed to controllable patterns of behavior (Anderson et al., 1983; Anderson & Arnoult, 1985).

Fourth, there is consensus among researchers on the need to distinguish short-term bouts of loneliness from chronic states. Although short-term and chronic loneliness are often discussed as discrete categories, they more accurately reflect endpoints on a continuum (Suedfeld, 1982, p. 50). There is some evidence that short-term loneliness may motivate social behavior, while chronic loneliness may be associated with social apathy (Gerson & Perlman, 1979). Short-term and chronic loneliness may also have different precipitating causes. Short-term loneliness is most likely to be brought about by events external to the individual, such as divorce, the death of a loved one, and mobility (Young, 1982). Factors likely to lead to chronic loneliness include personal characteristics such as a lack of social skills, negative dispositional tendencies, physical handicaps, and social stigmas.

## Measuring Loneliness

By virtually all definitions, loneliness is a person-centered construct. The investigation of individual differences such as loneliness requires measures of the condition. Until recently, adequate measures of loneliness have not been available. The major consequence was a corresponding paucity of empirical research (Peplau & Perlman, 1982; Russell, 1982). Although several graduate students developed measures of loneliness in the 1960s, the first scale was not published until 1978. In that year, Russell and his colleagues (Russell et al., 1978) published the UCLA Loneliness Scale. Two years later, this scale was modified slightly and the Revised UCLA Loneliness Scale was born (Russell et al., 1980). In subsequent years, other self-report measures of loneliness have been developed (Asher et al., 1984; Jong-Gierveld, 1978; Paloutzian & Ellison, 1982; Schmidt & Sermat, 1983; Young, 1982; see Russell, 1982, for a review of the various operationalizations; see Borys & Perlman, 1985, for an examination of the effects of gender on self-reports of loneliness). However, the vast majority of investigations of loneliness have utilized the UCLA Loneliness Scale (hereafter referenced as the UCLALS) in its original or revised format. This scale consists of 20 items that describe a feeling conceptually related to the experience of loneliness (e.g., "People are around me but not with me"). Respondents indicate the frequency with which they experience the feeling described (response options: never, rarely, sometimes, often). Scores on the earlier version of this scale have been shown to be very stable over time (Russell et al., 1978). Thus the instrument may be biased toward the assessment of chronic loneliness.

At this point, studies of social involvement and loneliness will be examined. The review is organized around five subsections: social contacts and activities, social inhibition, self-disclosure, self-focus, and interpersonal judgments. For the sake of convenience, the specific measure of loneliness employed in these studies will be mentioned only when it is *not* the UCLALS.

## Social Contacts and Activities

Perhaps the most basic measures of social involvement are those pertaining to the qualitative and quantitative nature of individuals' social networks. The assessment of these networks has taken two forms within the loneliness literature. Several scholars have examined the correlation between loneliness and recollections of past social contacts. This approach has been criticized on the grounds that people are not able to produce accurate recalls of the frequency and nature of their interactions (Wheeler, Reis, & Nezlek, 1983). Indeed, in one study of conversational memory, people were able to recall only 10% of the ideas within a dyadic exchange after a lapse of a mere five minutes (Stafford & Daly, 1984). The second, presumably more reliable, assessment approach is the self-monitoring method in which subjects record the details of their conversations in interaction diaries.

Several investigations of loneliness and perceived/recollected social contact have been published to date. Russell et al. (1980) asked students to estimate how frequently they had participated in various solitary behaviors during the two weeks prior to the study. Loneliness correlated positively with students' recalls of the amount of time they spent alone, the number of times they had eaten alone, the number of times they were alone on a weekend night, the number of social activities they participated in with friends, and the number of close friends they felt they had. Williams and Solano (1983) found no relationship between loneliness and number of "best friends" for a group of college students. The best friends of lonely subjects were just as likely to reciprocate these nominations as were the best friends of nonlonely subjects. However, lonely subjects and their best friends thought these relationships were of low intimacy relative to the ratings of nonlonely subjects and their best friends. Williams and Solano also found no difference between lonely and nonlonely people in the number of "friends" they believed they had. However, the "friends" of lonely people were less likely to return this friendship nomination than were the friends of nonlonely people. Rubenstein (1979; Rubenstein & Shaver, 1980) undertook a newspaper survey of loneliness in three northeastern U.S. cities. Respondents' scores on the New York University Loneliness Scale had very small but significant correlations with the frequency of seeing close friends and the number of hours per week spent socializing. Hoover, Skuja, and Cosper (1979) found trivial but positive correlations between college students' ratings of loneliness (the nature of the instrument was not reported) and two measures of aloneness—time alone and time studying alone. A small inverse relationship was found for dating frequency.

Three empirical investigations of the relationship of loneliness to social contact have been reported for samples of elderly people. Arling (1976) compared the relative importance of involvement with family, neighbors, and friends to the loneliness of over four hundred elderly widows. Loneliness was measured with a single-item, three-point scale. Family involvement was conceptualized as close proximity to other family members. Involvement with friends and neighbors was operationalized in terms of frequency of visits. The reported absence of loneliness was more strongly related to involvement with friends than to involvement with children, other relatives, or neighbors. Kivett (1979) investigated discriminators of loneliness in a sample of rural elderly adults. Subjects reported their level of loneliness on a one-item, three-point scale (often lonely, sometimes lonely, almost never lonely) and made ratings on a number of variables thought to be predisposing factors to loneliness for older people. Among the more important discriminators were three measures of social contact: frequency of telephoning, organizational activity, and the availability of a confidant. The most important discriminator was transportation problems. Presumably, difficulties in transportation could increase the social isolation of older people, especially in a rural setting. Finally, Rook (1984) studied the relative impact of positive and negative social involvement on a group of widowed women aged 60 or more. She found that the number of supportive ties these women reported was significantly related to loneliness. However, when skewness in her social ties measure was corrected via a data transformation, this significant relationship disappeared.

Three studies using the diary method have been undertaken. The obtained correlations between loneliness and social integration for these studies have usually been higher (range: .30 to .60) than for those studies utilizing recollections of past social contacts. This may be due to the greater reliability of the diary method. Jones (1981) had college students with known loneliness scores complete a brief questionnaire for every conversation they participated in of at least one minute in length over several days. For female subjects, loneliness correlated positively with the proportion of interactions with acquaintances and the diversity of people with whom conversations were held. Loneliness was negatively related to the proportion of interactions with family members. Among male subjects, loneliness was positively related to the proportion of interactions with strangers, the diversity of interaction partners, and the number of people with whom interaction took place. Loneliness correlated inversely with the proportion of interactions with family and friends and the rated emotional quality of the communication.

Corty and Young (1981) had college students complete Bradley's (1969) Loneliness Scale and keep a diary of every interaction they participated in over the course of one week. Participants also made ratings of the level of social support they received from friends and family. Loneliness was negatively related to the number of interactions for males, but not for females. Loneliness was inversely related to social support from family for both males and females, and to support from friends for males. In a replication study, 56 male college students completed the UCLALS and the measures included in the initial study. In this second investigation, loneliness scores on the Bradley measure were unrelated to frequency of social contact but significantly correlated with perceived social support from family and friends. Scores on the UCLALS were also unrelated to social contact and significantly related to support from family and friends.

Wheeler et al. (1983) had college students complete the Rochester Interaction Record for every conversation in which they were involved of at least 10 minutes in length for a two-week period. For male subjects, loneliness was negatively related to the number of interactions per day with females, the average amount of time per day spent interacting with females, the percentage of interactions with females, and the average length of interactions with females. Loneliness was positively related to proportion of interactions with other males. For female participants, loneliness was inversely related to the percentage of interactions that were with females and positively related to the number of interactions with males. Loneliness was also inversely related to the amount of time spent each day talking with females and the number of interactions per day with females. The pattern of relationships suggests that female interactional partners may be better equipped to meet the social and relational needs of both males and females.

Several investigators have examined the relationship of loneliness to media use. It has been suggested that lonely people may use mass media as a surrogate companion (e.g., Austin, 1985). Conversely, Flanders (1982) has argued that excessive media use may lead to loneliness by displacing time that might otherwise be spent in social contact with others. Rubenstein and Shaver (1982) have found that some individuals cope with loneliness by turning to reading, television, movies, and music. Perlman et al. (1978) found higher levels of TV viewing by lonely senior citizens than by nonlonely seniors. Hoover et al. (1979) found no relationship between loneliness and TV viewing in a sample of college students. Austin (1985) found no relationship between loneliness and the frequency of moviegoing, magazine reading, book reading, or TV viewing in a group of college students. Counter to prediction, Austin found small but significant *inverse* relationships between loneliness and newspaper readership and radio listening.

## Social Inhibition

Several investigators have explored the relationship of loneliness to dispositional measures of social-communicative inhibition. These investigations provide compelling evidence that lonely people tend toward communication avoidance. That loneliness is strongly related to social passivity is well illustrated by a study comparing the interpersonal problems of lonely and nonlonely people. Horowitz and French (1979) found that lonely people report difficulty making friends, introducing themselves at social gatherings, initiating social activity, and being friendly and sociable.

Four studies have examined the relationship of loneliness, as measured with the UCLALS, and various measures of shyness within samples of college students (Bell, in press; Jones et al., 1981; Maroldo, 1981; Russell et al., 1978). The obtained correlations for these studies ranged from .45 to .53. In a particularly insightful study, Cheek and Busch (1981) administered the UCLALS and Cheek and Buss's (1981) shyness scale to almost one hundred college students at the beginning and end of a new semester. Shy people reported significantly more loneliness than nonshy people for both time periods. However, shy individuals showed a significantly greater decline in loneliness from Time 1 to Time 2 than did nonshy people. Loneliness has also been shown to be positively associated with other aspects of social inhibition, including introversion (Bell & Daly, 1985; Russell et al., 1980), unassertiveness (Bell & Daly, 1985; Jones et al., 1981), low social adaptability (Hansson & Jones, 1981), affiliative tendencies, sensitivity to rejection, and social risk taking (Russell et al., 1980).

Several studies have investigated the relationship of loneliness to various dimensions of social anxiety and distress, including self-consciousness, social anxiety, and communication apprehension. Jones et al. (1981) found a moderate correlation between loneliness and public and private self-consciousness (women only) in a sample of college students. Bell and Daly (1985) found significant, positive correlations between loneliness and the Personal Report of Communication Apprehension (PRCA; McCroskey, 1978), as well as a measure of social anxiety (Fenigstein, Scheier, & Buss, 1975). Zakahi and Duran (1982) found that the PRCA did not account for any of the variance in the loneliness scores of a group of college students above and beyond that accounted for by a measure of communication competence. Unfortunately, Zakahi and Duran did not report the bivariate correlation between the PRCA and loneliness. Jones et al. (1981) found a moderate correlation between Fenigstein et al.'s (1975) social anxiety measure and loneliness.

## Self-Disclosure

Several observers of social behavior have given attention to self-disclosure and loneliness. Sullivan (1953) believed that loneliness is linked to social skills deficits brought about by poor interaction with parents. The effect is that the child fails to develop chums with whom intimate information can be disclosed. This failure to meet adolescent intimacy needs is assumed to cause loneliness in later life. Rogers (1973) observed that loneliness results when individuals, fearing rejection, supplant open communication with social facades. Through self-disclosure, Rogers believes that people can be made aware of their loneliness and then rescue themselves from it. Jourard (1968) has suggested that lonely individuals are characterized by a willingness to reveal their "real selves" to others. More recently, Derlega and Margulis (1982) have developed a privacy model of loneliness in which self-disclosure is a central component.

Research to date, while not always consistent, is generally supportive of the hypothesized relationship between low self-disclosure and loneliness. For instance, when Sermat and Smyth (1973; see also Sermat, 1980) asked 400 individuals to describe their loneliness, 75% of the respondents "spontaneously attributed their loneliness experience to difficulties or breakdowns in personal communication with other people" (p. 306). Other studies have also demonstrated the importance of confidants in the prevention and alleviation of loneliness. As noted earlier, the availability of a confidant was found by Kivett (1979) to discriminate groups of low-lonely, moderate-lonely, and high-lonely senior citizens. Likewise, Perlman, Gerson, and Spinner (1978) obtained a negative relationship between loneliness and the availability of a confidant in a sample of elderly people. They also found that loneliness was correlated with a desire to *receive* more personal information from other people.

Chelune et al. (1980) asked female college students to complete the Self-Disclosure Situations Survey (SDSS) and the UCLA Loneliness Scale and then participate in a role-playing exercise designed to assess social competence. Two scores are derived from the SDSS: dispositional self-disclosure and disclosure flexibility. The flexibility score, which is based on a comparison of subjects' responses to normative standards, reflects people's willingness to disclose appropriately. Greater loneliness was related to lower dispositional disclosures. The results also indicate that among medium disclosers, loneliness was highest for those individuals who did not disclose normatively. Thus the disclosures of the lonely women in this study were less intimate and less appropriate than the disclosures of the nonlonely subjects. However, peer and observer ratings of social skills, while positively related to dispositional willingness to self-disclose, were unrelated to loneliness.

Jones et al. (1981) found no significant relationship between loneliness and Jourard's (1971) measure of self-disclosure. Solano, Batten, and Parish (1982), however, obtained significant correlations ranging from −.33 to −.65 between loneliness and several subscales of the Jourard measure. They found a significant inverse relationship between current feelings of loneliness and past self-disclosure with an opposite-sex friend for both males and females. For females, there was a significant negative relationship between loneliness and past disclosures to a same-sex friend. The results for the self-disclosure ratings of the male subjects on the six topics revealed a negative correlation between loneliness and intimate disclosures about personality to a close female friend. For the female subjects, there were significant negative correlations between loneliness and disclosures to a close male friend about their attitudes, tastes, work and study, and personality. Notable correlations were also obtained for female respondents' disclosures about attitudes to a close female friend, disclosures about attitudes to their mothers and fathers, and disclosures about work and study to their mothers and fathers.

Berg and Peplau (1982) administered the UCLALS, three self-report measures of self-disclosure, and an androgyny scale to a group of college students. The measures of self-disclosure were the Miller Topic Inventory, a measure of past self-disclosure; the SDSS (Chelune, 1976); and the Openers Scale, a measure of self-disclosure *eliciting* abilities (Miller, Berg, & Archer, 1983). Loneliness did not correlate with any of the self-disclosure measures for male subjects. For women participants, loneliness was related to past disclosure to a same-sex friend, the SDSS, and the openers scale. Bell and Daly (1985) found a small but significant correlation between loneliness and the openness subscale of

Norton's (1978) Communicator Styles Measure. Franzoi and Davis (1985) found a modest inverse correlation between a short version of the UCLALS and the Self-Disclosure Index (Miller et al., 1983) for female high school students, but not for male students. No significant correlations were obtained between loneliness and self-disclosure to mothers or fathers for either sex. The results suggest that high private self-consciousness may facilitate self-disclosure to peers, which in turn leads to feelings of nonloneliness.

In all of these studies, self-disclosure was operationalized via self-reports of typical disclosure behavior. Two studies have examined the relationship of loneliness to self-disclosure within actual interactions. Solano et al. (1982) paired lonely and nonlonely students with a nonlonely "partner" to create dyads. Each dyad was given a list of discussion topics previously scaled for intimacy. Each subject and partner alternatively spoke for one minute on twelve topics. Lonely subjects selected less intimate topics than did nonlonely subjects. There was also evidence that the lonely people may have elicited fewer disclosures from their partners. Also important was the finding that nonlonely people were more disclosing to opposite-sex partners than to same-sex partners, which is consistent with the self-disclosure norm for college students (Davis, 1976), while lonely subjects self-disclosed more to same-sex partners. Lonely subjects were rated as less well known by their partners than were nonlonely subjects. In the diary study of Wheeler et al. (1983), described earlier, loneliness was strongly and inversely related to subjects' ratings of conversation "meaningfulness."

Expressive communication is certainly not restricted to verbal channels. People also divulge information about their feelings, reactions, and emotional states via nonverbal cues. Gerson and Perlman (1979) examined differences in the nonverbal expressiveness of nonlonely people, chronically lonely people, and situationally (recently) lonely people. Chronic loneliness and situational loneliness were measured with modified versions of the UCLALS. Expressiveness was measured with a slide-viewing technique developed by Buck (1978). The situationally lonely were more expressive than the chronically lonely and nonlonely subjects. The last two groups did not differ in expressiveness. Gerson and Perlman (1979) suggest that situational loneliness may be motivationally arousing. These results were not replicated in a study by Grace, Joshi, and Roberge (1983) of nonverbal expressiveness in separated and divorced women. No significant correlations were found between nonverbal expressiveness and measures of chronic or short-term loneliness.

## Self-Focus

The issue of whether lonely people are self-focused in their conversations with other people has received considerable discussion. Jones et al. (1982) note that lonely people seem to interact "with less awareness of or concern for others, with less responsiveness, and in a more self-focused or self-absorbed manner" (p. 685). Peplau and Perlman (1982) also believe that "the behavior of lonely people may reflect a greater self-focus than that of nonlonely people" (p. 12). Rook and Peplau (1982) suggest that lonely people may "focus excessively on themselves and their internal experiences" (p. 354).

There have been five investigations of loneliness and self-focus. Goswick and Jones (1981) obtained a moderate correlation between a self-report measure of dispositional self-focus in interactions and loneliness. Bell and Daly (1985) found significant, inverse relationships between loneliness and two subscales of the Interaction Involvement Scale (Cegala et al., 1982), responsiveness and attentiveness.

Three studies have examined loneliness and self-focus through content analyses of actual conversations. Jones, Hobbs, and Hockenbury (1982) paired lonely and nonlonely people with opposite-sex partners and instructed them to discuss things that attracted them to persons of the opposite sex. Their conversations were videotaped and coded for several partner-attention behaviors. People in the high lonely group made fewer partner references, were more likely to change the topic of discussion, asked fewer questions, and made fewer partner-attention statements. In a second study, Jones et al. (1982) taught partner-attention skills to a group of lonely people who then engaged in conversations with other individuals. Analyses of these conversations revealed that the training led to increased use of these behaviors and to decreases in reported loneliness.

Sloan and Solano (1984) examined the conversational behaviors of 10 lonely and 10 nonlonely males in videotaped interactions with a roommate and a stranger. The results draw a clouded picture of loneliness and self-focus. On the one hand, lonely subjects were less talkative than nonlonely subjects. On the other hand, lonely subjects were more attentive in their verbal behavior when talking with roommates. They used more back-channels (e.g., mmm-hm, oh), asked more questions, and made more statements of interpretation, reflection, and acknowledgment. Given the small sample size, these results should be interpreted with extreme caution.

Bell (in press) explored differences between 60 chronically lonely and 60 nonlonely people on a number of involvement behaviors indicative of self-versus other-focus. Each participant had a 10-minute videotaped conversation with an opposite-sex partner. Afterward, subjects recalled as many details of their conversations as possible. Lonely subjects had lower rates of talkativeness, interruptions, and, unlike subjects in the Sloan and Solano (1984) study, vocal back-channels. They also recalled fewer details of their conversations than did their non-lonely counterparts. Partners also rated lonely subjects as less involved than nonlonely subjects.

### Interpersonal Judgments

As the preceding review indicates, there is strong support for the proposition that lonely and nonlonely people vary systematically in their level of social involvement. It is thus quite surprising that studies to date have only occasionally identified differences in the evaluations others make of lonely and nonlonely individuals. However, loneliness does appear to be related to the tendency to judge others negatively.

Jones et al. (1981) found no differences in how lonely and nonlonely individuals were perceived after brief (15-minute) get-acquainted conversations. Lonely subjects did, however, attribute negative characteristics to their conversational partners and were less attracted to their partners. In another study, Jones et al. (1981) studied the relationship between loneliness and the judgments of students enrolled in human relations classes. Measures of loneliness and interpersonal evaluations were administered on the third class period and on the last day of classes. For the initial test period, a significant inverse relationship was obtained between students' level of loneliness and classmates' evaluations of them. By the last day of class, however, these interpersonal evaluations were unrelated to loneliness. The study suggests that lonely people may make poor initial impressions that they overcome, given an extended period of interaction. Jones, Sansone, and Helm (1983) examined inter-personal judgments in mixed-sex dyads composed of high- and low-lonely college students. Dyads interacted for 15 minutes and then completed a postinteraction inventory. Lonely men were rated more negatively than nonlonely men; no differences in evaluations received were found for lonely and nonlonely females. In terms of judgments given, lonely subjects, relative to nonlonely subjects, rated themselves more negatively and expected to be evaluated more negatively by their partners. The partners of lonely male subjects were also rated more nega-tively than the partners of other subjects. In addition, the lonely subjects were perceived by their partners as more likely to evaluate themselves negatively.

Differences in interpersonal judgments of lonely and nonlonely people have been identified in two studies. Asher, Hymel, and Renshaw (1984) found modest but significant relationships between a scale developed for the assessment of loneliness in children and the socio-metric status of over five hundred third through sixth graders. In Bell's (in press) study of conversational involvement and loneliness, lonely and nonlonely subjects and their partners were asked to make several inter-personal evaluations after generating their memory protocols. While no differences were found between the lonely and nonlonely groups in partners' satisfaction with the conversation, partners of lonely subjects did report less interpersonal attraction, fewer desires for friendship, and less interest in future interaction. Lonely subjects were not perceived as having fewer desires for future interaction than nonlonely subjects. However, lonely males were perceived by partners as having fewer desires for friendship than were lonely females and nonlonely subjects. When subjects' evaluations of partners were examined, lonely subjects reported less satisfaction with their conversations than did nonlonely subjects. Lonely subjects did not report less liking for their partners or fewer desires for future interaction and friendship. They did feel, however, that their partners had fewer interests in future interaction.

The tendency for lonely individuals to expect that they will be seen in a negative light led Jones et al. (1981) to ask whether loneliness is related to a generalized dislike for humanity and society. These scholars had a group of college students complete the UCLALS and several measures of attitudes toward people and the social environment. Loneli-ness was negatively related to acceptance of others, acceptance to others, the belief that the world is just, trust in human nature (women only), altruism, and total favorability toward humanity (men only). Loneliness correlated positively with external locus of control (men only), power-lessness (women only), normlessness (women only), and social isolation. No significant correlation was found for Machiavellianism. However, Bell and Daly (1985) did find a positive relationship between loneliness and Machiavellianism. Interestingly, Machiavellianism was more strong-ly related to loneliness for females than for males, indicating that manipulative behavior may be less negatively sanctioned when coming from men than from women. Hojat (1982) also found positive, though small, relationships between loneliness and external locus of control in two groups of Iranian college students. He also found positive correla-tions between misanthropy, a measure of mistrust and dishonesty (Rosen-berg, 1965), and loneliness in these two groups. Baum (1982) found no significant relationship between loneliness and locus of control in his sample of senior citizens. Finally, Nerviano and Gross (1976) did not find a significant relationship between scores on the Bradley loneliness scale and locus of control in a sample of chronic alcoholic men.

## SUMMARY AND INTEGRATION

This chapter has reviewed several frameworks for the study of social involvement. Studies of the various conceptualizations provide rather consistent evidence that social involvement is associated with a high level of communication activity, social integration, and communication competence.

While there are points of convergence among the perspectives considered, it is unfortunate that investigators operating from each have seldom taken advantage of the insights of the other approaches. The involvement pie has typically been sliced into small pieces (variables) that are then examined without regard to the other slices. A preferred approach would be to consider how these pieces fit together into a coherent whole. It is thus critical that the reviewed bodies of literature be compared and contrasted. *Facet design* provides a useful method for definitionally integrating the literatures discussed in this chapter (Levy, 1981). It also provides a foundation for future research.

A *facet* is an aspect or dimension of a construct on which observations may vary. An inspection of the constructs and research examined in this chapter suggests that observations of social involvement may be distinguished on the basis of at least five fundamental content facets. These facets have been incorporated into a *mapping sentence*, reported in Figure 5.1, which provides a definitional system for classifying (mapping) observations of social involvement.

The first content facet in the mapping sentence, Facet A, discriminates observations of involvement made by subjects under study (A1) from observations of these individuals made by others (A2). A1 observations constitute virtually all of the extant research on interaction involvement, self-monitoring, rhetorical sensitivity, and loneliness. In contrast, most of the research on empathic responding deals with other-judged involvement—with perceived empathy (A2 observations).

The second dimension, represented by Facet B, distinguishes observations of situationally bound social involvement (B1) from observations of dispositional involvement (B2). While the primary concern of this chapter has been with dispositional levels of involvement, a comprehensive understanding of social involvement will necessitate an integration of findings of both situational and dispositional involvement. Indeed, the many investigations of situational social involvement—carried out under

The extent to which person (x) is   (1. self-)    perceived to   (1. situationally)    (1. approach)

                                      **A**

                                      (2. other-)                   (2. dispositionally)    (2. avoid)

                                    **B**          **C**

**D**

others in a  (1. cognitive)    behavioral modality with respect to his/her   (1. interactions)

            (2. affective)                                          **E**   (2. relationships)

            (3. instrumental)

**R**

   (very high)   social involvement.

        to

 →  (very low)

**Figure 5.1: Mapping Sentence for Observations of Social Involvement**

such rubrics as mutual influence, speech accommodation, and communication rhythms—must provide the foundation for studies of dispositional involvement. The research on interaction involvement, self-monitoring, and rhetorical sensitivity is of a dispositional nature. Subjects are assigned scores on the basis of their responses to scales assumed to measure typical patterns of communication behavior. While most of the literature on loneliness has employed the UCLA Loneliness Scale, which has been shown to produce scores that are temporally stable, loneliness has also been examined as a situational (short-term) construct. Empathic responding could conceivably be investigated as a situational or a dispositional construct. One could study situational factors that facilitate emotional involvement between individuals or, conversely, one might examine people's dispositional tendencies to make emotional contact with others.

Facet C, which is taken from Cappella (1982), separates observations of avoidance behaviors from observations of approach behaviors. Cegala's (1981) 18-item interaction involvement scale, for instance, is composed of nine observations of the C1 type and nine observations of the C2 kind. An example of an approach item from the IIS is "I carefully observe how others respond to me during my conversations" (item 4). An example of an avoidance observation from the IIS would be "Often I feel 'unplugged' from the social situation of which I am part; that is, I'm uncertain of my role, others' motives, and what's happening" (item 14). The fact that avoidance observations (i.e., negatively worded items) may be "reversed" in scoring self-report measures of social involvement does not deny the fact that these observations are qualitatively different from approach observations in terms of the frame of reference required of respondents. When researchers sum across these items to construct a more general observation of interaction involvement, it may be fair to say that the resultant value reflects approaching tendencies.

Facet D identifies three forms of behavior through which social involvement may be indicated: cognitive, affective, and instrumental. Each has received consideration in the social involvement literature. Cognitive involvement (D1) encompasses observations of the extent to which an individual mentally approaches or avoids another. For example, Cegala's attentiveness and perceptiveness subscales tap social involvement of a cognitive nature. Affective involvement (D2) refers to the extent to which individuals approach another emotionally. While it was not given much attention in this chapter, a good example of affective involvement would be studies of the vicarious experience of another's emotional state. A second example would be studies of emotional loneliness and isolation. Instrumental involvement (D3) includes observations of overt approach/avoidance actions, examples of which include intercommunicator distance, head nods, and talkativeness. On the basis of Levy's (1981) discussion of these three modes of behavior, we might speculate that Facet D is ordered in terms of involvement strength; cognitive involvement is "weak," affective involvement is of intermediate strength, and instrumental involvement is "strong."

The final facet distinguishes interactional involvement from relational involvement. Of the constructs reviewed in this chapter, only loneliness deals with relational involvement. Interaction involvement, empathic responding, self-monitoring, and rhetorical sensitivity are each concerned with social involvement within interactions. This predominant concern for interaction-level involvement suggests that an understanding of relational involvement may presuppose an understanding of inter-action-level involvement.

On the basis of this discussion, it is possible to represent the various involvement constructs in terms of *structuples*. A structuple shows how each construct fits into the Cartesian set ABCDE, which is defined by the five facets. There are several benefits from such representations. First, these may make evident similarities and differences among the approaches. Second, the identification of missing structuples suggests areas for future inquiry. A consideration of the various constructs led to the assignment of the following struct values for each construct:

| | |
|---|---|
| Short-Term Loneliness—Emotional | A1B1C2D2E2 |
| Short-Term Loneliness—Social | A1B1C2D3E2 |
| Chronic Loneliness—Emotional | A1B2C2D2E2 |
| Chronic Loneliness—Social | A1B2C2D3E2 |
| Interaction Involvement—Attentive | A1B2C1D1E1 |
| Interaction Involvement—Perceptive | A1B2C1D1E1 |
| Interaction Involvement—Responsive | A1B2C1D3E1 |
| Self-Monitoring | A1B2C1D3E1 |
| Rhetorical Sensitivity | A1B2C0D3E1 |
| Empathic Responding | A2B0C1D3E1 |
| Mutual Influence Studies | A2B1C0D3E1 |

An examination of these structuples indicates that attentiveness and perceptiveness are closely related constructs, as are responsiveness and self-monitoring. The classifications suggest that research has been most concerned with self-reports of dispositional levels of instrumental involvement behaviors within interaction. Relatively little attention has been given to involvement within a cognitive or affective modality. Relational involvement has also been given comparatively little attention. These appear to be potentially fruitful areas for future study.

It was not possible to assign values to particular structs for three of the constructs. Rhetorical sensitivity, for example, may lead to approach or avoidance responses. Likewise, mutual influence research has been concerned with both approach and avoidance behaviors. Empathic responding has been conceptualized as both a situational or dispositional construct.

## CONCLUSION

Social involvement is an important individual difference that is inherently communicative. Involvement is a general class of social behavior and a common theme running through many communication constructs that have usually been examined in isolation. Clearly, the topic has received an impressive amount of attention by scholars of social interaction. While the present review suggests that social involvement research is rapidly accelerating, our understanding of involvement is not likely to progress as quickly unless scholars adopt an eclectic outlook on the topic. This chapter has advanced a faceted design for an integrated perspective on social involvement.

## REFERENCES

Adams, G.R., Schvaneveldt, J.D., & Jenson, G.O. (1979). Sex, age and perceived competency as correlates of empathic ability in adolescence. *Adolescence, 14*, 811-818.

Ajzen, I., Timko, C., & White, J.B. (1982). Self-monitoring and the attitude-behavior relation. *Journal of Personality and Social Psychology, 42*, 426-435.

Anderson, C.A., & Arnoult, L.H. (1985). Attributional style and everyday problems in living: Depression, loneliness, and shyness. *Social Cognition, 3*, 16-35.

Anderson, C.A., Horowitz, L. M., & French, R. de (1983). Attributional style of lonely and depressed people. *Journal of Personality and Social Psychology, 45*, 127-136.

Argyle, M., & Cook, M. (1976). *Gaze and mutual gaze.* Cambridge: Cambridge University Press.

Argyle, M., & Dean, J. (1965). Eye contact and affiliation. *Sociometry, 28*, 289-304.

Arling, G. (1976). The elderly widow and her family, neighbors, and friends. *Journal of Marriage and the Family, 38*, 757-768.

Asher, S.R., Hymel, S., & Renshaw, P.D. (1984). Loneliness in children. *Child Development, 55*, 1456-1464.

Austin, B.A. (1985). Loneliness and use of six mass media among college students. *Psychological Reports, 56*, 323-327.

Bahr, H.M., & Harvey, C.D. (1979). Correlates of loneliness among widows bereaved in a mining disaster. *Psychological Reports, 44*, 367-385.

Barnett, M.A. (1984). Perspective taking and empathy in the child's prosocial behavior. In H.E. Sypher & J.L. Applegate (Eds.), *Communication by children and adults*. Beverly Hills, CA: Sage.

Barrett-Lennard, G.T. (1981). The empathy cycle: Refinement of a nuclear concept. *Journal of Counseling Psychology, 28*, 91-100.

Baum, S.K. (1982). Loneliness in elderly persons: A preliminary study. *Psychological Reports, 50*, 1317-1318.

Bell, R.A. (in press). Conversational involvement and loneliness. *Communication Monographs*.

Bell, R.A., & Daly, J.A. (1984). The affinity-seeking function of communication. *Communication Monographs, 51*, 91-115.

Bell, R.A., & Daly, J.A. (1985). Some communicator correlates of loneliness. *Southern Speech Communication Journal, 50*, 121-142.

Bell, R.G. (1956). Alcohol and loneliness. *Journal of Social Therapy, 2*, 171-181.

Bercherer, R.C., & Richard, L. M. (1978). Self-monitoring and consumer behavior. *Journal of Consumer Research, 5*, 159-162.

Berg, J.H., & Peplau, L.A. (1982). Loneliness: The relationship of self-disclosure and androgyny. *Personality and Social Psychology Bulletin, 8*, 624-630.

Berger, C.R., & Douglas, W. (1981). Studies in interpersonal epistemology III: Anticipated interaction, self-monitoring, and observational context selection. *Communication Monographs, 48*, 183-196.

Bergin, A.E., & Suinn, R.M. (1975). Individual psychotherapy and behavior change. *Annual Review of Psychology, 26*, 509-556.

Berscheid, E., Graziano, W., Monson, T., & Dermer, M. (1976). Outcome dependency: Attention, attribution and attraction. *Journal of Personality and Social Psychology, 34*, 978-989.

Borys, S., & Perlman, D. (1985). Gender differences in loneliness. *Personality and Social Psychology, 11*, 63-74.

Bradburn, N. (1969). *The structure of psychological well-being*. Chicago: Aldine.

Bradley, R. (1969). *Measuring loneliness*. Unpublished doctoral dissertation, Washington State University.

Brady, D., Rowe, W., & Smouse, A.D. (1976). Faciliative level and verbal conditioning: A replication. *Journal of Counseling Psychology, 23*, 78-80.

Brandt, D.R., Miller, G.R., & Hocking, J.E. (1980). Effects of self-monitoring and familiarity on deception detection. *Communication Quarterly, 28*, 3-10.

Brennan, T., & Auslander, N. (1979). *Adolescent loneliness: An exploratory study of social and psychological predisposition and theory*. Boulder, CO: Behavioral Research Institute.

Briggs, S.R., Cheek, J.M., & Buss, A.H. (1980). An analysis of the self-monitoring scale. *Journal of Personality and Social Psychology, 38*, 679-686.

Brockner, J., & Eckenrode, J. (1979). Self-monitoring and the actorobserver bias. *Representative Research in Social Psychology, 9*, 81-88.

Buck, R. (1978). The slide-viewing technique for measuring nonverbal sending accuracy: A guide for replication. *JSAS Catalog of Selected Documents in Psychology, 8*, 63 (No. 1723).

Burstein, J.W., & Carkhuff, R.R. (1968). Objective therapist and client ratings of therapist offered faciliative conditions of moderate to low functioning therapists. *Journal of Clinical Psychology, 24*, 240-244.

Buss, A.H., & Briggs, S.R. (1984). Drama and the self in social interaction. *Journal of Personality and Social Psychology, 47*, 1310-1324.

Cahn, D.D., & Shulman, G.M. (1980). An exploratory study of the relationship between rhetorical sensitivity, leadership effectiveness, and rank in a military organization. *Michigan Speech Association Journal, 15*, 1-11.

Cappella, J.N. (1982). Conversational involvement: Approaching and avoiding others. In J.M. Wiemann & R.P. Harrison (Eds.), *Nonverbal interaction*. Beverly Hills, CA: Sage.

Cappella, J.N., & Greene, J.O. (1982). A discrepancy-arousal explanation of mutual influence in expressive behavior for adult and infant-adult interaction. *Communication Monographs, 49*, 89-114.

Caracena, P.F., & Vicory, J.R. (1969). Correlates of phenomenological and judged empathy. *Journal of Counseling Psychology, 16*, 510-515.

Cargan, L. (1981). Singles: An examination of two stereotypes. *Family Relations, 30*, 377-385.

Carkhuff, R. R. (1966). Counseling research, theory and practice—1965. *Journal of Counseling Psychology, 13*, 467-480.

Cavior, N., & Marabotto, C. M. (1976). Monitoring verbal behaviors in a dyadic interaction. *Journal of Consulting and Clinical Psychology, 44*, 68-76

Cegala, D.J. (1981). Interaction involvement: A cognitive dimension of communicative competence. *Communication Education, 30*, 109-121.

Cegala, D.J. (1984). Affective and cognitive manifestations of interaction involvement during unstructured and competitive interactions. *Communication Monographs, 51*, 320-338.

Cegala, D.J., Savage, G.T., Brunner, C.C., & Conrad, A.B. (1982). An elaboration of the meaning of interaction involvement: Toward the development of a theoretical concept. *Communication Monographs, 49*, 229-248.

Chapman, A.J. (1975). Eye contact, physical proximity, and laughter: A reexamination of the equilibrium model of social intimacy. *Social Behavior and Personality, 3*, 143-155.

Cheek, J.M., & Busch, C. M. (1981). The influence of shyness on loneliness in a new situation. *Personality and Social Psychology Bulletin, 7*, 572-577.

Cheek, J. M., & Buss, A. H. (1981). Shyness and sociability. *Journal of Personality and Social Psychology, 41*, 330-339.

Chelune, G. J. (1976). The Self-Disclosure Situation Survey: A new approach to measuring self-disclosure. *JSAS Catalog of Selected Documents in Psychology, 6,* 111-112.

Chelune, G. J., Sultan, F. E., & Williams, C. L. (1980). Loneliness, self-disclosure, and interpersonal effectiveness. *Journal of Counseling Psychology, 27,* 462-468.

Corty, E., & Young, R. D. (1981). Social contact and perceived loneliness in college students. *Perceptual and Motor Skills, 53,* 773-774.

Crabb, W. T., Moracco, J. C., & Bender, R. C. (1983). A comparative study of empathy training with programmed instruction for lay helpers. *Journal of Counseling Psychology, 30,* 221-226.

Cutrona, C. E. (1982). Transition to college: Loneliness and the process of social adjustment. In L. A. Peplau & D. Perlman (Eds.), *Loneliness: A sourcebook of current theory, research and therapy.* New York: Wiley-Interscience.

Dabbs, J. M., Evans, M. S., Hopper, C. H., & Purvis, J. A. (1980). Self-monitors in conversation: What do they monitor? *Journal of Personality and Social Psychology, 39,* 278-284.

Danheiser, P. R., & Graziano, W. G. (1982). Self-monitoring and cooperation as a self-presentational strategy. *Journal of Personality and Social Psychology, 42,* 497-505.

Darnell, D. K., & Brockriede, W. (1976). *Persons communicating.* Englewood Cliffs, NJ: Prentice-Hall.

Davis, J. D. (1976). Self-disclosure in an acquaintance exercise: Responsibility for level of intimacy. *Journal of Personality and Social Psychology, 33,* 787-792.

Davis, M. H. (1983a). Measuring individual differences in empathy: Evidence for a multidimensional approach. *Journal of Personality and Social Psychology, 44,* 113-126.

Davis, M. H. (1983b). The effects of dispositional empathy on emotional reactions and helping: A multidimensional approach. *Journal of Personality, 51,* 167-184.

Derlega, V. J., & Margulis, S. T. (1982). Why loneliness occurs: The interrelationship of social psychological and privacy concepts. In L. A. Peplau & D. Perlman (Eds.), *Loneliness: A sourcebook of current theory, research and therapy.* New York: Wiley-Interscience.

DeWever, M. K. (1977). Nursing home patients' perceptions of nurses' affective touching. *Journal of Psychology, 96,* 163-171.

Douglas, W. (1983). Self-monitoring: When does being a high self-monitor really make a difference? *Human Communication Research, 10,* 81-96.

Douglas, W. (1984). Initial interaction scripts: When knowing is behaving. *Human Communication Research, 11,* 203-219.

Eadie, W. F., & Paulson, J. W. (1984). Communicator attitudes, communicator style, and communication competence. *Western Journal of Speech Communication, 48,* 390-407.

Edinger, J. A., & Patterson, M. L. (1983). Nonverbal involvement and social control. *Psychological Bulletin, 93,* 30-56.

Elliott, G. C. (1979). Some effects of deception and level of self-monitoring on planning and reacting to a self-presentation. *Journal of Personality and Social Psychology, 37*, 1282-1292.

Elliott, R., Filipovich, H., Harrigan, L., Gaynor, J., Reimschuessel, C., & Zapadka, J. K. (1982). Measuring response empathy: The development of a multicomponent rating scale. *Journal of Counseling Psychology, 29*, 379-387.

Epstein, N., & Jackson, E. (1978). An outcome study of short-term communication training with married couples. *Journal of Consulting and Clinical Psychology, 46*, 207-212.

Evans, R. L., Werkhoven, W., & Fox, H. R. (1982). Treatment of social isolation and loneliness in a sample of visually impaired elderly persons. *Psychological Reports, 51*, 103-110.

Feinman, J. A., & Feldman, R. S. (1982). Decoding children's expressions of affect. *Child Development, 53*, 710-716.

Feldstein, S. & Welkowitz, J. (1978). A chronography of conversation: In defense of an objective approach. In A. W. Seigman & S. Feldstein (Eds.), *Nonverbal behavior and communication.* Hillsdale, NJ: Erlbaum.

Fenigstein, A., Scheier, M. F., & Buss, A. H. (1975). Public and private self-consciousness: Assessment and theory. *Journal of Consulting and Clinical Psychology, 43*, 522-527.

Fischer, M. J., & Apostal, R. A. (1975). Selected vocal cues and counselors' perceptions of genuineness, self-disclosure, and anxiety. *Journal of Counseling Psychology, 22*, 92-96.

Flanders, J. P. (1982). A general systems approach to loneliness. In L. A. Peplau & D. Perlman (Eds.), *Loneliness: A sourcebook of current theory, research and therapy.* New York: Wiley-Interscience.

Franzoi, S. L., & Davis, M. H. (1985). Adolescent self-disclosure and loneliness: Private self-consciousness and parental influences. *Journal of Personality and Social Psychology, 48*, 768-780.

Fretz, B. R., Corn, R., & Tuemmler, J. M. (1979). Counselor nonverbal behaviors and client evaluations. *Journal of Counseling Psychology, 26*, 304-311.

Furnham, A. (1981). Self-monitoring and social perception. *Perceptual and Motor Skills, 52*, 3-10.

Gabrenya, W. K., & Arkin, R. M. (1980) Self-monitoring scale: Factor structure and correlates. *Personality and Social Psychology Bulletin, 6*, 13-22.

Gaushell, H. (1982). Effect of empathic communication and use of paralanguage. *Perceptual and Motor Skills, 54*, 522.

Geizer, R. S., & Rarick, D. L. (1977). Deception and judgment accuracy: A study in person perception. *Personality and Social Psychology Bulletin, 3*, 446-449.

Gerson, A. C., & Perlman, D. (1979). Loneliness and expressive communication. *Journal of Abnormal Psychology, 88*, 258-261.

Giles, H., & Smith, P. M. (1979). Accommodation theory: Optimal levels of convergence. In H. Giles & R. St. Clair (Eds.), *Language and social psychology.* Baltimore, MD: University Park Press.

Gladstein, G. A. (1983). Understanding empathy: Integrating counseling, developmental, and social psychology perspectives. *Journal of Counseling Psychology, 30*, 467-482.

Goffman, E. (1967). *Interaction ritual: Essays in face-to-face behavior.* Chicago: Aldine.

Goldfarb, N. (1978). Effects of supervisory style on counselor effectiveness and faciliative responding. *Journal of Counseling Psychology, 25*, 454-460.

Gordon, S. (1976). *Lonely in America.* New York: Simon & Schuster.

Goswick, R. A., & Jones, W. H. (1981). Loneliness, self-concept, and adjustment. *Journal of Psychology, 107*, 237-240.

Grace, G. R. de, Joshi, P., & Roberge, L. (1983). Loneliness and nonverbal communication in separated or divorced women: An exploratory study. *Psychological Reports, 53*, 151-154.

Gurman, A. A. (1973). Effects of therapist and patient mood on the therapeutic functioning of high- and low-faciliative therapists. *Journal of Consulting and Clinical Psychology, 40*, 48-58.

Haase, R. F., & Tepper, D. T. (1972). Nonverbal components of empathic communication. *Journal of Counseling Psychology, 19*, 417-424.

Hammer, A. L. (1983). Matching perceptual predicates: Effect on perceived empathy in a counseling analogue. *Journal of Counseling Psychology, 30*, 172-179.

Hansen, J. C., Moore, C. D., & Carkhuff, R. R. (1968). The differential relationship of objective and client perceptions of counseling. *Journal of Clinical Psychology, 24*, 244-246.

Hansson, R. O., & Jones, W. H. (1981). Loneliness, cooperation, and conformity among American undergraduates. *Journal of Social Psychology, 115*, 103-108.

Harrigan, J. A., & Rosenthal, R. (1983). Physicians' head and body positions as determinants of perceived rapport. *Journal of Applied Social Psychology, 13*, 496-509.

Hart, R. P., & Burks, D. M. (1972). Rhetorical sensitivity and social interaction. *Speech Monographs, 39*, 75-91.

Hart, R. P., Carlson, R. E., & Eadie, W. F. (1980). Attitudes toward communication and the assessment of rhetorical sensitivity. *Communication Monographs, 47*, 1-22.

Hartog, J. (1980). The anatomization, In J. Hartog, J. R. Audy, and Y. A. Cohen (Eds.), *The anatomy of loneliness.* New York: International Universities Press.

Hodge, E. A., Payne, P. A., & Wheeler, D. D. (1978). Approaches to empathy training: Programmed methods versus individual supervision and professional versus peer supervisors. *Journal of Counseling Psychology, 25*, 449-453.

Hojat, M. (1982). Loneliness as a function of selected personality variables. *Journal of Clinical Psychology, 38*, 137-141.

Hoover, S., Skuja, A., & Cosper, J. (1979). Correlates of college students' loneliness. *Psychological Reports, 44*, 1116.

Horowitz, L. M., & French, R. (1979). Interpersonal problems of people who describe themselves as lonely. *Journal of Consulting and Clinical Psychology, 47*, 762-764.

Horowitz, L. M., French, R. de S., & Anderson, C. A. (1982). The prototype of a lonely person. In L. A. Peplau and D. Perlman (Eds.), *Loneliness: A sourcebook of current theory, research and therapy*. New York: Wiley-Interscience.

Ickes, W., & Barnes, R. D. (1977). The role of sex and self-monitoring in unstructured dyadic interactions. *Journal of Personality and Social Psychology, 35*, 315-330.

Ickes, W., Layden, M. A., & Barnes, R. D. (1978). Objective self-awareness and individuation: An empirical link. *Journal of Personality, 46*, 146-161.

Jaffe, J., & Anderson, S. (1979). Communication rhythms and the evaluation of language. In A. W. Siegman & S. Feldstein (Eds.), *Of speech and time*. Hillsdale, NJ: Erlbaum.

Jones, W. H. (1981). Loneliness and social contact. *Journal of Social Psychology, 113*, 295-296.

Jones, W. H. (1982). Loneliness and social behavior. In L.A. Peplau & D. Perlman (Eds.), *Loneliness: A sourcebook of current theory, research and therapy*. New York: Wiley-Interscience.

Jones, W. H., Freemon, J. E., & Goswick, R. A. (1981). The persistence of loneliness: Self and other determinants. *Journal of Personality, 49*, 27-48.

Jones, W. H., Hobbs, S. A., & Hockenbury, D. (1982). Loneliness and social skills deficits. *Journal of Personality and Social Psychology, 42*, 682-689.

Jones, W. H., Sansone, C., & Helm, B. (1983). Loneliness and interpersonal judgments. *Personality and Social Psychology Bulletin, 9*, 437-441.

Jong-Gierveld, J. de, & Raadschelders, J. (1982). Types of loneliness. In L. A. Peplau & D. Perlman (Eds.), *Loneliness: A sourcebook of current theory, research and therapy*. New York: Wiley-Interscience.

Jourard, S. M. (1968). *Disclosing man to himself*. New York: Van Nostrand Reinhold.

Kivett, V. R. (1979). Discriminators of loneliness among the rural elderly: Implications for intervention. *Gerontologist, 19*, 108-115.

Kraut, R. E., & Poe, D. (1980). Behavioral roots of person perception: The deception judgments of customs inspectors and laymen. *Journal of Personality and Social Psychology, 39*, 784-798.

Kulik, J. A., & Taylor, S. E. (1981). Self-monitoring and the use of consensus information. *Journal of Personality, 49*, 75-84.

Lambert, M. J., DeJulio, S. S., & Stein, D. M. (1978). Therapist interpersonal skills: Process, outcome, methodological considerations, and recommendations for future research. *Psychological Bulletin, 85*, 467-489.

Lamont, L. (1979). *Campus shock*. New York: Dutton.

Levinger, G. (1977). The embrace of lives: Changing and unchanging. In G. Levinger & H. L. Raush (Eds.), *Close relationships: Perspectives on the meaning of intimacy*. Amherst: University of Massachusetts Press.

Levy, S. (1981). Lawful roles of facets in social theories. In I. Borg (Ed.), *Multidimensional data representations: When and why.* Ann Arbor, MI: Mathesis Press.

Libow, J. A., & Doty, D. W. (1976). An evaluation of empathic listening in telephone counseling. *Journal of Counseling Psychology, 23*, 532-537.

Lippa, R. (1976). Expressive control and the leakage of dispositional extraversion during role-played teaching. *Journal of Personality, 44*, 541-559.

Lippa, R. (1978). Expressive control, expressive consistency, and the correspondence between expressive behavior and personality. *Journal of Personality, 46*, 438-461.

Lynch, J. J. (1971). *The broken heart: The medical consequences of loneliness in America.* New York: Basic Books.

Maroldo, G. K. (1981). Shyness and loneliness among college men and women. *Psychological Reports, 48*, 885-886.

Maurer, R. E., & Tindall, J. H. (1983). Effects of postural congruence on client's perception of counselor empathy. *Journal of Counseling Psychology, 30*, 158-163.

McCann, C. D., & Hancock, R. D. (1983). Self-monitoring in communicative interactions: Social cognitive consequences of goal-directed message modification. *Journal of Experimental Social Psychology, 19*, 109-121.

McCroskey, J. C. (1978). Validity of the PRCA as an index of oral communication apprehension. *Communication Monographs, 45*, 192-203.

McWhirter, J. J. (1973). Two measures of the faciliative conditions: A correlation study. *Journal of Counseling Psychology, 20*, 317-320.

McWhirter, J. J., & Marks, S. E. (1972). An investigation of the relationship between the faciliative conditions and peer and group leader ratings of perceived counselor effectiveness. *Journal of Clinical Psychology, 28*, 116-117.

Mehrabian, A. (1969). Some referents and measures of nonverbal behavior. *Behavioral Research Methods and Instrumentation, 1*, 203-207.

Michela, J. L., Peplau, L.A., & Weeks, D. G. (1982). Perceived dimensions of attributions for loneliness. *Journal of Personality and Social Psychology, 43*, 929-936.

Miller, G. R., deTurck, M.A., & Kalbfleisch, P.J. (1983). Self-monitoring, rehearsal, and deceptive communication. *Human Communication Research, 10*, 97-117.

Miller, L.C., Berg, J. H., & Archer, R. L. (1983). Openers: Individuals who elicit intimate self-disclosure. *Journal of Personality and Social Psychology, 44*, 1234-1244.

Murphy, H. B., & Rowe, W. (1977). Effects of counselor faciliative level of client suggestibility. *Journal of Counseling Psychology, 24*, 6-9.

Nerviano, V. J., & Gross, W. F. (1976). Loneliness and locus of control for alcoholic males: Validity against Murray need and Cattell trait dimensions. *Journal of Clinical Psychology, 32*, 479-484.

Newman, F. (1971). *Report on higher education.* Washington, DC: U.S. Department of Health, Education and Welfare.

Norton, R. W. (1978). Foundation of a communicator style construct. *Human Communication Research, 4*, 99-112.

Norton, R. W. (1983). *Communicator style: Theory, application, and method.* Beverly Hills, CA: Sage.

Ostrov, E., & Offer, D. (1980). Loneliness and the adolescent. In J. Hartog, J. R. Audy, & Y. A. Cohen (Eds.), *The anatomy of loneliness.* New York: International Universities Press.

Paloutzian, R. F., & Ellison, C. W. (1982). Loneliness, spiritual well-being, and the quality of life. In L. A. Peplau & D. Perlman (Eds.), *Loneliness: A sourcebook of current theory, research and therapy.* New York: Wiley-Interscience.

Paloutzian, R. F., Janigian, A., & Van Mouwerik, S. (1982). *Is loneliness a discrepancy between desired and achieved social interaction?* Paper presented before the annual meeting of the American Psychological Association.

Parmelee, P., & Werner, C. (1978). Lonely losers: Stereotypes of single dwellers. *Personality and Social Psychology Bulletin, 4*, 292-295.

Patterson, M. L. (1982). A sequential functional model of nonverbal exchange. *Psychological Review, 89*, 231-249.

Patterson, M. L. (1983a). *Nonverbal behavior: A functional perspective.* New York: Springer-Verlag.

Patterson, M. L. (1983b). Theoretical approaches to nonverbal exchange: A brief historical perspective. *Academic Psychology Bulletin, 3*, 375-388.

Patterson, M. L. (1985). The evolution of a functional model of nonverbal exchange: A personal perspective. In R. L. Street & J. N. Cappella (Eds.), *Sequence and pattern in communicative behavior.* Baltimore, MD: Edward Arnold.

Peplau, L. A., Miceli, M., & Morasch, B. (1982). In L. A. Peplau & D. Perlman (Eds.), *Loneliness: A sourcebook of current theory, research and therapy.* New York: Wiley-Interscience.

Peplau, L. A., & Perlman, D. (1979). Blueprint for a social psychological theory of loneliness. In M. Cook & G. Wilson (Eds.), *Love and attraction: An international conference.* New York: Pergamon Press.

Peplau, L. A., & Perlman, D. (1982). Perspectives on loneliness. In L. A. Peplau & D. Perlman (Eds.), *Loneliness: A sourcebook of current theory, research and therapy.* New York: Wiley-Interscience.

Perlman, D., Gerson, A. C., & Spinner, B. (1978). Loneliness among senior citizens: An empirical report. *Essence, 2*, 239-248.

Perlman, D., & Peplau, L. A. (1981). Toward a social psychology of loneliness. In S. Duck & R. Gilmour (Eds.), *Personal relationships 3: Personal relationships in disorder.* New York: Academic Press.

Perlman, D., & Peplau, L. A. (1982). Theoretical approaches to loneliness. In L. A. Peplau & D. Perlman (Eds.), *Loneliness: A sourcebook of current theory, research and therapy.* New York: Wiley-Interscience.

Pilkonis, P. A. (1977). Shyness, public and private, and its relationship to other measures of social behavior. *Journal of Personality, 45*, 585-595.

Rahaim, S., Waid, L. R., Kennelly, K. J., & Stricklin, A. (1980). Differences in self-monitoring of expressive behavior in depressed and nondepressed individuals. *Psychological Reports, 46*, 1051-1056.

Rarick, D. L., Soldow, G. F., & Geizer, R. S. (1976). Self-monitoring as a mediator of conformity. *Central States Speech Journal, 27*, 267-271.

Rogers, C. R. (1957). The necessary and sufficient conditions of therapeutic personality change. *Journal of Consulting Psychology, 21*, 95-103.

Rogers, C. R. (1973). The lonely person—and his experiences in an encounter group. In C. R. Rogers, *Carl Rogers on encounter groups*. New York: Harper & Row.

Rook, K. S. (1984). The negative side of social interaction: Impact on psychological well-being. *Journal of Personality and Social Psychology, 46*, 1097-1108.

Rook, K. S., & Peplau, L. A. (1982). Perspective on helping the lonely. In L. A. Peplau & D. Perlman (Eds.), *Loneliness: A sourcebook of current theory, research and therapy*. New York: Wiley-Interscience.

Rosenberg, M. (1965). *Society and the adolescent self-image*. Princeton, NJ: Princeton University Press.

Rubenstein, C. (1979). *A questionnaire study of adult loneliness in three U.S. cities*. Unpublished doctoral dissertation, New York University.

Rubenstein, C., & Shaver, P. (1980). Loneliness in two northeastern cities. In J. Hartog, J. R. Audy & Y. Cohen (Eds.), *The anatomy of loneliness*. New York: International Universities Press.

Rubenstein, C., & Shaver, P. (1982). The experience of loneliness. In L. A. Peplau & D. Perlman (Eds.), *Loneliness: A sourcebook of current theory, research and therapy*. New York: Wiley-Interscience.

Rubin, Z. (1982). Children without friends. In L. A. Peplau & D. Perlman (Eds.), *Loneliness: A sourcebook of current theory, research and therapy*. New York: Wiley-Interscience.

Russell, D. (1982). The measurement of loneliness. In L. A. Peplau & D. Perlman (Eds.), *Loneliness: A sourcebook of current theory, research and therapy*. New York: Wiley-Interscience.

Russell, D., Cutrona, C. E., Rose, J., & Yurko, K. (1984). Social and emotional loneliness: An examination of Weiss's typology of loneliness. *Journal of Personality and Social Psychology, 46*, 1313-1321.

Russell, D., Peplau, L. A., & Cutrona, C. E. (1980). The revised UCLA loneliness scale: Concurrent and discriminant validity evidence. *Journal of Personality and Social Psychology, 39*, 472-480.

Russell, D., Peplau, L. A., & Ferguson, M. L. (1978). Developing a measure of loneliness. *Journal of Personality Assessment, 42*, 290-294.

Sampson, E. E. (1978). Personality and the location of identity. *Journal of Personality, 46*, 552-568.

Schmidt, N., & Sermat, V. (1983). Measuring loneliness in different relationships. *Journal of Personality and Social Psychology, 44*, 1038-1047.

Schutz, W. C. (1960). *FIRO: A three-dimensional theory of interpersonal behavior*. New York: Holt, Rinehart & Winston.

Sermat, V. (1978). Sources of loneliness. *Essence, 2,* 271-276.

Sermat, V. (1980). Some situational and personality correlates of loneliness. In J. Hartog, J. R. Audy, & Y. A. Cohen (Eds.), *The anatomy of loneliness.* New York: International Universities Press.

Sermat, V., & Smyth, M. (1973). Content analysis of verbal communication in the development of a relationship: Conditions influencing self-disclosure. *Journal of Personality and Social Psychology, 26,* 332-346.

Shaffer, D. R., Smith, J. E., & Tomarelli, M. (1982). Self-monitoring as a determinant of self-disclosure reciprocity during the acquaintance process. *Journal of Personality and Social Psychology, 43,* 163-175.

Shapiro, J. G., Krauss, H. H., & Traux, C. B. (1969). Therapeutic conditions and disclosure beyond the therapeutic encounter. *Journal of Counseling Psychology, 16,* 290-294.

Shaver, P., & Rubenstein, C. (1980). Childhood attachment experience and adult loneliness. In L. Wheeler (Ed.), *Review of personality and social psychology* (Vol. 1). Beverly Hills, CA: Sage.

Sieck, W. A., & McFall, R. M. (1976). Some determinants of self-monitoring effects. *Journal of Consulting and Clinical Psychology, 44,* 958-965.

Sloan, W. W., & Solano, C. H. (1984). The conversational styles of lonely males with strangers and roommates. *Personality and Social Psychology Bulletin, 10,* 293-301.

Smith-Hanen, S. S. (1977). Effects of nonverbal behaviors on judged levels of counselor warmth and empathy. *Journal of Counseling Psychology, 24,* 87-91.

Snyder, M. (1974). Self-monitoring of expressive behavior. *Journal of Personality and Social Psychology, 30,* 526-537.

Snyder, M. (1979). Self-monitoring processes. In L. Berkowitz (Ed.), *Advances in experimental social psychology* (Vol. 12). New York: Academic Press.

Snyder, M., & Cantor, N. (1980). Thinking about ourselves and others: Self-monitoring and social knowledge. *Journal of Personality and Social Psychology, 39,* 222-234.

Snyder, M., & Gangestad, S. (1982). Choosing social situations: Two investigations of self-monitoring processes. *Journal of Personality and social Psychology, 43,* 123-135.

Snyder, M., & Monson, T. C. (1975). Persons, situations, and the control of social behavior. *Journal of Personality and Social Psychology, 32,* 637-644.

Snyder, M., & Simpson, J. A. (1984). Self-monitoring and dating relationships. *Journal of Personality and Social Psychology, 47,* 1281-1291.

Snyder, M., & Swann, W. B. (1976). When actions reflect attitudes: The politics of impression management. *Journal of Personality and Social Psychology, 34,* 1034-1042.

Snyder, M., & Tanke, E. D. (1976). Behavior and attitude: Some people are more consistent than others. *Journal of Personality, 44,* 501-517.

Solano, C. H. (1980). Two measures of loneliness: A comparison. *Psychological Reports, 46,* 23-28.

Solano, C. H., Batten, P. G., & Parish, E. A. (1982). Loneliness and patterns of self-disclosure. *Journal of Personality and Social Psychology, 43*, 524-531.

Spitzberg, B. H., & Canary, D. J. (1983). *Attributions of loneliness and relational competence.* paper presented at the annual meeting of the International Communication Association, Dallas.

Stafford, L.A., & Daly, J. A. (1984). Conversational memory: The effects of recall mode and memory expectancies on remembrances of natural conversations. *Human Communication Research, 10*, 379-402.

Stern, D.N. (1974). Mother and infant at play: The dyadic interaction involving facial, vocal and gaze behavior. In M. Lewis & L. Rosenblum (Eds.), *The effect of the infant on its caregiver.* New York: John Wiley.

Stern, D. N. (1977). *A first relationship: Mother and infant.* Cambridge, MA: Harvard University Press.

Strayer, J. (1980). A naturalistic study of empathic behaviors and their relation to affective states and perspective-taking skills in preschool children. *Child Development, 51*, 815-822.

Street, R. L., & Giles, H. (1982). Speech accommodation theory: A social cognitive approach to language and speech behavior. In M. Roloff & C. Berger (Eds.), *Social cognition and communication.* Beverly Hills, CA: Sage.

Suedfeld, P. (1982). Aloneness as a healing experience. In L. A. Peplau & D. Perlman (Eds.), *Loneliness: A sourcebook of current theory, research and therapy.* New York: Wiley-Interscience.

Sullivan, H. S. (1953). *The interpersonal theory of psychiatry.* New York: Norton.

Sypher, B. D., & Sypher, H. E. (1983). Perceptions of communication ability: Self-monitoring in an organizational setting. *Personality and Social Psychology Bulletin, 9*, 297-304.

Tepper, D. T., & Haase, R. F. (1978). Verbal and nonverbal communication of faciliative conditions. *Journal of Counseling Psychology, 25*, 35-44.

Teyber, E. C., Meese, L. A., & Stollak, G. E. (1977). Adult responses to child communications. *Child Development, 48*, 1577-1582.

Thauberger, P. C., & Cleland, J. F. (1979). Avoidance of ontological confrontation of loneliness and some epidemiological indices of social behavior and health. *Perceptual and Motor Skills, 48*, 1219-1224.

Therrien, M. E. (1979). Evaluating empathy skill training for parents. *Social Work*, 417-419.

Tobey, E. L., & Tunnell, G. (1981). Predicting our impressions on others: Effects of public self-consciousness and acting, a self-monitoring subscale. *Personality and Social Psychology Bulletin, 7*, 661-669.

Tunstall, J. (1967). *Old and alone.* New York: Humanities Press.

Weeks, D. G., Michela, J. L., Peplau, L. A., & Bragg, M. E. (1980). Relation between loneliness and depression: A structural equation analysis. *Journal of Personality and Social Psychology, 39*, 1238-1244.

Weiss, R. S. (1973). *Loneliness: The experience of emotional and social isolation.* Cambridge, MA: MIT Press.

Weiss, R. S. (1974). The provisions of social relationships. In Z. Rubin (Ed.), *Doing unto others*. Englewood Cliffs, NJ: Prentice-Hall.

Weiss, R. S. (1982). Issues in the study of loneliness. In L.A. Peplau & D. Perlman (Eds.), *Loneliness: A sourcebook of current theory, research and therapy*. New York: Wiley-Interscience.

Wenz, F. V. (1977). Seasonal suicide attempts and forms of loneliness. *Psychological Reports, 40*, 807-810.

Wheeler, L., Reis, H., & Nezlek, J. (1983). Loneliness, social interaction, and sex roles. *Journal of Personality and Social Psychology, 45*, 943-953.

Williams, J. G., & Solano, C. H. (1983). The social reality of feeling lonely: Friendship and reciprocation. *Personality and Social Psychology Bulletin, 9*, 237-242.

Wish, M. (1976). Comparisons among multidimensional structures of interpersonal relations. *Multivariate Behavioral Research, 11*, 297-327.

Wish, M., D'Andrade, R. G., & Goodnow, J. E. (1980). Dimensions of interpersonal communication: Correspondences between structures for speech acts and bipolar scales. *Journal of Personality and Social Psychology, 39*, 848-860.

Wish, M., Deutsch, M., & Kaplan, S. J. (1976). Perceived dimensions of interpersonal relations. *Journal of Personality and Social Psychology, 33*, 409-420.

Wish, M., & Kaplan, S. (1976). Toward an implicit theory of interpersonal communication. *Sociometry, 40*, 234-246.

Woodall, W. G., & Hills, S.E.K. (1982). Predictive and perceived empathy as predictors of leadership style. *Perceptual and Motor Skills, 54*, 800-802.

Young, D. W. (1980). Meaning of counselor nonverbal gestures: Fixed or interpretive? *Journal of Counseling Psychology, 27*, 447-452.

Young, J. E. (1982). Loneliness, depression and cognitive therapy: Theory and application. In L. A. Peplau and D. Perlman (Eds.), *Loneliness: A sourcebook of current theory, research and therapy*. New York: Wiley-Interscience.

Zahn-Waxler, C., Friedman, S. L., & Mark, E. (1983). Children's emotions and behaviors in response to infants' cries. *Child Development, 54*, 1522-1528.

Zakahi, W. R., & Duran, R. L. (1982). All the lonely people: The relationship among loneliness, communicative competence, and communication anxiety. *Communication Quarterly, 30*, 203-208.

Zanna, M. P., Olson, J. M., & Fazio, R. H. (1980). Attitude-behavior consistency: An individual difference perspective. *Journal of Personality and Social Psychology, 38*, 432-440.

# 6

# Style

## VIRGINIA EMAN WHEELESS
## WILLIAM B. LASHBROOK

Much research in interpersonal communication centers on the view that personality traits are stable, consistent predispositions that contribute in some manner to communication outcomes. Mischel's (1968) introduction of the controversial hypothesis that inconsistency, not consistency, is the norm for behavior has had profound implications on the study of personality and communication. Mischel's personality approach rests on the assumptions that people are active participants in the learning process (Bandura, 1971) and that cognitive social learning references the construction of adaptive behaviors that will produce beneficial consequences (Mischel, 1973). In terms of communication, Mischel seems to be referring to an individual's ability to construct diverse communication behaviors under appropriate conditions—in short, adaptability. The concept of behavioral adaptation has long been noted by interpersonal communication scholars, but has recently become a primary concern (see Spitzberg & Cupach, 1984).

Adaptability in human encounters depends on one's perceptions of self, others, and the context of the relationship. It is, in part, a function of consistent behavior in interaction with situational variables that demand the selection of responses among alternatives the person is capable of enacting. This explanation is referred to as "situational templating" by Bem (1983).

One way to understand adaptive communication behavior is to examine the "style" dimension of personality. Style is viewed as a "multidimensional, hierarchical system that integrates and modulates information by coordinating cognition affect, and by selection of particular modes of processing" (Royce & Powell, 1983, p. 11). Simply put, style determines the combination of traits that are activated when alternative possibilities exist. All individuals have repertoires of behavior patterns comprising knowledge structures which are activated through an interaction of the situation and the person's cognitive systems. Communication scholars refer to this "activation" as adaptability, flexibility, style flexing (Spitzberg & Cupach, 1984), and versatility (W. B. Lashbrook & Lashbrook, 1980). All such terms refer to an individual's ability to discern the relevant characteristics of a situation and integrate them with his or her available and accessible patterns of adaptive response.

Style has been recognized as an important communication variable. It has been studied as linguistic style (Scotton, 1985), management communication style (Richmond & McCroksey, 1979), styles used to gain compliance (Cody, McLaughlin, & Jordan, 1980), and as that level of communication which gives form to content (Norton, 1983). This chapter focuses on the latter. Our approach assumes that inconsistency is the norm in communication behavior, and to explain this inconsistency phenomenon, we explore three perspectives that have been labeled "styles." These perspectives were chosen because, by definition, they fit our conceptualization of style and offer an opportunity to examine specific variables that affect self-perceptions and perceptions of others, both of which ultimately affect communication. In terms of self-schema theory, the following style perspectives deal with "generalizations derived from past experience that organize and guide information processing about ourselves and others in our social experience" (Smith, 1982, p. 28) and that affect communication.

First, communicator style is considered a basic communication construct that addresses the use of different components of style in various contexts. Second, using the parameters of self-schema theory, we identify gender orientation, and particularly androgyny, as a style perspective that explains inconsistent behavior. From this perspective, individuals are seen as acquiring knowledge structures based on definitions of masculinity and femininity, and use of the appropriate repertoires in different situations is activated according to the individual's ability to adapt to situational demands. Finally, we consider style as something assigned by others based on observations of assertive and responsive behaviors exhibited over a variety of situations. Thus we examine the social style perspective.

We approach our task by first describing conceptually what is meant by each style perspective. We then examine the research used to test these conceptualizations and link them to the adaptive nature of interpersonal communication. Finally, we compare and contrast the three systems and offer some conclusions about the study of style and interpersonal communication.

## COMMUNICATOR STYLE

The concept of "communicator style" is found in various forms, and under different labels and operationalizations, across the social science literature. The definition and operationalization most frequently used in the study of interpersonal communication is Norton's (1978) communicator style construct. It is defined as "the way one verbally, non-verbally, and paraverbally interacts to signal how literal meaning should be taken, interpreted, filtered, or understood" (p. 99). While Norton (1983) advocates that one's style is a "function of consistently recurring communicative associations" (p. 19), an individual does not have one permanent style, but rather aspects of many styles. Thus the concept is congruent with our conceptualization of the style dimension of personality, and with our assumption that inconsistency is the rule for behavior.

Beginning with Watzlawick, Beavin, and Jackson's (1967) assumption that communication exists on content and relationship levels, Norton (1983) develops a style profile that summarizes the "signals that are used to help process, interpret, filter, or understand literal meaning" (p. 47) on the relationship level. In a comprehensive summary of the conceptualization and operationalization of communicator style, Norton (1983) gives credit to the work of Leary (1957), Schutz (1958), Mann, Gibbard, and Hartman (1967), Bales (1970), and Lieberman, Yalom, and Miles (1973) as beginning points for his work. Norton synthesizes these works and advances a style concept that is observable, multifaceted, multicollinear, and variable yet consistent. This latter characteristic portrays Norton's view that style is used both as a norm while consistent *and* as a deviation from the norm while variable (Norton, 1983).

Norton (1978) defines communicator style according to nine independent subconstructs (dominant, dramatic, contentious, animated, impression-leaving, relaxed, attentive, open, and friendly) and one dependent subconstruct (communicator image; for a complete description of communicator style, see Norton, 1983). It should be noted that later uses of the communicator style measure (CSM) show use of a tenth independent subconstruct—precise (Bednar, 1982).

Norton (1983) reports that impression-leaving, open, and dominant are the best predictors of communicator image. Least effective predictors are animated, contentious, and dramatic. Other researchers report that openness is also related to self-disclosure, control, trust, and intimacy (Millar & Rogers, 1976), and that dominant and open are additionally related to attractiveness (Norton & Pettegrew, 1977).

Three important communication constructs related to communicator style help verify that the subconstructs are important in different contexts. These are communicative competence, communication apprehension, and rhetorical sensitivity. In an attempt to identify communicator style behaviorally, Brandt (1979) found that the impression-leaving, openness, attentive, animated, and relaxed dimensions elicit perceptions of social and task attractiveness and perceived communicative competence in the areas of active listening, supportiveness, openness and candor, faciliation of conversations, and producing a relaxed atmosphere. Porter (1982) tested the relationship of communicator style and communication apprehension and found that high and low communication apprehensives are best discriminated by the style dimensions of dominance, impression-leaving, relaxed, and dramatic. Additionally, Talley and Richmond (1980) reported that communication apprehension and shyness accounted for an average 27% of the variance in communicator style. An example of research that examines the relationship between communicator style and rhetorical sensitivity is that reported by Eadie and Paulson (1984). In this investigation, rhetorical sensitives were perceived as more dominant, open, and friendly than were rhetorical reflectors, who are defined as archetypes with no "real" self-view. However, reflectors were perceived to be more precise and impression-leaving than the sensitives. Reflectors and noble selves, "the representative of the 'I take care of myself first' school of communication thought" (Eadie & Paulson, 1984, p. 390), attempted to leave an impression without being too dominant.

From research about the communicator style construct and its original conceptualization, Norton has developed three style profiles "because of the wide-ranging issues each one raises" (Norton, 1983, p. 13)—open, attentive, and dramatic. Norton and his colleagues continue to refine the definitions of these styles. "Open communication is the process of transmitting information about the self" (Montgomery, 1982, p. 28). According to Norton (1983), "Open style essentially signals that the message is personal, private, unambiguous, and explanatory. The way the person 'openly' communicates indicates that the message should be taken, filtered, or understood to be representational of the self and isomorphic with what the self knows the self to be" (p. 105).

Norton (1983) operationalizes the open style by five categories of behavior developed across a series of investigations. Negative openness is showing disagreement. Emotional openness references the expression of feelings, and receptive openness shows that the person is open to others' communication. General style openness represents Norton's overall, gestalt judgment of open behavior (Norton, 1978). In an attempt to refine the definition of the open style, Montgomery (1984) examined the relationship of verbal immediacy to the five open behavior categories. Results verified the conceptualization of openness by defining it in terms of verbal immediacy, nonverbal openness, emotional openness, receptive openness, and general style openness.

The attentive style is characterized by feedback given, listening, and empathy. The type of feedback inherent in this style is one that indicates involvement, interest, and affect. Listening refers to active listening, not merely hearing the sound of words, and empathy is "a combination of understanding the other's feelings and indicating that understanding to the other" (Norton, 1983, p. 158). Norton and Pettegrew (1979) refined the attentive style definition by identifying behavioral attributes of the style, finding that the most significant predictors of attentiveness were posture, restatement and nondirective responses, and direct eye behavior. Attentiveness is demonstrated by the verbal and nonverbal tendency to show interest. "The attentive communicator focuses his/her regard toward the other while simultaneously signaling verbally and paraverbally that interest, concern, sensitivity, and notice are being shown" (Norton & Pettegrew, 1979, p. 26).

Dramatic style is characterized by a communicator who "manipulates messages through exaggerations, fantasies, stories, metaphors, rhythm, voice, and other stylistic devices to highlight, understand, or alter literal meaning" (Norton, 1983, p. 129). The dramatic style is operationalized for effective teaching by entertaining behaviors, double takes, stories, laughter by others, sarcasm, and mood control (Norton & Nussbaum, 1980). In an examination of students' self-perceived communicator styles, Norton (1983) found that the "dramatic communicator vividly, emotionally, or strikingly signals that literal meaning is being emphasized to manipulate mood, change energy, and/or seek attention" (p. 151). The central elements of the dramatic style are playing the roles of fantasizer, performer, dramatizer, insulter, information distributor, gossiper, and storyteller.

While Norton and Nussbaum asserted in 1980 that communicator style is different from personality because style can be manipulated across situations, Norton (1983) fits communicator style into the personality style domain. Use of different components of communicator style in different situations simply refers to one's behavioral flexibility. "Certain communicator styles are likely to be perceived as more effective in particular interactions" (Norton, 1983, p. 91). One way to examine such an assertion is to review the research dealing with style of communication across contexts. Of particular interest are those suggested by Norton (1983)—organizations, marital dyads, education, and medicine.

In organizations, the definition of communicator style is most frequently labeled "managerial communication style." According to our conceptualization of style, managers use a combination of different traits according to what they are capable of enacting and what the situation demands. Thus Blake and Mouton's (1978) Managerial Grid speaks in terms of a manager's concern for production and for people and describes five types of managers (impoverished, country club, organization man, authority-obedience, and team) as utilizing different communication styles to gain compliance. A similar schema is used by Likert (1961) with the "four systems" approach. Richmond and McCroskey (1979) introduced the tell, sell, consult, and join styles of management communication in an attempt to combine communication behaviors with management behavior. Richmond and McCroskey (1979) and Wheeless, Wheeless, and Howard (1984) report that a more consulting/participatory style is associated with perceived job satisfaction among subordinates.

The influence aspect of managerial style is further examined in the compliance-gaining style literature. Influence tactics are investigated in the leadership literature (Barlow, Hansen, Fuhriman, & Finley, 1982; Fleishman, 1973; Halpin & Winer, 1952) and more recently as compliance-gaining tactics used to influence employees. Using Marwell and Schmitt's (1967) 16 compliance-gaining techniques, Kipnis, Schmidt, and Wilkinson (1980) provided a six-factor description of how managers get subordinates to comply and found that the type of tactic used varied with the reasons for exercising influence. For example, to improve performance, the most successful style was one that used assertive behaviors such as demanding, ordering, and setting deadlines. Yukl and Taber (1983) found that different uses of power were effective for obtaining commitment or compliance, or for reducing resistance. Authority and reward power worked best when seeking compliance, expert and referent power for gaining commitment, and coercive power for overcoming resistance to be influenced. Wheeless, Hudson, and Wheeless (1985) have reported that the lack of an intimidating style contributed the most to subordinates' job satisfaction, trust in supervisors, and organizational commitment.

Three reports have specifically examined managerial style as it relates to Norton's communicator style. Bradley and Baird (1977) used Norton and Miller's (1975) definition of communicator style as "characteristic predispositions toward an interactive situation" (p. 196). Using a modified version of the Communicator Style Measure, they reported that a democratic manager is perceived to be relaxed, animated, attentive, and friendly. A laissez-faire style if perceived as relaxed, friendly, and attentive. And, as expected, the authoritative manager is perceived to be dominant. Bradley and Baird (1977) conclude that management style and communicator style are highly correlated.

Bednar (1982) extended this finding and examined the degree to which managers' and supervisors' communicator styles systematically covary with performance. Bednar defined "outstanding and definitely above average" managers according to their communicator style using performance data. Managers in an insurance company were perceived to be outstanding when they were open, precise, and had a more positive overall communicator style. Managers in a hospital were called outstanding when they were less contentious, more animated, attentive, and had a more positive overall communicator style. Bednar (1982) suggests that the "specific role sets, contexts, objectives, and procedures of different organizations may have unique communicator style requirements for managers and supervisors" (p. 71).

Infante and Gorden (1982) found that supervisors who are perceived as higher on the components of relaxed, impression-leaving, and dominance, and lower on contentious and dramatic are rated as more effective. Subordinates are generally more satisfied with supervisors who are similar in terms of dramatic style and animation, but different in terms of being relaxed, open, and attentive.

The second context where the literature discusses communicator style is in the marital dyad, although use of Norton's conceptualization or operationalization is sparse. Mitchell (1982) reports that when married couples use different styles of communication, special attention must be given to acceptance of this difference for the relationship to continue. Honeycutt, Wilson, and Parker (1982) report that a friendly style accounts for the most variance in defining the good communicator in a marital relationship. A relaxed, friendly, open, dramatic, and attentive communicator style is used by happily married couples. Wives are also reported to prefer less of a controlling style in husbands than husbands prefer in themselves. Husbands value a conventional style in wives less than wives value it in themselves (Hawkins, Weisberg, & Ray, 1980).

Perhaps the context most examined by those interested in communicator style is education. Norton (1983) has provided an excellent summary of work by Finkbeinder, Lathrop, and Schuerger (1973), Rico (1971), Isaacson, McKeachie, Milholland, Lin, Hofeller, Baerwaldt, and Zinn (1964), Frey (1973), Meredith (1975), and Greenwood, Bridges, Ware, and McLean (1973) which outlines the important variables in teaching effectiveness. Norton describes three studies that further illustrate which components of communicator style contribute to effective teaching. The ineffective teacher is not animated, does not signal attentiveness or friendliness, is neither precise or relaxed, and does not use a dramatic style. Specific tests of the dramatic style show that getting others to fantasize, tell stories, be entertaining, use energy, catch attention, and manipulate the mood are related to effective teaching.

In an examination of how communicator style relates to different kinds of learning, Anderson, Norton, and Nussbaum (1981) report three important findings which illustrate the use of different style components in teaching. First, communicator style is related to affective and behavioral learning, but not cognitive learning. Second, the best predictors of affective learning are impression-leaving and contentiousness. Third, behavioral learning is predicted by communicator image and impression-leaving. Fourth, the good teacher is characterized by the style components of openness, relaxed, and impression-leaving.

Although it is generally documented that the most effective teaching style is the dramatic style, perceptions between students and teachers are not always consistent. Norton (1977) indicates that when teachers rate themselves, they say the best predictors of effectiveness are communicator image, attentiveness, and impression-leaving. Students also include the characteristics of being relaxed, not dominant, friendly, and precise.

Examinations of communicator style in the field of medicine generally center on the physician. Patients generally want doctors who are open, receptive, and who show concern (Korsch, Gozzi, & Vida, 1968). Patients also favor doctors who show personal interest in them (Geerston, Gray, & Ward, 1973), use person-oriented communication (Hargrove, 1974; Kalisch, 1973; Schulman, 1978), exhibit caring (DiMatteo & DiNicola, 1982), show sympathy and friendliness (Korsch & Negrete, 1972), and communicate empathy (Freeman, Negrete, Davis, & Korsch, 1971; Korsch et al., 1968; Vida, Korsch, & Morris, 1969). In a recent attempt to examine female patient and physician communication, Wheeless (1985) operationalized physician receptivity by combining Norton's (1978) open and attentive dimensions of communicator style. However, physician receptivity was not a significant predictor of patient likelihood to discuss health care topics with the physician or patient knowledge about gynecological health needs, and it accounted for only minimal variance in feelings toward the physician at the time of the examination. Variables that did contribute to these factors were patient communication apprehension and trust in the physician.

While the above-mentioned research verifies communicator style as an important construct in the study of the style dimension of personality and as evidence of the inconsistency norm of communication behavior, use of measures operationalizing the construct has not been without criticism. One criticism centers on the use of ten separate subconstructs/ dimensions of Norton's Communicator Style Measure (1978). Talley and Richmond (1980) found that the "self-reported communicator-style variables are highly interrelated, so highly interrelated that they may represent only a single dimension of response" (p. 337). Jablin (1985) also reported that when the top loading items on Norton's entire Communicator Style Measure instrument were used, low zero-order correlations emerged between items and the subdimensions. When the subdimension composite scores were factor analyzed, only two dimensions emerged— receptive-responsive and communicator activity. In addition, only three of the 45 Communicator Style Measure items have reversed polarity, which Talley and Richmond (1980) indicate may be producing a response bias artifact. Thus the utility of using the Norton measure in its original form and with its traditional scoring patterns may be problematic, and future research should scrutinize its use.

## GENDER ORIENTATION STYLE

Communication research on gender has concentrated on comparing the behavior of females and males. While research findings show that identifying individuals as men or women accounts for variance in a variety of criterion variables, within-group differences among females and males have focused attention on the introduction of gender identity, often referred to as gender orientation. Such emphasis provides an initial point from which to discuss gender orientation as a style perspective that explains inconsistency in behavior.

Mussen's work in the early 1960s provided evidence that males differ from each other in degrees of masculinity and dominance, among other variables. Mussen (1961) reports that 17- and 18-year-old males differ in their association with masculinity, and a longitudinal study, reported in 1962, showed that over a period of 20 years males changed in their levels of dominance, self-acceptance, and leadership abilities. In other words, males differ in gender identity and in some behaviors. Mere classification as a male does not adequately explain why males behave as they do.

While research with females appears to be less consistent, evidence has shown that they too differ from each other in terms of identification with femininity (Cosentino & Heilburn, 1964; Gray, 1957; Webb, 1963). These within-group gender differences have motivated the academic community to ask "why?" Some answers have questioned commonly held assumptions that it is "good" for males to be masculine and females to be feminine. As a result, the gender orientation construct was introduced to refer to one's basic sense of masculinity (instrumental/ agency) *and* femininity (expressive/communion). Important to understanding the construct is the recognition that individuals develop a style of behavior based on their identification with both masculine and feminine traits. Like Leary's (1957) interpersonal styles, masculinity is associated with a dominant style and femininity with a submissive style. Regardless of anatomical sex, individuals develop styles associated with varying degrees of both dominance and submissiveness. When females identify to a higher degree with femininity and males with a higher degree of masculinity, they are referred to as "sex-typed" individuals. When males identify more with feminine traits than masculine and females more with masculine traits than feminine, they are called "cross-sex-typed" or "reversed-sex-typed."

According to Kagan (1964) and Kohlberg (1966), the highly sex-typed person is motivated to behave according to rigid sex-role standards. Behavior defined as sex-inappropriate is eliminated from possible activation. When people view themselves as less sex-typed, their experiences vary and provide a wider repertoire of behaviors from which to choose. The widest repertoire belongs to the androgynous person who identifies to a high degree with both masculinity and femininity and whose behavioral style is based on an interaction of self-traits and the situation. Thus, by definition, gender orientation can be viewed as a "style." Masculinity and femininity constitute the knowledge structures used to activate behavior. This concept is best described by examining the tenets of gender schema theory.

Using the basic tenets of cognitive schemata theory (Bartlett, 1932), Bem (1981) explains gender orientation in terms of gender schema theory. This theory "construes perception as a constructive process wherein what is perceived is a product of the interaction between the incoming information and the perceiver's preexisting schema" (Bem, 1981, p. 355). When gender is viewed as the schema, individuals will have a readiness to encode, organize, and process information based on sex-linked associations (Markus, Crane, Bernstein, & Siladi, 1982). Two significant research endeavors provide investigations of the theory. Bem (1981) operationalized organizing and processing information according to various gender-related schemata by recalling words defined as male, female, masculine, and feminine and in a second study by how subjects used masculine and feminine adjectives to describe themselves. Results indicated that masculine males and feminine females (sex-typed individuals) clustered words on the basis of gender and also made faster gender-schema-consistent judgments about themselves than did non-sex-typed people.

Markus et al. (1982) report some support for Bem's findings and interpret them from a gender orientation style perspective. Masculine schematics processed information using masculine self-schemata, and feminine schematics used feminine self-schemata. The person who did not differ in the processing of feminine and masculine attributes, but recalled as many of one as the other, was the androgynous individual. Thus, to the androgynous person, both masculine and feminine knowledge structures were available for processing information.

Gender orientation as a style of personality can be further explained by examining the origin of schemata. Markus et al. (1982) explain that self-schemata are "summaries and constructions of past behavior" (p. 49). Past experiences help form knowledge structures around which rules for processing information about self and others are made (Smith, 1982). Identification with masculine and feminine traits affects the range of available behavioral alternatives.

> The masculine schematic individual and the high androgynous individual may both think of themselves as assertive and attach similar meaning and examples to that attribute, but the high androgynous individual is also likely to have the attributes "understanding" and "compassionate" as defining features of the self-concept. These other attributes of the self may well modify or constrain the range of behavioral alternatives that follow from thinking of one's self as assertive. Somewhat more subtly these additional features of the self-concept may influence the style and manner in which one acts in accordance with the attribute assertive. (Markus et al., 1982, p. 49)

The gender orientation construct can also be viewed from a style perspective through its original conceptualization. Accordingly, androgynous persons' self-concepts and behaviors are not formed or driven by gender experiences or gender schema and are thus more behaviorally flexible (Bem, 1974). Conceptually, sex-typed individuals, because of their narrow trait association, are restricted in their behavior and seldom vary from a dominant or submissive style. Cross-sex-typed individuals, while less rigid in their behaviors, express submissive or dominant behaviors across some situations. Because androgyny involves the adoption of a wide repertoire of traits and associated behaviors, this person acquires what Mischel (1968) refers to as the inconsistent norm—adaptation to situations, not rigid behaviors. The situation moderates the relationship between gender orientation traits and outcomes. Numerous research findings support the hypothesis that androgyny is related to adaptability.

Bem (1975) first provided support for the adaptability/androgyny hypothesis by examining how well masculine, androgynous, and feminine subjects perform masculine and feminine behaviors. Bem and Lenney (1976) extended such findings using sex-typed, androgynous, and sex-reversed subjects to specify which of 60 different masculine, feminine, or neutral activities they would be willing to perform for pay while being photographed.

Additionally, contemporary research—using more precise definitions of instrumental and expressive behavior—continues to support the assumption that androgyny is related to adaptability. Androgynous females report significantly less discomfort in situations demanding assertiveness and a significantly higher probability of engaging in asser-tive behavior than do sex-typed females (Gayton, Havu, Baird, & Ozman, 1983). Androgynous marital couples (or when at least one spouse is androgynous) have fewer sexual problems because of their adaptability and flexibility (Safir, Yochanan, Lichenstein, Hoch, & Shepher, 1982), and androgynous parents demonstrate more ''child-centered'' (as opposed to strict responsive/feminine or firm/masculine) child-raising approaches (Baumrind, 1982).

In research more clearly testing the relationship of adaptability in communication to androgyny, Wheeless and Duran (1982) and Brunner and Phelps (1980) have found that androgynous individuals demonstrate the highest levels of self-reported adaptability in communication compe-tence. Wheeless and Wheeless (1982) also report a significant positive correlation between both self-perceived and other-perceived social adapt-ability with androgyny. Further, Wheeless (1984) reports that androg-ynous individuals adapt to situations by using language similar to the behavioral cues of the other (i.e., masculine language to masculine behavior and feminine language to feminine behavior). Such adaptation is not always apparent for feminine or masculine individuals.

''It seems reasonable to conclude that, in the aggregate, both self-assertive and interpersonally oriented qualities tend to confer benefits on their possessers. In this sense, the men and women who exhibit both sets of personal characteristics . . . typically have an overall advantage over others'' (Spence, 1984, p. 79). Several research findings support such a conclusion. Androgynous adolescents show higher levels of self-esteem than do feminine or undifferentiated subjects (Lamke, 1982). For adult subjects, androgyny is positively related to self-esteem, self-acceptance, and acceptance of others (Eman & Morse, 1977; Wetter, 1975). Androgyny and masculinity in female students is also related to body satisfaction and sexual satisfaction (Kimlicka, Cross, & Tarnai, 1983). Androgynous individuals report that they are less lonely than masculine, feminine, or undifferentiated individuals (Avery, 1982; Berg & Peplau, 1982). Not only do androgynous individuals report better personal adjustment, but others also rate them high in adjustment (Jackson, 1983; Major, Carnevale, & Deaux, 1981).

Because of the popularity of examining the gender variable from the gender orientation perspective, researchers have devoted considerable time and effort to improving the conceptual meaning and operational measures of the construct. Spence (1984) has provided an extensive summary of the conceptual and operational changes made over the years. In terms of the gender orientation perspective as a style dimension of personality, the crucial questions revolve around the conceptualization of androgyny.

Spence and Helmreich (1979) use the term "androgyny" as a mnemonic for identifying high-high score combinations of masculinity and femininity, while Bem (1979) uses the scoring as a representation of the high masculinity and high femininity conceptualization of androgyny. The high-high combination operationalization would seem to place the androgynous concept in a double-bind. If high masculine males and high feminine females (sex-typed) are rigid in their behaviors, why wouldn't the androgynous person who is high in both be even more rigid? The answer seems to lie in our explanation of gender orientation from a style perspective. Sex-typed individuals have no alternative outside the narrow confines of masculine or feminine knowledge structures. They have developed masculine or feminine information constellations which serve as relevant knowledge when communicating. The androgynous person, on the other hand, is equally responsive to both masculine and feminine attributes and is able to cognitively integrate these traits with the situation and behave accordingly. The key is that *both* masculine and feminine knowledge structures are available. Markus et al. (1982) and Wheeless (1984) provide support for this theoretical explanation.

Markus et al. (1982) examined subjects' recall of masculine and feminine adjectives, use of masculine and feminine words to describe self, confidence in self-descriptions, and behavioral evidence of the self-descriptions. For all variables, feminine subjects associated with feminine self-schema and masculine subjects with masculine self-schema. The androgynous individual endorsed both equally.

Wheeless (1984) observed individuals' responses to situations by analyzing language used to respond to different people in various situations. Feminine individuals used predominantly feminine-typed language across all situations. However, both masculine and androgynous people used masculine language when confronted with a male exhibiting masculine behavior and feminine language when confronting a female exhibiting feminine behavior. Masculine and androgynous subjects did differ, however, when confronted with a female exhibiting masculine behavior. The masculine subjects still resorted to the use of feminine language, while the androgynous subjects responded with masculine language. Wheeless (1984) concluded that the sex-typed masculine person sees females in a stereotypic feminine manner, regardless of whether they exhibit dominant or submissive behaviors.

An attempt to examine directly the relationship of androgyny and schemata is provided by McMahan and Stacks (1984) using the cognitive complexity variable. This construct highlights social cognition learning by showing that individuals acquire personal cognitive construct systems through their interactions with others and the environment. These cognitive systems then provide parameters from which to view and interact with others. McMahan and Stacks compare cognitive constructs to Bem's (1979) gender schemata. Because the cognitively complex individual had previously demonstrated flexibility and adaptability to a variety of social stimuli, McMahan and Stacks proposed a positive relationship between cognitive complexity and androgyny. They found a significant, but low, positive correlation. However, it should be noted that the statistical analyses used in this study were low power correlations using continuous and categorical data in the same correlation model. Further, cognitive complexity was operationalized as the quantity of constructs used to describe two people, which may or may not represent the gender constructs held by the subject. The definition of androgyny does not assume the possession of many schemata but focuses on the gender schemata of masculinity and femininity. Of greater significance to the conceptualization of androgyny is the cognitive integration dimension of cognitive complexity. A key assumption of androgyny is that such individuals are able to integrate new information from situations with existing cognitive structures which are less narrow and restricted than those of sex-typed people (Mischel, 1973). Examination of gender orientation as a style personality dimension, which necessitates a look at this integrative ability, would help us to better understand the androgyny construct.

A question raised occasionally about the androgyny conceptualization refers to its adaptive nature. Is the androgynous individual only conforming to and mirroring others when responding in a like manner, or is he or she really adapting to the situation? Mischel (1973) explains such adaptation in terms of behavior for beneficial consequences and as a discriminative facility to respond appropriately, which connotes an active decision-making process. Adaptation can be considered a mix of assimilation and accommodation in terms of which sex-typed people are limited. Their knowledge structures do not allow accommodation, since only a narrow focus is available to contribute to limited alternative behaviors. Wheeless (1984) explains the adaptive nature of the androgynous individual as a type of convergence: "The adaptable androgynous individual, instead of feeling a need for approval, empathizes with the other and uses a language that demonstrates a type of 'task homophily.' For feminine cues, they demonstrate cooperation and sincerity; for masculine cues, they show a kind of expertise and energy necessary to accomplish a task" (pp. 18-19).

In the area of operationalizing the gender orientation construct, the two most frequently used operational measures of gender orientation are the Personal Attribute Questionnaire (PAQ; Spence, Helmreich, & Stapp, 1975), which refers to the two M. (masculine) and F (feminine) dimensions as self-assertive and interpersonal skills, and the Bem Sex-Role Inventory (BSRI; Bem, 1974), which simply calls the dimensions masculine and feminine. Regardless of the labels, the PAQ and the BSRI are used to measure personality traits associated with gender identities.

General objection to the measures, and in particular to the BSRI, revolves around use of subjects' self-reports as an accurate view of the self (Pedhazur & Tetenbaum, 1979), use of identification with personality traits without inclusion of situational contingencies (Putnam, 1982), the assertion that the measures are related to apparent social desirability (Silvern & Ryan, 1979), and the factor structure of the measure (Pedhazur & Tetenbaum, 1979). However, researchers continue to dispell such allegations.

Using the Crowne-Marlowe Measure of Social Desirability (Crowne & Marlowe, 1960), Dierks-Stewart (1980) found a slight correlation (.14) with masculinity and a low correlation with femininity (.35). Wheeless and Wheeless (1982) report a low correlation with only a self-measure of femininity and no significant correlations with perceptions of others. In addition, Wheeless's (1984) study demonstrated that situational contingencies can be used as a part of research designs examining gender orientation. The dimensional structure of the BSRI has been refined by Bem (1979), Dierks-Stewart (1980), and Wheeless and Wheeless (1982) to include a 20- or 30-item measure with two dimensions, masculinity and femininity, and high internal reliabilities.

Different scoring methods have been advocated for the BSRI since the *t* ratio method was first used. The most commonly used is the median split method where a combination of scores above and/or below the median determines classification as masculine, feminine, androgynous, or undifferentiated. A new formula, the androgyny score (A-score), developed by Wheeless and Wheeless (1982), was an attempt to provide a statistical way to combine the contributions of masculinity and femininity to form a continuous androgyny score. Use of the formula demonstrated superiority over the traditional masculine and feminine median split method in accounting for variance in social adaptability. Other researchers, such as Wheeless and Duran (1982), have used masculinity and femininity in regression models to examine the unique contribution of each to significant communication criterion variables.

Indictments of the operationalization of the measure of gender orientation have been addressed, and research has shown that masculine and feminine personality traits are response predispositions that have considerable transsituational significance for behavior (Spence & Helmreich, 1979). Androgyny has not been offered as a construct referring to a lack of sex identification, but instead has been conceptualized as the use of schemata based on *both* dimensions of gender identity, masculinity and femininity, which allows for the maximum integration of situations and cognitive systems. Such a conceptualization fits most definitions of "style" and research findings help explain the inconsistent nature of behavior.

## SOCIAL STYLE

The style personality perspectives of communicator style and gender orientation generally examine self-perceptions and interactions with situations. A construct that allows us to look at style as something that is assigned by others is social style. One of the basic assumptions underlying social style is that the judgments that one person makes of another are based primarily on observations of the subject's behavior exhibited across a variety of interpersonal contexts. Finally, those who interact with the subject will tend to agree on the type of category to which the person should be assigned, thus giving an individual's social style a fairly high degree of stability. Factor analytic research dealing with measurements of assertiveness and responsiveness viewed from the other perspective lends considerable support to this position.

When a person's social style is determined, it is based on consensus judgments of between three and five observers of his or her assertiveness and responsiveness. Once aggregated, the mean values assigned by the raters are used to place the person in one of four social styles—

analytical, driver, amiable, or expressive. An *analytical* is a person perceived to be low in both assertiveness and responsiveness. A *driver* is perceived to be high in assertiveness and low in responsiveness. An *amiable* is seen as low in assertiveness but high in responsiveness. Finally, the *expressive* is perceived to be high in both attributes.

One common reaction to the Social Style Matrix is that it is just another way to stereotype people. To the degree that stereotyping and generalizing are related, there may be some merit in this line of argument. However, there are two reasons to suggest that there is more dissimilarity than similarity in the two processes. First, social styles are based on consensus among observers on noncategorical variables. Second, social style assignment is supposedly based on actual interactions between observers and an observee. Stereotyping makes no such requirements. The best way of thinking about social style is that it represents a set of generalizations that can be made about an individual once he or she has been classified in terms of levels of assertiveness and responsiveness. In terms of viewing social style from the style dimension of personality, assertiveness and responsiveness become the knowledge structures used to make judgments.

Within the context of a social style, assertiveness is defined as the perceived effort (by others) that a person makes to influence or control the thoughts and actions of others (V. Lashbrook & Lashbrook, 1980). Responsiveness is defined as the effort a person makes (as perceived by others) to control his or her emotions and feelings when relating to others (V. Lashbrook & Lashbrook, 1980).

Perceived assertiveness has been found to be related to attempts to control or influence others and is often viewed as a task-oriented dimension of interpersonal communication. Highly assertive individuals are seen as active, confident, aggressive, ambitious, challenging, competitive, fast-paced, risk-taking, opinionated, and directive. Low assertive persons are described as reserved, easygoing, submissive, private, quiet, deliberate, risk-avoiding, and unaggressive. It is easy, we think, to see how such perceptions can be used in the analysis and rationalization of why and how a given communication may have transpired. It would appear possible for an individual to plan his or her communication to take into consideration the possible assertive reactions of the person being communicated with.

Research conducted (primarily by the Wilson Learning Corporation) over the past decade has consistently shown a person's perceived levels of assertiveness and responsiveness to be independent of one another (Lashbrook, 1974; Lashbrook & Lashbrook, 1979; Wiley & Lashbrook, 1984). All of these studies have involved the factor analysis of scales used to operationalize assertiveness and responsiveness and have reported low to zero-order correlations between consistently calculated factor scores. It is important to note that this research has been primarily psychometric in nature and has utilized the characteristics ascribed to the social styles as the scales used to operationalize the defining concepts.

Studies conducted in the late 1970s lend independent support for the relationship between assertiveness and responsiveness and sets of specific distinguishing characteristics. Sullivan (1977), investigating relationships among people in business settings, found that highly assertive individuals (in addition to being perceived as such) were also described as being more powerful and more competent than low assertive persons. Snavely (1981), in a more interpersonal context, found that highly assertive individuals were perceived to be more extroverted, more powerful, more versatile, and more similar in terms of values than their low assertive counterparts. Knutson and Lashbrook (1976) found highly assertive persons to have less communication apprehension than low assertive individuals. In general, there has been considerable support for predictable differences between high and low assertive people as perceived by others.

Similar findings have been reported for differences between high responsive and low responsive individuals. Sullivan (1977) found responsiveness to be positively associated with sociability, versatility, trust, social attraction, character, composure, interpersonal satisfaction, task attraction, and interpersonal solidarity. High responsive individuals were also perceived to be less dogmatic than low responsive persons. Similarly, Snavely (1981) found that high responsive persons are perceived to be more versatile, sociable, extroverted, and trustworthy than low responsive persons. Other researchers (Lashbrook & Lashbrook, 1979; Lashbrook, Knutson, Parsley, & Wenberg, 1976; Lashbrook, Lashbrook, & Buchholz, 1977) found a positive correlation between responsiveness, versatility, and interpersonal trust. In general, responsiveness appears to be positively related to various relationship-oriented dimensions of person perception, many of which predict behaviors during and following communication encounters.

Research dealing with the style profiles themselves supports the same ranges for assigned characteristics ascribed to differences in assertiveness and responsiveness. That is, the describing perceptions cluster to support four distinctive categories that can be labeled *analytical, driver, amiable,* and *expressive.* In actual use, the Social Style Matrix (see Figure 6.1) takes into account quartile breaks with respect to both assertiveness and responsiveness.

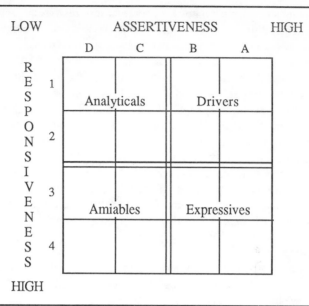

**Figure 6.1  The Social Style Matrix**

The combination of letters (D-A for levels of assertiveness) and numbers (1-4 for levels of responsiveness) actually allude to 16, rather than four, distinguishable styles. Again, in actual use, the primary social style of an individual is determined based on aggregated scores at or above the median or below on standardized measures of assertiveness and responsiveness. This means that, by design, the primary styles have equal percentages of assignees (25%). Within each primary style, there are four categories that mirror the overall matrix. Thus an analytical style (low in assertiveness and low in responsiveness) really stands for four categories of observed behaviors (D1, D2, C1, and C2). A D1 is characterized as an "analytical analytical" and a C2 as an "expressive analytical." It is important to note that while substyles are talked about in the training programs that use the Social Style Matrix, the research that supports the classification scheme has been limited to the four primary styles.

Lashbrook, Limbach, Morical, Habegger, Mullaney, Pechpel, Raiche, and Carns (1984) studied the context of sales involving people of known social styles. The study involved 70 interviews with buyers and sellers representing a cross-section of geographical locations, industries, and social styles. The intent of the research was to investigate buyer expectations and sales practices for people of different social styles. The study concluded that there are a great deal of similarities among buyers of the same social style in terms of buyer-sales relationships. There are also significant differences across styles. Likewise, there are both similarities and differences among salespeople in the way they approach the sales situation and develop relationships with buyers. Again, the similarities are with salespeople of the same style and the differences primarily across styles. The interesting thing to note is that when participants reported feeling discomfort with the sales process, it was expressed in terms of perceived differences in the assertiveness and responsiveness of the buyer or seller.

One of the major premises of social style is that once style is determined, and because determination itself is based on consistent behaviors viewed reliably by others, a person's primary style is stable. However, the system in use does permit movements within style based on a concept called "versatility." It is this latter concept that makes the social style construct more situational and personality dependent on (or, as we would argue, more representative of) the combination of trait personality characteristics and situational variables.

Perceived versatility refers to a person's willingness to adapt to other styles and various situations. It is conceptualized as a dimension that mediates the effectiveness of one's own social style (V. Lashbrook & Lashbrook, 1980). Although each person usually behaves in a manner consistent within his or her social style, to be viewed as more similar to another person affects perceptions of his or her versatility and the effectiveness of communication with the other person. Factor analytic research lends support for perceived versatility being distinguishable from levels of assertiveness and responsiveness, despite the fact that there appears to be a low to moderate correlation (.20-.40) between measures of responsiveness and versatility (Wiley & Lashbrook, 1984). Highly versatile individuals (regardless of style) are conceptualized to be generalists, adaptable, tolerant of ambiguity, negotiable, flexible, and multidimensional in their thinking. Persons with low versatility, on the other hand, are described as specialists, single-minded, predictable, intolerant of ambiguity, and inflexible (W. B. Lashbrook & Lashbrook, 1980).

One reason versatility has received such good press among the users of social style is that it has been found to be subject to influence through training (Burgess, Lashbrook, Wenberg, Larsen, & Lashbrook, 1980). Research has continually found that people, regardless of their primary social style, can be taught techniques which result in their being perceived to have high levels of versatility. The research goes on to suggest that it is the perceived "effort" to adapt that is the key to one's perceived versatility, and not the success of the effort nor its influence base. Versatility is something that seems to be appreciated when demonstrated in those situations that demand adaptation to others. Thus, while a person's social style may be relatively stable and consistent, his or her versatility may change as situations change. As something like a personality variable, versatility is a perceived willingness to change as much as possible without sacrificing those attributes that make a person most predictable and identifiable. Given this, it seems clear why the versatile person provides evidence of the inconsistent norm that is central to our definition of the style dimension of personality.

## CONCLUSIONS

This chapter is based on the premise that the style personality dimension provides one explanation for why individuals behave in inconsistent ways. This inconsistency is viewed as the norm, according to Mischel (1973), and through the concept of communication adaptability, three style perspectives have been examined. These style perspectives—communicator style, gender orientation style, and social style—allow for an examination of individuals' abilities to encode, process, integrate, and use information. Inherent in understanding style are the person-situation interaction demands in any communication act. Individuals have schemata, repertoires, and knowledge structures that are integrated with situational demands by a person's style. To varying degrees, the three style perspectives help explain this phenomenon. Communicator style uses subconstructs of behavior, gender orientation uses masculinity and femininity, and social style uses assertiveness and responsiveness as knowledge structures which can be activated according to situational demands. The three perspectives were chosen because they differ in their knowledge bases and because two, gender orientation and communicator style, allow for the examination of self-identity, while one, social style, allows for examination of the view from others' perceptions of behavior.

One aspect of all three perspectives should be noted. Basically, all three provide fundamental typologies with associated characteristics that give to each the look of a metaphoric, rather than a theoretical, reference. However, from the theoretical assumptions about the dominance/submissive axis of the interpersonal circumplex (Leary, 1957), at least the gender orientation dimensions of masculinity and femininity and the social style dimensions of of assertiveness and responsiveness appear congruent to this interpersonal communication theoretical grounding. While not defined in the same manner, these dimensions appear to have some conceptual overlap. In addition, we would suggest that all three perspectives—gender orientation, social style, and communicator style—are useful in terms of their heuristic and pragmatic value. For all three, evidence indicates that they are helpful in learning why some people are better able than others to integrate traits and situations and adapt accordingly. The introduction of the gender orientation high-high combination of masculinity and femininity and the versatility dimension of social style are further indications of the utility of these style perspectives in explaining adaptability in interpersonal communication.

It is difficult to evaluate communicator style in this context. Indeed, most researchers in this area do not even treat adaptation as an important process of the style perspective. While they do say that an individual has aspects of many styles, most researchers do not make it clear whether the combinations are unique or if the adaptation process is characteristic of all combinations. Norton (1983) adds to the confusion by stating, as an asset of the typology, its dependence on multicollinearity, leaving the reader with no real knowledge of either how differing styles are to be defined or the conditions under which people assume the characteristics of many styles. While research has dealt with the issue of how the communicator style construct relates to people in particular roles (i.e., teachers), to date it has not justified the use of the construct across a true situational base. When the Communicator Style Measure (Norton, 1978) was compared with a measure of the adaptability dimension of communicative competence (Duran & Zakahi, 1985), the two were only minimally related. Thus Duran and Zakahi concluded that communicator style and adaptability are conceptually different. The former was believed to be more descriptive and the latter more prescriptive. In other words, communicator style, rather than being a system itself, corresponds to how people describe systems of personality. In the end, the work on communicator style at best makes a case for matching styles to effect communication better, but not a basis for adaptation to others or to situations.

The gender orientation style research distinguishes combinations which are reasonable and which people seem to perceive differently. The system does allow for a type of co-orientation that is best considered an adaptive response. It is our belief that the degree to which a person is seen by self or by others as androgynous is a measure of his or her willingness to adapt to the gender orientation of another or, importantly, to situations that require something other than a typical gender-based response.

It would appear that those who study the social style construct have already begun the process of defining its usefulness in the adaptation arena in view of the treatment of versatility. Regardless of one's social style, versatility can range from low to high (W. B. Lashbrook & Lashbrook, 1980). Research has indicated that people with less than high perceived versatility can be trained to effect increasing amounts of the attribute. Given that versatility is conceptualized as the effort a person is *believed* to be making to adapt to the style of another person, or to the demands of a situation, the variation of the concept becomes one of its most desirable features. That a person can be versatile without changing his or her perceived levels of assertiveness and responsiveness would seem to give to social style the prime characteristics of a system. The link between versatility and interpersonal trust, the changeable nature of versatility, its distributional characteristics within quadrants of the Social Style Matrix, and is situational variability give emphasis to the concept of a trait in interaction with a set of communication demands that can be conceived of as adaptive response.

We have attempted in this chapter to take an alternative view of personality and interpersonal communication by focusing on the style perspective. All three style perspectives examined here provide a means to view more precisely the knowledge structures used to adapt to situations. In addition, gender orientation and social style have gone beyond surface explanations with the introduction of androgyny and versatility which provide further understanding of the adaptive nature of communicators. From our view of the study of personality, it is easy to see and appreciate the interaction between factors that keeps personalities stable while at the same time allowing them to adapt. We believe that in the long run, the adaptive response of a personality to its general environment is a viable way to talk about how one activates traits in different interpersonal communication situations.

## REFERENCES

Anderson, J., Norton, R., & Nussbaum, J. (1981). Three investigations exploring relationships among perceived communication style, perceived teacher immediacy, teaching effectiveness and student learning. *Communication Education, 30*, 377-392.

Avery, A. W. (1982). Escaping loneliness in adolescence: The case for androgyny. *Journal of Youth and Adolescence, 11*, 451-459.

Bales, R. (1970). *Personality and interpersonal behavior.* New York: Holt, Rinehart & Winston.

Bandura, A. (1971). *Social learning theory.* Morristown, NJ: General Learning Press.

Barlow, S., Hansen, W. D., Fuhriman, A. J., & Finley, R. (1982). Leader communication style: Effects on members of small groups. *Small Group Behavior, 13*, 518-531.

Bartlett, F. C. (1932). *Remembering: A study in experimental and social psychology.* London: Cambridge University Press.

Baumrind, D. (1982). Are androgynous individuals more effective persons and parents? *Child Development, 53*, 44-75.

Bednar, D. A. (1982). Relationships between communicator style and managerial performance in complex organizations: A field study. *Journal of Business Communication, 19*, 51-76.

Bem, D. J. (1983). Toward a response style theory of persons in situations. In M. M. Page (Ed.), *Nebraska Symposium on Motivation 1982: Personality, current theory and research.* Lincoln: University of Nebraska Press.

Bem, S. L. (1974). The measurement of psychological androgyny. *Journal of Consulting and Clinical Psychology, 42*, 155-162.

Bem, S. L. (1975). Sex role adaptability: One consequence of psychological androgyny. *Journal of Personality and Social Psychology, 31*, 634-643.

Bem, S. L. (1979). Theory and measurement of androgyny: A reply to the Pedhazur-Tetenbaum and Locksley-Colten critiques. *Journal of Personality and Social Psychology, 37*, 1047-1054.

Bem, S. L. (1981). Gender schema theory: A cognitive account of sex typing. *Psychological Review, 88*, 354-364.

Bem, S. L., & Lenney, E. (1976). Sex-typing and the avoidance of cross-sex behavior. *Journal of Personality and Social Psychology, 33*, 48-54.

Berg, J. H., & Peplau, L. A. (1982). Loneliness: The relationship of self-disclosure and androgyny. *Personality and Social Psychology Bulletin, 8*, 624-630.

Blake, R. R., & Mouton, J. S. (1978). *The new managerial grid.* Houston: Gulf.

Bradley, P. H., & Baird, J. E., Jr. (1977). Management and communicator style: A correlational analysis. *Central States Speech Journal, 28*, 194-203.

Brandt, D. R. (1979). On linking social performance with social competence: Some relations between communicative style and attributes of interpersonal attractiveness and effectiveness. *Human Communication Research, 5*, 223-237.

Brunner, C. C., & Phelps, L. A. (1980, May). *Interpersonal communication competence and androgyny.* Paper presented at the annual meeting of the International Communication Association, Acapulco, Mexico.

Burgess, W., Lashbrook, W., Wenberg, J. R., Larsen, D., & Lashbrook, V. (1980) An experimental study of the effects of training in managing interpersonal relationships (MIR). *Training and Development in Australia, 2*, 14-16.

Cody, M. J., McLaughlin, M. L., & Jordan, W. J. (1980). A multidimensional scaling of three sets of compliance-gaining strategies. *Communication Quarterly, 28*, 34-46.

Cosentino, F., & Heilbum, A. B. (1964). Anxiety correlates of sex-role identity in college students. *Psychological Reports, 14*, 729-730.

Crowne, F., & Marlowe, D. (1960). A new scale of social desirability independent of psychopathology. *Journal of Consulting Psychology, 24*, 348-354.

Dierks-Stewart, K. (1980). *The psychometric adequacy and desirability bias of the Bem Sex-Role Inventory*. Unpublished doctoral dissertation, Department of Interpersonal & Public Communication, Bowling Green State University.

DiMatteo, M. R., & DiNicola, D. D. (1982). *Achieving patient compliance: The psychology of the medical practitioner's role*. New York: Pergamon Press.

Duran, R. L., & Zakahi, W. R. (1985). Competence or style: What's in a name? *Communication Research Reports, 1*, 42-47.

Eadie, W. F., & Paulson, J. W. (1984). Communicator attitudes, communicator style and communication competence. *Western Journal of Speech Communication, 48*, 390-407.

Eman, V. A., & Morse, B. W. (1977, November). *A multivariate analysis of the relationship between androgyny and self-esteem, self-acceptance, and acceptance of others*. Paper presented at the annual meeting of the Speech Communication Association, Washington, D.C.

Finkbeinder, C., Lathrop, J., & Schuerger, J. (1973). Course and instructor evaluation: Some dimensions of a questionnaire. *Journal of Educational Psychology, 64*, 159-163.

Fleishman, E. A. (1973). Twenty years of consideration and structure. In E. A. Fleishman & J. G. Hunt (Eds.), *Current developments in the study of leadership*. Carbondale: Southern Illinois University Press.

Freeman, B., Negrete, V. F., Davis, M., & Korsch, B. M. (1971). Gaps in doctor-patient communication: Doctor-patient interaction analysis. *Pediatrics Research, 5*, 298-311.

Frey, P. (1973). Student ratings of teaching: Validity of several rating factors. *Science, 182*, 83-85.

Gayton, W. F., Havu, G., Baird, J. G., & Ozman, K. (1983). Psychological androgyny and assertiveness in females. *Psychological Reports, 52*, 283-285.

Geerston, H. R., Gray, R. M., & Ward, R. (1973). Patient non-compliance-within the context of seeking medical care for arthritis. *Journal of Chronic Disorders, 26*, 689-698.

Gray, S. W. (1957). Masculinity-femininity in relation to anxiety and social acceptance. *Child Development, 28*, 203-214.

Greenwood, G., Bridges, C., Ware, W., & McLean, J. (1973). Student evaluation of college teaching behaviors instrument: A factor analysis. *Journal of Higher Education, 44*, 596-604.

Halpin, A. W., & Winer, B. J. (1952). *Studies in aircrew composition: The leadership behavior of the commander*. Columbus: Ohio State University, Personnel Research Board.

Hargrove, D. S. (1974). Verbal interaction analysis of empathic and non-empathic responses of therapists. *Journal of Consulting and Clinical Psychology, 42*, 305-310.

Hawkins, J. L., Weisberg, C., & Ray, D. W. (1980). Spouse differences in communication style: Preference, perception, behavior. *Journal of Marriage and the Family, 42*, 585-593.

Honeycutt, J. M., Wilson, C., & Parker, C. (1982). Effects of sex and degrees of happiness on perceived styles of communication in and out of the marital relationship. *Journal of Marriage and the Family, 44*, 395-406.

Infante, D. A., & Gorden, W. I. (1982). Similarities and differences in the communicator styles of supervisors and subordinates: Relations to subordinate satisfaction. *Communication Quarterly, 30*, 56-66.

Isaacson, R., McKeachie, W., Milholland, J., Lin, Y., Hofeller, M., Baerwaldt, J., & Zinn, K. (1964). Dimensions of student evaluations of teaching. *Journal of Educational Psychology, 55*, 344-351.

Jablin, F. M. (1985). An exploratory study of vocational organizational communication socialization. *Southern Speech Communication Journal, 50*, 261-282.

Jackson, L. A. (1983). The perception of androgyny and physical attractiveness: Two is better than one. *Personality and Social Psychology Bulletin, 9*, 405-430.

Kagan, J. (1964). Acquisition and significance of sex-typing and sex-role identity. In M. L. Hoffman & L. W. Hoffman (Eds.), *Review of child development research* (Vol. 1). Beverly Hills, CA: Sage.

Kalisch, B. J. (1973). What is empathy? *American Journal of Nursing, 73*, 1548-1552.

Kimlicka, T., Cross, H., & Tarnai, J. (1983). A comparison of androgynous, feminine, masculine, and undifferentiated women on self-esteem, body satisfaction, and sexual satisfaction. *Psychology of Women Quarterly, 7*, 291-294.

Kipnis, D., Schmidt, S., & Wilkinson, I. (1980). Intraorganizational influence tactics. *Journal of Applied Psychology, 65*, 440-452.

Knutson, P., & Lashbrook, W. (1976, December). *Communication apprehension as an antecedent to social style.* Paper presented at the annual meeting of the Speech Communication Association, San Francisco.

Kohlberg, L. (1966). A cognitive developmental analysis of children's sex-role concepts and attitudes. In E. E. Maccoby (Ed.), *The development of sex differences.* Stanford, CA: Stanford University Press.

Korsch, B. M., Gozzi, E. K., & Vida, F. (1968). Gaps in doctor-patient interaction and patient satisfaction. *Pediatrics, 42*, 855-871.

Korsch, B. M., & Negrete, V. F. (1972). Doctor-patient communication. *Scientific American, 227*, 66-74.

Lamke, L. K. (1982). The impact of sex-role orientation on self-esteem in early adolescence. *Child Development, 53*, 1530-1535.

Lashbrook, V., & Lashbrook, W. B. (1980). *Social style as a basis for adult training.* Paper presented at the annual meeting of the Central States Speech Communication Association, Chicago, April.

Lashbrook, V. J., Limbach, M. P., Morical, K. E., Habegger, P. J., Mullaney, P. J., Pechpel, B. J., Raiche, J. J., & Carns, C. L. (1984). *Social style implications for buyer-seller relationships.* Eden Prairie, MN: Wilson Learning Corporation.

Lashbrook, W. B. (1974). *Toward the measurement and processing of the social style profile*. Eden Prairie, MN: Wilson Learning Corporation.

Lashbrook, W. B., Knutson, P. K., Parsley, M. L., & Wenberg, J. R. (1976, November). *An empirical examination of versatility as a consequence of perceived social style*. Paper presented at the annual meeting of the Western Speech Communication Association, San Francisco.

Lashbrook, W. B., & Lashbrook, V. (1980). *An empirical study of the differences between supervisor and peer perceptions of versatility*. Eden Prairie, MN: Wilson Learning Center.

Lashbrook, W. B., Lashbrook, V. J., & Buchholz, S. W. (1977). *The statistical adequacy of the social style profile*. Eden Prairie, MN: Wilson Learning Corporation.

Leary, T. (1957). *Interpersonal diagnosis of personality*. New York: Ronald Press.

Lieberman, M., Yalom, I., & Miles, M. (1973). *Encounter groups: First facts*. New York: Basic Books.

Likert, R. (1961). *New patterns of management*. New York: McGraw-Hill.

Major, B., Carnevale, P. J., & Deaux, K. (1981). A different perspective on androgyny: Evaluations of masculine and feminine characteristics. *Journal of Personality and Social Psychology, 41*, 988-1001.

Mann, R., Gibbard, G., & Hartman, J. (1967). *Interpersonal styles and group development*. New York: John Wiley.

Markus, H., Crane, M., Bernstein, S., & Siladi, M. (1982). Self-schema and gender. *Journal of Personality and Social Psychology, 42*, 38-50.

Marwell, G., & Schmitt, D. R. (1967). Dimensions of compliance-gaining behaviors: An empirical analysis. *Sociometry, 30*, 350-364.

McMahan, E. M. & Stacks, D. W. (1984). The relationship between androgyny and cognitive complexity: An exploratory investigation. *Southern Speech Communication Journal, 49*, 229-240.

Meredith, G. (1975). Structure of student-based evaluation ratings. *Journal of Psychology, 91*, 3-9.

Millar, F. E., & Rogers, L. E. (1976). A relational approach to interpersonal communication. In G. R. Miller (Ed.), *Explorations in interpersonal communication*. Beverly Hills, CA: Sage.

Mischel, W. (1968). *Personality and assessment*. New York: John Wiley.

Mischel, W. (1973). Toward a cognitive social learning reconceptualization of personality. *Psychological Review, 80*, 252-283.

Mitchell, C. E. (1982). Recognizing and accommodating different communication styles in marriage. *Family Therapy, 9*, 227-230.

Montgomery, B. M. (1982). Verbal immediacy as a behavioral indicator of open communication content. *Communication Quarterly, 30*, 28-34.

Montgomery, B. M. (1984). Behavioral characteristics predicting self and peer perceptions of open communication. *Communication Quarterly, 32*, 233-242.

Mussen, P. H. (1961). Some antecedents and consequences of masculine sex-typing in adolescent boys. *Psychological Monographs, 75*, No. 506.

Mussen, P. H. (1962). Long-term consequence of masculinity of interests in adolescence. *Journal of Consulting Psychology, 26*, 435-440.

Norton, R. (1977). Teacher effectiveness as a function of communicator style. In B. Ruben (Ed.), *Communication yearbook 1*. New Brunswick, NJ: Transaction.

Norton, R. (1978). Foundation of a communicator style construct. *Human Communication Research, 4*, 99-112.

Norton, R. (1983). *Communicator style: Theory, applications, and measures*. Beverly Hills, CA: Sage.

Norton, R., & Miller, L. (1975). Dyadic perception of communicator style. *Communication Research, 2*, 50-67.

Norton, R., & Nussbaum, J. (1980). Dramatic behaviors of the effective teacher. In B. Ruben (Ed.), *Communication yearbook 4*. New Brunswick, NJ: Transaction.

Norton, R., & Pettegrew, L. (1977). Communication style as an effective determinant of attraction. *Communication Research, 4*, 257-282.

Norton, R., & Pettegrew, L. (1979). Attentiveness as a style variable. *Communication Monographs, 46*, 12-27.

Pedhazur, E. J., & Tetenbaum, T. J. (1979). Bem Sex-Role Inventory: A theoretical and methodological critique. *Journal of Personality and Social Psychology, 37*, 996-1016.

Porter, D. T. (1982). Communicator style perceptions as a function of communication apprehension. *Communication Quarterly, 30*, 237-244.

Putnam, L. L. (1982). In search of gender: A critique of communication and sex-role research. *Women's Studies in Communication, 5*, 1-9.

Richmond, V. P., & McCroskey, J. C. (1979). Management communication style, tolerance for disagreement and innovativeness of employee satisfaction: A comparison of single-factor, two-factor approaches. In D. Nimmo (Ed.), *Communication yearbook 3*. New Brunswick, NJ: Transaction.

Rico, G. (1971). College students' perceptions of teacher effectiveness along given postulated dimensions. *St. Louis University Research Journal, 2*, 363-438.

Royce, J. R., & Powell, A. (1983). *Theory of personality and individual differences: Factors, systems, and process*. Englewood Cliffs, NJ: Prentice-Hall.

Safir, M. P., Yochanan, P., Lichenstein, M., Hoch, Z., & Shepher, J. (1982). Psychological androgyny and sexual adequacy. *Journal of Sex and Marital Therapy, 8*, 228-240.

Schulman, E. D. (1978). *Intervention in human services* (2nd ed.). St. Louis: Mosby.

Schutz, W. (1958). *FIRO: A three-dimensional theory of interpersonal behavior*. New York: Holt, Rinehart & Winston.

Scotton, C. M. (1985). What the heck, sir: Style shifting and lexical colouring as features of powerful language. In R. L. Street, Jr. & J. N. Cappella (Eds.), *Sequence and pattern in communicative behavior*. London: Edward Arnold.

Silvern, L., & Ryan, V. (1979). Self-rated adjustment and sex-typing on the Bem Sex-Role Inventory: Is masculinity the primary predictor of adjustment? *Sex Roles, 5*, 739-763.

Smith, M. J. (1982). *Persuasion and human interaction.* Belmont, CA: Wadsworth.

Snaveley, W. B. (1981). The impact of social style upon person perception in primary relationships. *Communication Quarterly, 29*, 132-143.

Spence, J. T. (1984). Masculinity, femininity, and gender-related traits: A conceptual analysis and critique of current research. In B. A. Maher & W. B. Maher (Eds.), *Progress in experimental personality research* (Vol. 13). New York: Academic Press.

Spence, J. T. & Helmreich, R. L. (1979). On assessing "androgyny." *Sex Roles, 5*, 721-738.

Spence, J. T., Helmreich, R. L., & Stapp, J. (1975). Ratings of self and peers on sex-role attributes and their relation to self-esteem and conceptions of masculinity and femininity. *Journal of Personality and Social Psychology, 32*, 29-39.

Spitzberg, B. H., & Cupach, W. R. (1984). *Interpersonal communication competence.* Beverly Hills, CA: Sage.

Sullivan, D. L. (1977). *Exploration in stylistic interpersonal communication: A conceptual framework and empirical strategy.* Unpublished doctoral dissertation, University of Nebraska-Lincoln, Department of Speech Communication.

Talley, M. A., & Richmond, V. P. (1980). The relationship between psychological gender orientation and communicator style. *Human Communication Research, 6*, 326-339.

Vida, F., Korsch, B. M., & Morris, M. J. (1969). Gaps in doctor-patient communication. *New England Journal of Medicine, 280*, 535-540.

Watzlawick, P., Beavin, J., & Jackson, D. (1967). *Pragmatics of human communication: A study of interactional patterns, pathologies, and paradoxes.* New York: W. W. Norton.

Webb, A. P. (1963). Sex-role preferences and adjustment in early adolescents. *Child Development, 34*, 609-618.

Wetter, R. E. (1975, October). *Levels of self-esteem association with four sex role categories.* Paper presented at the annual meeting of the American Psychological Association, Chicago.

Wheeless, L. R., Hudson, D. C., & Wheeless, V. E. (1985, February). *An examination of the relationships among management communication style, compliance-gaining styles, and organizational outcomes.* Paper presented at the annual meeting of the Western Speech Communication Association, Fresno.

Wheeless, L. R., & Wheeless, V. E. (1982). Attribution, gender orientation, and reconceptualization, measurement, and research results. *Communication Quarterly, 30*, 56-66.

Wheeless, L. R., Wheeless, V. E., & Howard, R. (1984). The relationships of communication with supervisor and decision participation to employee job satisfaction. *Communication Quarterly, 32*, 222-232.

Wheeless, V. E. (1984). A test of the theory of speech accommodation using language and gender orientation. *Women's Studies in Communication, 7*, 13-22.

Wheeless, V. E. (1985). Communication apprehension and trust as predictors of willingness to discuss gynecological health topics. *Communication Research Reports, 1*, 117-122.

Wheeless, V. E., & Duran, R. L. (1982). Gender orientation as a correlate of communicative competence. *Southern Speech Communication Journal, 48*, 51-64.

Wiley, J., & Lashbrook, V. (1984). *Social style profile update: Summary and analysis*. Eden Prairie, MN: Wilson Learning Corporation.

Yukl, G. A., & Taber, T. (1983). The effective use of managerial power. *Personnel, 60*, 37-44.

# Part IV
# INFORMATION-PROCESSING ORIENTATIONS

# 7

# Self-Conception and Social Information Processing

## CHARLES R. BERGER

Although the self-concept has assumed a central role in the thinking of a number of psychologists and sociologists (Allport, 1955; Cooley, 1902; James, 1890; Mead, 1934; Rogers, 1951; Sullivan, 1953), it has rarely been invoked by communication researchers as an explanatory construct for communication phenomena. One notable exception to this generalization is the work of Cushman and his associates (Cushman, Valentinsen, & Dietrich, 1982) in which it is argued that the self is an information processing system that generates and coordinates human action. McGuire and his colleagues (McGuire, McGuire, Child, & Fujioka, 1978; McGuire, McGuire, & Winton, 1979; McGuire & Padawer-Singer, 1976) have pointed to at least two reasons for the generally disappointing showing of the self-concept in social psychological research. First, most of the research reported in the area of self-conception has investigated self-esteem or the evaluative component of the self (see Wylie, 1961, 1974, 1979, for landmark reviews of self-concept research). However, McGuire and Padawer-Singer (1976) found that less than 10% of children's spontaneous thoughts about themselves could be classified as evaluative. Thus a considerable portion of what constitutes the self-concept has been ignored by researchers. Second, McGuire suggests that the use of reactive measurement methods in which the investigator has research participants evaluate themselves on dimensions selected by the researcher has produced distorted and inconsistent findings. Researchers need to determine whether or not persons actually evaluate themselves on particular dimensions and how salient these dimensions are to them before relationships between self-conception and other variables can be tested meaningfully (McGuire & Padawer-Singer, 1976).

The aim of the present chapter is to explore the linkages among self-conception, social information processing, and the generation of social action. Consistent with Cushman et al. (1982), it is assumed that the self-concept is a critical mediator between information input and action generaticn. Having said that, however, it is necessary to specify what the self-concept is, how it processes information, and how it is implicated in the generation of social action. In order to achieve this specification, the first part of this chapter will examine different definitions of self-concept. In the following section of the chapter, the role of the self in information processing will be explored. Finally, the relationships between self-conception and social interaction generation will be sketched. The discussion will focus on aspects of the self that are non-evaluative in nature, since Wylie's extensive reviews on the self-concept literature (Wylie, 1961, 1974, 1979) have more than adequately dealt with evaluative dimensions of the self. Attention will be paid to the potential role that affect about the self plays in the processing of social information. One caveat should be introduced at this point. While it is certainly the case that the self-concept plays an important role in the processing of social information, it is also true that the self-concept is not implicated in the processing of all information. This point will be clarified in later sections of the chapter.

## CONCEPTUALIZING THE SELF-CONCEPT

For William James (1890), the self consisted of two interrelated aspects, the self as known (the Me) and the self as knower (the I). He further argued that the Me comprises the material Me (a person's body, clothing, and home), the social Me (the recognition that persons get from those around them), and the spiritual Me (the entire collection of one's conscious states). James asserted that with reference to the social Me, a person has "*as many social selves as there are individuals who recognize him* and carry an image of him in their mind" (p. 294). James conceived of the I as that which at any given moment is *conscious*, whereas the Me is only one of the things of which the I is conscious. According to James, the stability of the self is achieved by the ability of the I to think in terms of both the present and the past.

There are several important features of James's (1890) conception of the self that have influenced subsequent discussions of the nature of the self-concept. First, the distinction between the objective (the Me) and subjective (the I) aspects of the self has been employed by later self theorists (e.g., Mead, 1934). Second, the tension between the ideas of the self as a singular entity and the self as a multiplicity of aspects (the social self) is an issue that persists to this day in conceptualizing the self. Related to this issue is the problem of the mutability of the self. Is the self-concept relatively enduring, or is it susceptible to change (Shrauger & Schoeneman, 1979; Swann & Ely, 1984; Swann & Hill, 1982; Swann & Read, 1981b)? This question is central to those who attempt to alter self-conceptions through therapeutic interventions. Thus many of James's ideas about the nature of the self and the issues he raised are still central to self-concept theory and research today.

Cooley (1902) defined the self as "that which is designated in common speech by the pronouns of the first person singular, 'I,' 'me,' 'mine,' and 'myself' " (p. 168). Cooley emphasized the role that "self-feeling" plays in the defining of oneself. Self-feeling is generated when, for any number of reasons, individuals differentiate themselves from their environment. He also asserted that there can be no sense of self or "I" without a sense of someone *else*. Moreover, his concept of the "looking glass self," or the view a given individual imagines another person to hold of him or her, was included in his thinking as a mechanism of social control for dampening the selfish impulses of the I.

Like Cooley, Mead (1934) emphasized the role that language and communication play in the development of the self-concept. He too recognized that the self as an object differs from other objects in that it can be an object unto itself (the I and the Me). Mead traced the development of the self through childhood and emphasized the importance of social interaction in the formation of the self. One result of the self's interactions is the formation of a concept of the "generalized other," which, like Cooley's "looking glass self," acts to curb selfish and/or antisocial behavior by making the individual cognizant of community standards for conduct. In Mead's view, it is through the "generalized other" and social interaction that social groups can coordinate their efforts to solve problems confronting them.

Rogers (1951) offers the following definition of the self-concept from his phenomenal perspective of personality and psychotherapy:

> The self-concept or self-structure may be thought of as an organized configuration of perceptions of the self which are admissible to awareness. It is composed of such elements as the perceptions of one's characteristics and abilities; the percepts and concepts of the self in relation to others in the environment; the value qualities which are perceived as associated with experiences and objects; and goals and ideals which are perceived as having positive or negative valence. (pp. 136-137)

In spite of the phenomenal orientation of this definition, Rogers recognized that there might be aspects of the self about which the individual could be unconscious. He felt that one of the aims of psychotherapy is to make the client aware of the unconscious aspects of the self through interaction with the therapist. One important feature of Rogers's definition of the self-concept is the inclusion of both affective and cognitive components of the self. The latter part of his definition emphasizes the affective dimension of the self, while "perceptions of one's characteristics" could include a host of relatively value-free perceptions of oneself. Rogers's therapeutic approach assumed that persons could make more realistic evaluations of themselves and their relationships with others if they could increase their intake of data from the environment. Thus Rogers not only posited an important relationship between affect and cognition but saw the importance of information processing in changing self-conceptions as well.

Sullivan (1953) conceived of the self-system as consisting of three personifications: the good-me, the bad-me, and the not-me. Sullivan felt that children did not develop these personifications by introjecting them from their mother. Rather, he hypothesized that these personifications developed as a result of the inevitable clash between the socially unacceptable behaviors that children might exhibit in response to various needs (e.g., genital manipulation) and the efforts of the "mothering one" to discourage these behaviors. Sullivan argues that the self-system develops as a way of coping with the anxiety induced by the mothering one's efforts to educate the child. Thus, unlike Cooley and Mead, who emphasized the role played by the "looking glass self" and the "generalized other" in encouraging cooperative behavior, Sullivan saw the passage from childhood to adulthood and the development of the self-system to be a difficult task because of the potential for numerous confrontations between children and significant others. In his *Interpersonal Theory of Psychiatry*, Sullivan (1953) attempts to explain the development of mental disorders in later life by recourse to the anxieties generated by interactions between children and significant others.

In his discussion of the self, Allport (1955) proposes that the self can be viewed to consist of the eight facets of a *proprium*. These are facets of persons' lives that are "peculiarly theirs." These facets are:

(1) *Bodily Sense*—Sense of self arising from bodily sensations.
(2) *Self-Identity*—Sense of self derived from being named, clothed, and so on.
(3) *Ego Enhancement*—Self-seeking nature of the person, pride.
(4) *Ego Extension*—Loyalties to others and causes or ideals.
(5) *Rational Agent*—Ability to solve problems and perceive accurately.
(6) *Self-Image*—Ideal self versus actual self.
(7) *Propriate Striving*—Striving for future goals.
(8) *The Knower*—Not a separate self, but part of what is known.

Allport (1955) alerted personality theorists to the problem of employing the self as an explanation for conduct. He saw the possibility that the self could become a homunculus residing within each of us that could be invoked to explain all manner of human behavior. In the present context, this possibility has already been anticipated by the caveat discussed earlier; that is, the self-concept is not always implicated in social information processing or the generation of social action.

This nonexhaustive review of various definitions of the self and self-conception demonstrates both commonalities and diversities in views of the self. All of the self-theorists cited here recognized that the self has both affective and cognitive components. Moreover, they saw the self as an important force in the generation of social behavior. Some theorists stressed the differences between the self as known (the Me) and the self as knower (the I) (James, 1890; Mead, 1934), whereas others (Rogers, 1951) focused on the self as known and avoided the problem of the self as knower, or argued that the I and the Me are not separate selves (Allport, 1955). Given the breadth and richness of these conceptual efforts, it is difficult to understand why, with few exceptions (Bugental & Zelen, 1950; Kuhn & McPartland, 1954; McGuire & Padawer-Singer, 1976; McGuire et al., 1978; McGuire et al., 1979), most research has focused exclusively on self-esteem and self-evaluation to the exclusion of the other aspects of the self-concept postulated by these theorists. One potential answer to this question is that much of the research in the self-concept area has been done by clinical psychologists and other researchers interested in psychotherapeutic effects. Frequently, a desired psychotherapeutic outcome is the enhancement of self-evaluations—hence the focus on this particular aspect of the self.

## SELF-CONCEPTION AND INFORMATION PROCESSING

In this section I consider recent theory and research that examines the relationship between self-conception and information processing. I first discuss the central construct in this research—the schema, then examine the role that self-schemata play in the processing of information.

### The Nature of Schemas

Space limitations preclude an exhaustive discussion of the history of the schema concept; however, Taylor and Crocker (1981) present such a discussion and offer the following definition of the schema construct:

A schema is a cognitive structure that consists in part of the representation of some defined stimulus domain. The schema contains general knowledge about the domain, including a specification of the relationships  among its attributes, as well as specific examples or instances of the  stimulus  domain. As such, one of the chief functions of the schema is to provide an answer to the question, "what is it?" (p. 91)

Taylor and Crocker (1981) then delineate three classes of social schemas. *Person schemas* include person prototypes such as extrovert-introvert (Cantor & Mischel, 1977), person impressions, and self-schemata (Markus, 1977; Markus & Smith, 1981). *Role schemas* encompass schemata for various occupations or social groups. Finally, *event schemas* are cognitive representations of routine action sequences, such as initial interactions between strangers, which have a scriptlike structure (Abelson, 1981; Bower, Black, & Turner, 1979; Schank & Abelson, 1977).

Taylor and Crocker (1981) suggest several functions that schemas serve. First, schemas enable persons to make their environment and the behavior of persons in it meaningful; that is, they enable persons to comprehend what is going on around them. Second, schemas influence what information is encoded and/or retrieved from memory. Third, schemas help to determine the rate at which information is processed. Fourth, schemas may provide information that is missing from an array of input information; that is, schemas may help perceivers "fill in the gaps." Fifth, schemas can be the basis for evaluating experiences. Finally, schemas can provide the basis for developing and enacting behavioral routines to meet goals. While the conceptual territory covered by the schema construct is impressive, Fiske and Linville (1980) have cautioned that unless the construct is embedded within an information-processing model, its scientific utility is limited.

## Self-Schemata and Information Processing

Of interest in the present context are person schemas in general and self-schemata in particular. In defining self-schemata, Markus (1977) states,

> Self-schemata are cognitive generalizations about the self, derived from past experience, that organize and guide the processing of self-related information contained in the individual's social experiences. (p. 64)

In further describing the nature of self-schemata, she asserts,

> Self-schemata are constructed from information processed by the
> individual in the past and influence both input and output of information
> related to the self. They represent the way the self has been differentiated
> and articulated in memory . . . Self-schemata can be viewed as a
> reflection of the invariances people have discovered in their own social
> behavior. (p. 64)

In later papers (Markus, Crane, Bernstein, & Siladi, 1982; Markus &
Smith, 1981), it is suggested that the self-concept is a system of
self-schemata. Moreover, Markus and Smith (1981) argue that
self-representations are stored together in one self-system that is linked
with other concepts in memory. General self-representations include
such features as one's name, age, marital status, and so on. Other
concepts may be irrelevant to the self (e.g., windows and tables) or may
intersect with the self through repeated associations (e.g., tennis). When
the self and another concept begin to overlap, a self-schema with respect
to the concept is formed. Thus if a person begins to think of the self as
independent or aggressive, that person is becoming schematic with
reference to these concepts.

To assess the role played by self-schemata in processing information
about the self, Markus (1977) compared the performances of persons
classified as independent, dependent, or aschematic on a number of
information-processing tasks. Independents were persons who gave themselves extreme ratings on three scales related to the independence-
dependence dimension *and* rated these dimensions as important.
Dependent persons were those who rated themselves to be extremely
dependent on the same three dimensions *and* rated these three dimensions as important. Aschematics were persons who placed themselves in
the mid-ranges of the three independence-dependence dimensions *and*
rated these dimensions to be unimportant to them.

In one task, research participants were asked to judge whether words
that described independence or dependence were or were not descriptive
of themselves. On this task, independent persons judged significantly
more "independent" words to be descriptive of themselves than did
dependent persons; the latter judged significantly more "dependent"
words to be self-descriptive than did independent persons. Moreover,
independents and dependents showed significantly shorter reaction times
in making their judgments when the words being judged were consistent
rather than inconsistent with their self-schemas. By contrast, aschematic
persons showed no difference in their reaction times to independent
versus dependent words. Apparently, aschematics are able to label
themselves as either independent or dependent with equal facility. In a

group of words not related to independence-dependence, there were no differ ences between the three groups, both in terms of the number of words selected as self-descriptive and the response latency of the choices. Thus persons who are schematic with reference to one content domain may not be schematic with reference to another.

In a second task, persons were shown various adjectives related to independence and dependence and asked to provide descriptions of their own past behavior that were consistent with the adjective shown. Results for this task showed that independent persons wrote more behavioral descriptions for independent words than did persons in the other two groups. Dependents wrote more behavioral descriptions for dependent words than did members of the other two groups. Aschematics supplied about equal numbers of behavioral descriptions for both kinds of words; moreover, in general this group generated fewer descriptions than did the independents or the dependents.

The third task involved making behavioral predictions. Research participants were given a series of behavioral descriptions that had been judged previously to be indicative of independence or dependence by another sample of students. Experimental participants were asked to indicate the likelihood that they would behave in a manner consistent with each behavioral description. The results indicated that independents assigned a higher probability to independent behaviors than dependent behaviors. Dependent persons showed the opposite pattern. Aschematics showed no differences in the likelihood that they would enact independent or dependent behaviors.

Finally, Markus (1977) found that schematic persons (independents and dependents) were significantly more resistant to information that was inconsistent with their schemas than were the aschematics. In addition, aschematics demonstrated considerably less consistency in their pattern of endorsement of self-descriptive words over time than did the schematics. These findings indicate that persons who have poorly developed schemas along a particular dimension are potentially more susceptible to change on that dimension than are persons who have highly differentiated schemas. Thus it should be easier to persuade persons who lack schemas with reference to the dimension creative-uncreative that they are creative than to persuade successfully persons who have well-developed uncreative self-schemata.

Several of the preceding findings were replicated in a study concerned with the influence of gender schemata on information processing (Markus et al., 1982). This study revealed that masculine schematics remembered more masculine than feminine attributes, endorsed more masculine qualities, displayed shorter processing times for "me" judgments to masculine attributes than to other types of attributes, and showed more confidence in their judgments. Feminine schematics displayed a parallel pattern of results for feminine attributes. Persons classified as androgynous did not show differential memory, response times, or levels of confidence for masculine versus feminine items; however, a comparison of high and low androgynous participants suggested that only low androgynous persons should be considered aschematic.

The findings of this study were interpreted as conflicting with Bem's (1981) cognitive account of sex typing. This theory argues that sex-typed persons (masculine or feminine schematics) should be especially sensitive to *any* information related to gender. Both Markus (1977) and Markus et al. (1982) suggest that schematic persons are especially sensitive *only* to information that is consistent with their schemas; schema-inconsistent information is not processed as quickly or remembered as well. For a more detailed discussion of this debate, the reader should consult Bem (1982) and Crane and Markus (1982). In a related study, Mills (1983) reported that masculine and feminine schematic persons showed shorter response latencies and better recall for words that were sex-role-congruent than for sex-role-incongruent words.

In summary, this body of research demonstrates that when persons have well-articulated self-schemata along a particular dimension, they are: (1) more attuned to pick up schemata-consistent information, (2) able to process schema-consistent information more quickly, (3) more likely to be able to recall the schema-consistent information, and (4) more likely to enact behaviors that are consistent with their schemas. By contrast, aschematics are not sensitive to informational differences along the dimensions on which they are aschematic. Moreover, they are not likely to show differential memory for information, and their behavior is likely to be unstable across situations and time with reference to the aschematic dimensions.

## Self-Reference and Memory

A line of research closely related to the self-schemata studies just described has examined how self-reference influences memory. For example, Rogers, Kuiper, and Kirker (1977) had research participants judge adjectives along four dimensions. In the *structural* task, participants were asked to judge the size of the letters of the word presented. A second task (*phonemic*) asked persons to judge whether the target adjective rhymed with another word. In the *semantic* task, participants were asked to judge whether the target adjective meant the same as another adjective presented with it. Finally, in the *self-reference* task, persons were asked to judge whether the adjective described themselves. Each participant in the experiment rated 10 adjectives under each of the four judgment tasks. After completing their ratings, they were given a blank sheet of paper and asked to recall as many as possible of the 40 adjectives they had judged. The results showed a strong effect for self-referencing. Persons recalled significantly more of those adjectives judged under the self-referencing instructions than adjectives judged under the three other task conditions. In addition, adjectives that were judged to be descriptive of the self were recalled better than adjectives that were judged not to be self-descriptive. Finally, analyses of the time to make judgments showed that self-reference judgments took longer to make than the other three types of judgments.

The findings of this study have been interpreted as support for the depth-of-processing explanation for memory effects (Craik & Lockhart, 1972; Craik & Tulving, 1975). These researchers argue that the degree to which words are deeply encoded in semantic memory at presentation corresponds to the extent to which they will be recalled; deeper encoding involves more semantic involvement. The study by Rogers et al. (1977) not only found the best recall for self-reference words but also that words judged in the semantic task were recalled better than words judged under the phonemic or structural tasks. Judgment time data followed this same trend, with less time required for the structural and phonemic tasks. Thus both the recall findings and the judgment time findings tend to support a depth of processing explanation, since the words encoded under self-reference instructions were recalled the best *and* took the longest judgment times. The longer judgment times could, of course, be taken as evidence for deeper encoding of these adjectives.

In a follow-up study, Kuiper and Rogers (1979) compared recall for adjectives encoded under structural, semantic, self-referent, and other referent tasks. The first three conditions were similar to those used in Rogers et al. (1977); however, the other referent task asked participants to indicate whether the word presented to them described the experimenter running the study. Again, adjectives judged under self-referent instructions were recalled better than adjectives judged under the other three tasks. In addition, participants were most confident of their judgments under self-reference instructions and found the self-reference task the easiest of the four. These findings suggest that the superiority of self-reference encoding observed in Rogers et al.'s (1977) study was not merely due to the fact that the self-reference condition involved thinking about a person while the other tasks did not. Apparently, the self plays a unique role in the encoding of personally relevant information, since the other-referent encoding condition failed to produce recall levels similar to those of the self-referent condition. Rogers, Rogers, and Kuiper (1979) present data which suggest that the self is a prototype that affects memory performance. Their study revealed that persons showed more errors in a recognition task as the degree to which the words were self-descriptive increased. This demonstration of the "false alarms effect" was taken as support for the notion that the existence of a self-prototype induces persons to make recognition errors.

Although the research reviewed here suggests that the self-reference effect is quite robust, there have been those who have disagreed with the depth-of-processing explanation offered for it. For example, Bower and Gilligan (1979) found that while the usual self-reference judgment task produced enhanced incidental recall for adjectives when compared with adjectives judged for their descriptiveness of Walter Cronkite ("Does this adjective describe Walter Cronkite?"), two other judgment tasks produced recall that was as good as self-reference recall. One of these was a self-reference episodic task ("Can you access a personal experience in which you exemplified this trait?"), and the other was a mother-reference episodic task ("Can you access an incident, either directly experienced by you or told to you, in which your mother exemplified this trait?"). These findings led Bower and Gilligan (1979) to conclude: "Any well differentiated cognitive structure can serve as a 'hitching post' for evaluating and attaching to the items to be remembered. In this sense, the self is not a uniquely distinguished conceptual structure" (p. 492). In addition, Bower and Gilligan (1979) argue that their findings support the notion that the self, as well as *any* well-differentiated conceptual structure (e.g., one's mother), can serve as a *retrieval cue* that will aid in recall. This explanation contrasts with the depth of processing account, which emphasizes the advantage to recall of deeper encoding of information into memory during acquisition.

Keenan and Baillet (1980) report findings that also question the depth-of-processing explanation for the self-reference effect. In one of their experiments, persons judged whether adjectives were descriptive of themselves, their best friend, a parent, a friend, a teacher or boss, or Jimmy Carter. These researchers reasoned that a continuum of conceptual elaboration, ranging from highly elaborated in the case of self to relatively low elaboration in the case of Jimmy Carter, underlies the person categories used. Consistent with their predictions, they found progressively better recall for adjectives judged at increasingly higher levels of conceptual elaboration. However, contrary to the depth of processing expectation, judgment times were progressively *shorter* at higher levels of conceptual elaboration. Better memory was associated with *shorter* encoding times in this experiment. This finding led Keenan and Baillet to conclude that the memorability of personally and socially significant events is due to the highly elaborated schemata associated with the self and personally significant others. In a second experiment, Keenan and Baillet (1980) found that the advantages of self-reference for memory are not present when persons make factual judgments. According to the researchers, factual judgments do not require that the full richness of a schema be tapped to make the judgment, whereas evaluative judgments require that the item be encoded with reference to much of the information of the schema.

Lord (1980) reports the usual self-reference effect in memory for adjectives; however, when persons were asked to construct mental images of *nouns* using either a self-referent image, a father referent image, a Walter Cronkite referent image, or a tree referent image, the self-referent image condition was the *least* effective of the four in promoting recall; all of the remaining three conditions promoted superior recall. These findings were taken as support for the notion that verbal and iconic encoding of social information takes place in two different modes. In the verbal mode, self-reference facilitates recall; however, in the iconic mode reference to other persons and objects, not self-reference, acts to heighten recall. Kendzierski (1980) has also found evidence for the self-reference effect. In her experiment participants judged adjectives in terms of their: (1) structure (whether or not they were printed in large letters), (2) semantic similarity to another word, (3) degree of fit in a sentence frame describing a social situation (e.g., "He was very_____on his first date"), and (4) ability to describe the self. Incidental recall of the adjectives followed the order of the four conditions, with self-reference best and structure the worst. Interestingly, although the third scriptal task produced recall that was better than the structural or semantic tasks, it was *not* as effective as self-reference in promoting recall.

As we have seen so far in this brief review, Bower and Gilligan (1979) explain the self-reference effect by recourse to the notion that the self, like any well-differentiated conceptual structure, allows potentially more entry points into a semantic network at retrieval. Increased access leads to better recall. This principle is derived from Anderson and Bower's (1973) HAM model of semantic memory. By contrast, Rogers and his associates (Kuiper & Rogers, 1979; Rogers et al., 1977; Rogers et al., 1979) explain the effect by reference to the depth of processing notion (Craik & Lockhart, 1972; Craik & Tulving, 1975), which emphasizes the differential effects of depth of encoding into memory on later recall. Both Bower and Gilligan (1979) and Keenan and Baillet (1980) reject the depth of processing explanation. In the latter experiment, better recall was associated with shorter judgment times, a result that directly conflicts with the depth of processing prediction.

Both Greenwald (1981) and Rogers (1981) have attempted to reconcile these competing explanations. Greenwald (1981) feels that the role of the self in memory can be explained by the notion that the self is a particularly well-differentiated conceptual structure (Bower & Gilligan, 1979; Keenan and Baillet, 1980). However, he also feels, unlike Bower and Gilligan, that the self has special properties not shared by other conceptual structures. These special properties include self-activation, a tendency toward the biased retrieval of positive information about the self, and privileged treatment given to information concerning self-evaluation or performance on persisting tasks. Rogers (1981) argues that the reaction time data from Keenan and Baillet (1980) and Kuiper and Rogers (1979) casts doubt on the ability of the HAM model to account for the self-reference effect. In both of these studies, reaction times for self-judgments were significantly shorter than those for other judgments.

According to Rogers (1981), these results run contrary to the prediction that a HAM model would make concerning judgment time in highly elaborated semantic networks—that is, the more complex the network, the greater the judgment time. He favors an availability/computational explanation similar to that proffered by Keenan and Baillet (1980). This explanation suggests that input items or adjectives that are relevant to dimensions of the self-concept are processed quickly because the relevant judgmental dimensions are highly available in memory (Tversky & Kahneman, 1973). However, words that cannot be associated with relevant dimensions of the self-concept require a series of computations or guesses to determine a response, thus increasing judgment time. These arguments are very similar to those employed by Markus (1977) and Markus and Smith (1981) to explain the greater processing efficiency of information congruent with self-schemata.

Research has suggested that tasks other than self-reference can enhance recall as much as the self-reference task. For example, Ferguson, Rule, and Carlson (1984) report that adjectives judged for their social desirability were recalled in about the same proportions as adjectives judged for self-descriptiveness. This finding led to the conclusion that self-reference judgments are simply one kind of evaluative judgment (Osgood, Suci, & Tannenbaum, 1957). Ferguson et al. (1984) employed a between-subjects design in which difference groups made the social desirability and self-reference judgments. Using a within-subjects design in which all persons made all types of judgments, McCaul and Maki (1984) found that adjectives judged for self-reference were recalled better than those rated for social desirability. They argue that since the judgmental context was held constant in their study, as opposed to Ferguson et al.'s experiment, their findings constitute a better comparison of the two tasks.

Bellezza (1984) suggests that internal cues that possess the properties of constructibility and associability will enhance recall even if they are not related to the self. Constructible cues are those that are available during learning and retrievable during recall. Associability refers to the degree of fit between new information and existing conceptual structures. This study found that personal experiences were better cues to the recall of trait words than were body parts; however, there were no differences between the two types of cues when concrete nouns were used as stimuli. These findings were explained in terms of the greater associability of personal experiences to traits. Wells, Hoffman, and Enzle (1984) have adduced data suggesting that the conditions under which information is retrieved from memory can modify the self-reference effect. They found that memory performance for information encoded under self-reference conditions was diminished significantly when persons retrieved the information under other-reference conditions. Thus the degree of consistency between learning and retrieval conditions appears to be an important determinant of the strength of the self-reference effect.

The advantages of self-reference in memory appear to be related to the fact that the self is a particularly well-differentiated conceptual structure with which personally relevant information can easily be associated, thus aiding retrieval of the information. However, we have seen that the self as a schema is not implicated in the processing of all types of information (Bellezza, 1984; Keenan & Baillet, 1980; Lord, 1980). Furthermore, it now appears that retrieval conditions as well as encoding conditions can influence the role that the self plays in social information processing. In spite of these qualifications and limitations, the self-concept plays an important role in the processing of personally relevant information. In the section that follows we consider several effects that the self-concept has on social interaction. These effects are directly related to the ways in which the self-concept processes social information.

## SELF-CONCEPTION AND
## SOCIAL INTERACTION

Of primary importance to students of social interaction is the relationship between the ways in which persons process social information and the ways in which they behave during their interactions with others. In the previous section, attention was focused upon the self as an information processing system. In this section, we will examine the potential effects the self system has upon the judgments, decisions and behaviors that persons generate during their interactions with others. Specifically, we will consider the ways in which the self-concept as an information processing system influences judgmental biases, social information seeking, self-verification and self-confirmation, social influence, and social comparison.

### Judgmental Biases

That persons remember more of what they say in a group than what other group members say has been demonstrated in a number of studies. Brenner (1973) found that individuals remembered words they had read to a group better than words that had been read by other group members. Similarly, Jarvella and Collas (1974) report that persons acting out a dialogue remembered sentences they had spoken themselves more accurately than sentences that were spoken to them. Sandelands and Calder (1984) found that in dyads in which persons were asked to make associations in response to stimulus words read by their partner, those who were induced to focus their attention on themselves remembered more of their own associations relative to the total number made by both persons than did persons who were instructed to attend to their partner during the session. These findings were replicated when self-focused attention was created by having individuals see themselves on a videotape monitor during the session. One study suggests that the findings of these studies may not be as robust as one might hope. Stafford and Daly (1984) report that in natural conversations, persons remembered slightly more of what their partners said than what they themselves said during the course of their interactions.

If persons are biased toward accurate recall of their own contributions in a group context, it is reasonable to suppose that the increased availability of instances in their own memories should affect their judgment of how frequently they make contributions in a group (Tversky & Kahneman, 1973). Persons should overestimate their own contributions and, as a result, see themselves as more responsible for the group's outcomes. Ross and Sicoly (1979) report a series of studies that persuasively demonstrate this point. They found that spouses overestimated the degree to which they took responsibility for household tasks, and when asked for specific instances of their own as well as their spouse's contributions, they tended to list more examples of their own contributions. In a group discussion situation, group members tended to overestimate their individual contributions to the group even when the group was told it did not do a very good job. In the previously cited Sandelands and Calder (1984) study, persons who performed the association task under self-focus conditions judged more of their own associations to be unique than did persons in the other focus condition. Ross and Sicoly (1979) have entertained a number of alternative explanations for these egocentric biases in judgment and attributions of responsibility. They point out that while there is no demonstrated causal link between availability and bias, it seems that availability is a potentially important factor in producing egocentric bias.

Another bias closely related to those observed by Ross and Sicoly (1979) is the false consensus effect (Ross, Greene, & House, 1977; van der Pligt, 1984). This bias involves the tendency for persons to believe that a majority of others would make the same behavioral choices as themselves in a given situation. Thus, if a person opposes legalized abortion, he or she is likely to believe that a large percentage of others feel the same way on the issue. In fact, false consensus effects have been observed in public opinion polling data (Fields & Schuman, 1976; van der Pligt, 1984). Ross et al. (1977) found that when individuals chose behavioral options that were discrepant from those they thought many others would choose, they made more extreme trait inferences about these persons than when they made choices that they believed were shared by a large proportion of other persons. While these findings are consistent with the notion that counternormative or out-of-role behavior is more informative about the dispositions of others (Jones & Davis, 1965), van der Pligt (1984) was unable to replicate the pattern of trait inferences found by Ross et al. (1977). However, he did find strong evidence for the false consensus effect itself.

Like the egocentric bias observed by Ross and Sicoly (1979), the false consensus effect may be explained in a number of alternative ways. Again, availability might be invoked to explain this effect by arguing that since persons tend to surround themselves with those who share their views, they tend to recall these instances easily and thus assume that "persons in general" would make the same choice they have made. However, Ross et al. (1977) also point to the possibility that motivational factors, as well as the strategies that persons use to cope with ambiguity, may be at the root of the false consensus effect.

In addition to the memory and judgment biases discussed so far, there is evidence to suggest that persons employ traits that are salient in their own self-evaluations to make judgments about others (Lemon & Warren, 1974; Shrauger & Patterson, 1974). Although such a strategy facilitates comparisons between the self and others, it is potentially misleading, since persons with whom individuals are comparing themselves may not evaluate themselves on the same set of dimensions or see the same set of dimensions as relevant to their self-concepts. Thus persons may make judgments of similarity or dissimilarity between themselves and others that are distorted, leading to potential disruptions of their interactions with others.

In summary, there is ample evidence to suggest that the self biases memory for events in such a way that more of what the self says and does is remembered. These memory biases may be partially responsible for the attributional egocentricities discussed in this section. Distorted estimates of the frequency of contributions to groups and responsibility for group outcomes can have profound effects on social interaction. Indeed, the basis of many conflicts may be the intersection of these egocentric biases. False consensus biases can lead social actors and actresses to interact with others, assuming that the others share their attitudes and behavioral choices when in fact they may not. The potential consequences of attributional disjunctions between social actors and actresses are obvious. Although it may be relatively easy for us to use ourselves an anchor points for making judgments about others because we have easier access to self-knowledge than to knowledge about others, the "self-as-anchor-point" strategy has the potential of producing considerable judgmental bias and significant interaction problems.

## Social Information Seeking

There is considerable evidence to suggest that when persons are asked to ascertain whether or not a target individual possesses a particular trait, they are prone to ask questions that are likely to confirm rather than to disconfirm the existence of the trait (see Snyder, 1981, for review). Thus, if a person is asked to determine whether another person is an introvert, he or she is likely to ask questions that will lead to the

conclusion that the target person is an introvert. A more optimal information-seeking strategy would be to ask both introvert and extrovert
questions. Although there have been several demonstrations of this
confirmatory bias in question asking, Trope and Bassok (1982) found
that under some conditions persons will seek diagnostic information
rather than confirmatory information when seeking information from
others.

There are a number of studies supporting the notion that persons tend
to seek information that confirms rather than disconfirms their
self-conceptions. Swann and Read (1981a) found that persons with
varying levels of self-perceived assertiveness and emotionality tended to
choose to ask another person questions that would confirm their
self-conceptions on these traits. Fong and Markus (1982) identified
persons who were extrovert schematics, introvert schematics, and
aschematics and gave them lists containing questions that had previously
been rated as being introvert, extrovert, or irrelevant to both introversion
and extroversion. Study participants then selected 12 questions that they
would ask in order to get to know a stranger. Although there was an
overall tendency for extrovert questions to be chosen more than introvert
or neutral questions, introvert schematics chose significantly more
introvert questions than did the extrovert schematics. This pattern of
question choice was reversed for extrovert questions. Aschematics chose
significantly more neutral questions than did either extrovert or introvert
schematics.

Riggs and Cantor (1984) found that persons who rated themselves as
anxious were more likely to ask their potential game partners questions
that would reveal anxiety than were persons whose levels of self-rated
anxiety were low. In this study, the correlation between self-rated
anxiety and the propensity to ask questions that would or would not
reveal anxiety was .61. This study, as well as those cited earlier,
provides ample support for the notion that well-differentiated
self-schemata can bias information-seeking strategies in ways that are
consistent with the self-schemata.

An important by-product of biased social information gathering is the
possibility that the targets of such biased strategies may begin to conform behaviorally to the bias that is present in the questions being asked.
Fazio, Effrein, and Falender (1981) found this to be the case. In their
study, persons were asked questions that were biased toward either extroversion or introversion. After being asked the questions, they interacted
with a confederate who was unaware of the kinds of questions that had
been asked earlier. Results revealed that persons who were asked
extroverted questions rated themselves as more extroverted than did

persons who were initially asked introverted questions. In addition to changing self-perceptions, the questions changed behaviors and the perceptions of others. Specifically, both confederates' and judges' ratings of the experimental participants on the introversion-extroversion dimension showed that persons who were initially asked extroverted questions were perceived to be more extroverted than persons who were asked introverted questions. Persons asked extroverted questions were also more likely to initiate conversations with the confederate and were more talkative than persons asked introverted questions. Persons asked extroverted questions also placed their chairs closer to the confederate than did those asked introverted questions. Thus the types of questions put to target individuals caused them to behave in ways that were consistent with the bias of the questions.

Riggs, Monarch, Ogburn, and Pahides (1983) tested the durability of the effect reported by Fazio et al. (1981) by replicating their study and extending it. Riggs et al. (1983) had persons answer either extroverted or introverted questions and then interact with a confederate who was blind to the experimental conditions of the research participants. In addition, the behavior of the confederates was systematically varied such that confederates behaved in either an extroverted or introverted manner. Self-ratings by participants replicated the Fazio et al. (1981) study; that is, persons asked extroverted questions rated themselves as more extroverted than persons asked introverted questions. This effect persisted in spite of the behavior of the confederate; thus, even after persons asked extroverted questions were exposed to an introverted confederate (or vice versa), the persons who were asked extroverted questions perceived themselves as more extroverted than did persons who were initially asked introverted questions. There was, however, a tendency for all persons to shift their self-descriptions toward the behavior that the confederate displayed.

As discussed earlier, Riggs and Cantor (1984) found that persons who scored high in anxiety were more prone to ask questions of conversational partners that would make them appear to be more anxious. Low-anxiety persons showed the opposite tendency. Furthermore, judges' ratings of the target persons' self-disclosures revealed that those persons who had interacted with highly anxious persons were judged to be significantly more anxious than were those targets who had interacted with the low- anxious persons. Apparently, the bias present in the questions put to the targets induced them to behave in a manner consistent with the line of questioning.

Taken as a whole, these studies make a persuasive case for the assertion that persons with self-schemata are likely to seek information that is consistent with those schemata. One result of this biased information seeking is that it induces interaction partners to behave in ways that are consistent with the schemata of their partners. Although such consistency is likely to give rise to perceptions of "similarity," these perceptions are likely to be illusory, thus leading to potential problems in the relationship being formed. Of course, these perceptions of similarity, while illusory, may promote a short-run attraction between information seekers and the targets of their information-seeking attempts.

## Self-Verification

Given the proclivities of self-schematics to bias their information searches in ways that bring out self-consistent behaviors in their conversational partners, it is but a small step to argue that persons have a tendency to verify or confirm their self-conceptions. In support of this general hypothesis, Swann and Read (1981b) found that persons who liked themselves (self-likables) and persons who disliked themselves (self-dislikables) both spent more time reading feedback from a potential interaction partner when they were led to believe that their potential partner evaluated them in a way that was inconsistent with their self-schemata. In addition, during ongoing interactions, self-likables who believed that their partners viewed them unfavorably elicited more favorable impressions from their partners than did self-likables who were led to believe that their partners had a favorable view of them. Self-dislikables who thought that their partners had a favorable impression of them elicited more unfavorable impressions from their partners than did self-dislikables who thought that their partners already had an unfavorable impression of them. Finally, this study revealed that self-likables tended to recall more positive than negative statements about themselves. There was a nonsignificant tendency for the reverse to be true for the self-negatives. These findings provide general support for the view that persons are prone to elicit, attend to, and remember information that is consistent with their self-conceptions, especially when they believe that others hold a view of them that is discrepant from their own.

Swann and Ely (1984) devised a situation in which one person (a perceiver) held an expectancy concerning his or her partner's (target) level of introversion or extroversion that was either accurate or erroneous. In addition, the certainty with which the expectancy was held was varied. Analyses of the target person's behaviors indicated that self-verification always occurred when the targets were certain of their self-conceptions. Perceivers were successful at inducing targets to confirm their expectations only when the perceivers were certain of their expectancies and targets were uncertain of their self-conceptions. This study suggests that when persons are schematic with reference to a particular dimension, it is difficult for others to alter their behavior to conform to an expectation that is discrepant from their self-conception. When persons do not have well-formed self-schemata, they are susceptible to fulfilling others' prophecies regarding their behavior.

## Social Influence

While the role that self-schemata play in the persuasion process has not received much research attention, at least one study has examined how message characteristics interact with self-schemata to influence persuasion outcomes (Cacioppo, Petty, & Sidera, 1982). These researchers exposed persons who had either religious or legalistic schemata to weak, proattitudinal arguments on issues about which the subjects held contrary attitudes. The persuasive messages were written in such a way that some of them reflected a religious approach to the issue, while others were based on a legalistic line of argument regarding the same issue. The messages were equated for their persuasiveness using a separate sample of persons. After reading these messages, persons rated them along a number of dimensions and listed all of the thoughts they had during the reading of the message.

The results of this study demonstrated that persons receiving messages consistent with their schemata rated the messages as more persuasive than did persons who received messages that were at variance with their self-schemata. Thus persons with legalistic schemata found legalistic messages more persuasive than religious messages. The opposite was true for persons with religious self-schemata. In addition, persons receiving schema-consistent messages listed more favorable thoughts than those receiving schema-inconsistent messages. Schemata-consistent message recipients also rated the source of their message as more articulate than did those who received schemata-inconsistent messages. The findings for the thought-listing phase of the study suggest that schema-consistent messages may produce greater access to long-term memory than schema-inconsistent messages, thus increasing the potential for significant persuasion to occur.

## Social Comparison

Miller (1984) has shown that persons with self-schemata related to gender make social comparison choices that are different from those made by aschematic individuals. Before taking an ability test, subjects were informed that the test they were about to take was one on which males and females did equally well or one on which either males or females excelled. After completing the test, research participants were asked whether they wished to see male, female, or combined male and female norms in order to assess their own standing on the test. Analyses of these choices showed that aschematics chose to see the norms of the same-sex group when sex was related to performance on the test; however, when sex was not relevant to test performance, aschematics tended not to choose the same-sex norms. By contrast, schematic persons chose to see the norms for the same-sex comparison group regardless of whether sex was related to performance on the test. Apparently, persons who organize their self-conceptions around gender tend to use gender as an important basis for choosing others with whom to compare themselves. Persons who do not organize their self-conceptions around gender are more likely to shift their bases for selecting comparison others according to the relevance of the attribute to performance on the task.

## Summary

In this section we have seen how the development of well-articulated self-schemata can bias social judgments in such a way that the self appears to be more influential than it actually is. Because of these egocentric biases, individuals tend to believe that other persons share their beliefs and would choose to behave the way they would in decision-making situations. Such biases are probably at the root of numerous interpersonal conflicts. Self-schemata can also induce persons to seek information about others in ways that make the other person appear to be similar to themselves. Biased information seeking can influence persons to behave in ways that are consistent with the bias. There also appears to be a tendency for persons to behave in ways that will elicit from others behavior that confirms their self-conceptions. This is especially true when persons believe that their interaction partners hold views of them that are discrepant from their own self-conceptions. In addition, persons who are certain of their self-conceptions will resist attempts by others to alter their behaviors in ways that are discrepant with those self-conceptions.

Persons with self-schemata are apparently more susceptible to persuasive communications that couch persuasive attempts in ways that are consistent with their self-conceptions. Self-schematic individuals also tend to be less sensitive to the potential relevance of the schematic dimension in the selection of others for the purpose of making ability comparisons.

Aschematics appear to be considerably more sensitive to the issue of relevance. In general, these diverse research areas demonstrate the considerable impact that self-schemata can exert in ongoing social interactions.

## SOME IMPLICATIONS FOR COMMUNICATION RESEARCH

In this section we consider how the research reviewed in this chapter might inform the study of communication processes. In their everyday lives, persons sometimes engage in interactions during which they have occasion to discuss various aspects of their self-conceptions with others. Moreover, persons frequently make remarks to others about aspects of themselves, (e.g., "You are really XXX today," where XXX refers to some emotional state or other self-attribute). Such comments, even though they are made *en passant*, can have the effect of making salient certain self-schemata or leading the individual toward the formation of a new self-schema on that attribute. Finally, simply being in specific social situations, such as parties, may raise the salience of particular self-schemata. While these are some of the social conditions that may raise the salience of various aspects of the self, there are a number of potential effects that self-schemata can have on subsequent communicative conduct in these situations. These effects involve consistency, confidence, and representativeness.

### Consistency

Given the self-schema research reviewed in this chapter, we would expect persons with self-schemata on an attribute to behave consistently across situations, at least until such time that their self-conceptions change with reference to that particular attribute. Thus persons who are extroverted schematics should display extroverted communication behavior across a number of social situations. However, it is possible that schematic individuals might alter their self-schemata so that their behavior will no longer display such consistency. By contrast, aschematics should show considerably more situational variation in their communicative conduct. We assume here, of course, that the attribute in question is potentially "displayable" in the situation. For example, it would be difficult to ascertain the extent to which communicative behavior is driven by an extrovert self-schema by observing persons at a funeral. Situational constraints may either dampen behavior along an attribute dimension or render other attribute dimensions more relevant. These issues are related to the general problem of the ability of trait measures to predict behavior consistently. The general conclusion to be drawn here is that trait measures are likely to predict behavior consistently for persons who have self-schemata for the trait in question.

Researchers interested in the study of self-schemata have paid virtually no attention to how such schemata are formed in the first place. In the experiments described in this chapter, subjects (almost always college students) are assessed for schemasticity at the time of measurement. There is no concern for how they arrived at that particular state. It is clear, however, that interactions with others and the environment are critical information sources for the development of self-schemata. For example, assume that a given individual takes up a new sport, such as cross-country skiing. The individual begins to affiliate with others who participate in the sport. Friends of the target individual begin to refer to him or her as "the cross-country skier." It is through such interactions that persons develop self-schemata involving concepts that were formerly not associated with the self. These interactions are worthy of research attention.

## Confidence

Persons who are self-schematic with reference to a particular attribute should be able to instantiate that self-schema easily when environmental demands call for behavior that is consistent with the self-schema. Persons who are schematic in ways that are inconsistent with environmental demands, or persons who are aschematic, should have more difficulty calling up self-schemata to guide their conduct. Thus the extrovert schematic should be able to meet the situational demands of a party more quickly than introvert schematics or aschematics.

The differential ability of schematics and aschematics to instantiate schemata relevant to a given situation should be reflected in their communication behavior. Specifically, persons who are schematic in ways that are consistent with situational demands should show fewer pauses in their speech, higher speech rates, fewer nonfluencies, and fewer adaptors than persons who are either aschematic or those whose self-schemata are inconsistent with behaviors or interaction styles that are typically expected in a given social situation. This line of reasoning suggests that one source of communication anxiety may be the lack of fit between the self-schemata of the individual and the behavioral demands of the social situation.

## Representativeness

In the present context, representativeness refers to the extent to which overt behavior is taken by social perceivers to be prototypical of a given personality type. It is similar to the construct of correspondent inference (Jones & Davis, 1965). Given the consistency of the behavior of self-schematic individuals and the confidence with which they enact schemata-consistent behaviors, we would expect observers of their behavior to be better able to perceive them as representative of a prototype than would observers of aschematic targets or targets enacting schemata-inconsistent behaviors. Thus observers should be able to pick out persons who are schematic introverts or schematic extroverts more easily than they could identify aschematics.

The preceding hypothesis assumes, of course, that the schematic individuals are enacting behaviors that are consistent with their schemas and not engaging in self-presentational behaviors that are at variance with their self-schemata. As noted earlier, situational demands may induce persons to engage in behaviors that are at variance with their self-schemata, thus making it difficult to test the hypothesis in a clear-cut fashion. A somewhat less direct way to test this hypothesis would be to determine whether persons with different self-schemata prefer to find themselves in social situations that call for behaviors consistent with their schemata. Under this hypothesis, for example, we would expect schematic extroverts to show a preference for situations in which extroversion is expected and perhaps valued (e.g., parties, sales situations), whereas schematic introverts should prefer situations in which introversion is normative. (e.g., monasteries, libraries). In theory, aschematics should show no differential preferences for these situations. If relationships between situational preferences and schema type were found, one might infer that these situations were picked so that persons would have the opportunity to display the kinds of behaviors they are most apt to enact. The general idea underlying this hypothesis is that persons with self-schematas involving a particular attribute can be viewed as "experts" in that particular domain (Fong & Markus, 1982).

## *SUMMARY*

In this chapter we have deviated from the usual treatments of the self-concept and viewed the self as an information-processing system. Our review has revealed that the self can exert considerable influence on the speed with which information about the self is processed, the amount of information that is stored in memory, and the ease with which that information can be retrieved from memory. The self can bias judgments in ways that induce individuals to believe that they are more influential in group activities than they actually are. Moreover, self-conceptions can drive persons to seek information from others that is likely to confirm or verify their own views of themselves. This biased information seeking can also alter the behavior of the person from whom the information is being sought. Finally, we suggested that the salience of self-schemata can be raised in a variety of ways during social interactions and that once a self-schema is instantiated, a person's communicative behavior is likely to become more consistent, confident, and representative.

## REFERENCES

Abelson, R. P. (1981). Psychological status of the script concept. *American Psychologist, 36*, 715-729.

Allport, G. W. (1955). *Becoming: Basic considerations for a psychology of personality.* New Haven: Yale University Press.

Anderson, J. R., & Bower, G. H. (1973). *Human associative memory.* Hillsdale, NJ: Erlbaum.

Bellezza, F. S. (1984). The self as a mnemonic device: The role of internal cues. *Journal of Personality and Social Psychology, 47*, 506-516.

Bem, S. L. (1981). Gender schema theory: A cognitive account of sex typing. *Psychological Review, 88*, 354-364.

Bem, S. L. (1982). Gender schema theory and self-schema theory compared: A comment on Markus, Crane, Bernstein, and Siladi's "Self-schemas and gender." *Journal of Personality and Social Psychology, 43*, 1192-1194.

Bower, G. H., & Gilligan, S. G. (1979). Remembering information related to one's self. *Journal of Research in Personality, 13*, 420-432.

Bower, G. H., Black, J. B., & Turner, T. J. (1979). Scripts in memory for text. *Cognitive Psychology, 11*, 177-220.

Brenner, M. W. (1973). The next-in-line effect. *Journal of Verbal Learning and Verbal Behavior, 12*, 320-323.

Bugental, J.F.T., & Zelen, S. L. (1950). Investigations into the self-concept—the W-A-Y technique. *Journal of Personality, 18*, 483-498.

Cacioppo, J. T., Petty, R. E., & Sidera, J. A. (1982). The effects of a salient self-schema on the evaluation of proattitudinal editorials: Top-down versus bottom-up message processing. *Journal of Experimental Social Psychology, 18*, 324-338.

Cantor, N., & Mischel, W. (1977). Traits as prototypes: Effects on recognition memory. *Journal of Personality and Social Psychology, 35*, 38-48.

Cooley, C. H. (1902). *Human nature and the social order.* New York: Scribners.

Craik, F.I.M., & Lockhart, R. S. (1972). Levels of processing: A framework for memory research. *Journal of Verbal Learning and Verbal Behavior, 11*, 671-684.

Craik, F.I.M., & Tulving, E. (1975). Depth of processing and the retention of words in episodic memory. *Journal of Experimental Psychology: General, 104*, 268-294.

Crane, M., & Markus, H. (1982). Gender identity: The benefits of a self-schema approach. *Journal of Personality and Social Psychology, 43*, 1195-1197.

Cushman, D. P., Valentinsen, B., & Dietrich, D. (1982). A rules theory of interpersonal relationships. In F.E.X. Dance (Ed.), *Human communication theory*. New York: Harper & Row.

Fazio, R. H., Effrein, E. A., & Falender, V. J. (1981). Self-perceptions following social interaction. *Journal of Personality and Social Psychology, 41*, 232-242.

Ferguson, T. J., Rule, B. G., & Carlson, D. (1984). Memory for personally relevant information. *Journal of Personality and Social Psychology, 44*, 251-261.

Fields, J. M., & Schuman, H. (1976). Public beliefs about the beliefs of the public. *Public Opinion Quarterly, 40*, 427-448.

Fiske, S. T., & Linville, P. W. (1980). What does the schema concept buy us? *Personality and Social Psychology Bulletin, 6*, 543-557.

Fong, G. T., & Markus, H. (1982). Self-schemas and judgments about others. *Social Cognition, 1*, 191-204.

Greenwald, A. G. (1981). Self and memory. In G. H. Bower (Ed.), *The psychology of learning and memory*. New York: Academic Press.

James, W. (1890). *The principles of psychology*. New York: Holt.

Jarvella, R. J., & Collas, J. G. (1974). Memory for the intentions of sentences. *Memory and Cognition, 2*, 185-188.

Jones, E. E., & Davis, K. E. (1965). From acts to dispositions. In L. Berkowitz (Ed.), *Advances in experimental social psychology* (Vol. 2). New York: Academic Press.

Keenan, J. M., & Baillet, S. D. (1980). Memory for personally and socially significant events. In R. S. Nickerson (Ed.), *Attention and performance VIII*. Hillsdale, NJ: Erlbaum.

Kendzierski, D. (1980). Self-schemata and scripts: The recall of self-referent and scriptal information. *Personality and Social Psychology Bulletin, 6*, 23-29.

Kuhn, M. H., & McPartland, T. S. (1954). An empirical investigation of self attitudes. *American Sociological Review, 19*, 68-76.

Kuiper, N. A., & Rogers, T. B. (1979). Encoding of personal information: Self-other differences. *Journal of Personality and Social Psychology, 37*, 499-514.

Lemon, N., & Warren, N. (1974). Salience, centrality and self-relevance of traits in construing others. *British Journal of Social and Clinical Psychology, 13*, 119-124.

Lord, C. G. (1980). Schemas and images as memory aids: Two modes of processing social information. *Journal of Personality and Social Psychology, 38*, 257-269.

Markus, H. (1977). Self-schemata and processing information about the self. *Journal of Personality and Social Psychology, 35*, 63-78.

Markus, H., & Smith, J. (1981). The influence of self-schemata on the perception of others. In N. Cantor & J. F. Kihlstrom (Eds.), *Personality, cognition, and social interaction.* Hillsdale, NJ: Erlbaum.

Markus, H., Crane, M., Bernstein, S., & Siladi, M. (1982). Self-schema and gender. *Journal of Personality and Social Psychology, 42,* 38-50.

McCaul, K. D., & Maki, R. H. (1984). Self-reference versus desirability ratings and memory for traits. *Journal of Personality and Social Psychology, 47,* 953-955.

McGuire, W. J., McGuire, C. V., Child, P., & Fujioka, T. (1978). Salience of ethnicity in the spontaneous self-concept as a function of one's ethnic distinctiveness in a social environment. *Journal of Personality and Social Psychology, 36,* 511-520.

McGuire, W. J., McGuire, C. V., & Winton, W. (1979). Effects of household sex composition on the salience of one's gender in the spontaneous self-concept. *Journal of Experimental Social Psychology, 15,* 77-90.

McGuire, W. J., & Padawer-Singer, A. (1976). Trait salience in the spontaneous self-concept. *Journal of Personality and Social Psychology, 33,* 743-754.

Mead, G. H. (1934). *Mind, self, and society.* Chicago: University of Chicago Press.

Miller, C. T. (1984). Self-schemas, gender, and social comparison: A clarification of the related attributes hypothesis. *Journal of Personality and Social Psychology, 46,* 1222-1229.

Mills, C. J. (1983). Sex-typing and self-schemata effects on memory and response latency. *Journal of Personality and Social Psychology, 45,* 163-172.

Osgood, C. E., Suci, G. T., & Tannenbaum, P. H. (1957). *The measurement of meaning.* Urbana: University of Illinois Press.

Riggs, J. M., & Cantor, N. (1984). Getting acquainted: The role of self-concept and preconceptions. *Personality and Social Psychology Bulletin, 10,* 432-435.

Riggs, J. M., Monarch, E. M., Ogburn, T. A., & Pahides, S. (1983). Inducing self-perceptions: The role of social interaction. *Personality and Social Psychology Bulletin, 9,* 253-260.

Rogers, C. R. (1951). *Client-centered therapy.* Boston: Houghton Mifflin.

Rogers, T. B. (1981). A model of the self as an aspect of the human information processing system. In N. Cantor & J. F. Kihlstrom (Eds.), *Personality, cognition, and social interaction.* Hillsdale, NJ: Erlbaum.

Rogers, T. B., Kuiper, N. A., & Kirker, W. S. (1977). Self-reference and the encoding of personal information. *Journal of Personality and Social Psychology, 35,* 677-688.

Rogers, T. B., Rogers, P. J., & Kuiper, N. A. (1979). Evidence for the self as a cognitive prototype: The "false alarms effect." *Personality and Social Psychology Bulletin, 5,* 53-56.

Ross, L., Greene, D., & House, P. (1977). The "false consensus effect": An egocentric bias in social perception and attribution processes. *Journal of Experimental Social Psychology, 13,* 279-301.

Ross, M., & Sicoly, F. (1979). Egocentric biases in availability and attribution. *Journal of Personality and Social Psychology, 37,* 322-336.

Sandelands, L. E., & Calder, B. J. (1984). Referencing bias in social interaction. *Journal of Personality and Social Psychology, 46*, 755-762.

Schank, R., & Abelson, R. P. (1977). *Scripts, plans, goals and understanding: An inquiry into human knowledge structures.* Hillsdale, NJ: Erlbaum.

Shrauger, J. S., & Patterson, M. B. (1974). Self-evaluation and the selection of dimensions for evaluating others. *Journal of Personality, 42*, 569-585.

Shrauger, J. S., & Schoeneman, T. J. (1979). Symbolic interactionist view of self-concept: Through a looking glass darkly. *Psychological Bulletin, 86*, 549-573.

Snyder, M. (1981). Seek and ye shall find. Testing hypotheses about other people. In E. T. Higgins, C. P. Herman, & M. P. Zanna (Eds.), *Social cognition: The Ontario Symposium on Personality and Social Psychology.* Hillsdale, NJ: Erlbaum.

Stafford, L., & Daly, J. A. (1984). Conversational memory: The effects of recall mode and memory expectancies on remembrances of natural conversations. *Human Communication Research, 10*, 379-402.

Sullivan, H. S. (1953). *The interpersonal theory of psychiatry.* New York: Norton.

Swann, W. B., Jr., & Ely, R. J. (1984). A battle of wills: Self-verification versus behavioral confirmation. *Journal of Personality and Social Psychology, 46*, 1287-1302.

Swann, W. B., Jr., & Hill, C. A. (1982). When our identities are mistaken: Reaffirming self-conceptions through social interaction. *Journal of Personality and Social Psychology, 43*, 59-66.

Swann, W. B., Jr., & Read, S. J. (1981a). Acquiring self-knowledge: The search for feedback that fits. *Journal of Personality and Social Psychology, 41*, 1119-1128.

Swann, W. B., Jr., & Read, S. J. (1981b). Self-verification processes: How we sustain our self-conceptions. *Journal of Experimental Social Psychology, 17*, 351-372.

Taylor, S. E., & Crocker, J. (1981). Schematic basis of social information processing. In E. T. Higgins, C. A. Herman, & M. P. Zanna (Eds.), *Social cognition: The Ontario Symposium on Personality and Social Psychology.* Hillsdale, NJ: Erlbaum.

Trope, Y., & Bassok, M. (1982). Confirmatory and diagnosing strategies in social information gathering. *Journal of Personality and Social Psychology, 43*, 22-34.

Tversky, A., & Kahneman, D. (1973). Availability: A heuristic for judging frequency and probability. *Cognitive Psychology, 5*, 207-232.

van der Pligt, J. (1984). Attributions, false consensus, and valence: Two field studies. *Journal of Personality and Social Psychology, 46*, 57-68.

Wells, G. L., Hoffman, C., & Enzle, M. E. (1984). Self- versus other-referent processing at encoding and retrieval. *Personality and Social Psychology Bulletin, 10*, 574-584.

Wylie, R. C. (1961). *The self-concept: A critical survey of pertinent research literature.* Lincoln: University of Nebraska Press.

Wylie, R. C. (1974). *The self-concept: A review of methodological consider-ations and measuring instruments* (Vol. 1). Lincoln: University of Nebraska Press.

Wylie, R. C. (1979). *The self-concept*. Lincoln: University of Nebraska Press.

# 8

# Cognitive Complexity

## BRANT R. BURLESON

During the last 10 years, researchers working with the "constructivist" theoretical perspective (e.g., Delia, O'Keefe, & O'Keefe, 1982) have conducted a series of studies assessing the contributions of social cognitive abilities to functional communication skills. The constructivist perspective represents an individual-difference approach to the study of communicative abilities; hence the central question addressed in most of these studies has concerned the extent to which individual differences in social cognitive skills are related to individual differences in a variety of communication skills (e.g., persuading others, comforting others, informing others, and regulating or disciplining others). Constructivism is thus similar to other theoretical positions, such as cognitive developmental theory (e.g., Feffer, 1970; Flavell, 1968; Looft, 1972), which emphasize the contributions of individual differences in social cognitive skills to the production of sophisticated forms of communication.

The distinctiveness of the constructivist approach lies in its specific conceptualization and assessment of "social cognitive ability," its specific conceptualization and assessment of "sophisticated communicative behavior," and its specific conceptualization of the relationship between social cognition and communication. The basic concept in the constructivist analysis of social cognitive ability is "interpersonal cognitive complexity," while the basic concept in the constructivist analysis of sophisticated functional communication is "person-centered communication." Briefly, cognitively complex individuals possess relatively differentiated, abstract, and organized systems of cognitive structures for interpreting the thoughts and behavior of others. Person-centered communication refers to message behavior that reflects an awareness of and adaptation to the subjective, affective, and relational aspects of communicative contexts.

Constructivist researchers have had considerable success in demonstrating the existence of a moderate positive relationship between interpersonal cognitive complexity and various forms of person-centered communication. More than 40 studies (reviewed in this chapter) have found statistically significant correlations between assessments of these variables. The central thesis of this chapter is that extant research has firmly established the existence of a significant, stable, and substantial relationship between cognitive complexity and person-centered communication; no further research directed simply at demonstrating this relationship needs to be undertaken. Instead, researchers now need to focus on understanding and explaining this relationship. That is, additional effort needs to be directed at developing and testing more sophisticated and detailed accounts of the relationship between cognitive complexity and person-centered communication.

This thesis should not be interpreted as implying that constructivist researchers have been unconcerned with providing theoretically meaningful accounts of their empirical findings. Indeed, the great majority of constructivist research has been motivated by the explicit desire to test theoretical claims. However, as is the case with any research area and any research tradition, further advances in understanding are often crucially dependent on theoretical revisions, extensions, and elaborations. Some constructivist researchers have suggested alternative ways of interpreting the empirical relationship between cognitive complexity and person-centered communication (e.g., Applegate, Burke, Burleson, Delia, & Kline, 1985; O'Keefe & Delia, 1982).

Because the direction and value of future empirical work are dependent on the development of clear theoretical positions, the aim of the present chapter is to review and evaluate several different explanatory accounts for the empirically established relationship between cognitive complexity and person-centered communication. Toward this end, the first section of the chapter reviews the methods and findings of constructivist studies assessing the relationship between cognitive complexity and person-centered communication. The second section presents and critiques several distinct accounts for the empirical relationship observed between these variables. The concluding section considers some general problems that need to be addressed in future constructivist studies of person-centered communication.

## COGNITIVE COMPLEXITY AND
## PERSON-CENTERED COMMUNICATION

### The Constructivist Analysis of Social Cognitive Ability

#### *Personal Constructs and Their Development*

The constructivist analysis of social cognitive ability is based on an integration of the personal construct psychology of Kelly (1955) and the structural developmental theory of Werner (1957). Following Kelly, the basic unit or element of cognitive structure is termed the "personal construct." Kelly characterized the personal construct as a bipolar cognitive dimension used in the interpretation, evaluation, and anticipation of events. Werner's developmental theory provides a way of dealing with systematic differences in the structure of individuals' personal constructs. According to Werner (1957), all things said to develop do so in accord with the "orthogenetic principle": "Wherever development occurs, it proceeds from a state of relative globality and lack of differentiation to states of increasing differentiation, articulation, and hierarchic integration" (p. 126). Applied to personal constructs, Werner's orthogenetic principle suggests that over the course of childhood and adolescence, persons will develop more differentiated (i.e., numerically larger) construct systems, more articulated systems (i.e., systems composed of more refined and abstract elements), and more integrated (i.e., organized) systems. This general prediction has been supported by substantial empirical research. Numerous studies have found that, with development, children's construct systems become increasingly differentiated, abstract, and organized (e.g., Barenboim, 1977, 1981; Biskin & Crano, 1977; Livesley & Bromley, 1973; Peevers & Secord, 1973; Scarlett, Press, & Crockett, 1971).

For both Kelly and Werner, development is seen to occur in specific domains of activity and involvement. Thus it is quite possible for a particular individual to possess a highly developed system of *interpersonal* constructs (constructs used in the interpretation, evaluation, and anticipation of people and their thoughts and behavior) while simultaneously possessing a relatively undeveloped system of constructs for other phenomenal domains (e.g., automobiles, furniture).

Because development is viewed as proceeding in specific domains of activity and involvement, the constructivist perspective provides a way of addressing systematic individual differences in interpersonal construct system development. That is, any particular group of individuals (either adults or children of the same age) is likely to contain both persons with relatively differentiated, abstract, and organized systems of interpersonal constructs and others with relatively sparse, concrete, and unorganized systems of interpersonal constructs. The reasons for these individual differences in interpersonal construct system development are not entirely clear, though some evidence suggests that such differences may begin relatively early in childhood (e.g., Jennings, 1975; Little, 1972) and may be due to such factors as parental socialization practices (e.g., Applegate & Delia, 1980; Burleson, 1983a; Shure & Spivack, 1978) and frequency of social interaction, especially with peers (e.g., Crockett, 1965; Nahir & Yussen, 1977; Rubin & Maioni, 1975; Strayer & Mashal, 1983). In any event, the available empirical evidence indicates that relatively stable individual differences in interpersonal construct system development are present in groups of both children (e.g., Delia, Burleson, & Kline, 1979) and adults (e.g., Crockett, 1965; O'Keefe, Shepherd, & Streeter, 1982).

### The Theory and Measurement
### of Cognitive Complexity

From the constructivist point of view (e.g., Crockett, 1965; Delia, 1976), developmentally advanced systems of constructs can be characterized as relatively complex. That is, persons with relatively differentiated, abstract, and organized systems of constructs in a particular domain (such as people) are considered *cognitively complex* in that domain. Thus, for example, someone with a relatively differentiated, abstract, and organized system of *interpersonal* constructs would be regarded as having a relatively high level of "interpersonal cognitive complexity." This analysis led Crockett (1965) to formulate the role category questionnaire (RCQ) as a tool through which interpersonal cognitive complexity could be assessed. In its most common form, the RCQ instructs persons to articulate their impressions of two well-known peers, one liked and one disliked. Subjects may be asked to produce these impressions either orally or in writing. When producing their impressions, persons are specifically instructed to describe each peer in as much detail as possible, focusing on his or her habits, beliefs, mannerisms, ways of treating others, traits, and personality characteristics. Such impressions have most frequently been scored for the number of interpersonal constructs they contain (according to a set of rigorous and highly reliable scoring procedures; see Crockett, Press, Delia, & Kenny, 1974).

When only the number of constructs contained in the elicited impressions is coded, the resulting score is most properly regarded as an index of *interpersonal construct differentiation*. Procedures are also available for coding the abstractness of interpersonal constructs (e.g., Applegate, 1980a; Burleson, 1984a; Delia, Clark, & Switzer, 1974) and the degree of organization among interpersonal constructs (Crockett et al., 1974). Interpersonal construct differentiation scores have frequently been found to be moderately to highly associated with abstractness and organization scores derived from RCQ impressions (see the review by O'Keefe & Sypher, 1981). Consequently, the differentiation score obtained from Crockett's RCQ has been regarded as a good overall index of interpersonal cognitive complexity. It has also been found, however, that under some circumstances construct abstractness or system organization is a theoretically more appropriate index of construct system development than differentiation (e.g., Delia, Kline, & Burleson, 1979; O'Keefe & Delia, 1979). Thus the specific measure of construct system development used has been a function of the theoretical issues addressed by particular studies.

The reliability and validity of constructivist measures of construct abstractness, organization, and especially differentiation (or complexity) have been documented in numerous studies (e.g., Delia et al., 1974; O'Keefe et al., 1982; see also O'Keefe & Sypher, 1981). In particular, the RCQ measure of interpersonal cognitive complexity has been shown to be superior to several alternative measures of cognitive complexity (O'Keefe & Sypher, 1981). Moreover, the RCQ procedure for assessing cognitive complexity has repeatedly been shown to be free from such potentially confounding influences as verbal intelligence, verbal fluency, loquacity, general intellectual abilities (IQ), grade point average, performance on standardized tests such as the SAT, narrative writing skill, and writing speed (Applegate et al., 1985; Burleson, Applegate, & Neuwirth, 1981; Burleson & Rowan, 1985; Burleson, Waltman, & Samter, 1985; Crockett, 1965; Delia, 1978; Delia & Crockett, 1973; Hale, 1980; Press, Crockett, & Rosenkrantz, 1969; Scarlett et al., 1971; Sypher & Applegate, 1982). In particular, although some researchers (e.g., Beatty & Payne, 1984; Powers, Jordan, & Street, 1979) have alleged that the RCQ procedure for assessing cognitive complexity may be confounded by "loquacity" (i.e., the propensity to talk) or other verbal abilities, several studies (e.g., Burleson et al., 1981; Burleson et al., 1985) have found little relationship between RCQ assessments of cognitive complexity and independent measures of loquacity, verbal fluency, and verbal intelligence (for a fuller discussion of this issue, see Delia et al., 1982, pp. 174-176; O'Keefe & Sypher, 1981).

## Construct System Development and
## Social Perception Skills

Constructivist theory distinguishes between *social perception processes* and *social cognitive structures*. Social perception processes are the mental activities through which persons perceive and interpret the qualities, thoughts, states, and behaviors of others. Typical social perception processes include such activities as making causal attributions, inferring dispositional qualities from behavior, identifying affective states, forming overall impressions of others, organizing and integrating information about others, evaluating aspects of others' conduct and traits, and inferring the perspective of others ("role-taking"). Social cognitive structures are the mental elements or schemes through which various social perception processes are carried out. As noted earlier, constructivist theory views the interpersonal construct as the basic element of social cognition. Consequently, constructivism maintains that all social perception processes occur through the application of interpersonal constructs.

The notion that all social perception processes occur through the application of interpersonal constructs has important empirical implications. In particular, it has been proposed that individuals with more developmentally advanced systems of interpersonal constructs will possess more sophisticated social perception skills than persons with less developed construct systems. This general prediction has been tested and supported by numerous empirical studies. Specifically, indices of interpersonal construct system development (most frequently cognitive complexity) have been found to be positively associated with: (1) the ability to infer multiple causes for and consequences of the actions of others (e.g., Clark, O'Dell, & Willinghanz, 1983; O'Keefe, Murphy, Meyers, & Babrow, 1983) (2) the ability to recognize and understand the affective states of others (e.g., Burleson, 1982a); (3) the ability to form more dispositionally and motivationally oriented impressions (e.g., Delia, 1972; Delia et al., 1974); (4) the ability to reconcile and integrate potentially inconsistent information about others (e.g., Nidorf & Crockett, 1965; Rosenbach, Crockett, & Wapner, 1973); (5) less reliance on global evaluation and simplifying social schemes (e.g., affective balance schemes) in understanding patterns of interpersonal relationships (e.g., Delia & Crockett, 1973; Press et al., 1969); and (6) the ability to represent and understand the cognitive, affective, and motivational features of others' perspectives (e.g., Burleson, 1982a; Hale & Delia, 1976) (for a more detailed review of constructivist research on social perception processes, see Delia et al., 1982). Thus there is substantial evidence that individual differences in interpersonal construct system development underlie individual differences in a wide array of distinct social perception processes. This evidence suggests that a general assessment of social cognitive ability can be obtained by tapping aspects of interpersonal construct system development.

## The Constructivist Analysis of Person-Centered Communication

The constructivist analysis of functional communication skill is based on an integration of the sociolinguistic theory of Bernstein (1975), the cognitive developmental theories of Piaget (e.g., 1926) and Werner (1957), and the "Chicago School" of symbolic interactionism (Blumer, 1969; Goffman, 1967). Since the nature of this theoretical integration has been discussed in detail elsewhere (e.g., Applegate & Delia, 1980; Clark & Delia, 1979; Delia et al., 1982; B. O'Keefe & Delia, 1982, in press), it will only be sketched here.

### Foundations for a Theory of Person-Centered Communication

Bernstein's (1975) sociolinguistic theory suggests that people embrace one of two fundamental orientations to the social world— either a person-centered orientation or a position-centered orientation. These two orientations reflect distinct, deeply tacit assumptions about the nature of persons, the organization of social relationships, and the psychological experiences of interactants involved in communicative episodes. Person-centered individuals view others as psychological entities possessing covert intentions, feelings, and perspectives; conceive of social relationships as based on negotiated and emergent understandings; and assume that others with whom they communicate are psychologically distant from themselves. These tacit assumptions lead person-centered individuals to employ what Bernstein terms an "elaborated code." The elaborated code is characterized by the relatively explicit statement and articulation of intentions, motives, lines of reasoning, feelings, perspectives, and beliefs. These features of self and other receive relatively extensive elaboration in talk, since it is assumed that these covert psychological states are the essential qualities that characterize individuals, and thus must be mutually understood for interaction to be coordinated and efficacious.

Position-centered individuals are more inclined to view others in terms of relatively concrete characteristics such as physical qualities, demographic categories, and especially socially defined roles; conceive of social relationships as established and governed by implicit sets of socially shared rules; and assume that others with whom they communicate are psychologically similar to themselves. These tacit assumptions result in position-centered individuals utilizing what Bernstein (1975) terms a "restricted code." Speech within the restricted code emphasizes culturally shared situational definitions, role expectations, and behavioral rules or norms. Such speech is "restricted" in reflecting the assumption that meanings can be shared adequately in communication by simply indexing the preexistent, culturally shared understandings appropriate for specific role relationships. Within the position-centered orientation, then, communication is viewed as a process of social roles interacting in accordance with culturally shared norms. There is no need to elaborate "individual" perspectives since it is assumed that the perspective of the individual is (more or less) coextensive with the culturally defined perspective of the social role being enacted.

According to Bernstein, the assumptions of the person-centered orientation are fostered by the socioeconomic circumstances (i.e., modes and relations of production) characteristic of the middle classes in advanced industrial societies, whereas the assumptions of the position-centered orientation are fostered by the socioeconomic circumstances typical of the working or lower classes. Moreover, Bernstein maintains that the elaborated and restricted codes constitute the mechanisms through which their respective person- and position-centered orientations are transmitted from one generation to the next. Consequently, the two sociolinguistic codes discussed by Bernstein are, at once, the *products* of underlying orientations toward persons and social relationships and the *means* through which these underlying orientations are reproduced in subsequent generations.

Bernstein's analysis of sociolinguistic codes provides (1) a way of conceptualizing major qualitative differences in communicative behavior, (2) an understanding of how such qualitative differences are tied to underlying conceptions of persons, relationships, and the activity of communication, (3) a framework for addressing cultural influences on communication, and (4) a mechanism for explaining the socialization of communicative orientations. There are, however, several important limitations on this analysis. First, the simple dichotomy between elaborated and restricted codes (or person-centered and position-centered communication) is not sufficiently fine-grained, particularly for cultures such as that of the United States, where the social class system is less rigid and defined than in Bernstein's native England. In relatively heterogeneous cultures, it is probably more useful to view person-centered and position-centered communication as ideal types defining the poles of a continuum rather than as exhaustive categories. Second, Bernstein's framework contains no analysis of individual psychological structure. Thus, although Bernstein's approach can easily accommodate cultural differences in communicative behavior, it contains no mechanism for understanding and explaining individual differences in communication. Third, most of Bernstein's work has focused on the lexical and syntactic manifestations of elaborated and restricted codes, while relatively little attention has been given to the strategic or rhetorical levels of communication.

Constructivist researchers have attempted to overcome some of these limitations by integrating Bernstein's analysis with aspects of the cognitive developmental theories proposed by Piaget (1926) and Werner (1957; Werner & Kaplan, 1963). As is well known, Piaget (1926) conceived the course of communicative development as involving a shift from relatively egocentric forms of speech to progressively more socialized forms. Egocentric speech consists of utterances that fail to consider or adapt to the perspectives of listeners, while socialized speech not only considers but also actively adapts to the perspectives of others. Somewhat similarly, Werner and Kaplan (1963) propose that the course of communicative development is marked by a progression toward increasingly "autonomous speech," which enables the individual "to communicate adequately with an audience psychologically quite distant from the addressor" (p. 49). Thus the approaches of both Piaget and Werner suggest that the qualitative changes in communicative behavior occurring over the course of development can be represented on a continuum. With development, the child's utterances become increasingly more adapted to the characteristics, needs, and qualities of listeners. Such development implies that the maturing child should be an increasingly flexible, appropriate, and effective communicator. Moreover, both Piaget and Werner view developmental changes in the quality of communication as a function of more general cognitive developments. That is, the shift from relatively egocentric speech to more socialized or autonomous speech is viewed as being due to the progressive differentiation and integration of underlying cognitive structures. These developing cognitive structures enable the child to represent the relevant features of persons and communicative situations and, hence, to adapt to these features in the process of producing messages.

The cognitive developmental view of communication development contributes three important ideas that help extend Bernstein's analysis of communication. First, cognitive developmental theory suggests that the concepts of person- and position-centered communication can be viewed as poles of a continuum along which different message forms can be arrayed. Second, the cognitive developmental perspective suggests that it may be fruitful to consider person-centered communication as a developmental accomplishment. As should now be clear, there are important similarities in Bernstein's description of person-centered communication and in Piaget's and Werner's descriptions of socialized or autonomous speech. Third, since cognitive developmental theory maintains that communicative development occurs as a function of underlying cognitive developments, this perspective provides a way of approaching the study of individual differences in person-centered communication. Specifically, cognitive developmental theory suggests that developments in underlying cognitive structures are at least partially responsible for the emergence of more person-centered forms of communication. Consequently, individuals with more developed (i.e., differentiated, articulated, and integrated) systems of cognitive structures should possess a greater capacity to engage in person-centered forms of communication.

The third leg of the constructivist analysis of person-centered communication is contributed by the symbolic interactionist theoretical perspective. Grounded in the writings of Mead (1934) and elaborated by such theorists as Blumer (1969) and Goffman (1967), the symbolic interactionist perspective suggests that communication is strategic, contextual, and multifunctional. Communication is strategic, not necessarily in the sense of being consciously planned at a high level of reflective awareness, but rather in the sense of being *functional*; communication is viewed as an instrumental activity directed at the achievement of goals (which often may be diffuse or implicit).

According to the symbolic interactionist perspective, communicative behaviors flow, most generally, from an individual's "definition of the situation," a person's answer to the question, "What is going on here?" A person's definition of the situation—his or her answer to the what, who, and why of a communicative encounter—calls forth general goals which shape the broad texture of the interaction and, further, inform the mobilization of specific communicative intentions. Both situational definitions and specific communicative intentions are shaped by features of the interactional context. Cultural, institutional, functional, and performance factors all contribute to the character of specific communicative contexts (for a detailed analysis of these contextual factors, see Applegate & Delia, 1980). Finally, symbolic interactionism maintains that a situational definition not only specifies the instrumental nature of the interaction but also presents answers to questions regarding who is involved in an interaction and how these persons are related to one another. Consequently, communicative interactions have a multifunctional character: In addition to pursuing instrumental goals, participants in a communicative encounter must also attend to identity management and relational goals.

The symbolic interactionist perspective contributes three important ideas to the constructivist analysis of person-centered communication. First, this perspective suggests that analyses of communication must be sensitive to the instrumental goals pursued by actors. Concretely, this means that a person-centered orientation is instantiated somewhat differently depending on the particular instrumental goal being pursued. Thus different systems of analysis sensitive to the peculiarities of distinct instrumental goals (e.g., comforting, persuading, informing) need to be developed and employed. Second, since concrete communicative behaviors are organized by emergent situational definitions and attendant context-relevant beliefs, these behaviors should not be strongly predicted by general levels of cognitive development. Rather, only moderate associations should be expected between cognitive development and communicative behavior, since the developmental level of relevant cognitive structures is only one influence (albeit an important one) on the character of the context-relevant beliefs chanelizing situated action. Moreover, appreciation of the role of contextual factors on situated communicative behavior suggests the desirability of distinguishing between the *competence* to engage in highly person-centered forms of communication and actual behavioral *performance*. Because level of cognitive development should be predictive of the capacity to engage in person-centered communication, the strongest empirical relations between cognition and communication should be observed when factors known to depress communicative functioning (e.g., stress, anxiety, and exhaustion) are minimized. Third, recognition of the multifunctional nature of communication implies that a complete analysis of communicative behavior in any context must consider not only how individuals pursue instrumental goals but also how they pursue subsidiary goals, such as identity management and relationship protection and, further, how they integrate concern for these latter goals with instrumental ends. More specifically, recognition of the multifunctional nature of communication suggests the need for developing coding procedures sensitive to degrees of person-centeredness in managing identities and relationships, as well as degrees of person-centeredness in pursuing various instrumental objectives.

By infusing Bernstein's analysis of person-centered communication with aspects of cognitive developmental theory and symbolic interactionism, the constructivist perspective provides a rich framework for the detailed analysis of individual differences in person-centered communication in a variety of contexts. The next section sketches the methods employed in empirical analyses of specific forms of person-centered communication.

## Methods for Assessing Person-Centered Communication

The constructivist conceptualization of person-centered communication has resulted in a distinctive approach to message analysis. Perhaps the most characteristic methodological feature of constructivist empirical studies is the use of hierarchically structured coding systems to assess the person-centered quality of message behavior (see Clark & Delia, 1979). Different hierarchically ordered coding systems have been employed in the analysis of persuasive messages (Clark & Delia, 1976; Delia & Clark, 1977; Delia, Kline, et al., 1979), comforting messages (Applegate, 1980a; Burleson, 1982b; Ritter, 1979), regulative or disciplinary messages (Applegate, 1980a; Applegate et al., 1985), conflict management messages (Samter & Ely, 1985), and informative or explanatory messages (Kline & Ceropski, 1984; Rowan, 1985). Hierarchical systems have also been used to code messages for the extent to which person-centeredness is exhibited in pursuing such subsidiary communicative objectives as relationship maintenance (Applegate, 1980a) and face-support or identity management (Applegate, 1982a; Kline, 1981a, 1981b), as well as for the extent to which the pursuit of instrumental objectives is integrated with a concern for relational and identity goals (O'Keefe & Shepherd, 1983). Moreover, hierarchical coding systems have been used to assess the person-centered quality of the rationales or justifications people use when explaining their choice of persuasive messages (Burke & Clark, 1982; O'Keefe & Delia, 1979), comforting messages (Applegate, 1980a; Burleson, 1980), and regulative messages (Applegate, 1980a).

All of these hierarchical coding systems share a number of common features. All view person-centeredness as a continuous quality; thus all are composed of multiple categories hierarchically ordered for the degree of person-centeredness manifested. Categories for each system are defined by specifying features of messages (or rationales) that presumably embody particular levels of person-centeredness (see Clark & Delia, 1979). The unit of analysis focused on by each system is the "message strategy," which can be defined as a single, coherent line of verbal behavior directed at the accomplishment of a particular end.

While there are similarities among these hierarchical systems, there are also important differences. The constructivist analysis of person-centered communication suggests the need for sensitivity to the specific instrumental goals pursued in communication—in other words, the manner in which person-centeredness is manifested will vary as a function of instrumental goal. Thus, for example, a high level of person-centeredness is exhibited in *persuading* (Clark & Delia, 1976; Delia, Kline, et al., 1979) when the speaker seeks to gain compliance by framing the persuasive request so as to accommodate the needs, interests, and goals of the persuadee (rather than focusing only on his or her own needs and goals). A high level of person-centeredness is exhibited in *comforting* (Applegate, 1980a; Burleson, 1982b) when the speaker attempts to improve the affective state of a distressed other by acknowledging, elaborating, legitimizing, and placing into perspective the feelings of the other (rather than minimizing, ignoring, or challenging these feelings).

Person-centeredness is exhibited in *regulating* or *disciplining* (Applegate, 1980a; Applegate et al., 1985) when the speaker seeks to modify the norm-violating behavior of an offender by encouraging the offender to reason through the consequences—especially the interpersonal or social consequences—of his or her actions (rather than invoking rules, threatening punitive actions, or using force). In *managing interpersonal conflicts* (Samter & Ely, 1985), a high level of person-centeredness is manifested when the speaker seeks to resolve differences or disagreements by proposing solutions that respect the rights and accommodate the interests of both disputants (rather than attempting to force concessions from the other). Person-centeredness is exhibited as well in *informing* or *explaining* (Kline & Ceropski, 1984; Rowan, 1985) when the speaker seeks to enhance understanding by encouraging the listener to reason through how new information is consistent and/or inconsistent with the listener's existing beliefs (rather than simply asserting that some set of propositions about the relevant topic is "true" and should be believed).

Finally, a high level of person-centeredness is exhibited for such subsidiary communicative goals as *identity management* and *relationship enhancement* (Applegate, 1982a; Kline, 1981a, 1981b) when the speaker seeks to protect the face of the listener by framing messages so they convey a positive evaluation of the other and preserve the other's autonomy (rather than conveying a negative evaluation and/or limiting the other's behavioral options). Because the manner in which person-centeredness is manifested varies as a function of communicative goal, different hierarchical coding systems have been employed when studying distinct forms of communication.

## Validity of Constructivist Coding Systems

The constructivist analysis of person-centered communication suggests several empirical criteria that can be used to assess the construct validity of these hierarchical coding systems. For example, Bernstein's analysis of the sociocultural bases of the elaborated and restricted codes suggests that there should be a positive association between socioeconomic status (social class) and the use of person-centered communication. Consistent with this prediction, socioeconomic status has been found positively correlated with the use of person-centered regulative, persuasive, and comforting messages (Applegate, 1980b; Applegate et al., 1985; Applegate & Delia, 1980; Church & Applegate, 1981; Jones, Delia, & Clark, 1981a; Kasch, 1984). Also following Bernstein, the constructivist analysis of person-centered communication suggests that children whose parents typically use person-centered communication should develop a person-centered orientation, while children whose parents typically employ position-centered forms of communication should develop a corresponding position-centered orientation. Findings from studies conducted by constructivist researchers (Delia, Burleson, et al., 1979; Jones, Delia, & Clark, 1981b), as well as by other researchers (see the reviews of Applegate et al., 1985; Applegate & Delia, 1980; Burleson, 1983a), support this hypothesis.

Within the constructivist perspective, the competence to engage in sophisticated forms of person-centered communication is viewed as a developmental achievement. Thus there should be a positive association between person-centered communication and chronological age during childhood and adolescence. Consistent with this prediction, considerable research has documented developmental advances in children's persuasive skills (see review by Delia & O'Keefe, 1979), comforting skills (see review by Burleson, 1984b), referential or informative skills (see reviews by Asher, 1979; Glucksberg, Krauss, & Higgins, 1975), and conflict management or social problem-solving skills (e.g., Abrahami, Selman, & Stone, 1981; Marsh, 1982). More specifically, age has been found to be positively correlated with the use of person-centered persuasive messages (Burke & Clark, 1982; Clark & Delia, 1976; Delia & Clark, 1977; Delia, Kline, et al., 1979; Ritter, 1979), comforting messages (Burleson, 1980, 1982a, 1982b; Ritter, 1979), and conflict management messages (Samter & Ely, 1985).

The constructivist analysis of person-centered communication suggests that developmental and individual differences in social cognitive ability should be positively associated with the use of person-centered messages. The extensive empirical evidence linking indices of social cognitive ability to hierarchical codings of person-centered communication is reviewed in detail below.

Finally, the constructivist approach to message analysis suggests that messages coded as relatively high in person-centeredness should, at least in some circumstances, be more functional or successful than less person-centered messages. Messages exhibiting a high level of person-centeredness legitimize the other's perspective, accommodate the other's views or interests, and support the other's self-image. Thus such messages should be preferred by, elicit more favorable reactions from, and be more effective with listeners. Consistent with this line of reasoning, a series of studies undertaken by Burleson and his associates (Burleson, 1985; Burleson & Samter, 1985, in press; Samter, Burleson, & Basden, 1985) found that people rated highly person-centered comforting messages as more sensitive and effective than less person-centered messages and, further, evaluated the users of highly person-centered comforting strategies more positively than the users of less person-centered strategies. Burleson and Fennelly (1981) found that highly person-centered persuasive strategies were more effective than less person-centered strategies at getting children to share with others, a result consistent with findings reported by several other researchers (e.g., Dlugokinski & Firestone, 1974; Eisenberg-Berg & Geisheker, 1979). Shepherd and O'Keefe found that person-centered messages integrating relational concerns with instrumental objectives in natural persuasive interactions were as effective in changing the attitudes of a persuadee as messages focusing exclusively on instrumental objectives but resulted in a higher degree of liking for the persuader. Finally, research by Husband (1981) indicates that individuals in leadership positions who employ person-centered forms of communication are evaluated more positively by both supervisors and subordinates than individuals employing more position-centered forms of communication.

In sum, constructivist methods for assessing the person-centered quality of communication, especially hierarchical codings for the person-centeredness of message strategies, are appropriately associated with such variables as socioeconomic status, socialization outcomes, chronological age, social cognitive development, and functional effectiveness. Moreover, research has found hierarchical codings for the person-centeredness of message strategies to be generally unrelated to such potentially confounding variables as verbal intelligence, verbal fluency, and loquacity (e.g., Applegate, 1978; Applegate et al., 1985; Borden, 1979; Burleson & Delia, 1983; Hale, 1980). Taken together, the results of the studies reviewed here provide strong support for the validity of the methods employed by constructivist researchers to assess the person-centered quality of communication.

## Interpersonal Construct System Development and Person-Centered Communication

### *The Theoretical and Empirical Paradigm of the Studies*

As noted at the outset of this chapter, the relationship between individual differences in interpersonal construct system development and the use of person-centered communication has been a primary focus for constructivist research. More than 40 studies have assessed this relationship in some way. The basic theoretical notion underlying these studies has been that the use of person-centered message strategies (i.e., messages that reflect an awareness of and adaptation to the needs, interests, feelings, knowledge, or perspective on an individuated listener) is dependent on the ability to infer and internally represent relevant psychological characteristics of the listener. Interpersonal constructs constitute the fundamental cognitive mechanisms through which features of another's thoughts, behaviors, and communicatively relevant characteristics are inferred and represented. Hence, individuals with more developed (i.e., differentiated, abstract, and integrated) systems of interpersonal constructs ought to be better able to infer and represent the relevant qualities of a listener. Therefore, individuals with more developed systems of interpersonal constructs should be more capable of producing highly person-centered messages (for additional details regarding this theoretical relationship, see Delia et al., 1982).

Most studies assessing the relationship between interpersonal construct system development and person-centered communication have used basically similar procedures. The majority of studies have assessed construct system development through a two-role written version of Crockett's (1965) RCQ. Typically, responses to the RCQ have been scored for construct differentiation, or cognitive complexity. Orally administered versions of the RCQ have also been used, especially with populations (e.g., young children) that might have difficulty with the written version of this task. A number of studies (e.g., Burleson, 1983b) have assessed construct system development in terms of interpersonal construct abstractness. In these studies, constructs are elicited by either the RCQ or a modified version of Kelly's (1955) Role Construct Repertory Test (RCRT) and then hierarchically coded for degree of abstractness (i.e., degree of psychological centeredness). Still other studies (e.g., Applegate, 1982b; Burleson, 1984a) have included assessments of both construct differentiation and construct abstractness.

Messages used to assess the person-centered quality of communicative behavior have most frequently been elicited by having experimental participants respond to several hypothetical situations, the content of which varies according to participant characteristics and the type of communication being examined. For example, children have been asked to imagine persuading a parent to hold an overnight party, while college students have been asked to imagine persuading a friend to spend his or her vacation at a particular location. Children have been asked to imagine comforting a peer who is upset about not receiving an invitation to an acquaintance's party, while adults have been asked to comfort a friend who is upset about having been "dumped" by a dating partner. Mothers have been asked to imagine regulating the behavior of a child refusing to go to bed, while adults have been asked to imagine regulating the behavior of an employee who is consistently late for work. For each hypothetical situation presented, subjects have generally been asked to state (or write) exactly what they would say to accomplish the functionally relevant goal (i.e., persuade another, comfort another, and so on). In studies where communicative flexibility has been a variable of interest (e.g., Burleson, 1982b; Clark & Delia, 1976), subjects have been instructed to state everything they might say in response to a situation. These data then provide a basis for scoring the number and variety of strategies employed. Subjects have also been asked to provide justifications or rationales for the messages elicited. Hypothetical situations have been presented to subjects both orally and in writing.

There are several advantages associated with the use of hypothetical situations as a data collection device for message behavior (see Burleson, 1984b). For example, the use of hypothetical situations enables researchers to collect a large corpus of message behavior relatively easily and economically. Reliance on hypothetical situations also provides researchers with a degree of experimental control; within a given study, all subjects respond to the same situations, and researchers can tailor these situations to meet particular theoretical interests. Moreover, studies can employ multiple hypothetical situations to enhance the reliability of assessments of person-centered communication skills. Internal consistencies of .80 and higher have been reported for multiple-situation tests of person-centered communication skills (e.g., Applegate et al., 1985; Burleson, 1983b, 1984a).

Responses to hypothetical situations also appear to provide valid assessments of person-centered communication skills. In constructivist studies employing hypothetical situations, subjects have been required to construct or generate message strategies rather than rate preformulated strategies for likelihood of use. This is an important feature of constructivist research because the strategy construction and rating procedures generally yield different results, with the strategy rating procedure exhibiting little sensitivity to theoretically relevant variables (e.g., Burke & Clark, 1982; Burleson & Samter, in press; Clark, 1979; Renshaw & Asher, 1983).

A growing body of evidence indicates that messages constructed in response to hypothetical situations approximate those used in real-world situations. For example, Applegate (1980b) had a sample of day care teachers construct messages in response to hypothetical situations involving children who were either misbehaving or emotionally distressed. Applegate also observed these teachers' interactions with children at the day care center over a three-month period, specifically recording natural disciplinary and comforting acts. This researcher found that teachers producing highly person-centered disciplinary and comforting strategies in response to the hypothetical situations also tended to use highly person-centered strategies in real-world contexts, although they occasionally employed less person-centered strategies as well. On the other hand, teachers who produced less person-centered strategies in response to the hypothetical situations consistently employed less person-centered strategies in natural contexts.

In addition to supporting the validity of results obtained through hypothetical situations, Applegate's (1980b) findings also suggest that messages obtained in response to hypothetical situations can be viewed as tapping an individual's *competence* to engage in person-centered communication (for a fuller discussion of this issue, see Burleson, 1984b). In a different study, Applegate (1982b) found that the person-centered quality of the persuasive strategies produced by college students in response to hypothetical situations was positively associated (at a moderate level) with the person-centered quality of the persuasive strategies generated by the students in a real-world bargaining situation. Results similar to those obtained by Applegate (1980b, 1982b) have been reported by Kline and Ceropski (1984) in their study of the communicative strategies employed by medical students, and by Selman and his associates (e.g., Selman, 1980; Selman, Schorin, Stone, & Phelps, 1983; Stone & Selman, 1982) in studies of the conflict management behavior of children. In sum, there is good reason to believe that messages constructed in response to hypothetical situations constitute a valid assessment of real-world communicative behavior.

The messages elicited through hypothetical situations have been analyzed in a number of different ways by constructivist researchers. Most frequently, messages have been scored (within an appropriate hierarchical coding system) for the degree of person-centeredness exhibited in pursuing the relevant instrumental goal. In cases where a subject produces multiple strategies codable within different levels of the hierarchical system, most studies have focused on the highest-level strategy used in responding to the situation. This is because an individual's competence to engage in person-centered communication has been the focus of most research. As will be recalled, the constructivist analysis of person-centered communication suggests that level of cognitive development should be most strongly associated with the capacity to engage in highly person-centered forms of communication. Further, Loevinger and Wessler's (1970) analysis of different scoring procedures used in coding free-response data suggests that the highest-level response is the most appropriate coding when the characteristic under study is viewed primarily as a capacity.

In addition to being scored for the degree of person-centeredness exhibited in the pursuit of an instrumental goal, messages have also been scored for person-centeredness manifested with respect to such subsidiary goals as face-support and relationship enhancement (e.g., Applegate, 1980a, 1982a). Message rationales have also been coded for the extent to which message choices are justified in terms of specific features of the listener and the communicative situation (e.g., Applegate, 1980a; Burleson, 1980; O'Keefe & Delia, 1979). Finally, some studies have coded the number and/or variety of strategies employed by subjects to provide an index of the speaker's communicative flexibility (e.g., Burleson, 1982b; Clark & Delia, 1976; O'Keefe & Delia, 1979).

## Summary of Research Findings

The results of studies assessing the relationship between measures of interpersonal construct system development and various aspects of person-centered communication are summarized in this section. A more detailed review of much of this literature is presented by O'Keefe and Sypher (1981).

Eight studies have assessed the relationship between interpersonal construct system development and person-centered persuasive skills in children. The subjects in these studies have ranged from 5 to 18 years of age. Because interpersonal construct system development and person-centered persuasive skills are both positively associated with chronological age, adequate tests of the relationship between construct system development and persuasive skills must control for the effect of age, either through the statistical procedure of partialing or through the use of single-age, individual-difference research designs. When controlling for the effects of age in one of these manners, six studies (Clark & Delia, 1977; Clark, Willinghanz, & O'Dell, 1983; Delia & Clark, 1977; Delia, Burleson et al., 1979; Delia, Kline, et al., 1979; Sarver, 1976) have found significant positive associations between interpersonal construct differentiation and the use of person-centered persuasive messages. The magnitudes of these significant associations generally range from .30 to .60.

Only one study (Ritter, 1979) failed to detect a significant relationship between construct differentiation and the use of person-centered persuasive messages; however, Ritter notes that there was little variance in the construct differentiation scores of her sample. In addition, three studies (Clark, Willinghanz, et al., 1983; Delia, Burleson, et al., 1979; Delia, Kline, et al., 1979) found significant relationships between construct abstractness and the use of person-centered persuasive messages in samples of older children and adolescents. Because few abstract constructs are developed prior to late childhood, this dimension of construct system development should not emerge as a meaningful predictor of communicative functioning until the late childhood years. Supplementing the findings obtained with persuasive strategies, Burke and Clark (1982) found both construct differentiation and abstractness positively associated with the person-centeredness of rationales used to justify persuasive message selection, while two studies (Clark, Willinghanz, et al., 1983; Sarver, 1976) found positive relationships between construct system development and the number of different persuasive strategies employed.

Eight studies have investigated the relationship between construct system development and persuasive skills with samples of adults. Three studies (Applegate, 1982b; Borden, 1981a; Burke, 1979) found significant correlations between construct systems indices (differentiation and/or abstractness) and the use of person-centered persuasive strategies, with the associations ranging between .25 and .50. Sarver (1976) found only a marginally significant association ($r = .27$, $p < .10$) between construct differentiation and the person-centered quality of persuasive strategies employed by a sample of young mothers. Three studies (Applegate, 1982b; O'Keefe & Delia, 1979; Sypher & O'Keefe, 1980) report significant associations between construct differentiation and the number of strategies used in responding to hypothetical situations, while

O'Keefe and Delia (1979) found a positive relationship between the use of person-centered message rationales and "construct comprehensiveness," a variable conceptually similar to construct abstractness. Rowan (1981) detected a positive correlation between construct differentiation and the inclusion of listener-appropriate information in a persuasive message. Finally, Shepherd and O'Keefe (1984) found a significant association between construct differentiation and the use of persuasive strategies integrating concern for the primary persuasive objective with concerns for the listener's "face" and the relationship with the listener.

Four studies have examined the relationship between construct system development and children's person-centered comforting skills. When controlling for the confounding effects of age, Burleson (1984b) and Delia, Burleson, et al. (1979) found the use of person-centered comforting strategies positively associated with both construct differentiation and abstractness. Moreover, Burleson (1982a) found both differentiation and abstractness to be positively related to person-centered explanations of comforting strategy choices. Across these three studies, construct system development consistently explained about one-third of the variance in children's person-centered comforting skills. Ritter (1979) found no relationship between construct differentiation and the use of person-centered comforting strategies in a sample of adolescents; as noted earlier, however, there was little variability in the construct differentiation scores of Ritter's sample.

Nine studies have assessed the relationship between individual differences in adults' construct system development and person-centered comforting skills. The samples used in these nine studies have included groups of college students, mothers of young children, teacher trainees, day care center workers, and medical students. All nine studies (Applegate, 1978, 1980a, 1980b; Applegate et al., 1985; Borden, 1981b; Burleson, 1978, 1983b; Kline & Ceropski, 1984; Samter & Burleson, 1984) found significant relationships between the use of person-centered comforting messages and construct differentiation and/or abstractness. In addition, three studies (Applegate, 1978, 1980a, 1980b) found the quality of rationales justifying comforting strategy choices to be associated with construct abstractness.

Ten studies have examined the regulative or disciplinary communication skills of adults in such diverse groups as police officers, nurses, teachers, college students, and mothers of young children. Seven of these studies (Applegate, 1978, 1980a, 1980b; Applegate et al., 1985; Church & Applegate, 1981; Kasch, 1984; Kline & Ceropski, 1984) have found moderate-level (.40 to .65) positive associations between the use of person-centered regulative messages and measures of construct abstractness and differentiation. The other three studies (Applegate, 1982a; Kline, 1981a, 1981b) assessed the influence of construct system development on the use of regulative strategies attending to the "face" of the listener. In this latter group of studies, messages were coded for the extent to which they (1) conveyed a positive interpersonal evaluation of the listener and (2) protected the listener's autonomy of action. In all three studies, interpersonal construct abstractness was positively associated with both aspects of face management. Finally, Applegate (1980a) found construct abstractness to be positively associated with the extent to which teachers' regulative strategies demonstrated concern for maintaining a positive interpersonal relationship with students.

To date, six studies have examined the relationship between person-centered informative skills and construct system development. Four of the five studies employing an adult sample (Hale, 1980, 1982; Kline & Ceropski, 1984; Sarver, 1976) found positive relationships between construct differentiation and informative skill. The other study (Losee, 1976) employing an adult sample failed to detect a significant relationship between these variables. Delia, Kline, Burleson, Clark, Applegate, and Burke (1980) found children's performances on three different informative communication tasks to be positively associated with individual differences in construct differentiation. Sarver (1976), however, found construct differentiation and informative skill to be positively associated in a sample of seventh graders but unassociated in a sample of second graders.

Finally, Samter and Ely (1985) have investigated the relationship between construct differentiation and the use of person-centered conflict management strategies by children. Strategies were coded for the extent to which proposed solutions to the conflict accommodated the legitimate interests of both conflicting parties. Construct differentiation significantly predicted ($r = .50$) the use of person-centered conflict management strategies.

Although the great majority of studies assessing the relationship between construct system development and person-centered communication have elicited messages by having subjects respond to hypothetical situations, some studies have also assessed the relationship between construct development and messages produced during the course of real-world interactions. For example, Samter and Burleson, (1984) found construct differentiation to be positively associated with the person-centered quality of comforting strategies employed by college females during a natural interaction. Applegate (1982b) found college students' use of person-centered persuasive strategies during natural bargaining interactions to be associated with construct abstractness but not construct differentiation. Shepherd and O'Keefe (1984) found construct differentiation to be significantly associated with the use of persuasive strategies integrating concern for interpersonal and instrumental goals in a natural, mutual influence situation, and Kline and Ceropski (1984) found the construct differentiation of medical students to be positively associated with their use of person-centered informative strategies during actual admission interviews conducted with patients. Thus it appears that construct system development not only predicts qualities of the messages produced in response to hypothetical situations, but also the person-centered quality of communication in real-world, or natural, situations.

## Summary

The research reviewed here leaves little doubt that measures of interpersonal construct system development are moderately associated with measures tapping the person-centered quality of communication. Virtually all studies assessing this relationship have reported significant results, with obtained relationships generally ranging from .30 to .65. Moreover, the relationship between construct system development and person-centered communication appears to be quite general, having been found to hold across (1) diverse subject populations (including children, adolescents, college students, mothers of young children, teachers, day care workers, nurses, medical students, residence hall counselors, and police officers), (2) different instrumental goals pursued by speakers (persuading, comforting, regulating or disciplining, informing, and managing conflict), (3) different subsidiary objectives pursued by speakers (identity management or "face" protection, relationship maintenance), (4) different measures of construct system development (differentiation, abstractness), (5) different aspects of communicative behavior (quality of messages, quality of message rationales, number of messages, and variety of messages), (6) differences in the media or modality used to assess both construct system development and communicative behavior (oral modality, written modality), and (7) different means used to elicit communicative behavior (hypothetical situations, real-world situations).

The consistency of the results obtained in the studies reviewed here is particularly striking in light of the often contradictory and ambiguous findings reported in other investigations of the relation between social cognition and communication (see reviews by Burleson, 1984c; Shantz, 1981). Apparently, the distinct manner in which constructivist researchers have conceptualized and assessed social cognitive ability, person-centered communication, and the relationship between these variables has led to the highly consistent findings summarized earlier (see also Applegate et al., 1985, pp. 112-115).

In sum, there is a significant, stable, and substantial relationship between measures of interpersonal construct system development and indices of person-centered communication. It appears that individual differences in construct system development reliably account for 10% to 40% of the variance in the use of highly person-centered forms of communication. The evidence supporting the relationship between construct system development and person-centered communication seems so strong and consistent that no further research directed simply at demonstrating the existence of this relationship is needed. Rather, attention should be focused on producing more sophisticated and detailed theoretical accounts for this relationship. The next section of this chapter considers some different explanations for this relationship.

## CONSTRUCT SYSTEM DEVELOPMENT AND PERSON-CENTERED COMMUNICATION: EXPLANATORY ACCOUNTS

The "standard account" for the empirical relation between construct system development and person-centered communication has maintained that relatively sophisticated social cognitive abilities are needed for the production of messages adapting to the perspective and characteristics of an individuated other, and that interpersonal construct differentiation and abstractness are good general indices of social cognitive ability. The position taken here holds that this account is not so much wrong as it is unelaborated and lacking in detail. The limitations of the standard account were first detailed by O'Keefe and Delia (1982); since the publication of their paper, a number of more refined accounts for the relation between construct system development and person-centered communication have been proposed (e.g., Applegate et al., 1985; Burleson, 1984c; Kline & Ceropski, 1984; O'Keefe & Delia, in press). This section reviews and critiques two other substantive accounts that have been proposed to explain the relationship between construct system properties and communicative behavior. A third possible account for this relationship—one alleging that the relationship between these variables is spurious—is discussed initially.

### The Spurious Relationship Account

Virtually all studies investigating the relationship between construct system development and person-centered communication have employed correlational research designs. The use of correlational designs has been mandated by the nature of the variables under study. Clearly, a presumably stable individual-difference variable such as construct system development is not easily manipulated. While the use of correlational research designs has been appropriate, then, there is always a certain amount of ambiguity associated with such designs. For example, it is always possible that a correlation between two observed variables might not be due to actual covariation between these variables, but instead might be a function of the two observed variables each covarying with some underlying and unassessed third variable. In such cases, a spurious relation exists between the two observed variables. In the present case, this spurious relation account would maintain that the observed relationships between construct system development and person-centered communication are due to the influence of some unassessed third variable.

It is impossible to disprove fully the spurious relation explanation for the results summarized above, since such an effort would involve an attempt to prove the null hypothesis. However, as O'Keefe and Delia (1982) note, there is good reason for not taking the spurious relation account too seriously. First, as O'Keefe and Delia suggest, the relationship between construct system properties and person-centered communication is *developmental:* As interpersonal constructs become more differentiated and abstract over the course of development, people become better able to use highly person-centered forms of communication (e.g., Burleson, 1984a; Delia, Kline, et al., 1979). This fact implies that any proposed "third variable" would also have to change systematically over the course of development. This requirement eliminates many potentially confounding factors from consideration, including environmental factors and most personality traits.

Second, the effects of many potentially confounding "third variables" have been assessed and found not to attenuate the relationship between construct system development and person-centered communication. For example, Samter and Burleson (1984) found a zero-order correlation of .36 between construct differentiation and person-centered comforting in natural interactions. These researchers also obtained assessments of four other personality variables (locus of control orientation, emotional empathy, and two aspects of communication apprehension) and partialed out the effects of these variables from the relationship between construct differentiation and comforting behavior. The resulting fourth-order partial correlation of .34 was only slightly less than the zero-order correlation of .36. Other studies have found measures of construct system development, measures of person-centered communication, and/or relationships between these measures to be relatively unaffected by such variables as Machiavellianism, value orientations, control orientations, empathic disposition, rhetorical sensitivity, communication apprehension, and self-monitoring (e.g., Borden, 1979; Burleson, 1983b; Burleson & Samter, in press; Kline & Ceropski, 1984). In addition, measures of construct development and person-centered communication have been found to be unassociated with such developmentally related intellectual factors as verbal fluency and verbal intelligence (e.g., Applegate et al., 1985; Burleson & Delia, 1983; Burleson et al., 1981; Burleson et al., 1985; Hale, 1980; Sypher & Applegate, 1982).

While all possible spurious factors have not been studied, the variables most likely to produce spurious relationships between construct system properties and communicative behavior have been examined and found to exert little influence. Consequently, it appears reasonable to conclude that the relationship between construct system development and person-centered communication is not the product of some unassessed variable.

## The Role-Taking/Adapted Communication Account

Cognitive developmental theorists (e.g., Flavell, 1968; Piaget, 1926), as well as symbolic interactionists (e.g., Blumer, 1969; Mead, 1934), have long maintained that a crucial cognitive process underlying the production of messages adapted to the characteristics of listeners is "role-taking" or "social perspective taking." In particular, Piaget (1926) argues that the preoperational child's inability to infer another's perspective and coordinate it with his or her own perspective results in the production of unadapted, egocentric speech. However, with the onset of concrete operational thought, a stage of cognitive development marked by the ability to coordinate multiple dimensions of a situation, children become capable of sustaining both their own and another's view of a situation, and thus are able to adapt or tailor utterances to fit the characteristics of the others. From this perspective, then, the acquisition and elaboration of the ability to "take" (i.e., infer and internally represent) the perspective of another is regarded as the crucial cognitive development underlying the production of socialized or adapted speech.

As an explanatory account for the findings of constructivist studies, this position would view measures of construct system properties such as differentiation and abstractness as surrogate measures for role-taking skill, and measures of person-centered communication as surrogate measures of listener-adapted communication. Thus the findings of constructivist studies would be explained in terms of persons with highly developed construct systems being better able to take the perspective of the listener and therefore more capable of producing messages tailored to listener characteristics.

Some evidence supports the role-taking/adapted communication account of constructivist research findings. For example, several studies have found construct system properties moderately associated with measures of role-taking skill (e.g., Burleson, 1982a; Clark & Delia, 1977; Delia et al., 1980; Hale & Delia, 1976; Sarver, 1976; Sypher & O'Keefe, 1980). Moreover, some measures of person-centered communication skill appear to focus on the extent to which message behavior reflects listener adaptation. For example, the coding system for persuasive messages developed by Clark and Delia (1976) and elaborated by Delia, Kline, et al. (1979) hierarchically scores persuasive messages for the extent to which they "accommodate to the perspective of the target" (Delia, Kline, et al., 1979, p. 248). Further, virtually all coding systems for message rationales (Applegate, 1980a; Burke & Clark, 1982; Burleson, 1980; O'Keefe & Delia, 1979) score these justifications in terms of the extent to which specific characteristics and qualities of the listener are mentioned as a basis for strategy choice. Finally, specific measures of role-taking ability have been found to be moderately correlated with constructivist measures of person-centered communication skills in a number of studies (Burleson, 1982a, 1984a; Clark & Delia, 1977; Delia, Burleson, et al., 1979; Sarver, 1976).

Although some empirical evidence supports a role-taking/adapted communication account for the results of constructivist studies, there are also significant problems with this account. First, as a number of writers (e.g., Burleson, 1984c; Delia & Clark, 1977; Glucksberg et al., 1975) note, the construct of role-taking is not coherent either conceptually or empirically. Role-taking skills have been distinguished in terms of the content of role-taking tasks (i.e., whether making inferences about another's perceptual, conceptual, or affective perspective) and in terms of the type of cognitive operations required for performance on a task (i.e., recognition of another's perspective, sequential coordination of perspectives, simultaneous coordination of perspectives, or recursive coordination of perspectives). Most studies have found different measures of role-taking skill to be either uncorrelated or only weakly correlated (see Enright & Lapsley, 1980; Ford, 1979; Rubin, 1978). Similarly, various types of "adaptive communication skills" have been distinguished, but there appears to be little coherence among these skills. Several studies (e.g., Burleson & Delia, 1983; Kroll, 1978; Piche, Michlin, Rubin, & Johnson, 1975) have found only weak relationships among different measures of adaptive communication skill (see also

Burleson, 1984c). Because of the conceptual and empirical ambiguity associated with both the construct of role-taking and the construct of adaptive communication, it appears that little would be gained by interpreting the results of constructivist studies in terms of this account.

A second major reason for not accepting the role-taking/adapted communication account is that the concept of interpersonal construct system development is not exhausted by the notion of role-taking, nor is the concept of person-centered communication exhausted by the notion of listener adaptation. As noted earlier, constructivist theory views role-taking as only one of several distinct social perception processes, all of which are assumed to function through the application of interpersonal constructs. Constructivists (e.g., Delia & Clark, 1977; O'Keefe & Delia, 1982) have argued that multiple social perception processes (e.g., making causal and dispositional attributions, forming and organizing impressions, integrating information, as well as role-taking) probably figure in the production of sophisticated messages. Thus reducing construct system development to the single process of role-taking would have the effect of oversimplifying the contributions of social cognition to communication. Similarly, the complex concept of person-centered communication cannot be fruitfully reduced to the simple notion of listener adaptation. As Applegate et al. (1985, pp. 134-135) argue, the notion of person-centeredness refers to a general quality of communication having several separable aspects, including the following:

> (a) the extent to which a message is responsive to the aims and utterances of one's interactional partner, (b) the extent to which a message is adapted or tailored so as to meet the specific characteristics of a particular listener, (c) the extent to which the topic or content of a message deals with persons and their psychological and affective qualities, (d) the extent to which a message implicitly seeks to enhance interpersonal relationships or create positive interpersonal identities, and (e) the extent to which a message encourages reflection by another about his or her circumstance or situation.

On this view, listener adaptation is only one aspect of person-centered communication. Reduction of the notion of person-centeredness to the notion of listener adaptation would thus have the effect of excluding many significant features of person-centered messages from examination.

O'Keefe and Delia (1982) note that at least some versions of the role-taking/adapted communication account presuppose a model of the message production process that logically can apply to only a limited range of communicative encounters. These writers suggest that the role-taking/adapted communication account assumes that persons first generate a "kernel message," and then—through the process of role-taking—infer and consider relevant characteristics of the listener. Finally, they produce an "adapted message" by using the results of the role-taking process to generate appropriate modifications in the kernel message. Although such a complex, multistage process may characterize message production in some circumstances (particularly when the speaker is especially concerned about the consequences of his utterances), such circumstances are probably relatively rare and do not typify most everyday communicative encounters.

There are several other problems with the role-taking/adapted communication account. For example, at least some versions of this account fail to consider adequately the context-specificity of communicative behavior, fail to consider knowledge and processes other than role-taking needed for the production of effective messages, and fail to identify those types of communication where role-taking skill would be most pertinent (for a detailed discussion of these problems, see Burleson, 1984c).

Although there are certainly significant problems with the role-taking/adapted communication account, it may be possible to develop versions of this account that overcome some of the problems discussed earlier and that represent more adequately the contributions of social cognition to communication. For example, certain research has suggested the utility of viewing role-taking skill as a domain-specific ability, with only certain types of role-taking skill contributing to a limited range of communicative behaviors (see Burleson, 1984c). Moreover, some research findings suggest that it would be unwise to completely discard the role-taking/adapted communication account. For example, in studies where both construct system development and role-taking skill have been assessed and correlated with indices of person-centered communication, role-taking skills have frequently been a better predictor of communicative behavior than construct system development (e.g., Burleson, 1982a, 1984a; Clark & Delia, 1977; Delia, Burleson, et al., 1979; Sarver, 1976). In addition, one study (Burleson, 1984a) found a measure of role-taking skill to be significantly correlated with an index of person-centered communication even when controlling for the effects of both construct system differentiation and abstractness. This latter finding suggests that some aspect of cognitive development tapped by role-taking measures, but not construct system measures, contributes uniquely to the production of person-centered messages. Thus it would appear inappropriate at this time to reject outright the role-taking/adapted communication account.

## The Goal Complexity/Behavioral Complexity Account

In response to the inadequacies of the role-taking/adapted communication account, O'Keefe and Delia (1982, in press) have proposed an alternative explanation for the relationship between construct system development and the production of person-centered messages. The account offered by O'Keefe and Delia is quite complex, involving substantial reinterpretations of both the construct system measures and the communication measures used in prior research; only the broad outlines of this account are summarized here.

O'Keefe and Delia observe that many, if not most, communicative situations are attended by some degree of ambiguity and thus require definition by participants. Although many communicative situations are characterized by one or more instrumental goals being pursued by participants, the specific ways in which these goals can be pursued are not given or defined by culturally shared schemes for the situation. Rather, each participant is faced with the task of constructing his or her own specific line of activity and integrating this line with the other participants' unfolding lines of activity. In addition to developing lines of activity in the service of instrumental goals, there are other features of the situation (e.g., self-presentation, "face" support for the other, and relationship definition and maintenance) that may or may not be considered salient by participants. However, if these other features of the situation are considered salient, then lines of action must be developed that not only service instrumental goals but also attend to interpersonal identities and relationships. Thus many communicative situations have the inherent potential to be defined as "complex" by interactants. Such situations can be characterized as those involving multiple goals.

Complex situations require complex lines of action through which multiple goals can be addressed. O'Keefe and Delia introduce the term "behavioral complexity" to characterize the extent to which a line of action reflects concern for multiple goals. These researchers further contend that behavioral complexity is the basic construct tapped by the hierarchical scoring systems used to code person-centered communication. In other words, highly person-centered messages are behaviorally more complex than less person-centered messages because, in addition to demonstrating concern for a particular instrumental goal (e.g., persuading, regulating, or informing), they also reflect the pursuit of other, interpersonally oriented goals (e.g., protecting the other's "face," or maintaining/enhancing a social relationship with the other). Less person-centered forms of communication are less behaviorally complex in that such messages typically reflect concern for only the relevant instrumental goal.

It is important to note that O'Keefe and Delia are not claiming that most communicative situations are inherently complex. Rather, they maintain that most communicative situations have the inherent potential to be defined as complex (i.e., involving interpersonal as well as instrumental goals) by participants. O'Keefe and Delia suggest that it is precisely those persons who produce highly differentiated and psychologically centered (i.e., abstract) impressions on tasks such as Crockett's RCQ who are most likely to define communicative situations in a complex manner. That is, people who score relatively highly on traditional measures of construct differentiation and abstractness give evidence of spontaneously attending to the dispositional, motivational, and affective features of others, and this spontaneous inclination to attend to such psychological characteristics may result in consistently defining communicative situations in a relatively complex way. Thus persons scoring highly on measures of construct system development also tend to score highly on measures of person-centered communication because they generate complex definitions of the situation which include both instrumental and interpersonal goals, and thus develop complex lines of action that attend to these multiple goals.

It is important to note here that definitions of the situation are viewed as arising from the cognitive schemes or constructs employed. Thus it is a person's spontaneous cognitive structuring of the phenomenal field in a way that includes dispositional, motivational, and affective features of others that leads to complex situational definitions and consequent complex (i.e., person-centered) behaviors. Generalized value orientations, attitudes, and belief sets are not viewed as primary influences on situational definitions. This may explain in part why such variables as locus of control, emotional empathy, value orientation, and Machiavellianism are relatively poor predictors of person-centered communication.

The goal complexity/behavioral complexity account forwarded by O'Keefe and Delia is intriguing but as yet has little direct empirical support. Nevertheless, some research has found that the manner in which persons define situations does influence subsequent behavior. For example, Renshaw and Asher (1983) have found that differences in the types of goals children expressed for several social situations were related quite directly to differences in the types of behavior they suggested they would employ in those situations. However, no measures of construct system development were employed by these researchers, so it is unknown whether variations in situational definitions were a function of interpersonal constructs.

In an unpublished study, Kline (1982; cited by O'Keefe & Delia, 1982) presented subjects with a hypothetical situation that called for the regulation of a peer's behavior. Half of the subjects were instructed to attend to the peer's feelings and "face wants" in seeking to produce behavioral change, while the other half of the subjects were told only to address the peer's inappropriate behavior. Kline found that individual differences in construct system development were significantly associated with the use of face-saving strategies only in the group in which face saving was *not* explicitly mentioned as a goal. These findings suggest that persons with relatively developed construct systems spontaneously attend to features of communicative situations such as the other's face wants. However, the results of Kline's study are somewhat difficult to reconcile with the results of research on person-centered comforting (e.g., Applegate, 1980a; Applegate et al., 1985; Burleson, 1983b, 1984a). In this latter body of research, subjects were given explicit instructions to say everything they could to make a distressed other feel better about a particular situation. These situations typically involved circumstances in which the other's positive self-image had been violated. In spite of the explicit statement that the other was feeling "upset" or "depressed" and that the subject should "try to make the other person feel better about things," construct system development was consistently found to be positively associated with the use of person-centered ("behaviorally complex") comforting messages. At the minimum, then, it would appear that further research is needed to determine whether variations in the goal sets provided to people can influence the relationship between construct system development and the production of person-centered messages.

The goal complexity/behavioral complexity account suggests that while general features of construct system development should be somewhat predictive of behaviorally complex forms of communication, context-specific goals and intentions should be even more powerful predictors of behavior. This hypothesis was tested by Kline and Ceropski (1984) in their study of person-centered communication by medical students. Construct system development was assessed by a measure of construct abstractness, and person-centered communication was assessed by coding message strategies employed by the medical students during actual admission interviews with patients. In addition, Kline and Ceropski had the medical students complete a questionnaire in which they were asked to report their conceptions of the aims of medical interviews and their roles in them. Responses to this questionnaire were coded for "belief differentiation," or the number of specific goals or intentions mentioned. While both construct abstractness and context-relevant belief differentiation were positively related to message behavior, construct abstractness was (contrary to expectations) the more powerful predictor. Moreover, when controlling for the effect of construct abstractness, belief differentiation was unrelated to message behavior. Although methodological problems may partially account for these results (the validity of the belief differentiation measure has not been established), there is certainly some question whether context-specific intentions and goals are a better predictor of message behavior than more general aspects of construct system development.

The most direct test of the goal complexity/behavioral complexity account was carried out in a study by Shepherd and O'Keefe (1984). These researchers had pairs of college students who disagreed about some attitude-relevant topic (e.g., abortion) try to change one another's viewpoint during the course of a brief (15-minute) conversation. The message strategies employed by subjects during these persuasive conversations were coded for the way in which competing instrumental, interactional, and interpersonal goals were reconciled. Specifically, messages that focused on one objective to the exclusion of others were coded as *selection* strategies, messages that addressed multiple goals in a sequential (i.e., temporally or behaviorally separated) manner were coded as *separation* strategies, and messages designed so as to address multiple goals simultaneously were coded as *integration* strategies.

Consistent with predictions, construct system differentiation was found to be unassociated with the frequency of behaviorally simple selection strategies ($r = .01$), weakly associated with the frequency of separation strategies ($r = .29$), and strongly associated with the number of integration strategies ($r = .61$).

While these results certainly appear to support the notion that construct system development is related to behavioral complexity, it is not entirely clear why integration strategies are behaviorally more complex, and hence should be better predicted, than separation strategies. After all, both separation and integration strategies address multiple objectives. The major difference appears to be that the separation strategy does this sequentially, while the integration strategy does it simultaneously. Thus, while integration strategies may enjoy a formal advantage in terms of economy or efficiency, they do not appear to be functionally superior to separation strategies, since both strategy types address multiple goals. Here again, additional clarification of the features distinguishing separation and integration strategies may be needed.

The goal complexity/behavioral complexity account is theoretically sophisticated and holds promise of further illuminating the relation between social cognition and communication. As yet, however, this account has been subjected to few empirical tests, and what empirical evidence is available provides ambiguous support at best for the particulars of this account. Of course, this is hardly surprising given the recent emergence of this account and the need to develop and refine methods that will permit more adequate tests of the predictions derived from this account.

## *CONCLUSION*

Of the four explanatory accounts reviewed above, the goal complexity account would appear to have the greatest potential for providing a detailed and sophisticated understanding of the relationship between construct system properties and the production of person-centered communication. To date, however, only an initial formulation of the goal complexity account has been presented, and there is a clear need for further conceptual elaboration and empirical testing of this account. Moreover, none of the other accounts discussed above can be dismissed out of hand. The concepts and methods of the "standard account" have been rich enough to stimulate the generation of one of the most consistent bodies of findings in the area of interpersonal communication. The role-taking account, although beset by numerous conceptual problems, has in its favor empirical findings showing the dependency of person-centered message production on role-taking skills. And the spurious relationship account, while supported by little evidence, cannot be completely dismissed if only because of the logical impossibility of ever proving a generalized null hypothesis. In addition, it should be obvious that the four explanatory accounts discussed here are not the only possible accounts for the relation between construct system development and person-centered communication: With further conceptual and empirical advances, it is certain that still other theoretical accounts for this body of findings will emerge.

Not to be overlooked is the fact that there *is* a body of findings to be accounted for. As shown in the first section of this chapter, there is a stable and quite general relationship between measures of construct system development and indices of person-centered communication. Considerable evidence supports the validity of the methods and procedures used to generate this body of findings, and the relationship between construct system properties and assessments of person-centered communication is probably one of the most replicated relationships in the human communication literature.

While much future constructivist research can be expected to focus on elaborating and testing various theoretical accounts for the relation between construct system development and person-centered communication, several other problems also need to be addressed. For example, research focusing on the contributions of social cognition to the production of person-centered messages is limited in several significant ways. First, this research is limited in focusing on only one specific type of communicative behavior. Clearly, there is more to communication than the production of person-centered messages. Although some constructivist research has addressed such issues as the organization of conversational interaction (e.g., O'Keefe, Delia, & O'Keefe, 1980) and the content of initial interactions (e.g., Delia, Clark, & Switzer, 1979), these and other important topics have received comparatively little attention. Of course, it can be argued that progress in science depends on examining specific phenomena thoroughly and in detail. From such a perspective, the limited focus of constructivist research on person-centered communication can be regarded as a virtue.

There are, however, significant limitations even in the research focused on person-centered communication. While constructivist researchers have readily admitted that social cognition is only one influence on the production of person-centered messages (e.g., Delia & O'Keefe, 1979; Delia et al., 1982), few studies have examined how knowledge and processes other than social cognition influence the capacity to produce person-centered messages. Clearly, the research on person-centered communication would be enriched by examining how such variables as world knowledge and metacommunicative knowledge contribute to person-centered communication skills. In addition, most constructivist research has focused only on the *competence* to produce person-centered messages; little work has examined factors affecting the use of such messages in specific contexts. Some research findings suggest that a variety of situational, organismic, and motivational variables exert considerable influence on the situated use of person-centered communication skills (e.g., Applegate, 1980b; Samter & Burleson, 1984). Consequently, future research needs to examine how both competence and performance factors affect the production of person-centered messages.

Another general area that has received relatively little attention pertains to the effects or outcomes resulting from the use of person-centered communication. Some research suggests that highly person-centered messages are more effective than less person-centered messages in attaining such instrumental goals as persuasion and comforting (Burleson & Fennelly, 1981; Burleson & Samter, 1985), while other research suggests the relative effectiveness of person-centered messages with respect to such subsidiary goals as "face" protection and relationship maintenance (Samter et al., 1985; Shepherd & O'Keefe, 1985). Still other studies suggest that person-centered messages may have important long-term effects on the socialization of cognitive and communicative orientations in children (Applegate & Delia, 1980; Delia, Burleson, & Kline, 1979; Jones et al., 1981b) and on acceptance by the peer group (Burleson, 1985, in press). While intriguing, such findings cannot be regarded as more than suggestive at the present time. More research is needed on both the short- and long-term outcomes of person-centered communication.

Finally, the important question of whether person-centered communication skills can be taught needs to be addressed. Thus far, only two studies (Clark, O'Dell, & Willinghanz, 1983; Rowan, 1984) have attempted to train people in the use of person-centered messages, and the results of these studies are far from conclusive. However, if it is found that highly person-centered messages generally produce desirable short- and long-term outcomes, than a pragmatic rationale will have been established for training persons in the use of such messages.

Researchers interested in person-centered message production thus face a relatively lengthy agenda of issues. Certainly, research needs to focus on the precise manner in which social cognition contributes to the production of person-centered communication. In addition to this issue, however, research needs to examine other factors that contribute to the competence to produce person-centered messages, factors affecting the use of person-centered communication skills in various contexts, the utility of person-centered messages in achieving various instrumental and interpersonal goals, and the training of people in the use of person-centered skills. A comprehensive understanding of person-centered communication can be attained only if all of these issues are addressed.

## REFERENCES

Abrahami A., Selman, R. L., & Stone, C. (1981). A developmental assessment of children's verbal strategies for social action resolution. *Journal of Applied Developmental Psychology, 2*, 145-164.

Applegate, J. L. (1978). *Four investigations of the relationship between social cognitive development and person-centered regulative and interpersonal com-*

*munication.* Unpublished doctoral dissertation, University of Illinois at Urbana-Champaign.

Applegate, J. L. (1980a). Adaptive communication in educational contexts: A study of teachers' communicative strategies. *Communication Education, 29,* 158-170.

Applegate, J. L. (1980b). Person- and position-centered communication in a day-care center. In N. K. Denzin (Ed.), *Studies in symbolic interaction* (Vol. 3, pp. 59-96). Greenwich, CT: JAI Press.

Applegate, J. L. (1982a). *Construct system development and identity-management skills in persuasive contexts.* Paper presented at the Western Speech Communication Association Convention, Denver, February.

Applegate, J. L. (1982b). The impact of construct system development on communication and impression formation in persuasive contexts. *Communication Monographs, 49,* 277- 289.

Applegate, J. L., Burke, J. A., Burleson, B. R., Delia, J. G., & Kline, S. L. (1985). Reflection-enhancing parental communication. In I. E. Sigel (Ed.), *Parental belief systems: The psychological consequences for children* (pp. 107-142). Hillsdale, NJ: Erlbaum.

Applegate, J. L., & Delia, J. G. (1980). Person-centered speech, psychological development, and the contexts of language usage. In R. St. Clair & H. Giles (Eds.), *The social and psychological contexts of language* (pp. 245-282). Hillsdale, NJ: Erlbaum.

Asher, S. R. (1979). Referential communication. In G. J. Whitehurst & B. J. Zimmerman (Eds.), *The functions of language and cognition* (pp. 175-197). New York: Academic Press.

Barenboim, C. (1977). Developmental changes in the interpersonal cognitive system from middle childhood to adolescence. *Child Development, 48,* 1467-1471.

Barenboim, C. (1981). The development of person perception in childhood and adolescence: From behavioral comparisons to psychological constructs to psychological comparisons. *Child Development, 52,* 129-144.

Beatty, M. J., & Payne, S. K. (1984). Loquacity and quantity of constructs as predictors of social perspective-taking. *Communication Quarterly, 32,* 207-210.

Bernstein, B. (1975). *Class, codes, and control: Theoretical studies toward a sociology of language* (rev. ed.). New York: Schocken.

Biskin, D. S., & Crano, W. (1977). Structural organization of impressions derived from inconsistent information: A developmental study. *Genetic Psychology Monographs, 95,* 331-348.

Blumer, H. (1969). *Symbolic interactionism: Perspective and method.* Englewood Cliffs, NJ: Prentice-Hall.

Borden, A. W. (1979). *An investigation of the relationships among indices of social cognition, motivation, and communicative performance.* Unpublished doctoral dissertation, University of Illinois at Urbana-Champaign.

Borden, A. W. (1981a). *Interpersonal values, Machiavellianism, and social cognition as indicators of communicative competence in persuasive contexts.*

Paper presented at the Speech Communication Association Convention, Anaheim, CA, November.

Borden, A. W. (1981b). *An investigation of the relationships among social-cognitive indices, interpersonal values, and interpersonal communicative performance.* Paper presented at the International Communication Association Convention, Minneapolis, May.

Burke, J. A. (1979). *The relationship of interpersonal cognitive development to the adaptation of persuasive strategies in adults.* Paper presented at the Central States Speech Association Convention, St. Louis, April.

Burke, J. A., & Clark, R. A. (1982). An assessment of methodological options for investigating the development of persuasive skills across childhood. *Central States Speech Journal, 33*, 437-445.

Burleson, B. R. (1978). *Relationally oriented construct system content and messages directed to an affectively distressed listener: Two studies.* Paper presented at the annual convention of the Speech Communication Association, Minneapolis, November.

Burleson, B. R. (1980). The development of interpersonal reasoning: An analysis of message strategy justifications. *Journal of the American Forensic Association, 17*, 102-110.

Burleson, B. R. (1982a). The affective perspective-taking process: A test of Turiel's role-taking model. In M. Burgoon (Ed.), *Communication yearbook 6* (pp. 473-488). Beverly Hills, CA: Sage.

Burleson, B. R. (1982b). The development of comforting communication skills in childhood and adolescence. *Child Development, 53*, 1578-1588.

Burleson, B. R. (1983a). Interactional antecedents of social reasoning development: Interpreting the effects of parent discipline on children. In D. Zarefsky, M. O. Sillars, & J. R. Rhodes (Eds.), *Argument in transition: Proceedings of the third summer conference on argumentation* (pp. 597-610). Annandale, VA: Speech Communication Association.

Burleson, B. R. (1983b). Social cognition, empathic motivation, and adults' comforting strategies. *Human Communication Research, 10*, 295-304.

Burleson, B. R. (1984a). Age, social-cognitive development, and the use of comforting strategies. *Communication Monographs, 51*, 140-153.

Burleson, B. R. (1984b). Comforting communication. In H. E. Sypher & J. L. Applegate (Eds.), *Communication by children and adults: Social cognitive and strategic processes* (pp. 63-104). Beverly Hills, CA: Sage.

Burleson, B. R. (1984c). Role-taking and communication skills in childhood: Why they *aren't* related and what can be done about it. *Western Journal of Speech Communication, 48*, 155-170.

Burleson, B. R. (1985). *Communicative correlates of peer acceptance in childhood.* Paper presented at the biennial meeting of the Society for Research in Child Development, Toronto, April.

Burleson, B. R. (in press). Communication skills and childhood peer relationships: An overview. In M. L. McLaughlin (Ed.), *Communication yearbook 9.* Beverly Hills, CA: Sage.

Burleson, B. R., Applegate, J. L., & Neuwirth, C. M. (1981). Is cognitive complexity loquacity? A reply to Powers, Jordan, and Street. *Human Communication Research, 7*, 212-225.

Burleson, B. R., & Delia, J.G. (1983). *Adaptive communication skills in childhood: A unitary construct?* Paper presented at the biennial meeting of the Society for Research in Child Development, Detroit, April.

Burleson, B. R., & Fennelly, D. A. (1981). The effects of persuasive appeal form and cognitive complexity on children's sharing behavior. *Child Study Journal, 11*, 75-90.

Burleson, B. R., & Rowan, K. E. (1985). Are social-cognitive ability and narrative writing skill related? *Written Communication, 2*, 25-43.

Burleson, B. R., & Samter, W. (1985). Consistencies in theoretical and naive evaluations of comforting messages. *Communication Monographs, 52*, 103-123.

Burleson, B. R., & Samter, W. (In press). Individual differences in the perception of comforting messages: An exploratory investigation. *Central States Speech Journal.*

Burleson, B. R., Waltman, M. S., & Samter, W. (1985). *More evidence that cognitive complexity is not loquacity: A reply to Beatty and Payne.* Paper presented at the Speech Communication Association Convention, Denver, November.

Church, S. M., & Applegate, J. L. (1981). *Construct system development and person-centered communication in a police bureaucracy.* Paper presented at the International Communication Association Convention, Minneapolis, May.

Clark, R. A. (1979). The impact of self interest and desire for liking on selection of communicative strategies. *Communication Monographs, 46*, 257-273.

Clark, R. A., & Delia, J. G. (1976). The development of functional persuasive skills in childhood and early adolescence. *Child Development, 47*, 1008-1014.

Clark, R. A., & Delia, J. G. (1977). Cognitive complexity, social perspective-taking, and functional persuasive skills in second- to ninth-grade children. *Human Communication Research, 3*, 128-134.

Clark, R. A., & Delia, J. G. (1979). *Topoi* and rhetorical competence. *Quarterly Journal of Speech, 65*, 165-206.

Clark, R. A., O'Dell, L., & Willinghanz, S. (1983). *Cognitive and behavioral components of persuasive skill: A training study with fourth-graders.* Paper presented at the annual meeting of the Speech Communication Association, Washington, D.C., November.

Clark, R. A., Willinghanz, S., & O'Dell, L. (1983). *The relationship of construct systems to reconciliation of objectives and persuasive skills.* Paper presented at the University of Kansas Conference on Social Cognition and Interpersonal Behavior, Lawrence, KS, September.

Crockett, W. H. (1965). Cognitive complexity and impression formation. In B. A. Maher (Ed.), *Progress in experimental personality research* (Vol. 2, pp. 47-90). New York: Academic Press.

Crockett, W. H., Press, A. N., Delia, J. G., & Kenney, C. J. (1974). *The structural analysis of the organization of written impressions.* Unpublished manuscript, Department of Psychology, University of Kansas, Lawrence, KS.

Delia, J. G. (1972). Dialects and the effects of stereotypes on interpersonal attraction and cognitive processes in impression formation. *Quarterly Journal of Speech, 58*, 285-297.

Delia, J. G. (1976). A constructivist analysis of the concept of credibility. *Quarterly Journal of Speech, 62*, 361-375.

Delia, J. G. (1978). *The research and methodological commitments of a constructivist.* Paper presented at the Speech Communication Association Convention, Minneapolis, November.

Delia, J. G., Burleson, B. R., & Kline, S. L. (1979). *Person-centered parental communication and the development of social-cognitive and communicative abilities.* Paper presented at the annual meeting of the Central States Speech Association, St. Louis, April.

Delia, J. G., & Clark, R. A. (1977). Cognitive complexity, social perception, and the development of listener-adapted communication in six-, eight-, ten-, and twelve-year-old boys. *Communication Monographs, 44*, 326-345.

Delia, J. G., Clark, R. A., & Switzer, D. E. (1974). Cognitive complexity and impression formation in informal social interaction. *Speech Monographs, 41*, 299-308.

Delia, J. G., Clark, R. A., & Switzer, D. E. (1979). The content of informal conversations as a function of interactants' interpersonal cognitive complexity. *Communication Monographs, 46*, 274-281.

Delia, J. G., & Crockett, W. H. (1973). Social schemas, cognitive complexity, and the learning of social structures. *Journal of Personality, 41*, 413-429.

Delia, J. G., Kline, S. L., & Burleson, B. R. (1979). The development of persuasive communication strategies in kindergartners through twelfth-graders. *Communication Monographs, 46*, 241-256.

Delia, J. G., Kline, S. L., Burleson, B. R., Clark, R. A., Applegate, J. L., & Burke, J. A. (1980). *Social-cognitive and communicative skills of mothers and their children.* Unpublished manuscript, University of Illinois at Urbana-Champaign.

Delia, J. G., & O'Keefe, B. J. (1979). Constructivism: The development of communication. In E. Wartella (Ed.), *Children communicating* (pp. 157-185). Beverly Hills, CA: Sage.

Delia, J. G., O'Keefe, B. J., & O'Keefe, D. J. (1982). The constructivist approach to communication. In F.E.X. Dance (Ed.), *Human communication theory* (pp. 147-191). New York: Harper & Row.

Dlugokinski, E., & Firestone, I. J. (1974). Other-centeredness and susceptibility to charitable appeals: The effects of perceived discipline. *Developmental Psychology, 10*, 21-28.

Eisenberg-Berg, N., & Geisheker, E. (1979). Content of preachings and power of the model/preacher: The effect on children's generosity. *Developmental Psychology, 15*, 168-175.

Enright, R. D., & Lapsley, D. K. (1980). Social role-taking: A review of the construct, measures, and measurement properties. *Review of Educational Research, 50,* 647-674.

Feffer, M. H. (1970). Developmental analysis of interpersonal behavior. *Psychological Review, 77,* 197-214.

Flavell, J. H. (1968). *The development of role taking and communication skills in children.* New York: John Wiley.

Ford, M. E. (1979). The construct validity of egocentricism. *Psychological Bulletin, 86,* 1169-1188.

Glucksberg, S., Krauss, R., & Higgins, E. T. (1975). The development of referential communication skills. In F. D. Horowitz (Ed.), *Review of child development research* (Vol. 4, pp. 305-345). Chicago: University of Chicago Press.

Goffman, E. (1967). *Interaction ritual: Essays on face-to-face behavior.* New York: Anchor.

Hale, C. L. (1980). Cognitive complexity-simplicity as a determinant of communicative effectiveness. *Communication Monographs, 47,* 304-311.

Hale, C. L. (1982). An investigation of the relationship between cognitive complexity and listener-adapted communication. *Central States Speech Journal, 33,* 339-344.

Hale, C. L., & Delia, J. G. (1976). Cognitive complexity and social perspective-taking. *Communication Monographs, 43,* 195-203.

Husband, R. L. (1981). *Leadership: A case study, phenomenology, and social-cognitive correlates.* Unpublished doctoral dissertation, University of Illinois at Urbana-Champaign.

Jennings, K. D. (1975). People versus object orientation, social behavior, and intellectual abilities in preschool children. *Developmental Psychology, 11,* 511-519.

Jones, J. L., Delia, J. G., & Clark, R. A. (1981a). *Socio-economic status and the developmental level of second- and seventh-grade children's persuasive strategies.* Paper presented at the annual meeting of the International Communication Association, Minneapolis, May.

Jones, J. L., Delia, J. G., & Clark, R. A. (1981b). *Person-centered parental communication and the development of communication in children.* Paper presented at the annual meeting of the International Communication Association, Minneapolis, May.

Kasch, C. R. (1984). *Interpersonal competence, compliance, and person-centered speech: A study of nurses' and para-professionals' communicative strategies.* Paper presented at the Central States Speech Association Convention, Chicago, April.

Kelly, G. A. (1955). *The psychology of personal constructs.* New York: W.W. Norton.

Kline, S. L. (1981a). *Construct system development, empathic motivation, and the accomplishment of face support in persuasive messages.* Paper presented at the annual meeting of the Speech Communication Association, Anaheim, CA, November.

Kline, S. L. (1981b). *Construct system development and face support in persuasive messages: Two empirical investigations.* Paper presented at the annual meeting of the International Communication Association, Minneapolis, May.

Kline, S. L., & Ceropski, J. M. (1984). Person-centered communication in medical practice. In J. T. Wood & G. M. Phillips (Eds.), *Human decision-making* (pp. 120-141). Carbondale: Southern Illinois University Press.

Kroll, B. M. (1978). Cognitive egocentrism and the problem of audience awareness. *Research in the Teaching of English, 12*, 269-281.

Little, B. R. (1972). Psychological man as scientist, humanist, and specialist. *Journal of Experimental Research in Personality, 6*, 95-118.

Livesley, W. J., & Bromley, D. B. (1973). *Person perception in childhood and adolescence.* New York: John Wiley.

Loevinger, J., & Wessler, R. (1970). *Measuring ego development* (Vol. 1). San Francisco: Jossey-Bass.

Looft, W. R. (1972). Egocentrism and social interaction across the life span. *Psychological Bulletin, 78*, 73-92.

Losee, G. D. (1976). *An investigation of selected interpersonal and communication variables in marital relationships.* Unpublished doctoral dissertation, University of Illinois at Urbana-Champaign.

Marsh, D.T. (1982). The development of interpersonal problem-solving among elementary school children. *Journal of Genetic Psychology, 140*, 107-118.

Mead, G. H. (1934). *Mind, self, and society.* Chicago: University of Chicago Press.

Nahir, H. T., & Yussen, S. R. (1977). The performance of Kibbutz- and city-reared Israeli children on two role-taking tasks. *Developmental Psychology, 13*, 450-455.

Nidorf, L. J., & Crockett, W. H. (1965). Cognitive complexity and the integration of conflicting information in written impressions. *Journal of Social Psychology, 66*, 165-169.

O'Keefe, B. J., & Delia, J. G. (1979). Construct comprehensiveness and cognitive complexity as predictors of the number and strategic adaptation of arguments and appeals in a persuasive message. *Communication Monographs, 46*, 231-240.

O'Keefe, B. J., & Delia, J. G. (1982). Impression formation and message production. In M. E. Roloff & C. R. Berger (Eds.), *Social cognition and communication* (pp. 33-72). Beverly Hills, CA: Sage.

O'Keefe, B. J., & Delia, J. G. (in press). Psychological and interactional dimensions of communicative development. In H. Giles & R. St. Clair (Eds.), *Advances in language, communication, and social psychology.* London: Erlbaum.

O'Keefe, B. J., Delia, J. G., & O'Keefe, D. J. (1980). Interaction analysis and the analysis of interactional organization. In N. K. Denzin (Ed.), *Studies in symbolic interaction* (Vol. 3, pp. 122-155). Greenwich, CT: JAI.

O'Keefe, B. J., Murphy, M. A., Meyers, R. A., & Babrow, A. S. (1983). *The development of persuasive communication skills: The influence of develop-*

ments in interpersonal constructs on the ability to generate communication-relevant beliefs and a level of persuasive strategy. Paper presented at the annual meeting of the International Communication Association, Dallas, May.

O'Keefe, B. J., & Shepherd, G. (1983). *Defining the communication situation: Consequences for perception and action.* Paper presented at the annual convention of the Speech Communication Association, Washington, D.C., November.

O'Keefe, D. J., Shepherd, G. J., & Streeter, T. (1982). Role category questionnaire measures of cognitive complexity: Reliability and comparability of alternative forms. *Central States Speech Journal, 33*, 333-338.

O'Keefe, D. J., & Sypher, H. E. (1981). Cognitive complexity measures and the relationship of cognitive complexity to communication: A critical review. *Human Communication Research, 8*, 72-92.

Peevers, B. H., & Secord, P. F. (1973). Developmental changes in the attribution of descriptive concepts to persons. *Journal of Personality and Social Psychology, 27*, 120-138.

Piaget, J. (1926). *The language and thought of the child.* London: Routledge & Kegan Paul.

Piche, G. L., Michlin, M. I., Rubin, D. L., & Johnson, F. L. (1975). Relationships between fourth graders' performances on selected role-taking tasks and referential communication accuracy tasks. *Child Development, 46*, 965-969.

Powers, W. G., Jordan, W. J., & Street, R. L. (1979). Language indices in the measurement of cognitive complexity: Is complexity loquacity? *Human Communication Research, 6*, 69-73.

Press, A. N., Crockett, W. H., & Rosenkrantz, P. S. (1969). Cognitive complexity and the learning of balanced and unbalanced social structures. *Journal of Personality, 37*, 541-553.

Renshaw, P. D., & Asher, S. W. (1983). Children's goals and strategies for social interaction. *Merrill-Palmer Quarterly, 29*, 353-374.

Ritter, E. M. (1979). Social perspective-taking ability, cognitive complexity, and listener-adapted communication in early and late adolescence. *Communication Monographs, 46*, 40-51.

Rosenbach, D., Crockett, W. H., & Wapner, S. (1973). Developmental level, emotional involvement, and the resolution of inconsistency in impression formation. *Developmental Psychology, 8*, 120-130.

Rowan, K. E. (1981). *A Kinneavian model for research on adaptive discourse: Theory and an empirical test.* Paper presented at the National Council of Teachers of English Convention, New York, November.

Rowan, K. E. (1984). The implicit social scientist and the implicit rhetorician: An integrative framework for the introductory interpersonal course. *Communication Education, 33*, 351-360.

Rowan, K. E. (1985). *Explanatory writing skills: Theoretical analysis and an empirical investigation of individual differences.* Unpublished doctoral dissertation, Purdue University, West Lafayette, IN.

Rubin, K. H. (1978). Role taking in childhood: Some methodological considerations. *Child Development, 49*, 428- 433.

Rubin, K. H., & Maioni, T. L. (1975). Play preference and its relationship to egocentrism, popularity, and classification skills in preschoolers. *Merrill-Palmer Quarterly, 21*, 171- 179.

Samter, W., & Burleson, B. R. (1984). Cognitive and motivational influences on spontaneous comforting behavior. *Human Communication Research, 11*, 231-260.

Samter, W., Burleson, B. R., & Basden, L. (1985). *Effects of comforting strategy type, sex, and cognitive complexity on impressions of a speaker.* Unpublished manuscript, Purdue University, West Lafayette, IN.

Samter, W., & Ely, T. (1985). *Children's conflict management strategies: Assessments of individual and situational differences.* Paper presented at the Central States Speech Association Convention, Indianapolis, April.

Sarver, J. L. (1976). *An exploratory study of the antecedents of individual differences in second- and seventh-graders' social cognitive and communicative performance.* Unpublished doctoral dissertation, University of Illinois at Urbana-Champaign.

Scarlett, H. H., Press, A. N., & Crockett, W. H. (1971). Children's descriptions of peers: A Wernerian developmental analysis. *Child Development, 42*, 439-453.

Selman, R. L. (1980). *The growth of interpersonal understanding: Developmental and clinical analyses.* New York: Academic Press.

Selman, R. L., Schorin, M. Z., Stone, C. R., & Phelps, E. (1983). A naturalistic study of children's social understanding. *Developmental Psychology, 19*, 82-102.

Shantz, C. U. (1981). The role of role-taking in children's referential communication. In W. P. Dickson (Ed.), *Children's oral communication skills* (pp. 85-102). New York: Academic Press.

Shepherd, G. J., & O'Keefe, B. J. (1984). *Interpersonal construct differentiation and the production of messages addressing multiple aims in persuasive situations.* Paper presented at the Speech Communication Association Convention, Chicago, November.

Shepherd, G. J., & O'Keefe, B. J. (1985). *Securing task, interactional, and relational objectives in interpersonal persuasive interactions.* Paper presented at the Speech Communication Association Convention, Denver, November.

Shure, M. B., & Spivack, G. (1978). *Problem-solving techniques in child rearing.* San Francisco: Jossey-Bass.

Stone, C. R., & Selman, R. L. (1982). A structural approach to research on the development of interpersonal behavior among grade-school children. In K. H. Rubin & H. S. Ross (Eds.), *Peer relations and social skills in childhood* (pp. 163-184). New York: Springer-Verlag.

Strayer, J., & Mashal, M. (1983). The role of peer experience in communication and role-taking skills. *Journal of Genetic Psychology, 143*, 113-122.

Sypher, H. E., & Applegate, J. L. (1982). Cognitive complexity and verbal intelligence: Clarifying relationships. *Educational and Psychological Measurement, 49*, 537-543.

Sypher, H. E., & O'Keefe, D. J. (1980). *The comparative validity of several cognitive complexity measures as predictors of communication-relevant abilities.* Paper presented at the International Communication Association Convention, Acapulco, May.

Werner, H. (1957). The concept of development from a comparative and organismic point of view. In D. B. Harris (Ed.), *The concept of development* (pp. 125-146). Minneapolis: University of Minnesota Press.

Werner, H., & Kaplan, B. (1963). *Symbol formation: An organismic-developmental approach to language and the expression of thought.* New York: John Wiley.

# ABOUT THE CONTRIBUTORS

**Robert A. Bell** is Assistant Professor of Communication Studies at Northwestern University. He received his Ph.D. from the University of Texas at Austin.

**Charles R. Berger** is Professor of Communication Studies at Northwestern University. He received his Ph.D. from Michigan State University. He is a Fellow of the International Communication Association.

**Brant R. Burleson** is Associate Professor of Communication at Purdue University. He received his Ph.D. from the University of Illinois.

**John A. Daly** is Associate Professor of Speech Communication at the University of Texas at Austin. He received his Ph.D. from Purdue University.

**Dominic A. Infante** is Professor of Speech Communication at Kent State University. He also received his Ph.D. from that institution.

**William B. Lashbrook** is a Fellow of Wilson Learning Corporation. He received his Ph.D. from Michigan State University.

**James C. McCroskey** is Professor and Chairperson of the Communication Studies Department at West Virginia University. He received his Ed.D. from Pennsylvania State University. He is a Fellow of the International Communication Association.

**Virginia P. Richmond** is Professor of Studies Communication at West Virginia University. She received her Ph.D. from the University of Nebraska.

**Thomas M. Steinfatt** is Professor of Communication, University of Miami. He received his Ph.D. from Michigan State University.

**Virginia Eman Wheeless** is Associate Professor of Speech Communication at West Virginia University. She received her Ph.D. from the University of Nebraska.